CHINA TODAY,
CHINA TOMORROW

CHINA TODAY, CHINA TOMORROW

Domestic Politics, Economy, and Society

Edited by
Joseph Fewsmith

ROWMAN & LITTLEFIELD PUBLISHERS, INC.
Lanham • Boulder • New York • Toronto • Plymouth, UK

Published by Rowman & Littlefield Publishers, Inc.
A wholly owned subsidiary of The Rowman & Littlefield Publishing Group, Inc.
4501 Forbes Boulevard, Suite 200, Lanham, Maryland 20706
http://www.rowmanlittlefield.com

Estover Road, Plymouth PL6 7PY, United Kingdom

British Library Cataloguing in Publication Information Available

Library of Congress Cataloging-in-Publication Data

China today, China tomorrow : domestic politics, economy, and society / edited by Joseph
Fewsmith.
    p. cm.
  Includes bibliographical references and index.
  ISBN 978-0-7425-6706-1 (cloth : alk. paper) -- ISBN 978-0-7425-6707-8
(pbk. : alk. paper) -- ISBN 978-0-7425-6708-5 (electronic)
  1. China--Politics and government--1976-2002. 2. China--Politics and government--
2002- 3. China--Economic conditions--1976-2000. 4. China--Economic conditions--
2000- 5. China--Social conditions--1976-2000. 6. China--Social conditions--2000- I.
Fewsmith, Joseph, 1949-
  DS779.26.C473535 2010
  951.06--dc22   2010009029

Printed in the United States of America

Contents

Part Three: Politics

Part Four: Systemic Constraints

Tables and Figures

Tables

Figures

Acknowledgments

UNDERSTANDING THE IMPORTANCE OF CHINA to global development, the Frederick S. Pardee Center for the Study of the Longer Range Future at Boston University worked with the editor of this volume to find experts in various aspects of China's development to write a series of essays that would explore the implications for the future of domestic developments over the past three decades. The director of the Pardee Center, Adil Najam, was unstinting in his support for this project, and his staff, including Cynthia Barakatt, Georgia Iordanescu, and Lindsey Jones made the work seamless. All of the participants in this project are grateful for the generous support of Frederick S. Pardee and the center.

We also thank the administration of Boston University, including Provost David Campbell and Dean Virginia Sapiro, for their support, and appreciate the Center for the Study of Asia for its participation and efforts. Hopefully the quality of the chapters in this volume expresses our thanks for all this support.

The efforts of Susan McEachern, Carrie Broadwell-Tkach, and Alden Perkins at Rowman & Littlefield have also been terrific in supporting this project and getting it out in timely fashion.

Alas, any errors remain the responsibility of the authors and editor.

Introduction

Three Decades of Reform and Opening

Joseph Fewsmith

W HEN MAO ZEDONG DIED ON SEPTEMBER 9, 1976, leadership passed to vice chairman Hua Guofeng, then only fifty-five years of age and possessing none of the credentials of his revolutionary elders. Mao had purged Deng Xiaoping once again in April 1976 believing him to be responsible for the activities of the thousands who gathered in Tiananmen Square to mourn the recently deceased former premier, Zhou Enlai. Casting about the Politburo for possible replacements for Deng, Mao skipped over his wife, Jiang Qing, and the rest of the Gang of Four, and settled on the loyal if relatively inexperienced Hua Guofeng. Bolstering Hua's position in the leadership, Mao wrote the famous instruction, "with you in charge, I am at ease."[1] Following the chairman's death, Hua vowed to carry out Mao's policies and affirmed the correctness of the Great Proletarian Cultural Revolution. On February 7, 1977, the Communist Party's official paper, *People's Daily*, carried an editorial that famously declared that the party should "resolutely uphold whatever policy decisions Chairman Mao made, and unswervingly follow whatever instructions Chairman Mao gave" (a formulation that was quickly dubbed the "two whatevers"). On reading this, a young cadre by the name Zhu Jiamu, who would later serve as secretary to senior economic policy specialist Chen Yun, went to Deng Liqun and pointed out that if this policy were followed neither Deng Xiaoping nor other veteran cadres purged by Mao could return to office.[2] Deng Xiaoping soon declared that the "two whatevers" could not stand; Mao Zedong Thought needed to be understood comprehensively.[3] A year later, the Dengists were prepared to go further, declaring that "practice was the sole criterion of truth."[4] This declaration in a "special commentator's" article on the front page of *People's Daily* on May 9, 1978, set off a furious debate over the criterion of practice and, by implication, the direction of politics. By the time the CCP convened a work conference in November 1978, several senior cadres were prepared to act decisively.

Only two days after the start of the meeting, Chen Yun declared that the party had to confront and deal with several controversial cases, including the verdict on the Tiananmen incident, which needed to be reversed. Chen Yun's remarks changed the atmosphere of the meeting, and by the time the conference was over, it had been agreed that the verdict on the Tiananmen incident would be reversed, the discussion on practice as the sole criterion of truth would be affirmed, and the party's judgment on several party leaders would change.[5]

Thus, when the Third Plenary Session of the Eleventh Central Committee met December 18–22, 1978, the party was prepared to endorse the most important change in direction since the Zunyi Conference of 1935 had elevated Mao Zedong into the leadership. It publicly affirmed that the Tiananmen incident of 1976 was "revolutionary"; restored the political reputations of former military head Peng Dehuai and senior economic specialist Bo Yibo; "highly evaluated" the discussion on practice as the sole criterion of truth; added Chen Yun, Hu Yaobang, and others to the Politburo; and shifted the focus of the party's work to "socialist modernization."[6]

Three decades have passed since then, and those thirty years of economic growth and social change have changed the face of China and the place of China in the world. Indeed, China has gone from a largely autarkic, impoverished country to the second-largest economy in the world and the second-largest exporter.[7] Real GDP has expanded some thirteen times in that period, raising some 300 million people out of poverty. This growth rate has been built on a high savings rate, a correspondingly high investment rate, and a rapidly growing export sector.[8]

Such a rate of growth underlies the rapidly modernizing skylines of Beijing, Shanghai, and other cities that amaze visitors. But it also accounts for tensions that China faces; as China has focused single-mindedly on economic growth, it has neglected much—income equality, the environment, health care, and basic issues of governance. Such issues have fueled the growth of both protest and populist demands that social issues be addressed.

Thus, the book begins with societal issues, which lie at the heart of China's evolving political economy. We hear much these days about burgeoning "civil society" and "rights consciousness" in China, raising expectations that China might soon evolve into a liberal democratic society. Elizabeth Perry questions this thesis, putting social protest into historical context, including pre-1949 China, the Maoist period, and in reform China. Focusing on the rising tide of "mass incidents" in China, Perry argues that Chinese citizens today, like their predecessors in earlier times, are not challenging the system but rather using the rhetorical devices allowed them by the government to negotiate better terms with the state. Rather than challenging the rules governing state-society relations, they are "playing by the rules." This is sure to be a controversial thesis, challenging as it does the conventional academic and popular wisdom. But it is an important thesis, forcing us to think about a Chinese society evolving in ways quite different from Western assumptions about the inevitability of democratic transition.

Just as Perry concentrates on popular protest, Robert Weller and Sun Yanfei focus on another unintended consequence of reform—the striking and rapid growth of religiosity, and how that growth is challenging the way in which the state has thought of religion and the state's relationship to it. Particularly striking has been the growth of temple religion. This form of popular religion, with its attendant temple fairs, has grown rapidly despite its not being recognized by the state (which recognizes only five religions: Buddhism, Catholicism, Daoism, Islam, and Protestantism). The space allotted or not allotted by the state, the way religions interact with the economy, and the tremendous diversity of religion across China have all shaped the growth of religion and are forcing the state to reassess the way in which it governs religion. Given the rapid growth of religion, the state may become more tolerant toward religious activity,[9] while still taking a hard line on religious activities that seem to cross the line into politics.

China's political economy has not only generated protest but also a growing body of law that is increasingly shaping state-societal relations. In chapter 3, Jamie Horsley documents the strides law has made in China. There are now over 231 laws, 600 administrative regulations, and 7,000 local rules and regulations. Over the last three decades, China has built a legal infrastructure— lawyers, courts, and lawmaking institutions—out of practically nothing. The question is really one of whether the state can go beyond an instrumental view of the law, what is generally called "rule by law," to a system in which state and citizen are equally bound by the law—"rule *of* law." In this regard, Horsley is cautiously optimistic, noting the many efforts of the central and local states to develop law as a check on the abuse of state power (as in the Administrative Litigation Law and more recent open-government laws).

Turning to the economy, Barry Naughton and Sebastian Heilmann look at very different aspects of China's growth, while Carl Riskin examines the degree of inequality in contemporary China. Naughton notes the degree to which objectives other than economic growth have been subordinated to the goal of rapid development. However, as other needs—health care, welfare, environmental protection, and so forth—have emerged as pressing social issues, China has no choice but to slow its growth and divert economic resources to other needs. Similarly, long driven by investment, the Chinese economy must be reshaped to permit consumer spending to be a more important factor in its development. China's leadership has clearly recognized these needs, and, indeed, over the past five years has tried to attend to them. The economic juggernaut that has been constructed, however, is not easily diverted, and high-speed growth continued right up until the global economic crisis hit in the fall of 2008. The impact of the economic crisis is thus likely to be especially important in China, but the crisis may end up reinforcing the role of the government as the driver of the economy.

Sebastian Heilmann looks at the economy from a different perspective, arguing that as China faces a different era in policymaking, its political system gives it significant potential for "authoritarian upgrading"—including more inclusive, consultative policymaking, fostering innovation, and maintaining state control over central parts of the economy. Moreover, Heilmann believes that China has an experimental approach to finding ways to implement the priorities the state favors, and thus has been able to develop a unique combination of planning and experimentation that situate it well to respond not only to the current economic crisis but also to the likely demands of the global political economy of the twenty-first century.

Carl Riskin tackles the complicated and controversial issue of inequality. There are many different dimensions to inequality and measuring them is not easy, particularly because regional price differentials play such a major role. Although everyone is familiar with the gap between urban and rural living standards, it is nevertheless surprising that after three decades of reform, pre-reform era policies, particularly the household registration system (*hukou*) system, continue to haunt efforts to improve equality. Government policy, including the suppression of natural resource prices to support state-owned enterprises, has also been important. So the question is whether government policy can be directed at reducing these gaps. The administration of Hu Jintao and Wen Jiabao appear to be committed to doing so, but the legacy of the past is large and the impact of the current economic recession will no doubt have a negative impact.

In the political realm, Min Ye looks at the role social networks played in China's opening to the outside world, arguing that such networks go a long way in explaining not only why China opened itself to foreign direct investment (FDI) in the late 1970s, when the majority of the political elite opposed such a radical reorientation of the economy, but also why China has maintained openness at times when this policy has come under severe criticism, such as in 1982–1983 and 1989–1991. The interesting question looking forward is what role diaspora capital is likely to play in the future as China becomes wealthier and, perhaps, less dependent on foreign markets. Ye suggests that such capital will have less impact on national policies but is likely to have significant impact on the development of localities and in partnering with China's private enterprises.

Joseph Fewsmith suggests that the greater institutionalization of elite politics has been critical to the development of China's economy. The questions that need to be confronted are: How does one explain the creation of institutions? How do formal institutions reinforce or conflict with informal norms? And how stable are current arrangements? One can argue that in the 1980s, despite significant progress in developing new political institutions, the formal institutions simply were not strong enough to contain conflicts arising from informal politics. In the two decades since then, a more stable balance seems to have been achieved, in part because the top leadership does not have the political resources that would allow informal politics to overwhelm the institutional rules. Looking ahead, current arrangements appear reasonably stable, but they will face challenges from (1) their ability to face crises, (2) leadership succession, which is always a difficult issue in authoritarian political systems, and (3) societal challenges that will require a political response. One might say that either institutionalization moves forward or political conflict could still overwhelm it.

Economic development, migration, and the arbitrary wielding of political power have made local areas the sources of conflict. For two decades now, the Chinese government has been experimenting with various forms of political reform in an effort to absorb and contain these tensions. Yawei Liu notes that beginning in the late 1990s, electoral democracy began to make a "great leap" from the village level to the township level. This trend was touched off by the election in Buyun Township in Sichuan Province and has continued through several other important electoral contests in Sichuan and elsewhere. However, instead of progress being consolidated and advancing further, there has been notable stagnation in electoral democracy since the "color revolutions" of Ukraine, Georgia, and Kyrgyzstan in 2004–2005. Although there have been several efforts to promote local political reform since then, electoral democracy has stagnated. It is thus not clear how China will meet the challenge posed by continuing problems of social order.

Western observers rarely take the issue of ideology seriously, so Ren Jiantao's essay is a particularly interesting and revealing discussion of how ideology plays a role in the political system and how it has increasingly come under challenge in recent years. Ren notes that the development of reform, particularly political reform, has been severely constrained by the Stalinist framework that it has necessarily been built on. This has denied liberalism the sort of supportive role that it might otherwise have played and has allowed reform to be challenged by the New Left. Nevertheless, confronted by the economic need to continue reform, the Chinese Communist Party has continued to dilute Marxism.

Finally this volume turns to constraints that will influence the development of reform in the future. These constraints are both political and material. On the political side, thirty years of reform and opening have bequeathed China a very different relationship between the center and the localities. As Yongnian Zheng notes in chapter 11, de facto federalism spurred China's economic growth, but it has now become a barrier for national reforms. Decentralization is not a threat to the unity of China, but it can prevent the central government from further rationalizing the economic system.

On the material side, China is constrained by its energy needs and its deteriorating environment. Edward Cunningham notes that China is largely self-sufficient in energy (over 94 percent) and both its energy governance and energy markets are highly fragmented, but that this division has helped China meet most of its energy needs. The big question, both in the energy sector and the environment, is energy intensity. Despite earlier good trends, starting in 2002 energy consumption has grown faster than economic output. China's capacity to deal with this issue will greatly affect its ability to meet its ever-growing need for energy and to mitigate environmental consequences.

China has emerged as the largest emitter of CO_2—not the largest per capita emitter of CO_2 (that dubious honor belongs to the United States)—raising significant questions about its ability to manage environmental concerns and economic growth as it moves forward. The good news is that China's leaders "get it," and they have been doing much to bring down energy intensity (despite reversals in recent years) and to address environmental issues moving forward. As Joanna Lewis argues in chapter 13, China's environmental challenges are closely linked to its energy prospectus—particularly the fact that China draws some 70 percent of its energy needs from coal, which is highly polluting. The question is whether China can move significantly away from coal as a source of energy or substantially reduce the impact of coal on the environment by introducing various sorts of clean coal technology.

When China began to reform there was much talk of "crossing the river by feeling the stones." This saying expressed both a pragmatic sense of moving forward one step at a time and an idealistic, perhaps even naïve, sense that they would soon reach the "other side of the river." Of course, there were very different understandings even then of what the other side of the river would look like. Although everyone assumed it would include a more prosperous China, some saw that prosperity accompanied by, and indeed brought about by, a market-oriented economy supported by a strong legal system and some sort of democracy. Others had a more limited sense of a strong state preserving the values of "socialism" while generating greater wealth for the people and securing a higher standing in the world.

Three decades later China is indeed far wealthier than it was (and perhaps far wealthier than its leaders dreamed it could become in that time), but many of the same basic questions that stirred debate in the 1980s remain unresolved: What will be the role of the state in a market-oriented economy? How will different priorities of economic growth, environmental protection, health care, and other social justice issues be balanced? How much inequality is acceptable in Chinese society? What role will law play? And, of course, can the political system be perceived as just and legitimate for the vast majority of the citizens? The answers to these questions will shape the China of the future. The chapters that follow offer no predictions of what China will look like thirty years from now, but they do lay out the issues and constraints that will shape that future. In the conclusion, I try to pull together some of the implications of these chapters.

I
SOCIAL ORDER

1

Popular Protest

Playing by the Rules

Elizabeth J. Perry

A MONG THE MANY SURPRISES OF the post-Mao era has been the remarkable upsurge in popular protests that has accompanied the economic reforms. The Tiananmen Uprising of 1989 was the largest and most dramatic of these incidents, but it marked neither the beginning nor the end of widespread unrest in the reform period. In the first decade of reform, China experienced a steady stream of collective protests, culminating in the massive demonstrations in Tiananmen Square (and many other Chinese cities) in the spring of 1989.[1] Despite the brutal suppression of the Tiananmen Uprising, the frequency of protests has escalated in the years since June Fourth. According to official Chinese statistics, public disturbances in China increased tenfold during the period from 1993 to 2005, from 8,700 to 87,000.[2] Most observers believe that the actual figures are considerably higher than these official statistics—which the Chinese government ceased making public after 2005—would suggest.

More than a few China scholars, long accustomed to viewing collective action in the People's Republic of China (PRC) as a product of top-down state mobilization rather than an expression of bottom-up societal interests, have heralded the recent protest activity as a definitive break with the Maoist past that indicates a "rising rights consciousness" propelled by a newfound appreciation of "citizenship." The consequence, they suggest, could be a threat to both the legitimacy and the longevity of the Communist system. Kevin O'Brien and Li Lianjiang write of the Chinese countryside: "The notion of being a citizen is seeping into popular discourse. . . . We should not underestimate the implications of rising rights consciousness and a growing fluency

in 'rights talk' in a nation where rights have traditionally been weakly protected," on grounds that "today's rightful resistance could . . . evolve into a
much more far-reaching counterhegemonic project."[3] David Zweig also de-
tects an emerging "rights conscious peasantry."[4] The observation is not restricted to rural villagers. Mary Gallagher sees the new labor law, and related
urban legal institutions, as helping to generate "increased societal conflict and
rising rights-consciousness among Chinese workers."[5] Pei Minxin notes a "rising rights consciousness" within Chinese society at large. Summing up the
history of the reform era with an eye toward the future, Pei predicts that
"China's incipient opposition is likely to become more resilient, sophisticated
and adept in challenging the regime as the conditions for democratic resistance further improve."[6] Similarly, Merle Goldman argues that "by the century's end the sense of rights consciousness . . . had spread . . . beyond intellectual and elite circles . . . to the population at large. . . . The transition from
comrade to citizen in the People's Republic of China has begun."[7] In a booklet
commissioned by the Association for Asian Studies as a teaching aid intended
to summarize prevailing scholarly opinion on key issues, Goldman writes: "A
growing consciousness of citizenship and organized efforts to assert political
rights . . . signify the beginnings of a genuine change in the relationship between China's population at large and the state at the beginning of the twenty-
first century."[8]

There is considerable justification for emphasizing the role of "rights talk"
among Chinese protesters. An unmistakable discourse of "legal rights" (*hefa
quanli* 合法权利) permeates the manifestoes, petitions, and slogans put forth
by protesters in both city and countryside. Moreover, the protests are sometimes instigated by newly established grassroots citizens' organizations: environmental nongovernmental organizations (NGOs), homeowners' associations, Internet networks, house churches, and the like. But the temptation to
depict these features as indicative of an emergent "civil society" posing a growing challenge to the authority of the Chinese Communist state should probably be resisted.[9]

The tendency on the part of many analysts to frame the discussion of contemporary Chinese protest in terms of Western political concepts such as
"rights consciousness" and "citizenship"—unless very carefully distinguished
from their European and American counterparts—creates expectation of a
fundamental transformation in Chinese state-society relations that appears
unwarranted. When placed in historical perspective, the evidence that emerges
from an examination of the past three decades of popular protest does not, in
my view, offer grounds for an optimistic prognosis that state authoritarianism
is eroding under the pressures of a newly awakened and assertive society animated by alien conceptions of universal human rights.

To be sure, the protests that roil the contemporary Chinese landscape present significant challenges to the central leadership. Although most of the protests are directed in the first instance against grassroots officials, protesters often take their petitions to higher levels—including all the way to Beijing—if a local resolution is not forthcoming. Moreover, the protests can be highly disruptive of government operations as well as economic and social life when vociferous demonstrators surround government offices, march through city streets, stage sit-ins in public places, and block traffic on busy highways and railways.[10] Taking full advantage of international connections, media attention, and cyberspace contention to publicize their cause,[11] protesters have in time wrung some significant concessions from the state; for example, the historic abolition of the agricultural tax in 2006, the property rights law the following year, and the current move to privatize collective land ownership.

Yet, however visible and vocal (and sometimes violent) these protests may be, participants usually go to great lengths to demonstrate their loyalty to central policies and leaders. The breathless enthusiasm with which many journalists and some scholars have greeted the protests of recent years notwithstanding, contentious politics in post-Mao China continues to be highly circumscribed in its targets and stated ambitions. In these respects, today's protests perpetuate certain core features of both Mao-era and pre-Mao-era protests. Among these features is a pronounced penchant on the part of protesters to advance their claims within the "legitimate" boundaries authorized by the central state. To be sure, these boundaries have shifted in significant ways over time—as a result of state initiative as well as societal innovation. But whether we are talking about the pre- or post-1989 reform-era period or for that matter about the Maoist era (or even the Republican or imperial periods) that preceded them, Chinese protesters have shown a consistent tendency to "play by the rules." Although the language of "revolution" articulated by "comrades" in Mao's day has been supplanted by a language of "rights" proclaimed by "citizens" today, it is not readily apparent that most protesters in the two periods differ fundamentally in either their mentality or their relationship to the authoritarian state. Rather than interpret protest in contemporary China as emblematic of a seditious "rights consciousness," in which a new generation of citizens assert their autonomous interests against the state, I see these protests as reflecting a seasoned "rules consciousness" that expressly acknowledges, and thereby serves to undergird more than to undermine, the authority of the state.

It is of course extremely difficult, if not impossible, to gauge the genuine political sentiments of a populace living in an authoritarian system where expressions of antistate defiance carry substantial risk. Whether or not Chinese protesters, in their heart of hearts, accept the legitimacy of the Communist state, they generally behave as if they do. Even in the absence of a deeply rooted belief in state legitimacy, however, popular compliance may work to promote the stability of authoritarian regimes.[12] Moreover in China, where cultural norms have long valued "orthopraxy" (proper behavior) over "orthodoxy" (proper belief),[13] overt expressions of deference to political authority would seem to play an especially powerful role in sustaining the system.

Protest in Mao's China

To evaluate the political implications of reform-era protest, it is instructive to revisit earlier eras. Looking back on Mao's China (1949–1976) from the vantage point of today, there is a temptation to subsume that entire period under the rubric of totalitarianism and to interpret the repeated outbursts of popular contention that occurred in those years as state-sponsored mobilization rather than as socially generated protest. From the anti-American demonstrations of the Korean War through the Red Guard rampages of the Cultural Revolution, we are inclined to regard collective action under Mao as orchestrated by the central state, usually in the person of the Great Helmsman himself. But a closer examination of that era, with the aid of increasingly accessible archival sources, suggests that to discount the social power of collective action under Mao would be a serious misreading of the historical record. Crucial as state signals were in generating the mass movements of the Maoist era, the popular contention that erupted in the course of those political campaigns anticipated the contemporary scene both ideologically and organizationally.

The laws passed by the new People's Republic of China invited ordinary citizens to invoke legal authority in demanding redress for long-standing grievances. The Marriage Law of 1950, publicized through a series of mass campaigns in the early 1950s, generated an extraordinary level of popular turmoil as millions of Chinese took their cases to the courts and other newly established government agencies in order to seek divorces, property rights, and settlement of other civil claims in the name of revolutionary liberation.[14] But the tendency to play by the rules was visible not only in the initial years of the PRC, when the state explicitly encouraged its citizens to make use of new laws and legal channels. It could be seen throughout the Mao years.

Take the massive strike wave that rolled across urban China in 1956–1957.[15] In March 1957, the Chinese Communist Party issued a directive that acknowledged that labor strikes, student boycotts, and mass petitions and demonstrations had increased dramatically in the previous six months. Party Central estimated that more than ten thousand labor strikes had erupted across the country during this half-year period. Although the walkouts by industrial workers were certainly stimulated by Mao's Hundred Flowers Campaign, and in particular his speech "On the Correct Handling of Contradictions Among the People," the protests evidenced notable spontaneity and presented real challenges for factory managers, trade union cadres, and local party officials alike. The urban protests of that period were a popular response to fundamental changes in the structure of the economy.[16] Under the socialization of industry, private firms were replaced by so-called joint ownership enterprises. In Shanghai, of the more than 1,300 strikes that occurred in the approximately one hundred days from March to early June 1957 (the highpoint of the strike wave), nearly 90 percent were centered in newly formed joint ownership enterprises.

Typically, the labor disputes of that period began by raising repeated suggestions and demands to the factory leadership. When these were not dealt with, written petitions were lodged with higher authorities. The workers set deadlines by which they expected a satisfactory response and often staged rowdy meetings to publicize their grievances. If the demands did not meet with a timely response, the protest would often evolve into a strike, slowdown, collective petition movement, or forcible surrounding of cadres—activities that were categorized (then and today) as *naoshi* 闹市, or outright "disturbances."

Even at the height of the 1956–1957 strike wave, protesters demonstrated a preference for operating within the boundary of the law. Shanghai's pedicab drivers, for example, sought legal counsel to ascertain that their requests were consistent with state regulations. Other measures were also taken to impress the authorities that protesters were playing by the state's rules. With class status considered the litmus test of political propriety in Mao's China, elections for workers' representatives were held in which anyone from a "bad" class background (e.g., capitalist or landlord) was eliminated from the roster. Nevertheless, many of the protests grew larger and more ambitious over time—moving beyond requests for better welfare provisions or mild criticisms of local leadership attitudes to demands for the fulfillment of basic political and social claims.

The 1956–1957 strikes evinced a wide repertoire of protest behavior. Many workers put up big-character posters and wrote blackboard newspapers explaining their grievances; some went on hunger strike; some threatened suicide; some marched in large-scale demonstrations—holding high their workplace banners as they paraded vociferously through city streets; some staged sit-ins and presented petitions (often on bended knee) to government authorities; some mustered "pickets"—armed with staves and other makeshift weapons—to enforce public order; some organized action committees and liaison offices to coordinate strikes in different factories and districts. In many cases, workers surrounded grassroots cadres, raising various demands and imposing a deadline for a satisfactory response, refusing to disband until their requests had been met.

While we tend to think of Mao's China—in contrast to the post-Mao era—as a period of international isolation, the importance of foreign influences on the 1956–1957 strike wave was considerable. Just as the example of Poland's Solidarity movement would inspire Chinese workers in the 1980s, so at this earlier juncture the Hungarian revolt was a powerful stimulus for labor unrest. A popular slogan in the protests of 1957 was "Let's create another Hungarian Incident!" There was awareness—as would be the case in the Tiananmen Uprising of 1989—of China's being part of an international socialist world. Another slogan in 1957 was "We'll take this all the way from district to city to Party Central to Communist International." Some workers, hearing that Khrushchev was about to visit Shanghai, planned to present their grievances directly to him. Although it turned out that the Soviet leader did not make his trip until the following year—well after the antirightist crackdown had dashed any hopes of a direct encounter with restive workers—the parallel with 1989, when protesters tried to share their grievances with Gorbachev, is noteworthy.

As would be true in the reform era, the earlier strike wave offered evidence of a growing sophistication in protest strategies over time. Moreover, the organizational infrastructure of the protests indicated far more independence from state control than a totalitarian image of Mao's China would suggest. Workers printed up their own handbills and manifestoes to publicize their demands, and formed autonomous unions (often termed *pingnan hui* 评难会, or redress grievances societies) to press their claims. In one district of Shanghai, thousands of workers joined a "Democratic Party" (*minzhu dangpai* 民主党派) organized by three local workers. In this and other instances, "united command headquarters" were established by the strikers to coordinate "battle plans."

Despite this remarkable display of social ferment, it would be wrong to characterize the strikes of 1956–1957 as an expression of a protodemocratic civil society rising up in opposition to the authoritarian state. For one thing, the involvement of grassroots cadres in many of the incidents cautions against drawing a clear line between state and society. For another thing, the protesters were asking for an opportunity to enjoy fully the socialist promises of the new regime, not clamoring for its overthrow.

As would be the case in the post-Mao period, economic cleavages and concerns were fundamental to the outpouring of unrest, but such matters were inextricably linked to state policies (collectivization of agriculture and socialization of industry in the 1950s, decollectivization and privatization in the reform era). Ordinary people were fully aware that responsibility for economic policy and management rested squarely with the state. While demands for higher income and improved welfare dominated their requests, much of the protesters' wrath was directed against government cadres. Even so, local officials often acted as facilitators—if not outright instigators—in many of the incidents. As would be true more than thirty years later during the Tiananmen Uprising of 1989, union cadres saw in the disturbances an opportunity to shed their image as government patsies and forge a new closeness with the workers. A union report on the uprising at the Datong Oil Refinery in the spring of 1957 noted approvingly that when striking workers gathered at a teahouse, pounded their fists on the tables, and loudly cursed the cadres as "scabs," union officials listened respectfully to the complaints.

In cases where the protesters failed to gain a satisfactory response at the local level, they did not shy away from taking their grievances to higher levels. On July 1, 1957, the All China Federation of Trade Unions in Beijing issued a notice to provincial and municipal unions pointing out that it had been deluged with disgruntled petitioners from all over the country, and complaining that it often could not resolve the disputes for lack of full knowledge about the local situation. The central union called upon grassroots unions and officials to do a better job of settling grievances and defusing protests.

One might propose that the strike wave of 1956–1957 was merely an anomalous exception to the Maoist pattern of state-orchestrated mass campaigns were it not that we find very similar expressions of popular contention a decade later at the height of the Cultural Revolution—often regarded as the quintessential expression of totalitarian rule. The Cultural Revolution saw the unfolding of what political scientist Sidney Tarrow has termed a "cycle of protest." Tarrow observes of these cycles that "in the presence of such general periods of turbulence, even the poor and disorganized can draw upon opportunities created by the 'early risers' who trigger the cycle." In the winter of 1966–1967, months after the onset of Red Guard factionalism, a so-called wind of economism (*jingjizhuyi feng* 经济注意风) swept across China's industrial workforce.[17] The term referred to a spate of protests animated by socioeconomic grievances and demands. As had been the case during the Hundred Flowers Movement, these protests were accompanied by an impressive display of spontaneous social organization. In Shanghai alone, we have records of 354 unofficial labor associations that were formed in this period. In most cases, their names—albeit parroting the state-approved "revolutionary" language of the day—indicated their relatively modest objectives: "Rebel Revolutionary Headquarters for Housing Difficulties," which sought a resolution of housing complaints; "Rebel Headquarters for Revolutionary Bachelor Workers," which called for transfer to Shanghai of workers' families living in the countryside; "Revolutionary Rebel Headquarters for Permanent Residents with Temporary Household Registration," which demanded resolution of residency problems; and so forth.

The grievances expressed by these various Cultural Revolution grassroots organizations were long-standing concerns that had been simmering below the surface for years. However, they erupted into the public arena only after the Workers' General Headquarters (an initially unauthorized umbrella organization of rebel-worker outfits that had challenged their factory authorities) won a set of concessions from the Shanghai Party Committee in the so-called Anting Incident. The Anting Incident of November 1966 was the first disruption of rail traffic in the Cultural Revolution. It began when more than a thousand worker rebels, having staged an unsuccessful sit-in at the Shanghai Party Committee to demand recognition of their maverick union, decided to take their petition to Beijing. When Premier Zhou Enlai learned that the petitioners were Beijing-bound, he ordered that their train be grounded soon after it left Shanghai (at the Anting railway station) so that the dispute could be resolved locally. Lasting for over thirty hours, the Anting Incident halted nearly 150 trains headed to or from the industrial capital of Shanghai, and created a serious transportation snarl that triggered further intervention by central party leaders. In the end, Beijing agreed to recognize the Workers' General Headquarters as a "revolutionary and legal organization," thereby unleashing a surge of extrastate organizational activity on the part of a broad array of aggrieved social actors who claimed revolutionary legitimacy for their demands.

As had been the case during the strike wave of 1956–1957, rebel workers in the Cultural Revolution were led by a diverse mélange of party and league members, ordinary workers, and officially designated "activists" and "backward elements." Yet this complex intermingling of state and society at the grassroots level did not prevent the protests from presenting serious challenges to government authorities. The outcome was often surprisingly favorable to the protesters. During Shanghai's "wind of economism," the pressure of worker demands led cadres at all levels to turn over huge sums of money as restitution. The city of Shanghai as a whole paid out some 35 to 40 million yuan in the single month of January 1967 in the form of higher wages, subsidies, welfare provisions, divisions of union accumulation funds, factory dividends, and the like as part of the economist wind. The 160,000 workers in Shanghai's Number 2 Commercial Bureau, for example, were granted more than 1 million yuan in wage hikes and subsidies as a result of their "revolutionary" participation in the protests. In the name of "rebellion," restive workers also forcibly seized and occupied much of the city's housing supply.

Although most of the organizations that had formed spontaneously during the wind of economism were soon suppressed, a number of the demands raised in that period later came to be accepted as official policy. As a direct response to the demands of protesters, temporary workers who had entered Shanghai factories before 1966 were converted to permanent status and differences between union and nonunion members in medical and other welfare benefits were abolished by the Shanghai Labor Bureau.

The upsurges of 1956–1957 and 1966–1967 are but two examples of a much broader phenomenon that is observable throughout the duration of the Maoist era. From the earliest days of the new Communist regime to the final months of Mao's life, widespread popular protest was a continuing reality.[19] Often (but not only) stimulated by state-sponsored mass campaigns such as the Hundred Flowers Movement and the Cultural Revolution, the protests invoked central state authority (including of course the incendiary utterances of Chairman Mao himself) to justify their claims. These were classic cases of what Kevin O'Brien and Li Lianjiang have recently dubbed "rightful resistance"; yet they pointed not toward an incipient awakening of social citizenship in opposition to state control—but rather to a persistent attempt (traceable back to the imperial era) by Chinese protesters to work an authoritarian political system to their own advantage.[20]

Rural Protest in the Reform Era

The agricultural reforms of the early post-Mao period, which greatly reduced the power of the collectives in favor of returning control over farming to individual households, were accompanied by an upsurge in rural unrest. For the first several years of the reform period, rural contention primarily took the form of communal violence in which rival lineages and villages struggled for control over contracted land and other natural resources, often at the behest of local cadres.[21] By the late 1980s, however, as township and village governments imposed higher taxes and surcharges to compensate for the lack of revenue that followed in the wake of decollectivization, the target of rural unrest shifted from competing social units to grassroots agencies and officials. Tax riots blazed across the countryside in opposition to what farmers (taking their cue from central leaders) referred to as unfair and excessive "peasant burdens." As Thomas Bernstein and Xiaobo Lu explain, "On the burden issue, because of their concern with stability, the central authorities sided with the peasants, leading to an implicit alliance between the Center and the peasantry, in which the latter explicitly invoked the authority of Center regulations when protesting against the levies imposed by local officials."[22]

Villagers were quick to seize upon the language of democracy and law, popularized by the post-Mao state, to press their grievances against grassroots cadres. As a young farmer complained in 1988, "Isn't the state building democratic politics? We farmers also want to talk about democracy. . . . It is both reasonable and lawful to pay grain [taxes]. We farmers are not confused about this. But they just take money from us in some muddled way."[23] By the 1990s, tax resistance had reached alarming proportions, with frequent reports of beatings, property destruction, arson, and other violence targeting local cadres; instances of peasants killing cadres (and sometimes being hailed as heroes by their fellow villagers for doing so) were openly reported in the Chinese press.[24]

The public sympathy that such protests elicited derived in large part from the fact that they generally followed a series of recognized stages, in which villagers dutifully acknowledged the authority of the central state before devolving into localized violence. Most protests began with a collective petition, or letter of complaint, that chided grassroots officials for failing to abide by higher-level dictates. As O'Brien and Li write of rural petitioners,

> Letters of complaint may concern any grievance, but in practice they usually target rural cadres who have violated a Party policy, a law, or a state regulation. Express reference to official documents (or sometimes leadership speeches) is useful inasmuch as it makes it difficult for local officials to ignore a complaint. . . . Typical complainants do not question the legitimacy of central laws and policies, not to mention the right of unaccountable leaders at higher levels to promulgate laws and policies. Complainants, by and large, seem to direct their attacks at over-eager or dishonest grassroots cadres who have harmed their interests—and then, mainly those cadres who are vulnerable because they have proven themselves unwilling (or unable) to comply with directives issued by higher levels or the "spirit of the Centre."[25]

Despite the frequency and scale of these protests, they were constrained by protesters' pronounced willingness to play by the rules. As Bernstein and Lu note, "The peasants' positive orientation toward the Center legitimated but also limited protests. . . . Villagers' tactic of clothing protest in the authority of the Central Committee and State Council undoubtedly made it more difficult for local officials to assign negative political labels to such acts. But this limitation also meant that tax-and-fee collective actions did not turn into social movements."[26]

Despite its failure to "turn into a social movement," the rampant tax resistance was regarded very seriously by the Chinese leadership. When the central authorities responded in 2006 by taking the extraordinary step of abolishing the national agricultural tax, the focus of rural protest shifted from tax riots to land disputes. The lucrative sale of collective lands by corrupt village and township cadres who neglected to consult or adequately compensate their fellow villagers led to widespread—and often violent—protests. In the face of ambiguous government regulations that do not clearly specify the property rights of various agencies and actors, the latitude for confusion and conflict is great. As Peter Ho observes, "The local governments and courts walk a thin line between the protection of the state's interests and meeting the collectives' demands for social justice."[27] The 2007 property rights laws and subsequent high-level deliberations over land privatization are efforts to come to grips with this unresolved dilemma.

Urban Protest in the Reform Era

While the Chinese countryside has seethed with tax riots and land disputes in the post-Mao period, the cities have been no less immune to popular contention. The April Fifth Movement of 1976—which began in Tiananmen Square but quickly spread beyond Beijing to other cities—demonstrated the willingness of students and other urbanites to express (veiled) political criticism even before Chairman Mao had passed away.[28] Mourning for the late Premier Zhou Enlai turned into an opportunity for condemning the radical excesses of the Cultural Revolution. Shortly after Mao's death, the Democracy Wall Movement of 1978–1979 saw an outpouring of big-character posters and impromptu street lectures calling for elections and other political reforms. Student protests—some directed against Japanese militarism and others against domestic police brutality—continued throughout the 1980s.[29]

In the winter of 1986–1987, widespread student demonstrations (supported by sympathetic workers) swept across urban China. Although these incidents were swiftly suppressed when central leaders decided that they had outlived their political usefulness, they prefigured the Tiananmen Uprising of 1989 in important respects. In January 1987, the general-secretary of the Communist Party, Hu Yaobang, was removed from power when other top leaders accused him of being too kindhearted toward the protesters. The same fate would befall his successor, Zhao Ziyang, two years later. More significant for our concerns, in both cases students clamoring for "democracy" took pains to play by the state's rules.

A striking feature of the so-called democracy movement of 1989 (like the 1986–1987 demonstrations that preceded it) was the deference that students paid to state authority.[30] Aware that the state was particularly wary of worker-student connections, students scrupulously honored police cordons and even dispatched their own "pickets" (*jiucha dui* 纠察队) to ensure that workers remained outside their inner circles. Student petitioners who attempted (unsuccessfully) to gain a hearing with the top leadership went so far as to drop to their knees and kowtow up the stairs of the Great Hall of the People in a time-honored ritual of humble subjects showing their respect for government authority. Although the students' action could certainly be interpreted as an ironic critique of the Communist state (for resembling a "feudal" imperial regime that required such obsequious behavior of its people), the widely re-ported incident was presented by the Chinese (and foreign) press at the time as a clear indication of the students' respect for authority.

Paralleling the well-publicized "democracy" movements of the late 1970s and 1980s, Chinese cities witnessed an upsurge in labor protest. Like the stu-dent movements, worker unrest also predated Mao Zedong's death. The April Fifth Movement of 1976 included substantial participation by young workers in the mass demonstrations and riots that broke out in more than forty cities that spring. Under Deng Xiaoping, labor unrest continued apace. The example of Solidarity in Poland stimulated a Chinese strike wave in the fall of 1980, with dozens of strikes breaking out in Wuhan and Taiyuan, followed by dis-ruptive work stoppages in Shanghai, Tianjin, Kunming, Manchuria, and cities in Hubei and Shanxi. Still strongly influenced by the discourse of the Cultural Revolution, workers' demands were often framed in Maoist class terms. The local press described strikers at a Taiyuan steel mill as "labeling themselves 'the poorest workers in the world,' call[ing] for 'breaking down the rusted doors of socialism,' the right to decide their own fate, the end to dictatorship and the overthrow of the system of political bureaucracy."[31]

The pace of labor unrest accelerated in the years leading up to the Tianan-men Uprising. Official Chinese statistics reported ninety-seven strikes in 1987 and over one hundred the following year.[32] Although we usually think of the 1989 Uprising as a student movement, proletarian participation was substan-tial. As had been true in the April Fifth Movement a decade earlier, large con-tingents of workers took to the streets, marching behind banners emblazoned with the names of their factories. The official trade unions made substantial monetary donations to the student hunger strikers, and even threatened the possibility of a general strike. The specter of a worker-student alliance, along the lines of Solidarity, surely figured importantly in Deng Xiaoping's decision to call in the People's Liberation Army to crush the movement.

One might have expected urban protest to subside after the brutal suppres-sion of June Fourth. Yet the opposite occurred. Worker unrest grew in both frequency and scale, often spilling outside the factory doors into public spaces. As Ching Kwan Lee observes, "Labour protests in the post-Tiananmen decade witnessed a heightened tendency for workers to go beyond the confines of their workplace."[33] Protest marches down major city thoroughfares, sit-ins at government offices, barriers erected at key intersections, and other disruptive displays of discontent were common features of urban life in the 1990s. In 1995 alone, official statistics reported 1,620 large-scale demonstrations in more than thirty Chinese cities.[34]

Chen Xi has recently argued that these pervasive urban protests "trigger a bargaining process" with government authorities. Through a series of standard and well-recognized "troublemaking" tactics, protesters enhance their leverage by engaging in familiar performative acts, attempting to engage higher-level officials or the public. As Chen explains, although the Letters and Visits (*xinfang* 信访) system through which many of these protests channel their initial activity dates back to the Maoist era, it has been updated in response to contemporary challenges: "When collective petitioning became more frequent and more disruptive, party leaders adjusted the system to cope with popular mobilization."[35] Despite the state's expectation that reforms to sharpen the powers and streamline the procedures of the *xinfang* system would work to defuse popular protest, they appear to have had the reverse result. Protest has grown apace, often overstepping the bounds stipulated by the Letters and Visits system. Chen's analysis makes clear, however, that although Chinese petitioners may choose to disregard certain inconvenient laws and regulations, they observe an unwritten set of conventions that is tacitly acknowledged by protesters and officials alike.

Playing by the rules involves adopting official language to signal that one's protest does not question the legitimacy of the central state. Even in the unusual case of Falun gong, where confrontation between the spiritual sect and state authorities escalated into an exceptionally bitter and protracted struggle, the protest began with submissive petitions seeking government recognition and registration. In today's China, where the government trumpets "rule by law" and where bookstores and television and radio broadcasts are replete with government-supplied legal information, protesters routinely invoke laws and regulations to justify their demands. Ching Kwan Lee describes a protest by laid-off textile workers in Liaoning, who marched behind banners and presented a petition that made clear their "legal-mindedness and restraint." Their petition read in part,

> Here are the discrepancies between the Bankruptcy Law and the situations of our enterprise. First, the procedure of bankruptcy was illegal. According to Instructions on Bankruptcy of State-Owned Enterprises passed by the Liaoning People's Government Office . . . there must be approval by the Workers' Congress and the superior department of the enterprise. . . . None of this is true in our case. . . . Second, workers received absolutely no livelihood allowance and this is a violation of Clause Four in the Bankruptcy Law.[36]

The invocation of legal rights is a prominent feature of popular protest in contemporary China. But whether this points to a newfound rights consciousness, rather than a familiar practice of presenting one's demands in terms acceptable to the state in order to receive a sympathetic hearing, is debatable. When Ching Kwan Lee asked workers in Liaoning whether they were fighting for citizens' legal rights, she was greeted with scorn. One worker representative explained to her,

"Because you are talking to the government, you have to talk about laws and regulations. Otherwise, they can ignore you."[37] Just as "comrades" in Mao's China spoke the language of "revolution" to gain the ear of the ruling authorities, so today's "citizens" present their grievances as a matter of "legal rights."

Rules Consciousness in Historical Perspective

Contemporary Chinese protesters (like generations before them) play by the rules of a widely understood—albeit ever-evolving—game whose operating procedures are shaped by interaction with (and testing of) government authorities. The rules certainly vary over time in tandem with changes in state ideology and policies, and they also vary markedly according to the social composition and location of the challengers, but in the main Chinese protesters go to considerable lengths to demonstrate that their actions are intended to support and strengthen—rather than to subvert—the authority of the state. This they do through the self-conscious use of the state's own rhetoric, presenting their claims in terms authorized by the laws, policies, and statements of the central government and its leadership. This strategy is basically what O'Brien and Li refer to as "rightful resistance," a useful conceptualization with which I would have no quarrel were it not for the suggestion of (1) the novelty of this type of protest in the post-Mao era; and (2) its connection to a rising rights consciousness on the part of a citizenry poised to mount a counterhegemonic project.

China lays claim to one of the oldest and most robust traditions of protest of any country in the world. Passed down through such media as folk stories, legends, and local operas, familiar repertoires of popular resistance were for centuries a major means of alerting an authoritarian political system to the grievances of ordinary people. Under certain unusual conditions, endemic protest could escalate into the large-scale rebellions for which Chinese history is famous.[38] But it took the catalytic combination of charismatic rebel leadership, heterodox ideology, widespread economic crisis, foreign threat, and an unresponsive and incompetent central state to generate a serious threat to dynastic rule. And such a combination was rare. As an American observer wrote in 1895, "The Chinese people have in numberless instances risen in opposition to their local rulers, but it has been an uprising against abuses of the system of government, never against the system itself. They have been known to deal with a local magistrate . . . in a most democratic and unceremonious manner . . . but it was not because of the exercise on his part of lawful authority, but because he had exceeded it."[39]

Today scholars often portray contemporary China as distinguished by the advent of a legal consciousness unknown in earlier eras, but it is remarkable how many instances of collective protest during the imperial and Republican periods were connected with the filing of lawsuits. Nineteenth-century local gazetteers confirm that, even in the poorest regions of the country, court cases were routinely initiated by all sectors of rural society. As the 1882 gazetteer of Fengtai County in northern Anhui put it, "The people are frugal, wear rough clothing, and eat coarse food. However, they frequently gamble and file lawsuits. Households may easily be bankrupted in this way. Those who are able to take their complaints to the higher courts are regarded as local heroes. Relatives and friends think it normal to give money to support these ventures, which are pursued in hopes of profit."[40] Legal channels were a well-recognized means for villagers to advance collective interests. When such efforts failed to bring about the desired outcome, protest often ensued.[41]

The willingness of Chinese protesters to play by the rules is clear in an eyewitness account by another American writer in 1896, who describes nineteenth-century complainants as turning to (limited) "trouble-making" tactics only when their initial petition effort failed to produce the desired result:

> I once saw a procession of country people visit the yamens of the city mandarins. . . . Shops were shut and perfect stillness reigned as, twenty thousand strong, they wended their way through the streets, with banners flying. . . . "What is the meaning of this demonstration?" I inquired. "We are going to reduce the taxes," was the laconic answer. Petitions had been tried in vain and now, driven to desperation, they were staking everything on a last appeal. . . . The conflict was with the mandarins only; the rioters were under strict discipline, and still professed loyalty to the supreme government. . . . Entering the yamen . . . to watch the proceedings, I noticed a company of rioters guarding a portion of the building while their comrades were eviscerating the rest. Inquiring why they were mounting guard instead of joining the looting, they answered simply, "This is the treasury, and no man shall touch the emperor's money." Their grievance was not taxation, but excessive charges made by local officers.[42]

As this example suggests, imperial-era protests—like protests today—frequently began with the presentation of petitions, usually written in boilerplate language that referred to the authority and benevolence of the central state in order to condemn the illegal and venal behavior of local officials. If the petitions did not elicit a sympathetic response from the yamen, they might evolve into riots that would either be crushed by military force or resolved by some sort of compromise with higher-level authorities. So standard and predictable were the manifestation of these protests that the historian Hsiao Kung-ch'uan refers to them as "model riots."[43]

In Republican-era China, when the new Nationalist state called upon its people to act as modern citizens rather than as feudal subjects, this protest

tradition was updated—but not uprooted. In place of scribe-brushed petitions citing imperial edicts and the Qing legal code to justify their actions,
protesters in the Republican period produced printed manifestoes that invoked rights enshrined in Sun Yat-sen's *Three Principles of the People*. Rebecca
Nedostup and Liang Hong-ming, drawing upon a large number of Nanjing-
decade petitions culled from the Kuomintang Archives in Taipei, describe one
protest in which a group calling itself the Shanghai Association of Blind
Gentlemen submitted a petition to the Executive Yuan:

> Not only was their petition typeset and printed, rather than the standard hand-
> written communication, it was accompanied by an appeal they called, in the
> manner of Nationalist Party congresses, a "proclamation" (*xuanyan* 宣言). Fur-
> thermore, by writing under the name of something called a "public association"
> (*gonghui* 公会), a term usually used for commercial groups, the blind diviners
> rhetorically linked themselves to all the other professional associations and
> unions in the city. . . .
>
> The language of the petition and proclamation reveals a fairly thorough ab-
> sorption of the ideology of the Nationalist Party and the concept of tutelary
> government, mixed as it was with leftover conventions of the imperial state. Lac-
> ing the language of the humble memorials to the Emperor with the vocabulary
> of modern politics, the diviners wrote "on bended knee we beg the sages of the
> party-state, and the good people of society, to permit some help for our be-
> nighted and dark lives."

Of course not all Chinese protests were (or are) as orderly or obedient as
these particular incidents might suggest. Like that of other nations, China's
history is replete with indiscriminate mob violence and bloodletting; and, as
is also true elsewhere across the globe, such rampages still erupt today.[44] Yet
China differs from many other countries in that its dominant modes of unrest
have for centuries taken the form of highly scripted protest repertoires intended not only to register indignation, but also to signal an interest in negotiation with an authoritarian state that takes such deferential expressions of
popular discontent extremely seriously.[45]

Conclusion

The argument here is definitely *not* that China has not changed since imperial
or Republican days. It has of course been transformed, politically as well as
economically and socially, in amazing and almost unimaginable ways over the
last three decades—let alone the last three hundred years. My point is simply
that widespread popular protest targeting lower-levels of the government and

framed in the language of the central state (even as that language has fluctuated to reflect major changes in official ideology and policy) is more likely an indication of politics-as-usual than a harbinger of some tectonic shift in state-society relations. Under an authoritarian system in which the ballot box has never been an effective means of conveying popular concerns to the political leadership, protest has often served that purpose instead. As Peter Lorentzen points out, "Authoritarian governments have limited sources of information about either the actions of the bureaucrats at their lower levels or the discontent of their citizens. Permitting protests provides information about both, helping to limit corruption and to bring discontented groups of citizens out in the open rather than driving them underground."[46] So long as the central state responds sympathetically yet shrewdly to the grievances expressed in widespread protest, the political system is strengthened rather than weakened by its occurrence.

Chinese political theory—from Confucian notions of the Mandate of Heaven to Mao's injunction that "it is right to rebel"—recognizes popular revolt as an expected expression of social grievances. The successful management of disturbances was the sine qua non of long-lived dynasties. As the astute observer of Chinese popular protest, Thomas Taylor Meadows, wrote in 1856: "In China it is precisely the right to rebel . . . that has been a chief element of a national stability, unparalleled in the world's history."[47] This is not to say that Chinese authorities (with the notable exception of Chairman Mao) encouraged popular protest. Riots and revolts were ruthlessly repressed by imperial rulers, who feared such expressions of discontent as a cosmic sign that their grip on the Mandate of Heaven might be slipping. A similarly hostile attitude prevails today. Nevertheless, central leaders' willingness and capacity to respond sensitively to protesters' demands (by such actions as dismissing unpopular local officials, providing disaster relief, and other concrete remedial measures) has been a key determinant of their political longevity.

Of course Meadows reached his conclusion on the sources of systemic stability just as the Taiping rebels were mounting a fundamental challenge to the Chinese imperial order. Under the charismatic leadership of Hong Xiuquan (who claimed to be the younger brother of Jesus Christ), the quasi-Christian message of the Taipings helped to mobilize a rebellion unprecedented in scale that unleashed a century of revolutionary upheaval in China. In the twentieth century, both the Nationalists (inspired by Sun Yat-sen's *Three Principles of the People*) and the Communists (led by Marxist-Leninist Mao Zedong) drew heavily upon foreign inspiration to forge new state systems that departed dramatically from Confucian precedents and principles.

The fact that alien religious and political ideas have fueled revolutionary change in twentieth-century China underscores what is at stake in the contemporary debate over "rights consciousness." Over the past 150 years, Western ideologies of Christianity, nationalism, and Marxism-Leninism have played a key role in facilitating the efforts of disaffected Chinese to launch revolutionary challenges against a succession of authoritarian states. In the eyes of some analysts, the contemporary discourse of universal human rights harbors a similar potential. But these days, when the authoritarian Chinese state is itself largely responsible for publicizing and propagandizing the importance of "legal rights" among its "citizens," the invocation of such rights in protest movements would seem to carry conservative, rather than radical, political implications. There is little evidence at present of any of the elements whose explosive combination would portend a serious threat to political stability: a counterhegemonic ideology, a charismatic oppositional leader, a widespread economic crisis, a foreign military threat, and an unresponsive state.

To propose, as many observers do, that Chinese protesters are articulating a new understanding of state-society relations, in which Western conceptions of citizenship and legal rights are infusing and thereby altering popular consciousness so as to undermine state legitimacy, is to point toward the likelihood of bottom-up political transformation. An escalation in the number of protests is often equated with a rising civil society believed to be approaching some tipping point after which political liberalization, democratization (or in some scenarios regime collapse or revolution) becomes unavoidable. To suggest, as I have tried to do in this chapter, that what we are seeing in China today reflects a much older "rules consciousness," in which savvy protesters frame their grievances against grassroots cadres in officially approved terms in order to negotiate a better bargain with the authoritarian state, leads us to a less dramatic—but perhaps more realistic—expectation.

2

Religion

The Dynamics of Religious Growth and Change

Robert Weller and Sun Yanfei

CHINA'S REFORMS HAVE BEEN REMARKABLY effective in achieving many of its leaders' goals. Like any major policy change, however, they also brought many unintended consequences. One of the most striking among these has been a massive increase in religiosity. This has affected the entire country—east and west, urban and rural—but unevenly across the geographic and economic landscapes. The new religious world also ranges across the entire legal landscape, from strongly repressed groups viewed as dangers to national security to the five officially sanctioned national religious associations. The most lively realm, however, has been the one that falls in the intermediate zone—not sanctioned by law but recently more or less tolerated by officials at all levels.

While the rapid increase in religious activity obviously relates to the increased personal (but not political) space that opened up from the beginning of the reforms, it also has roots in earlier Chinese religious patterns and in the modern history of religious control. Much of what we now call religion in China fell into two separate categories in late imperial China. One was "worship" (拜神), which typified the loosely organized activities based around local temples. These usually had institutional structures that extended only through a village or town, and they lacked priestly leadership and canonized textual traditions (though priests would be hired to conduct rituals). This very loose and local structure is one of the keys to the rapid regrowth of these traditions during the reform period. The second category that we now call "religion" included the "teachings" (教), a category that subsumed organized forms of knowledge passed down by teachers. Most important of these was the teaching of the scholars (儒教, Confucianism), but Buddhism, Daoism, Islam, and eventually Christianity were also classified as teachings.[1]

State policy toward religion changed drastically in the early twentieth century. Both the Nationalist and Communist leaders embraced key nineteenth-century ideas about secularism, especially in the French version that saw a radical separation of Church and State and an attempt to undercut the economic power of religious organizations, often by taking their land. Separating religion from politics in part also meant defining religion as a separate category of thought. One immediate result of this was the coining of a word for "religion" (宗教) for the first time in Chinese, and its definition along roughly Protestant lines as something with a sacred canon, voluntary membership, and trained specialists. By this definition, popular temple worship was only superstition (迷信, another new usage). Confucianism also fell out of the list of religions, because its fit with the standard definition was precarious (as seen by continuing arguments about whether it is a "religion"), even though it was the most exalted example of a "teaching." This Kuomingtang (KMT) legacy continues today in the official sanctioning of just five religions in the People's Republic: Islam, Buddhism, Daoism, Protestantism, and Catholicism.

Marx's basic stand toward religion was that it was an escape for people made miserable by their class position—"the heart of a heartless world."[2] It would simply fade away, he thought, when communism swept away exploitation. When the Chinese Communists took power after 1949, it is perhaps not so surprising that their religious policy was roughly a continuation of the previous decades under KMT rule—distinctly unsympathetic but not determined to exterminate religion entirely. Temples certainly were closed in the 1950s, but in ways very much like what the KMT had done earlier. The most striking difference was that the Communists felt much less need to spare Christianity for diplomatic reasons, and indeed worked hard to excise its significant foreign presence. A more radical seed, however, had been planted by Mao in 1927, when he wrote of religion as one of the four thick ropes binding the Chinese people—an attitude very different from Marx's patronizing sympathy.[3] That seed matured with the Cultural Revolution, which brought a far more antireligious attitude than ever before, and succeeded in stamping out almost all public forms of religiosity and making China appear in polls as the least religious place on the planet.[4]

Although basic attitudes of high cadres toward religion did not change, the policy immediately loosened up with the reforms. Large numbers of small village temples had reopened in some areas by the middle of the 1980s. The most important signal of the new policy was the promulgation in 1982 of "Document 19," which reiterated the basic stand (first taken in the 1950s) of respect for and protection of freedom of religious belief, and the confidence that religion would wither away on its own. This allowed the eventual reopening and restoration of many religious buildings, the training of new religious specialists, and the renewed performance of their rituals. New regulations issued in 2005 (as well as the law on heretical sects passed after the Falun gong repression in 1999) further clarified many details, but did not offer a new departure. After three decades, much of the work of rebuilding and restoration has been accomplished. That process, however, is only a small part of the changes that have occurred, as we will discuss.

To some extent, the rapid growth of many religions has led the central state to begin reconsidering policy. While no fundamental changes have occurred since Document 19 was issued, there are many signs that a new policy may be possible within a few years. Some regions, for example, experimented with the possibility of registering local temples as a sixth official religion—"Popular Religion" (民间宗教). This did not become central policy, however, and the idea now seems to have been dropped in favor of treating local temples as repositories of Chinese culture and allowing their activities as a kind of folkloric revival. At the same time we see public calls from a few intellectuals for things like registering house churches independently from the official church, which would have been impossible to say a few years ago. The main government offices in charge of religion have also been reaching out. The United Front Department of the Communist Party, for example, has established religious research areas around the country (including temple religion as well as the officially recognized ones). In another sign of change, the State Religious Affairs Bureau has recently established exchange relations with religious studies programs in foreign universities.

While we will return to these long-term possibilities of change in the conclusion, most of this chapter addresses the rapidly evolving situation on the ground right now. For reasons of space, we will concentrate just on the groups that have changed most strikingly. We will begin with local temple religion. Although this rarely shows up in polls because it is not an officially recognized religion, we have evidence of its growth in rural areas across the country. Indeed, there are probably hundreds of millions of people in China who take part in such activities, at least a few times during the year, making this one of the largest (and least recognized) religions in the world. The others that stand out for their size and rate of growth are Buddhism and Protestantism. Numbers of adherents are again extremely uncertain, especially because the boundaries of Buddhism are so porous and because so many Protestants will not register with the official Three Self Patriotic Movement. Nevertheless, all observers agree that we have rapid growth in both cases involving at least many tens of millions of people.

We will spend little time with the other traditions or with issues of religion among China's many ethnic minorities, simply for reasons of space. Let us briefly note, though, that the past ten years have seen signs of Confucianism coming back in Chinese society: the restoration of ancestral halls and recompilation of genealogies in rural areas, a handful of high-profile intellectuals advocating that Confucianism reassume public roles, the movement to teach Confucian classics in urban centers, the fashion of wearing traditional Chinese robes among some college students, as well as revived state-sponsored sacrificial rites to traditional Confucian cultural icons. Nevertheless, two of the most vital social institutions of Confucianism—the lineage system and the civil service examination system based on the classics—are unlikely to reclaim their former centrality, which will limit the possibilities for a revival. In comparison with Buddhism and Protestantism, the growth of institutional Daoism during the reform era has been lethargic, if measured by the scanty numbers of young clerics and the slow increase of the population of formal lay disciples. For the minorities, Buddhism, Christianity, and Islam are all very important, but there is also a mosaic of other religious diversity among minorities—much more than we can begin to address here.

As we describe the developments of the three religions, we will focus on three broad issues that crosscut the religious denominations. The first of these is the relation between religion and the state. One of the crucial variables in explaining religious change in China is the kind of space the state has made available for religion, and the ways different traditions have been able to take advantage of it. Each of the five recognized religions was consolidated into a state-controlled association in the 1950s, and all five associations were revived after the Cultural Revolution. In the case of Buddhism and Daoism, which were not historically organized in congregations, these organizations have had relatively successful monopolies due to their control over monastic life and ordination. The Protestant and Catholic organizations, however, have been challenged from the beginning by "house churches" that refuse to accept state oversight and interference in theological matters. Temple religion is equally precarious, in this case because the state does not recognize it as religion at all.

The result is five conservative, careful religious associations with close ties to the State Administration for Religious Affairs. Among them, the Buddhists have probably been most successful at negotiating that position. At the other extreme, we have officially condemned "evil cults" (the term was resurrected from imperial language in the aftermath of Falun gong), which the state actively represses. These include various syncretic sects with long histories in China, and more recently a few radical and indigenous Christian groups. The vast majority of the growth, however, lies in between—a gray zone not technically legal but largely allowed to occur.[5] Repression is always a legal possibility, but in fact a wide range of such religious activity—from massive local temple rituals to large, clearly marked unofficial churches—can be seen across the country. The intermediate space shows up again in the wide array of government offices with some say over religion, but often with conflicting interests. These include local branches of the Religious Affairs Bureau, the Communist Party's United Front Department, the Tourism Bureau, and sometimes the Civil Affairs Bureau and other departments. The various religious traditions deal with the opportunities and risks of this intermediate zone in quite different ways, which has been crucial for understanding their different rates of growth and potentials for the future.

The second broad issue is the relation between economy and religion, especially with the rapid commercialization of life since the reforms. To what extent does religion shape economic behavior and to what extent does it change as a result of a new economy? Certainly religion has not been immune from the market—its increasing involvement in charity is one kind of response to perceived failures of the market, while increasing feelings that temples and clergy are corrupt is quite another kind of market involvement. One crucial factor here is the relatively low level of institutional control over religion over the past millennium in China, which helps create a high degree of flexibility and adaptability to new economic conditions. At the same time, as we will discuss, the perception of "modernity" has been important in attracting adherents to some religions, especially Protestantism.

Third, the data remind us yet again of China's enormous geographical and social diversity. We will thus be concerned to begin to outline—as far as possible right now when there is still little research on modern religion—some of the major variations. Christianity, Buddhism, temple religion, and the rest exist everywhere in the country, but each also has areas of particular strength. Religious conversion and activity similarly extend across all levels of society, but we sometimes see quite different dynamics between men and women, rural and urban, educated and uneducated, and so on.

Temple Religion

Temple religion suffered in China throughout the twentieth century. Officials considered many associated activities like spirit mediumship to be superstition at best and a dangerous con at worst. Spirit mediums, fortune tellers, *fengshui* experts, and the like had to practice underground or not at all. Gradual closings of temples continued policies from the KMT period. The only attempt at total repression, however, was during the decade of the Cultural Revolution. This was a relatively short period compared to what happened in the Soviet Union, for example. It was not long enough to break social memory.

Indeed, the repression never succeeded completely, even in the most radical years. Many places hid god images, to be worshipped in secret or pulled out of hiding when it became safe, even during the Cultural Revolution. Chau, for example, reports that in its early, most radical years, the spirit of Norman Bethune (widely studied and admired during the period thanks to an essay of Mao's) was performing miracle cures in northern Shaanxi. There was no temple, but people invoked the spirit by uttering his name and smoking his favorite *Yan'an* brand cigarettes.[6] Also in China's northwest, Jing reports that although all local temples at his field site had been dismantled in 1958, an early makeshift shrine had already been established by a female medium in 1975.[7]

Things began to change rapidly in the early years of the reforms. Probably the first thing to return in most areas was ancestor worship, especially where it could be done without a permanent public display (like an ancestral altar). "Sweeping" the graves at the Qingming Festival by offering incense and food and cleaning up the year's plant growth was an obvious candidate, in part because people could always claim quite secular motives if they had to, and partly because it involves no permanent religious structures. One local cadre in Guangxi explained that he was a Communist and an educated man (that is, an unsuperstitious atheist), but that shortly after the Cultural Revolution he had successfully consulted a spirit medium who helped him find his parent's grave so he could sweep it. He had lost track of it during the Cultural Revolution decade.[8]

Spirit mediums also came back relatively quickly in many areas, for similar reasons. Mediums do not need permanent religious structures and can easily work out of residences. They could operate under the radar of any cadres high enough to be concerned. Thus in rural Fujian, Dean reports that local areas that had not yet reconstructed their temples were able to send spirit mediums to festivals.[9] In many areas the initial mediums were all women, even when men had traditionally played that role. This was again because of the insecurities of those first years of opening up—cadres found it easier to ignore or dismiss what women were doing.[10]

Within a few years, however, temple festivals reappeared and temples began to be rebuilt or refurbished. These included a few famous tourist sites that had government support, but also many thousands more built in the full knowledge that there was no government support and that renewed repression was always a possibility. Typically, reconstruction began with the smallest temples (village shrines to earth gods), but in many cases eventually major temples of the past were recreated or even expanded.

Fujian has been one of the centers of this revival. Dean documents the reconstruction of various temples throughout the 1980s, and suggests that there were about a hundred such cases in one county alone.[11] Only a few of these had direct government support, but many drew support from Taiwanese devotees of the deities in these temples. Local officials often tended to stand aside because they were eager for other forms of Taiwanese investment to accompany the rebuilding of temples.

This may have encouraged a greater density of newly rebuilt temples in Fujian than most other places, but overseas connections were not necessary. One of us (Weller) saw dozens of new earth god temples (社坛) in remote parts of Guangxi in 1985, and major community temples had been rebuilt in many areas by then. In one area of northern Shaanxi, for example, the major temple festival had been revived in 1978—almost the first possible instant— and the temple was rededicated in 1982.[12] Also in the northwest, Jing documents that his field site had eight new or rebuilt temples by 1992, four of them the responsibility of female shamans.[13] Another festival, this time in northern Hebei, had been restored in 1979, as documented by Gao Bingzhong.[14] In this case there had never been a temple, but just a wooden board dedicated to a Dragon King. As the villagers got both wealthier and bolder, they created ever larger and more elaborate boards to substitute for the old one that had been hidden through the Cultural Revolution. They paid 30,000 RMB for the one carved in 1995, and they built a permanent structure for it in 1996, for the first time ever. They report that one hundred thousand people typically attend the annual festival, and this scale is not unusual by the standards of other temples for which we have studies.

We have too few studies to produce a good geography of local temple religion (historically as well as in contemporary times), but most observers would agree that the southeast coast has the greatest density of such activity and that we see at least some activity all across rural China. By the end of the 1990s the spate of rebuilding appeared to have run its course in many areas. In rural Zhejiang, for instance, consecration rituals for new village temples attracted thousands of believers from near and far earlier in the 1990s. By around 2000, however, enthusiasm began to wane and temples found themselves competing for attention.

In some areas, village solidarity has been so weakened that temples no longer have the kind of influence they once did. These temples have become simple profit-making enterprises or have simply given way to other forms of religion.[15] As Wu Keping reports from the highly developed Changzhou area (Jiangsu), for example, village resettlement as a result of rapid urban expansion has nearly wiped out local temple religion because the local communities of support have dissolved. Instead, religious life has been taken over by Buddhism and by spirit mediums.[16] Thus while temple religion thrives all across the country, it is probably most active on the southeast coast (especially Fujian) and less so in the rapidly urbanizing environment of the lower Yangtze valley.

Just as with the rebirth of spirit mediumship, women—especially older women—have often been crucial in the rebirth of temples by initiating the rebuilding, raising funds, and persuading men to help. Old age and female status provided them with a double layer of protection, making them relatively immune to suspicion and suppression from local cadres. This was especially important during the early years of the reforms when there was more repression. It offered women new visibility and power in the religious public sphere, which men had dominated in an earlier era.

In many cases women have retained these new forms of power after temples have been restored, but in others men have taken over again once the political risks diminished and the advantages for building social capital again became clear. One unforeseen consequence of this has been that women founders of temples have sometimes turned them over to Buddhist clergy rather than lose control to men as temples reenter systems of local social capital. This has been especially true in the lower Yangtze region, where Buddhism is thriving (see below). It also allows temples to avoid the difficulties of the unregistered gray zone that temples usually occupy in China today by allowing them to register with the Buddhist association. It is not yet at all clear whether this sort of Buddhist conversion is mere camouflage, or a Buddhist "superscription" on local religion, or the beginning of a fundamental change in religiosity.[17] In many wealthier parts of China, we can also find individuals becoming formal disciples of Buddhist or Daoist clergy. In some cases this is obviously a continuation of long-standing practices of lay devotees, but in others it appears to be simply a purchased document that allows activists in temple religion to make a formal claim that they are part of officially registered religions rather than victims of feudal superstition.

Entrepreneurs are a significant proportion of this last kind of devotee. Whether or not the end result will be a gradual move from temple religion to more standard forms of Buddhism or Daoism, these people remind us that temple religion has a comfortable relationship with the modern economy. Taiwan's temple religion boomed at the exact moment the island became rich. People continue to argue about how correlation and causation may be related in Taiwan's case, but at the very least it tells us that temple religion, in spite of its strong continuities with a much earlier China, is no hindrance at all to modern economic success.

Buddhism

As soon as the Cultural Revolution ended, the restoration of dilapidated Buddhist temples began. Monks were allowed to return to the temples and reassert the power to run them. As with temple religion, donations from Chinese expatriates, both clergy and laity, greatly aided rebuilding in the 1980s.

The deepening of economic reform since the early 1990s has had a major impact on Buddhism, creating both opportunities and problems. Especially after Deng Xiaoping's southern tour in the spring of 1992, economic development became the paramount objective for government at all levels, both motivating and pressuring officials to develop the local economy. Cadre promotion criteria in many counties have focused almost entirely on how much capital investment they can bring to the county from outside. Under such circumstances, local officials have been driven to exploit every possible resource to stimulate the local economy. Cadres in many areas have seen religion's potential to facilitate the tourist industry and, for some areas, to help bring in other forms of investment from overseas Chinese.

Buddhism has proved to be the most valuable resource for this strategy because of the location of many of its temples in famous scenic spots, its cultural appeal, and its widespread networks of devotees. Indeed, as rapid economic development led to growing affluence for many Chinese, endless streams of tourists and pilgrims swarmed daily to the sacred Buddhist mountains and famous temples. They gave rise to an economic chain that consists of hotels, restaurants, shops for religious goods, tour guides, taxi drivers, and other associated industries.

Local governments are thus responding favorably to initiatives of rebuilding Buddhist temples. In some cases, they themselves have initiated the process. Local government officials, for example, sometimes have tried hard to woo old monks with national fame to preside over the temples in their locality, because these eminent old monks have widespread disciple networks and are able to channel tremendous resources to any temple they help to rebuild. Let us give just one example of this "old monk effect." Fengxin County in Jiangxi Province is a relatively poor county not blessed with many economic resources. It is, however, the site of a historically significant temple where the eminent monk Baizhang in the Tang dynasty purportedly established an early set of rules for Chan monastic discipline. The local county government, interested in tapping into the developing Buddhist tourist economy, generously allocated 192 acres of land for the purpose of rebuilding the temple. In addition, the county officials paid five visits to the renowned monk Benhuan based in Shenzhen City. The ninety-eight-year-old monk finally agreed to assume the abbotship. He and his lay disciples poured 120 million yuan into temple construction. Within two years, a magnificent temple complex emerged from the bucolic surroundings. The temple, scheduled to open in early 2010, is expected to create an influx of pilgrims and tourists and help to boost the local economy.[18] Fengxin County has also invested heavily in the infrastructure of this promising tourist site. By the end of 2007, they had completed a 15-kilo-meter-long highway to replace the original zigzagging and bumpy dirt road leading to the location of the temple.

Corporate interests too covet the commercial value of Buddhism. These companies, which generally have strong government background, are partici-pating in projects to build giant Buddha statues and Buddhist theme parks or tourist complexes. Other groups that cash in on Buddhist temples include the nearby villagers who act as incense sellers, tourist guides, photo takers, and fortune tellers. Their unrestrained moneymaking activities often interfere with the operation of the temples. In the face of market forces, some Buddhist temples have taken the initiative and tried to exploit the commercial potential themselves. The most (in)famous example is the Shaolin Temple in Dengfeng City, Henan Province. Known as the legendary birthplace of both Chan prac-tice and martial arts, it became a cultural icon, thanks to some widely popular kungfu films and novels. Under the leadership of the monk Yongxin, who as-sumed the abbotship in 1987, Shaolin has taken advantage of its fame and made a series of commercial moves, including kungfu shows of Shaolin monks around the globe, film productions, hosting reality TV shows for kungfu stars, and online selling of Shaolin-related products from secret kungfu recipes to chopsticks. In 2006, the Dengfeng municipal government awarded Yongxin a German Volkswagen SUV for his "extraordinary contribu-tion to developing local tourism."[19]

This tendency toward internal commercial secularization intensified when the new generation of monks born in the 1950s and 1960s assumed abbot-ships. Unlike the old generation of monks who are withering away, many of these new leaders have little experience of Chan hall training but have strong administrative skills and great political finesse.[20] They have an affinity with the bureaucrats because they share the mindset of developmentalism.

Modern technology, management skills, and business development can serve religious ends, but much of the concern now is that religion is becoming simply a façade for business ventures and the bait for generous donation and spending. Furthermore, the means many Buddhist temples employ to acquire income (even if they try to justify the means in light of religious or charitable ends) are questionable, some in direct contradiction with the Buddhist spirit. The not uncommon practices of inveigling visitors into burning exorbitantly priced in-cense before Buddha statues, selling bell-tolling rights at New Year's Eve, and holding auctions of purportedly consecrated (开光) cell phone numbers have downgraded temples into moneymaking enterprises, clerics into salespersons.

In certain ways, this kind of entrepreneurial approach creates an economic win-win situation for Buddhist temples, their local government, and the neighboring community. Its economic value (combined, of course, with its recognition as one of the five official religions) has made state legitimation easier for Buddhist temples than for those in most other traditions. As a source of significant income, such temples can bargain with the state for a higher degree of autonomy. The economic value of Buddhism, however, is a double-edged sword. It makes Buddhism easy prey to various interest groups and is a source of conflict and contestation. Conflicts might rise over disagreements about profit distribution. Temples might bicker with Tourism Bureau or corporate interests on issues like the price of entry tickets, and who gets the bigger share of the income from tickets. Conflicts might also rise when Buddhist temples resist the forces encroaching on their autonomy and take radical actions to assert their religious identity. The first half of 2009 witnessed several such incidents: two important and vigorous Buddhist temples, the Bailin Temple in Hebei Province and the Famen Temple in Shaanxi Province, both announced that they would close the temples to public access as a protest against the predatory commercial forces that impinged on their autonomy. Without doubt, similar incidents will occur in the future. Some of the Buddhist temples are becoming stronger and more self-assertive about their religious identity. On the other hand, the local governments have not changed their attitude toward Buddhist temples, seeing them primarily as profit-generating machines. They still adopt a developmental mentality and authoritarian style when dealing with temples. Furthermore, capitalists looking for high-return investments covet the commercial value of Buddhist temples. They and the local government easily form allies. Often the local governments are the developers themselves. Thus, even though Buddhism has tended to be politically safe—not advancing into the gray zone where both temple religion and Christianity (see below) have thrived—it is still forced into extensive negotiation with the state.

The overt commercialization practices of some temples may bring wealth to temples in the short run, but they also risk overspending and abusing their "spiritual capital" and thus eating away the very foundation on which faith in temples and sangha is built. In effect, much of this damage has already been done. The Shaolin Temple, the pioneer of such commercialization, has found itself in the center of controversy. In several polls carried out by news websites, public opinion toward Shaolin's business moves and its abbot's accepting the German SUV was overwhelmingly negative and the netizens expressed their contempt, ridicule, and regret in chat rooms.[21] The recent Internet uproar shows that the public, Buddhist practitioners or not, holds some basic expectations of how a Buddhist monk or a temple should act. In adapting to modernity and riding the tide of market forces, many feel that Buddhism should at least uphold its religious core. The secularization has been so rampant that the former head of China's State Religious Affairs Bureau, Ye Xiaowen (not known as a man of great religious conviction himself), called on the Buddhist sangha to take the Vinaya (precepts and monastic rules) as their master (以戒为师) at an important meeting of the Buddhist Association of China in 2006.[22]

The Buddhist world is aware of the danger of commercial secularization. Some monasteries stress the importance of upholding the Vinaya rules, and they have earned the respect of Buddhist believers. Two monasteries in particular, the Pushou Temple on Mt. Wutai in the north, and the Pingxin Temple in Fujian in the south have emerged as new pilgrimage destinations for the Buddhist practitioners because of their strict adherence to the Buddhist precepts and ascetic practices.

There is also a type of temple that diligently preserves religious traditions but remains more actively engaged with society. The Bailin Temple in Hebei Province is a forerunner and one of the most successful examples of promoting the Buddhist Dharma through cultural and educational means. It publishes a Buddhist periodical and books, and organizes meditation retreats. The most noteworthy achievements have been the sixteen summer camps they have organized for college students since 1993. Other temples emulate the practices of the Bailin Temple, and summer camps organized by Buddhist temples are now sprouting across China. Some monasteries or lay Buddhist associations have also been involved in charitable work, from disaster relief to building old-age homes. They work to patch the gaps in people's lives that neither the market nor the state is currently filling. Even those temples being criticized for going too far down the road of commercialization have made efforts to return to their religious core in recent years. The Shaolin Temple, for example, partially salvaged its image within Buddhist circles by launching a meditation retreat in 2006, and sponsoring the grand ordination ceremony in 2007.

Protestantism

The growth of Protestantism in the past thirty years has been spectacular. Other religions have tried simply to recover from the wreckage of the Cultural Revolution, but Protestantism has far surpassed its 1949 level. It has been the fastest growing religion in the reform era.[23] Protestantism in China is divided into two segments: (1) the government-sanctioned churches that are associated with the committee of the Three Self Patriotic Movement (TSPM) and its ecclesiastical extension, the China Christian Council (CCC); and (2) the house churches not registered with the government. The TSPM and the CCC are commonly referred to as the "two committees." Like the Buddhist Association of China, they form the leadership structure of the official churches and are directed by the State Administration for Religious Affairs.

With a sea change in the CCP's religious policies after the Cultural Revolution, the government reinstalled the TSPM in 1979 and formed the CCC in 1980. The official church recovered much of its property, reopened sites for collective gatherings, ran seminaries, and published national Christian journals. The official 2006 membership figure of 16 million Protestants, compared with the 1949 figure of 870,000, indicated a growth of almost twenty times during the last three decades. However, this number does not take into account membership unaffiliated with the official churches. The growth of these unregistered house churches is even more vigorous than that of the state-sanctioned churches. As we now know, house churches, particularly in Henan, Anhui, Shandong, and Zhejiang, continued to meet in secret even during the most repressive time.[24] The liberalization of the state religious policy has enabled the house churches to engage in more open and active activities. Unlike the official churches, they refuse to be burdened by abiding by state policy constraints on evangelization, and recruit avidly. Also, the more intimate relationship among its members and the vigor it displays often makes a house church much more appealing to seekers.[25]

There are many strands within the category of house churches.[26] We will highlight three types, as they probably represent the three most influential or potentially influential models.[27] Each is a noticeable social phenomenon on its own terms and has distinctive leadership and organizational attributes. There is some commonality but also clear differences in each type's relationship with the state and its interaction with the market economy.

First, there are the house churches in rural Henan and Anhui, especially along the Huai River valley. Starting from the 1970s, this region has seen a remarkable spread of Protestantism. Illiterate or semi-illiterate itinerant evangelists made up a core of charismatic leaders and zealous preachers, who have been extremely successful in recruiting the rural poor. Then, by taking advantage of the converts' existing social bonds of family, friends, and neighbors, Protestantism expanded rapidly to the wider population. The tremendous increase of Protestantism in these areas actually owes a great deal to the Communist state because the state effectively wiped out or weakened the main local foes and competitors of Christianity—the lineage groups and the gentry class, and other religions and sects. Indeed, the peasants found Protestantism a good substitute for popular religion and were first attracted to it precisely because the kind of Protestantism trumpeted by the rural preachers had elements reminiscent of popular religion, for example, supernatural healing, exorcism, and petitionary prayers for health and wealth.[28]

As the rural churches further expanded, they began to be afflicted by a number of problems—lack of theological training of the preachers, personality cults, embezzlement of overseas donations, authoritarianism, conflicts between different sects, and some Christian offshoots that drifted far from their roots and sometimes into violence. The problem of these "heresies" has been recognized by some church leaders and members. In fact, one of the chief motivations behind the drafting of *The Manifesto of Chinese House Churches* (中国家庭教会宣言) by Henan house church leaders in 1998 was to facilitate doctrinal unity among different sects and churches, and to separate themselves from Christian sects they saw as heretical.

The fervent evangelization, the large scale of the churches, the firm control of a mother church over a number of smaller churches, together with the above-mentioned problems made local officials wary and unnerved. The Henan house churches have suffered intermittently from police raids and some church leaders were imprisoned. The tension with the state has reinforced the sectarian tendency of these rural churches. Their mistrust and antagonism toward the local state and the government-sanctioned Three Self churches are too deep-rooted for them to compromise easily.

The second major Protestant type is the Wenzhou model. The Wenzhou model of economic development, characterized by privately owned businesses thriving by producing and selling small merchandise, was used to explain the marvelous rise of Wenzhou from an impoverished rural town to one of China's most affluent cities and regional hub of global capitalism during reform-era China.[29] Perhaps less known to the world, Wenzhou also earned the nickname of "China's Jerusalem" during the same period. Located on China's east coast, Wenzhou became an important base of foreign missionary activities as early as the Qing dynasty, especially for the United Methodist Free Church and China Inland Mission. Wenzhou has also been deeply influenced by the "Local Church" movement led by Watchman Nee, one of the most influential Christian leaders in twentieth-century China. By 1949, Wenzhou already had approximately 70,000 Protestants. Geographically isolated and politically distant from the center, believers were able to keep their faith even during the turbulent years of the Cultural Revolution. Even before the Cultural Revolution ended, Wenzhou had already witnessed the dawn of a Protestant revival. Now the city is home to more than 1,200 churches and an estimated 700,000–1,000,000 Protestants, which amounts to very roughly 12 percent of the local population.[30] In comparison with the rural churches in Henan and Anhui, Wenzhou churches, with more than one hundred years of Protestant influence, are less vulnerable to sectarian offshoots. In addition, the inherited church structure has made Wenzhou churches less likely breeding grounds for charismatic and authoritarian leaderships.

One of the most distinctive features of the Wenzhou model of Protestantism is that the new generation church leaders are often at the same time successful private business owners. These "boss Christians" have made generous offerings to church coffers, aggressively acquired assets for churches, helped erect sumptuous church buildings, invited famous preachers from other areas to provide pastoral services, trumpeted prosperity theology in their congregations, orchestrated mass Christmas celebrations, and spread their faith by taking advantage of their widespread existing business networks.[31] Their enthusiasm in expansion and evangelization was boosted by their entrepreneurial pursuit for a bigger share in the market. Their audacity to think big and act bold was not only a reflection of the self-confidence based on their success in the market economy, but also an enactment of the developmentalism they fully embraced.

Unlike the Henan Christian leaders, who suffer from state repression and who are a marginalized social group, these affluent Wenzhou Christians, social elites in mainstream society, have adroitly built social connections with local cadres and used those connections to win some security from the state for house churches they built or managed. Sometimes they have also been able to secure the local state's permission or at least acquiescence to evangelize in the localities where they have business investments.

The third major form consists of urban house churches in Beijing and other cities. In recent years the house churches in metropolitan cities have risen in significance, not only because of their rapidly growing membership, but also because of their increasing social impact. These urban house churches, especially those in Beijing, have attracted well-educated professionals, college and graduate students, writers and artists.[32] Many of these believers or seekers are young people born after the 1970s. They find Christianity "liberating, democratic, modern, cosmopolitan, or universal."[33] These same traits made Christianity a favored religion among social activists and political dissidents. Although currently these urban church members constitute an insignificant percentage of the Christian population in China, they will be able to exert disproportionate influence on the Chinese Christian community in years to come. The emphasis on the importance of theological training and institution building by the urban churches has set an example for other churches to follow. They are open to dialogue with other intellectuals and government officials and would like Protestantism to become more actively engaged in the discursive arena of the public sphere instead of having to retreat to their sectarian enclave. These urban elite Christians are thus quite discontent with remaining in the gray area and in recent years are the most active Christian groups calling on the government to revise the current church registration system to allow house churches to register on a par with the TSPM churches rather than register under them.[34]

The urban house churches had little interference from the government until 2008 when a number of house churches in Beijing and Chengdu were raided by government agencies. As these churches are well connected with the overseas Christian community, these incidents immediately evoked an international outcry. Most noticeably, the Autumn Rain Church of Chengdu, headed by a social activist and lawyer, sued the county Religious Affairs Bureau for transgressing the appropriate legal procedure and violating the religious freedom guaranteed in the Constitution.[35] Using legal weapons to defend their rights has become a commonly accepted practice among the urban Christian churches.

The state in general remains uneasy with Protestantism, especially the house church movement, compared with its relatively relaxed attitude toward Buddhism and popular religion. Although they live within the same legal and regulatory framework set by the central state, the three types of house churches have very different relationships with the local officials, as we have seen above. It is the local state more than central policy that directly shapes the sociopolitical milieu in which they operate. Even within the same prefecture, the religious governance of neighboring counties can be drastically different. In spite of internal variations, as a rule, the Henan house churches have an antagonistic relationship with the repressive local government offices, while the relationship between the Wenzhou churches and the local cadres often is more harmonious. The urban churches led by elite intellectuals, on the other hand, are actively seeking to engage the state in dialogues and pushing for a fundamental change of the existing restrictive and discriminatory legal framework toward house churches.

Current religious policy appears unable to curb the growth of Protestantism at all. Unlike Buddhism and the more compliant TSPM churches, house churches exert little self-censorship in evangelization work, which contributes to their more rapid growth. The state's outright repressive measures are bound to elicit international criticism on human rights, which Beijing has to take into consideration. Moreover, the house church movement has already become a powerful social force, and the state cannot afford to further solidify and radicalize them.

Protestantism has been able to gain converts across China, from a wide range of age groups and from very different socioeconomic groups, from marginalized peasants, the new rich, the urban middle class, and elite intellectuals. What makes Protestantism the fastest growing religion in China today? First we would point to the inner drive of evangelicalism of Protestantism. In comparison with the enthusiastic proselytization efforts of Protestantism, Buddhism as a whole appears rather inert. Protestantism not only has many skillful and persistent evangelists who dedicate their lives to spreading the faith, it also prompts all believers to evangelize in the social networks in which they are embedded. Moreover, it devises strategies to recruit nonnetworked strangers.[36]

Protestantism has also been developing a much firmer base in the local communities than Buddhism. By appropriating personal ties—family members, neighbors, friends and colleagues—to spread its messages, Protestantism is able to encapsulate an increasingly wider but connected community. Such a move has also brought about long-term demographic change in the congregation. In the beginning of the 1980s, in the rural areas, both Buddhism and Protestantism appeared to be religions of old women. Now with the lapse of some twenty years, more young people have joined the Protestant community and the sex ratio has become more balanced, while Buddhism remains predominantly for middle-aged and old women. The pastoral care that Protestant churches are performing helps to stabilize the community of the faithful and binds them together. In contrast, while monks in small Buddhist temples make a living by performing rituals for local patrons, major Buddhist monasteries are primarily transterritorial entities in the sense that they value more their relationship with those socioeconomically advantaged patrons from afar. In both cases, little effort has been made to take care of the local communities in which Buddhist temples are embedded. Even believers who have already taken formal refuge with Buddhism are basically left to their own devices for spiritual growth.

The current restrictive religious policy actually has hampered the growth of the more compliant religions like Buddhism rather than unregistered Protestant churches. Although the state prohibits religious activities outside of the designated religious sites, underground Protestantism has exercised little self-restraint in evangelization. Instead, they invented ways to circumvent the radar of state surveillance, for example, door-to-door proselytizing in the countryside, cultural performances with Christian messages in the cities, and proselytization in overcrowded public spaces.[37]

The rapid growth of Protestantism in China, however, is accompanied by fission, discord, and disputes. Conflicts will continue to thwart any promise of unity in the future—not just those between government-sponsored and house churches, but also within the house church segment, like the conflicts between the conservative Local Churches and the charismatic movement, between self-regarded orthodoxy and heterodoxy, between the more conciliatory groups and the adamantly antistate groups, between the groups promoting Protestantism to become a public religion and the sectarian groups that accuse them of succumbing to the world.

Conclusion

One of the striking features of Chinese religions over the three decades of the reform period has been the speed of change. This involves significant new variations in every tradition, not simply recapturing earlier levels of religiosity. Along with these new adaptations we can see broad lines of regional variation that we have been able to mention only briefly. Thus, even though all the traditions we have discussed exist across the entire country (along with some others, like Islam or Catholicism), some areas have developed concentrations of particular traditions: Protestantism in the Huai River region, Buddhism in the lower Yangtze, and temple religion in the southeast coast.

One reason for this variability in time and space is the relative lack of very strong institutions of religious control in China ever since (pre-Christian) religion took roughly its current form in the Song dynasty. There is a striking historical contrast with the Orthodox Church in Russia, or the Roman Catholic Church in West Europe, or Islam in Saudi Arabia. Unlike those cases, central control over Buddhist or Daoist ritual practice, ordination, and textual interpretation was quite weak. For the temple religion that framed the lives of most people, there were no central institutions at all, with religious authority generally stopping at the temple in the nearby town or the relatively educated man down the street.

The lack of strong centralized traditions has allowed all kinds of religion to develop quickly and flexibly in China, in spite of a very new economic environment. This holds some ironies and some lessons for current government policy, which has in general pushed in just the opposite direction. Religious policy has changed greatly since the near complete repression of the Cultural Revolution, but has maintained the general attempt of the 1950s (pioneered much earlier by the KMT) to allow only religions with strong centralized control through the five official associations. The rapid growth and adaptation, however, has happened almost entirely at or beyond the boundaries of those official institutions.

We see this in every tradition we have examined. The empowerment of women in the rebuilding of village temples is one example. Temple religion itself, of course, is entirely beyond the State Administration for Religious Affairs because it does not meet their definition of religion. The experiments of a few years ago in registering temples as a sixth official religion appear now to have been abandoned. Instead, some local temples have been able to register as Buddhist or Daoist temples. The long-term consequences of this are still unclear, but it might lead to a push toward greater monastic control and, especially for the Buddhists, more widespread changes in ritual practice. Recently it has become common for temples to find some political legitimacy by claiming folkloric value as repositories of traditional culture. At the same time, Buddhist monasteries are increasingly experimenting with new social positioning, sometimes inspired by the enormous success of Taiwanese Buddhist groups in gathering support in Taiwan and around the world.

Protestants, although they have an official association, have been active above all in the gray zone, with churches that refuse to cooperate with the official Three Self Patriotic Movement and that even ordain their own ministers. These churches are no longer underground at all, in the sense that they often occupy large, clearly marked buildings that attract hundreds of worshippers, but they still completely reject the state religious project and could be legally subject (just like temple religion) to repression at any time. This sector is growing especially quickly, in part because Protestantism is so skilled at working in this gray zone. Much more than the Buddhists or Daoists, who have tended to recognize and live within the authority structures of the official associations, the Protestants have been able to capitalize on their ability to work the interstices of the system. One of the greatest unintended consequences of government policy has thus been the very rapid expansion of Christianity at the expense of older Chinese traditions that remain more clearly within the law. Protestants, for example, missionize among rural migrants to cities—a group that temple religion is not well placed to serve and that Buddhism has been too cautious to approach.

These limitations on the earlier traditions are very different from all other contemporary Chinese societies, which lack comparable policies. In Hong Kong, Chinese communities of Southeast Asia, and especially Taiwan the most rapid growth has been in temple religion and Buddhism rather than Christianity. The kinds of space left open by current state policy have thus had quite different implications for the different religious traditions. Large parts of Protestantism and temple religion have thrived in the gray zone, officially disapproved but usually permitted. Buddhism, on the whole, has maintained a congenial relationship with the government, staying within sanctioned boundaries and taking advantage of state support (as in the hosting of the 2007 and 2009 World Buddhist Forums). Buddhism's contribution to boosting local tourist industry has made local governments adopt policies favorable to the rebuilding and expansion of Buddhist temples. However, exploitation of the economic value of Buddhism has also led to consequences detrimental to the growth of the religion in the long run, especially the overcommercialization of temples.

The traditions also vary significantly in their relationship to the market economy that has increasingly characterized the last thirty years. To a great extent temple religion was already comfortable with the commodity aspect of China's earlier economy. Temples had long been run as shareholding corporations that depended on a "market" of donations, and worship was often for purely pragmatic goals (including market success). Combined with the relative lack of institutional constraints, this has allowed such practices to thrive in all modern Chinese societies, including the mainland after the reforms.

The situation has been more complex for the more institutionalized traditions like Buddhism or Daoism. They lost their earlier economic base in monastic landholding, and have had a greater adjustment to make. In addition, both have to work through the institutional inertia of the state-controlled associations. On the other hand, both can also offer a long legacy of moral thought, and this often appeals to people looking for an alternative to the perceived selfishness and greed they experience as the market economy comes to dominate. Here the Buddhists and the Christians have been far more nimble than the Daoists at taking over this position.

Most traditions evolve some combination of helping people with the new economy and offering alternatives to its failings through charity or by offering new moral worlds. Temple religion easily embraces the market, and also develops as part of the reemerging world of rural social capital. Buddhism has tended to concentrate on the other approach of offering a moral alternative, although the obvious commercialization of some monasteries tends to undercut the moral message, as we discussed above. The Protestants have managed to do both strategies at once with great success. On the one hand, the rural evangelical churches have satisfied people's needs for healing in particular, while urban churches have found champions in wealthy entrepreneurs who attribute their wealth to Christianity. At the same time, the churches preach a moral message that people find appealing as an alternative to the image of a tooth-and-claw market (just as they do in the United States). Perhaps most striking is the way that Protestants have successfully positioned themselves, especially in urban areas, as being the cultural key to modernity. This shows up both in intellectual calls for a relatively nontheistic "cultural Christianity" as well as in the Wenzhou entrepreneurs who keep their copy of Max Weber's *Protestant Ethic* next to their Bible.[38] There is nothing automatic about this positioning, and it has not happened in most other Chinese societies. We have seen a rekindled Buddhism able to take advantage of this niche in Taiwan, for example. This has so far not been possible in China because of the weight of government control over Buddhism, which the Protestants do not accept.

What will the next thirty years bring? There are, of course, far too many unknowns to try to answer with any confidence, although there is little reason to expect a return to the antireligion environment that dominated just before the reforms. Given China's history of great religious diversity, it also seems unlikely that we will see any one tradition come to monopolize the field. Still, the last thirty years have brought a major reproportioning in the strength of the various traditions. Actual rates of growth are impossible to determine, both because so much religious activity is unregistered and because adherence to any of the non-Christian traditions is extremely difficult to define. The overall trends seem clear enough, though. Protestantism has increased extremely rapidly, especially in some areas; Catholics are expanding much more slowly, but are important in a few places. Buddhism is increasing statistically although some of that surely represents adherents of temple religion. Institutional Daoism is struggling by comparison. Temple religion, while clearly thriving in many parts of the country, will stagnate eventually unless it is able to move beyond strong roots in rural villages.

Our closest comparative case to China is Taiwan. In Taiwan, as in many places, great success in the market economy also accompanied a religious boom. Temple religion there, which thrived as the economy grew rapidly several decades ago, has indeed suffered as migration weakened village ties. On the other hand, this has been counterbalanced by its successful rise in modern urban areas and by the central role that several temples (especially the cult of the goddess Mazu) play on an islandwide basis—much larger than the usual field of influence for a popular temple.

Most striking of all in Taiwan has been the rapid rise of the new humanistic Buddhist (人间佛教) groups, several of which claim millions of adherents and have spread around the world. This new Buddhism is seen as both consistent with modernity and as an antidote to the malaise of modernity. Moreover, Taiwanese Buddhist organizations have developed disciplinary practices to ensure the penetration of Buddhism into believers' daily lives. In China, on the other hand, Buddhism just embarked on the modernization project, but is now in danger of being bogged down in commercialization brought about by the unbridled market forces. On the mainland it is Protestants who have been far more successful so far in positioning themselves as the religion of modernity, especially in urban areas, while they remain moribund in Taiwan.

Much of this difference is due to government policy. Both governments inherited the early KMT antipathy to religion, especially temple religion. Both also developed roughly corporatist mechanisms to control religion. Both saw rapid growth in the resulting gray areas. In Taiwan, however, all of that ended in 1987 with democratization. While the major Buddhist groups existed before that, their rapid growth occurred at exactly the moment when the relationship between state and society changed, and the Buddhist Association of the Republic of China lost its grip over the religion. Freed up to behave like genuine social organizations in the public sphere, the Buddhists were able to rework their traditions into something with enormous appeal.

This has not happened in China because the current policy of tight nominal control but loose supervision of the gray area has handcuffed the cooperative Buddhists (and Daoists) and left the field open to others. A change in this situation within the next few years, however, seems plausible. We have already mentioned signs that the central organs in charge of religious policy (the State Administration for Religious Affairs and the United Front Department of the

CCP) have become much more open to new ideas. It seems to have become clear to policymakers that current policy is failing to control or even effectively monitor religious growth, and that the patterns of growth are unexpected.

Any fundamental change, however, will mean revising the monopoly power of the five religious associations. First, the condemnation of temple religion as "feudal superstition" has clearly not had the desired result of discouraging it. Moving away from the idea of legitimizing it as a sixth religion, the policy might turn to three current directions: (1) toward temples as folkloric repositories of Chinese culture (registered with local cultural departments); (2) toward temples as NGOs that provide services (registered with civil affairs departments or related units); and (3) affiliating, at least nominally, with the Buddhist or Daoist Association. In all cases the adjustments raise questions about the long-term effects on local practice. How much of a difference does it make that a temple also has a sign declaring it a museum of "dragon culture," that it runs an arboretum or school on the side, or that it has brought in a monk as manager?

Christianity poses the most difficult problem for the government, because the registration system is already clear, but it is so widely and openly resisted that it is hard to see how the registration system can be patched. One possibility is to give up on the attempt at institutional and theological unity through the five religious associations, and simply allow groups to register directly with the government. From the government's point of view, this would have several advantages. It would end a situation where tens of millions of Christians see themselves at least partially acting against the will of the state and it would allow far more effective monitoring. At the same time, applying the same policy to Buddhists would open up new space for them to develop as more plausible competitors to the Christians (as they have done so successfully in Taiwan).

Yet such a change will not be easy or obvious either. In part, officials worry that it will encourage dangerous sectarian offshoots (although that is happening anyway). More importantly, it would mark a change in how state and society relate to each other, where we would have large numbers of groups not directly under the control of any corporatist association—the beginnings of a genuine public sphere. This would solve many problems of religious policy, but will probably require a longer time frame than just the next few years.

3

The Rule of Law

Pushing the Limits of Party Rule

Jamie Horsley

THIRTY YEARS AGO AT THE HISTORIC Third Plenum of the Eleventh Central Committee in December 1978, the Chinese Communist Party adopted as part of its reform and opening platform the twin goals of "democratic institutionalization and legalization," launching China onto the path of establishing a modern legal system. Borrowing from a speech that had been delivered by Deng Xiaoping at the meeting, the Plenum Communiqué looked to law and democracy to defend against a resurgence of the violent and arbitrary Cultural Revolution politics of the 1960s and early 1970s:

> In order to safeguard people's democracy, it is imperative to strengthen the socialist legal system so that democracy is institutionalized and legalized, in such a way as to ensure the stability, continuity and full authority of this type of system and law; *there must be laws to follow, these laws must be observed, they must be strictly enforced and lawbreakers must be dealt with.*" [1]

Since the 1978 Third Plenum, "legalization" has been intertwined with China's political, economic, and social modernization. By the Seventeenth Communist Party Congress in October 2007, "ruling the country in accordance with law" had been enshrined in China's Constitution and was espoused as essential, alongside party leadership and the position of the people as masters of their own country, to the promotion of political development under "socialism with Chinese characteristics." [2] Nonetheless, thirty years after reform and opening, and ten years after making rule of law a constitutional principle, law and legal institutions are still unable to effectively manage the complex tensions and rising conflicts caused by China's wrenching transition from a command to a market economy and the emergence of a more pluralistic society.

While China has successfully established over the past three decades a respectable body of law to follow, its leaders are having great difficulty in achieving the other three interrelated goals expressed above: broad compliance with and enforcement of the law, and holding lawbreakers accountable. The challenges to making China a truly law-based nation are complex and multifaceted, and ultimately implicate the continued dominance and extralegal status of the Chinese Communist Party, which exerts influence both legitimately through state structures but also through parallel, nontransparent mechanisms that place it outside and above the law.

"There must be laws to follow . . ."

China's leadership moved quickly to establish the laws necessary to accomplish Deng's modernization vision, including what would be called the "socialist market economy." Focused on the goals of using law to safeguard the nation against future chaos, promote social stability, and spur economic development, the National People's Congress (NPC), China's lawmaking body, adopted in the next few years new criminal and criminal procedure laws, a trial civil procedure law, a provisional environmental protection law, domestic contract and tax regulations, trademark and patent laws, and beginning in 1979, a slew of laws and regulations to permit private foreign investment in China for the first time since the country's establishment in 1949.

China also revised its Cultural Revolution Constitution, adopting a new version in 1982 that replaced explicit party control of the state with party leadership and restored a system of government through state organs duly constituted through lawful procedures set forth in the Constitution. This Constitution called for the state to uphold the uniformity and dignity of the "socialist legal system," proclaimed that no organization, political party, or individual was above the Constitution and the law, articulated an impressive-sounding list of rights and duties of Chinese citizens, and formally endorsed the "open-door policy" for foreign trade and investment.

China's rapid and substantial economic reforms called for new legislation to regulate and guide China's transformation. Many laws and regulations were adopted on a "provisional" basis or "for trial implementation," to permit for trial and error. China's legal reform model, paralleling its economic approach, has been notable for its experimental and incremental approach of trying new ideas on an approved local or sectoral basis before applying them to the entire country. Chinese officials began cautiously to study foreign legal experience, especially with regard to how to regulate foreign companies and foreigners who were arriving in increasing numbers and setting up shop within China's borders.

Looking back over the past thirty years, China has done a remarkable job of creating a fairly complete system of substantive law. As of March 2009, China counts 231 laws, some 600 administrative regulations, and 7,000 local rules and regulations currently in force,[3] as well as roughly 600 regulations issued by the autonomous regions of China and "numerous" departmental rules at all levels that regulate different aspects of daily life.[4] Although China's Legislation Law differentiates between "laws" that can create rights and can only be passed by the NPC and local enactments passed by local people's congresses and governments, these legally binding, official documents are, following the Chinese practice, all generally referred to herein as "legislation" or "law."

China's domestic law is supplemented by a large number of bilateral and international treaties and agreements that China has joined, including forty-eight international conventions on environmental protection,[5] twenty-two international agreements on human rights,[6] and the World Trade Organization agreements, accession to which required China to commit to many changes in China's legal system and helped to promote China's move toward a more transparent governance model. China is becoming ever more engaged in the international economic and legal "order," although it reserves the right to adopt its own interpretations of these norms.

The 1982 Constitution has been amended four times. In 1999 the NPC added the principles that China exercises the rule of law and is "building a socialist country governed according to law" and, in 2004, that the state is to "respect and preserve human rights," as well as protect private property. While constitutional principles are important in articulating general aspirational principles, constitutional rights are not directly enforceable in Chinese courts. Realization of these rights normally requires enactment by the NPC of specific laws to provide the relevant details and procedures for carrying out these principles.

Over the years, lawmaking has also moved from emphasis on regulating the socialist market economy to achieving greater social fairness and justice. China's leadership recognizes that the legitimacy of its one-party rule depends not only on delivering economic growth but also on ensuring that its people are treated fairly and on creating a "harmonious society." In its embrace of the market economy, the government recognizes that it has withdrawn perhaps too far from such fundamental areas as public health and education. Recent NPC legislative plans have included more laws on social security, welfare and social relief, health insurance, labor protection, food safety, and the environment.

China's leaders have also come to realize that law is useful not only as a tool to regulate the economy and society but also to restrain abuse of state power by government bureaucrats. In the absence of direct elections or other effective mechanisms to hold government officials directly accountable to the public, corruption and abuse of power have led to widespread feelings of disaffection between the Chinese people and their "people's government." Reported incidents of mass unrest increased from 58,000 in 2003 to roughly 90,000 in 2006,[7] at which point the authorities stopped disclosing specific statistics on protests and other manifestations of unrest.

While local leaders continue to rely on heavy-handed tactics to put down disturbances, the central leadership realized the governance model had to change in order to better address the underlying causes of social unrest, including environmental degradation, illegal land seizures and forced relocations for urban development, unpaid wages, police malfeasance, and government and business corruption, as well as to better deal with that unrest. Recent central policies and legislation seek to provide clearer procedural restraints upon, and clearer rights in the public to protect their interests against, state power.

After a brief overview of how the legal institutions of the people's congresses, the government, the courts, and the legal profession have developed over the past thirty years, this chapter explores in more depth how the party-state is working through administrative reforms to transform the lawmaking and policymaking process, to improve administrative mechanisms to manage conflict, and to help achieve better compliance with the law by both the public and the state.[8]

". . . , these laws must be observed, they must be strictly enforced and lawbreakers must be dealt with."

Having lots of laws, even good laws, is not sufficient to ensure that the law is broadly complied with and enforced, that is, what we think of as the rule of law. In contrast with the traditional "rule of man" that characterized imperial China and the Maoist era, or the instrumentalist "rule *by* law" that arguably describes reform-era China, under which the state views and uses law as a tool to regulate the public, the concept of "rule of law" requires that the state itself—and the party—also be subject to law. The 1982 Constitution stipulated that in principle everyone—including the state, the military, and all political parties—must abide by the Constitution and the law and that no one is above the Constitution and the law.[9] It also provides for basic legal institutions including lawmaking congresses and governments at all political levels, and law-enforcing courts and procuracies, and articulates a list of basic rights of Chinese citizens. Even the party's own Constitution requires its members to abide by the laws and regulations of the state.[10]

Yet, despite its notable legislative and institutional accomplishments, Chinese leaders recognize that China's rule of law enterprise is not yet complete and admit that at least in some localities and departments "laws are *not* observed, they are *not* strictly enforced, and lawbreakers are *not* dealt with" (emphasis added).[11]

They have concluded that an important reason why the rule of law remains so elusive is that the formulation of laws and regulations has been insufficiently "scientific and democratic," resulting in laws that are inadequate to address the rapid economic, social, and political changes taking place in China and the lack of public support. Accordingly, the party-state is undertaking to make the lawmaking and law-enforcement institutions more professional, rules-based, participatory, and transparent.

The Legislative and Rulemaking Institutions

Under China's Constitution, all power ostensibly belongs to the people, and state power is to be exercised by the people through the "democratically elected" National People's Congress (NPC) and local people's congresses (together with the NPC, referred to collectively herein as "PCs") at the provincial, county, and township levels. The PCs make law and local regulations, supervise government organs, and approve the government budgets. PC elections are becoming incrementally more competitive, and PC deputies somewhat more assertive and representative, but the PC system is still heavily influenced by the party, which essentially controls the appointment and election of PC delegates and congressional and government leaders.

The NPC and local PCs now meet regularly, but only once a year. Standing committees make most of the PCs' decisions between annual meetings in close consultation with the party, which sets the annual agendas for the full PC meetings at its own party congresses. Full-time legislative affairs committees under the standing committees are responsible for drafting and submitting national and local laws for approval either by the relevant standing committee or the full PC. In recent years these legislative committees are increasingly staffed by legally trained employees, including former law professors, in an attempt to improve the quality of legislation.

The State Council, China's cabinet appointed by the NPC, is the highest executive body and the center of state power, headed by the premier. It oversees China's central government ministries and commissions and the work of local governments at each level. Legislative affairs offices (LAOs) at each level of government draft administrative rules and regulations to carry out and enforce the laws and to regulate the government bureaucracy, as well as handle administrative appeals brought by the regulated public. The party controls the appointment or "election" by the PCs of high-ranking government officials at the corresponding political level. However, lower-ranking staff are part of an increasingly competitive and merit-based civil service system, and the trend is for LAO personnel to be trained in law.

Both of these lawmaking institutions are also moving toward a more transparent and participatory legislative process involving the use of public hearings, advice from subject matter experts, and written public input, drawing on research into international practices and experimentation.[12] Public participation is encouraged, but not required, for legislation deemed to be of particular public interest under the Legislation Law and its implementing regulations.

The PCs have historically been somewhat more open than the government, utilizing discretionary mechanisms such as visiting localities to listen to the people's opinions directly and permitting the public to "audit" or observe their annual meetings. While local PCs started experimenting with legislative hearings in 1999, the NPC Standing Committee held its first public hearing in September 2005, on draft revisions to the Individual Income Tax Law. Prior to 2008, the NPC selectively released a number of draft laws since 1949, including the 1954 Constitution, for public comment. In April 2008, the NPC Standing Committee announced that, going forward, all drafts submitted to it for review and adoption will ordinarily be made public as a standard practice, observing that an open and transparent legislative process would better ensure the public's "right to know, participate, express and supervise" and provide the people with a better understanding of new laws through participation in their formulation.[13] It has also promised to continue to experiment with public hearings and the broadcasting of its deliberations.

Following initial experiments by some central ministries and local governments, the State Council LAO first released draft regulations for public comment in October 2002. Thereafter, it gradually increased the number of draft regulations that it made public each year, until it announced in 2008 that it and the central ministries should henceforth release virtually all draft rules and administrative regulations—other than those relating to state secrets or national security—for public comment. State Council Work Rules adopted in 2008 similarly call for increased public participation in major policy decisions and draft regulations, through written input as well as hearings when appropriate, and Premier Wen Jiabao directed in his 2008 Work Report that governments at all levels should henceforth release information about and hold public hearings before making major decisions.

The Courts

China's judicial system, which applies and enforces the law, comprises some 3,631 people's courts at four levels corresponding to the political structure, with the Supreme People's Court (SPC) at the apex, and staffed by roughly 200,000 judges. It also includes the 160,000-member procuracy that prosecutes cases and the public security apparatus, China's police.[14] The procuracy and public security organs primarily handle criminal cases.

Institutionally, the courts are not an independent branch of government but rather part of the government structure, subject to oversight by the procuracy and answerable to the PCs at the same political level. The NPC Standing Committee, rather than the SPC, has the authority to interpret national law, although the SPC issues judicial interpretations on questions arising out of specific application of law. Some of these interpretations are as a practical matter tantamount to supplemental legislation, and some draft interpretations have even been released for public comment, following the practice of government agencies and PCs in recent years.

Chinese courts are supposed to exercise their adjudicatory power independently, in principle through open trials and free from interference.[15] However, judges are appointed (in accordance with party guidance) and remunerated by the PCs at the corresponding governmental level, a system that fosters local protectionism and undue political influence. In practice, government officials may apply pressure on courts in particular cases, and the party may intervene through court-based adjudication committees that supervise the work of the judges and other channels. Consequently, the courts frequently decline to accept jurisdiction over sensitive cases, such as lawsuits relating to land seizures, official corruption, or "hot" social issues like government liability for the shoddily constructed elementary schools that collapsed and killed thousands of children in the Sichuan Province earthquake of May 2008.

In addition to institutional constraints on their authority and independence, the courts have traditionally been plagued by incompetence, lack of professionalism, and corruption, which undermine the public's trust. In the early days of the People's Republic, judges were frequently drawn from the ranks of the retired military and were not required to have any legal training. Now, new judges must hold university degrees and pass a national unified judicial exam, as well as participate in ongoing legal education programs. However, the quality of judicial personnel outside the major cities is still uneven, and low salaries contribute to widespread judicial corruption.

Lack of transparency in the judicial system also contributes to potential corruption. Since China follows a continental or civil law system, court decisions do not have binding precedential value as in a common law system like the United States, and legal opinions have not normally been made public, although selected decisions are published for reference by other courts and lawyers. Moreover, trials are frequently closed off to the public and media even though, in principle, they are supposed to be open to the public. The SPC announced reforms in early 2009 to introduce greater judicial transparency, including publishing court opinions and enforcement decisions online and permitting greater public access to trials,[16] as well as to prohibit acceptance of gifts and ex parte communication between judges and lawyers and to otherwise curb inappropriate and corrupt judicial behavior.

The appointment in March 2008 of Wang Shengjun as president of the SPC caused some pessimism about the road to judicial independence and rule of law. Wang's background was in party politics and public security rather than in law, and his appointment raised concern that the courts were being politicized. Continued momentum on a variety of judicial reforms, including some movement toward centralized funding of all courts to help overcome local protectionism, judicial transparency, and the promotion of judicial ethics, suggests that incremental progress toward a more professional and somewhat autonomous judiciary might continue.

Nonetheless, the party seems conflicted about the degree of judicial independence it wants to actually foster and it is not clear, thirty years after China began to develop a modern legal system, whether the courts will be permitted to effectively carry out their potentially critical role in resolving conflict, especially with the government, and in strengthening rule of law.

Lawyers

Of little relevance in traditional China, lawyers enjoyed a tenuous status in Republican China and the early years of the People's Republic. Less than 2,000 lawyers could be identified at the beginning of Reform and Opening in 1978. By the end of 2008, however, China had more than 600 institutions of higher learning offering bachelor's degrees in law, nearly 157,000 licensed lawyers, and over 14,000 law firms.[17]

The overall number of practicing lawyers for a country the size of China is still low (slightly more than one lawyer per one thousand people), and they are subject to the often strict "supervision and guidance" of local judicial bureaus under the Ministry of Justice (MOJ), which supervises the legal profession. Nonetheless, the legal profession is increasingly recognized as an important institution to help ensure that law is understood, observed, and enforced. Like lawyers around the world, Chinese lawyers not only handle a wide range of criminal, civil, and administrative cases and counseling; many lawyers and legal scholars also undertake "public interest" lawyering and get involved in drafting and proposing legislation.

Government agencies have begun to hire law graduates as "public service lawyers," although many of these seem to be assigned to perform legal aid for government-sponsored legal aid centers rather than fill the same kind of role as government lawyers do in the United States. Indeed, most legally trained officials working within government agencies are not technically qualified to be lawyers under the current Lawyers Law.

Government-supported and private legal aid are also developing rapidly. China's legal aid system dates back to 1994 but only began to flourish in recent years. The MOJ now requires all lawyers to handle a certain number of legal aid cases each year, and Chinese law now requires that criminal defendants must have access to legal assistance if they cannot afford it. Moreover, low-income citizens can apply for legal aid when seeking state compensation, social security, welfare, pensions, alimony, maintenance, child support, and labor payments.

Chinese trade unions are beginning to offer legal aid to migrant workers and others with labor disputes, and the government-supported All-China Consumers Association announced in early 2009 that it had received authorization to bring lawsuits. Law schools and nongovernmental organizations sponsor legal aid clinics that assist low-income citizens with criminal defense, employment discrimination, family disputes, juvenile justice, urban relocations, and rural land takings. Although rural areas remain significantly underserved, legal aid seems to be becoming firmly rooted in China's changing legal culture and helping to raise rights consciousness among sectors of society that have not had much access to the formal legal system in the past.

Chinese lawyers are also becoming more politically active. A lawyer was elected as a deputy to the NPC for the first time in 1988. Since then law school professors and lawyers increasingly seek posts on local PCs to promote their law reform agendas, sometimes winning appointment by the local party but sometimes running as independent candidates. As of 2008, some 519 lawyers reportedly served as deputies to the PCs at all levels, and 2,845 are members of various levels of the Chinese People's Political Consultative Conference, a political advisory body.[18]

A growing number of Chinese lawyers have begun to file "public interest" cases that highlight particularly difficult or widespread social problems. Some practitioners estimate there are only about 120 public interest lawyers throughout the country, although the establishment of a nationwide public interest lawyers network in March 2009 to share and tap into professional expertise,[19] taking advantage of the Internet in China, may expand these numbers. While these lawyers frequently lose their lawsuits, the public attention thereby drawn to the issues through litigation often leads to beneficial changes in law or policy.

In recent years, a small number of courageous lawyers—sometimes referred to as "rights defenders"—have taken on and publicized sensitive cases involving criminal defendants, peasant activists, displaced urbanites, religious worshippers, unpaid migrant laborers, and others who find themselves in conflict with the state. Such representation frequently places these lawyers in direct conflict with the local governments that license them. Criminal defense lawyers in particular and others who speak out on politically sensitive issues face the prospect of being jailed on such grounds as falsifying evidence or revealing state secrets and may lose their jobs and their licenses to practice law. As one prominent Chinese lawyer put it, "You cannot be a rights lawyer in this country without becoming a rights case yourself."[20]

Despite the sobering limitations on the role of the courts and the legal profession in helping realize rule of law in China, statistics show that these two institutions are in fact playing an ever greater role within Chinese society. In the five-year period 2003–2007, the courts heard approximately 26 million cases,[21] and the total number of cases heard in 2008 alone increased by 11 percent to over 10.7 million.[22] During this period, lawyers handled millions of criminal and civil cases, as well as administrative proceedings against the government, and provided a wide range of advisory services to both the public and the government.[23] Today, the coercive power of the party-state generally intervenes in the normal functioning of the judicial process only when a private interest is at odds with an important government or party interest. However, it is precisely these kinds of cases, involving state or party power, that most call into question the role of law in China and are most likely to cause wider-spread social unhappiness and unrest.

Law as an Instrument to Restrain State Power

The idea of using law to constrain state power is a relatively recent development in China. Traditional Chinese law contained numerous administrative regulations and codes, but these were primarily designed to regulate government practices, not to establish rights in the public to contest state actions. Only with adoption of the unprecedented Administrative Litigation Law (ALL) in 1989 were ordinary Chinese citizens for the first time given the right to challenge the legality of official action through lawsuits in the people's courts. Since then, China has been building a body of administrative law to better regularize government behavior and the government's interaction with the public.

Allowing the Chinese public to sue the government was heralded as a "revolution" in legal system development. The administrative tribunals have recorded a respectable plaintiff success rate of 20–40 percent over almost two decades. However, after an initial enthusiastic response, the number of administrative lawsuits leveled off, fluctuating around 95,000 per year. This flattening was attributed to a combination of lowered expectations due to the ALL's limits on what cases the courts can adjudicate and the reluctance of courts to accept complaints in more politically sensitive cases, rather than to a decline in grievances against the government.[24]

Nonetheless, plaintiffs (and groups of plaintiffs) have won some notable successes, including in the areas of enviromental protection and land takings, and the number of administrative lawsuits seems to be inching upward in recent years, exceeding 109,000 in 2008,[25] with a plantiff success rate of about 30 percent.[26] It is not clear whether this uptick in administrative lawsuits represents a long-term trend, but revision of the ALL is on the NPC's legislative agenda and many scholars and officials are working to broaden its scope to allow more cases to be heard in the courts.

The 1994 State Compensation Law permitted citizens to sue the government for monetary compensation for injuries caused by official action. Possibly due to its low levels of mandated compensation and some of the same limitations that discourage litigation against the government generally, relatively few compensation claims have been filed and only 34 percent of those awarded compensation, leading many to refer to it as the "State Non-Compensation Law." This law is also undergoing revision by the NPC.

As an alternative to suing the government, the 1999 Administrative Reconsideration Law (ARL) permits citizens aggrieved by unlawful or inappropriate government action to request review or "reconsideration" within the government agency itself. An average of slightly over 80,000 disputes—less than those taken to the courts—have been filed under the ARL every year since it came into effect.[27] Applicants can normally appeal the final administrative decision to the courts or bypass the administrative reconsideration (AR) system altogether and sue directly in the courts.

In principle, AR should be quicker than court proceedings, broadly accessible, and free of charge, and, because it is handled by career government personnel who may better understand the relevant regulatory background, potentially more professional. In practice, AR is fundamentally constrained by the same political environment that undermines the effectiveness of administrative litigation: the lack of truly independent or neutral adjudicators. While the officials who review the case may be somewhat removed from the issues in dispute, they are still within the same chain of agency command. Both the party and government leadership support reforms to make AR more professional and neutral, so the Chinese public will trust and accept the outcome, and begin to use this "in-house" dispute resolution mechanism more frequently.

Instead, a large number of disputants remain unsatisfied with both administrative litigation and reconsideration and have preferred resorting to a traditional petitioning or "letters and visits" system called *xinfang* 信访, which is governed by State Council Regulations on Letters and Visits. The State Council has a Letters and Visits Office, whose function is replicated throughout the bureaucracy at each level of government and in individual government agencies, the courts, the procuracies, and the PCs. While the courts nationwide heard close to 11 million cases in 2008, Chinese government agencies, including the courts themselves, have been flooded in recent years with upward of 11–12 million citizen petitions seeking assistance to resolve a range of grievances, including complaints about government behavior. Many Chinese legal scholars call for the abolition of the *xinfang* system altogether on the premise that it perpetuates disputes and undermines rule of law and the role of the courts, which need to be strengthened so that they can more effectively and finally resolve disputes.

The above laws seek to restrain Chinese state action by providing some redress to aggrieved citizens *after* the fact. Others seek to impose procedural constraints on government action *in advance* and have introduced unprecedented requirements of procedural due process.

The 1996 Administrative Penalties Law gave the Chinese public clear procedural rights for the first time, by requiring government agencies not only to publicize the range and standards for potential penalties, but also to give affected persons advance notice when the government proposes to impose a penalty, such as shutting down production, revoking a license, or levying a fine. This law further affords Chinese citizens the right to provide a defense to the charges and proposed penalty and to request a public hearing at no cost. The 1998 Price Law subsequently introduced the hearing into the broader administrative decision-making process, requiring that public hearings be held when government-set or guided prices are being determined or changed.

The 2003 Administrative Licensing Law also established procedural requirements for government action. Responding to a nationwide proliferation of government approval requirements that were unduly burdening both economic and social activity and fueling official corruption, it restricts government from imposing a license or permit requirement unless it can demonstrate that individual initiative, associations, or the market are not able to regulate the activity effectively. This law, which has no counterpart anywhere in the world, limits the government entities that have authority to issue licenses and the types of activity that can be so regulated. The law also stipulates procedures, including public hearings, to ensure transparency, fairness, and impartiality in the establishment and implementation of licensing requirements and in the licensing process. The number of matters requiring approvals at all levels has been nearly halved since the law's adoption, and some plaintiffs have successfully sued to stop polluting projects based on their failure to obtain required environmental licenses under this law.

Most recently, the State Council adopted nationally applicable regulations that require governments at all levels to disclose a broad range of records on their own initiative as well as upon request, albeit subject to broadly crafted exceptions for information constituting state secrets, commercial secrets, or privacy. The Regulations on Open Government Information (OGI), which took effect May 1, 2008, are yet another part of China's evolving administrative law and are seen as an important step toward a national law on information disclosure that will further promote government transparency.

Unlike many of the administrative laws discussed above, the OGI Regulations do specifically provide that agency failure to abide by their requirements can be appealed through administrative reconsideration or directly in the courts. Within the first seven days after they took effect, Chinese media reported seven cases brought by retired workers and peasants, in addition to lawyers and law professors. Many of the initial lawsuits were rejected or not acknowledged, but a few courts did rule that government agencies had to comply with the regulations and disclose the requested information. Moreover, the publicity surrounding some information requests pressured government to respond positively. For example, a Shanghai lawyer in January 2009 filed a request for details on China's stimulus plan to counter the global economic downturn starting in 2008 and, after he threatened to sue, the National Development and Reform Commission publicly pledged to disclose the plan on its website once it was approved by the NPC.

Other legislation to round out the administrative law framework and standardize government behavior is being drafted, including a law to regulate and prevent abuse of compulsory law enforcement measures, to regulate the imposition of administrative or user fees, and to require disclosure of civil servants' assets to curb corruption.

Law-based and Open Government

Recognizing that the remedies provided by the administrative laws described above were insufficient on their own to address the continuing failures in observance and enforcement of law as well as holding lawbreakers accountable, and that these failures were undermining the government's credibility, the party-state has begun to promote a Chinese version of "reinventing government" under the rubric of "administration in accordance with the law" (*yifa xingzheng* 依法行政). The State Council committed itself in 2004 to a ten-year reform program,[28] extending it down to the municipal and county levels in 2008. [29] The program calls for establishing clear rules on the scope of administrative power; fair, rational, and transparent administrative procedures to regulate the exercise of government power; more open government information and "scientific and democratic decision-making" with greater public participation; doing a better job of preventing and administratively resolving social tensions; introducing better law-enforcement mechanisms; and ensuring greater accountability for government actions. Some of these systems have been "legalized" through the administrative laws discussed above or in planned amendments thereto. Others are still at the policy stage.

Party Secretary Hu Jintao has promoted the complementary theme of party "governance in accordance with the law," calling for protection of the people's rights and interests and ensuring social fairness and justice in pursuit of a "harmonious society." He and Premier Wen have urged all segments of government and society to experiment with "innovations" in governance to "build a just, transparent, hard-working, efficient, honest, upright and clean government that follows a well-defined code of conduct, a government with which the people are satisfied."[30]

The party and the central government have identified reform of the way decisions are made and laws and regulations formulated as critical to improving the entire administrative process. Public participation and increased transparency in lawmaking were identified as key mechanisms to build trust in government, curb rampant corruption, and help maintain social stability. The 2008 Government Work Report to the NPC promised to improve the quality of legislation by seeking views from many sources and publishing drafts to solicit the public's opinions, as well as developing the positive role of civic organizations to expand public participation in government affairs and give voice to the concerns of the people.[31]

To be sure, the handling of various forms of public participation is still in the experimental stage. The solicitation of written public input on legislative drafts, while steadily spreading in practice, is not yet standardized. Legislative or decision-making hearings in China all too often suffer from inadequate openness, hand-picked participants who are not necessarily representative of the diversity of views on a matter, and the lack of a public record of the hearing proceedings. Both the written comment process and public hearings need to provide better feedback to the public on the impact of their input on the final decision. Chinese commentators complain that these proceedings are often just "for show" and call for more standardized and transparent procedures that would truly serve to curb arbitrary exercise of power and safeguard citizens' rights and interests.

Another area where China is introducing greater "open government" is in making various kinds of official meetings open to the public. Peoples' congresses have permitted citizens to "audit" or observe their meetings for a number of years. Some localities have begun experimenting with holding open government meetings, a "government under the sunshine" practice that is encouraged under Hunan Province's pioneering 2008 Administrative Procedure Provisions.[32] As another sign of increasing openness, many governors and mayors now provide mailboxes for public comments and questions on their official government websites and hold online chats to discuss current issues with the public, a modern channel for interacting with the people that has even been utilized by China's top leaders, Party Secretary and President Hu Jintao and Premier Wen Jiabao.

More recently, in a new model for better dealing with protests, high-level local officials have held hearings or informal meetings with aggrieved protesters to discuss their issues and promised to do a better job of soliciting their input to prevent future problems. A series of taxi strikes prompted by largely similar grievances concerning unlicensed competition, fuel prices, and fees unrolled in different cities throughout the country in November 2008. In one of the first, the party secretary of Chongqing Municipality held a televised and podcast open hearing with aggrieved taxi drivers following a citywide strike.[33] Quick action, promises to address the complaints, the meeting with the party secretary, and a government apology to the public for not having managed the taxi system effectively convinced most drivers to go back to work, while the responsive handling of the incident was reported to have improved the Chongqing government's credibility.[34]

In the wake of these taxi-driver strikes, and other well-publicized protests and riots in 2008, former public security minister and Politburo member Zhou Yongkang observed that "more channels should be opened to solicit public opinion and local governments should spare no effort to solve people's problems,"[35] so as to prevent these problems from intensifying and leading to social instability. Clearly, the benefits of greater transparency and interaction with the public are increasingly recognized by Chinese leaders, if not always implemented.

While public participation procedures are not yet legally mandated at the national level, their increasing use and adoption of the OGI Regulations seem to reflect a growing appreciation of how greater openness and consultation can elicit public support and compliance with law and policy, as well as a growing confidence on the part of the Chinese leadership about their ability to interact with, respond to, and manage conflict with the Chinese public.

The Next Thirty Years

Thirty years after launching the Reform and Opening program, China has achieved at least one important plank of its legal reform objectives, that of establishing a sound and fairly complete body of law and regulations for not only the people, but also the government, to abide by. Basic legal institutions, including the people's congresses, the courts, the legal profession, and government agencies themselves, are becoming more professional, transparent, and responsive to public concerns.

However, the Chinese leadership recognizes it continues to face formidable challenges in achieving the other three goals of general compliance with and strict enforcement of the law and accountability for violations of the law. The conclusion to China's 2008 white paper on establishing the rule of law observes:

> The development of democracy and the rule of law still falls short of the needs of economic and social development; the legal framework . . . calls for further improvement; in some regions and departments, laws are not observed, or strictly enforced, violators are not brought to justice; local protectionism, departmental protectionism and difficulties in law enforcement occur from time to time; some government functionaries take bribes and bend the law, abuse their power when executing the law, abuse their authority to override the law, and substitute their words for the law, thus bringing damage to the socialist rule of law.[36]

What the white paper does not acknowledge is that undoubtedly the largest obstacle to achieving those goals is the ambivalence of the party itself about how far it is willing to permit the country to move toward true rule of law. Despite continued lip service to the importance of rule of law and the principle that party members must also be subject to the Constitution and the law, the party remains unwilling to give judges the authority to decide cases independently and the legal profession the latitude to zealously help the public achieve justice, particularly when cases involve the party-state. Moreover, the party maintains its own parallel, secretive system of "justice," under which the Party Central Discipline Inspection Commission investigates corruption and other forms of wrongdoing by party members, subjects them to the extralegal *shuanggui* 双规 or "double treatment" system, and only at its discretion turns those cases over to the judicial system for disposition.

In part due to its reluctance to permit the courts to handle the rising number of increasingly complex social conflicts, the party is advocating "transformation" of the Chinese government. The premise is that enhanced transparency, participation, and accountability will make government more efficient and effective and thereby reduce and better resolve disputes over government actions and policies and achieve better compliance with laws and policies. With increasing confidence, the party-state is beginning to standardize the use of public participation in different forms in legislation and policymaking and has already issued executive regulations requiring government at all levels to disclose a wide range of information both on its own initiative and upon request by the public.

The party-state is experimenting with making more government decisions publicly available, holding face-to-face adjudicatory hearings, improving the use of negotiation or mediation to resolve administrative disputes, and making the in-house administrative reconsideration system more professional, effective, and credible. The goal of these reforms is to satisfactorily settle disputes with the government so the people feel they have been fairly treated and do not subsequently resort to overburdened and often unhelpful courts or the *xinfang* system.

China's legislative accomplishments, the cautious movement toward a new model of government administration that is regulated and constrained by law, the rise of the beleaguered but resilient "rights protection" lawyers movement, and the Chinese people's seeming enthusiasm for continuing to use the courts and other legal avenues even though the track record seems so dismal, all do reflect substantial progress over the past three decades. From this perspective, China can be said to be moving further along the continuum from the traditional rule of man that Deng Xiaoping denounced, beyond the instrumental concept of rule *by* law that appeared pervasive in the first years of Reform and Opening, toward a rule *of* law under which all citizens, government entities, and political parties are truly subject to law.

China had no tradition of either democracy or rule of law on which to draw when it began this journey. We have learned in the United States that democracy and law are not settled but are dynamic works in progress. Both China's leadership and the Chinese people are experimenting with new practices, adopting new perspectives, and continually refining their unique "legal system with Chinese characteristics."

Looking back to reflect on the legal reform accomplishments over the past thirty years, the Chinese have established a comprehensive, modern, and sometimes innovative body of law. They are professionalizing their legislative and enforcement institutions. They are cautiously "democratizing" the legislative and decision-making processes through greater transparency and public participation to better involve the public and obtain their compliance with the law, and they are moving to make the judicial system more transparent and accessible.

The continuation of the generally positive trends of the past thirty years is by no means inexorable. The paradox, of course, is that China's Communist Party continues to espouse a rule of law that also constrains state power while insisting on the primacy of the party. The tension between promotion of greater rule of law and one-party rule permeates the entire legal system.

However, the official rhetoric of legality and positive development of law and the legal institutions and processes discussed above, including the rapid growth of administrative law to not only regulate but also limit state power, is fostering a new culture of legality in the public and the party-state. These developments suggest that an increasingly transparent, participatory, and accountable China may well continue to progress further along the continuum toward rule of law.

II
ECONOMICS

4

Economic Growth

From High-Speed to High-Quality

Barry Naughton

CHINA HAS GROWN FASTER, LONGER THAN any other economy in history. China is thus unique, yet in its broad outlines, the Chinese growth experience also resembles other successful developing countries and, in particular, recapitulates earlier East Asian growth miracles. Developing countries can grow very rapidly for twenty or more years, but eventually growth must slow. Growth slows down, in the first place, for structural reasons: the transformation from a traditional rural economy to a mostly modern urban economy is completed when the vast majority of agricultural workers have transitioned into nonagricultural work. After this turning point, growth must slow and growth strategy must adapt to new conditions. In fact, there is no precise turning point, because in most countries growth strategy is already being adapted before this structural turning point. Policy starts to be driven by new imperatives, such as upgrading of labor skills and improvement of the natural and built environment. Moreover, policymaking around the time of the turning point usually takes place with a sharp increase in public participation, and sometimes even coincides with full-blown democratization. Third, and finally, these changes take place amidst rapidly changing external conditions that are often perceived as crisis. Growth and policy both adapt to these sharp changes in external conditions. It is hard to disentangle all these effects: the transition from high-speed growth to moderate growth is hardly ever smooth.

China today seems to be hurdling into just such a turning point. Growth has been consistently fast for thirty years, but then accelerated to "super-fast" growth rates above 10 percent per year between mid-2003 and mid-

2008. This five-year growth surge moved China toward the structural turning point much more quickly than most observers anticipated. Even Chinese policymakers were far from confident that growth at such a pace could be healthy or sustained. Since nearly the beginning of the five-year growth surge, Chinese policymakers have been talking about pursuing more "balanced" growth that is "higher quality" and more "friendly to the environment." However, this high-level talk has had little impact on the actual pattern of growth. By most measures, Chinese growth became *more* unbalanced throughout the five-year growth surge. Then, in the second half of 2008, the Chinese economy ran into a perfect storm: the US financial crisis caused a dramatic slowing of external demand just at the time when the domestic economic cycle was turning down. Faced with this challenge, Chinese policymakers moved decisively to reinstate the investment-driven growth that their system is particularly well suited to deliver (and which they understand so well). By the end of 2009, this policy had succeeded in stabilizing growth, and China was one of the first economies recovering from the global crisis.

As it emerges from the global financial crisis, China faces many immediate questions. Will China settle into a new growth trajectory with slower speeds and different characteristics? Will China's recovery be smooth, or must an additional crisis be overcome before the economy reaches a sustainable long-run growth path? While these questions are still open, China's long-run economic challenge is recognizably the same as what it was before the crisis. Having successfully powered through the developmental and systemic transitions at warp speed, China must now adapt to a new phase of growth. When the dust settles, we will see China making a shift from "quantity" (speed) to "quality," that is, to slower growth but with more than proportionate improvements in the quality of life.

How will China adapt to this potentially wrenching set of changes? In the following I address this question by first looking back on the experience of growth thus far. The first section examines the way that policymakers have subordinated nearly every consideration to the quest for economic growth, a quest that has been remarkably successful. The second section then looks at some of the most important concomitants of the "unbalanced" growth pattern that was followed. Quite obviously, rapid growth has had costs as well as benefits. I do not attempt a full analysis of the growth process, but confine myself to sketching some of the most important outcomes. The third section looks at the attempt of Chinese policymakers to move to a more balanced growth strategy, an attempt that today appears to have been too feeble to make much difference. I argue that the attempt at a radical recasting of Chinese growth strategy was probably doomed from the start, given China's institutional and economic environment. The fourth section looks at the impact of the economic crisis on China, while a fifth section looks to the future, and speculates about the coming transition to higher-quality economic growth.

Economic Growth before Everything Else

For thirty years, the Chinese leadership has subordinated every other consideration to the quest for economic growth. The beginnings of economic reform were inseparable from the burgeoning disillusionment with Maoism's failure to bring adequate economic development. Subsequently, at a key crossroads of the economic reform process, in late 1991, Deng Xiaoping declared, "Development is the only hard truth," and brought two years of vacillation and backsliding in the reform process to an end. When competing objectives confront Chinese policymakers, they have almost invariably chosen to give priority to economic growth over whatever the other objective has been. This can be seen in virtually any policy arena examined, and most crucially in those core policy realms where choices are made that shape the overall development process. For example, China's foreign policy has been shaped by the desire to avoid overt confrontations with the dominant powers—in practice, the United States—and to maintain a positive environment for China's economic growth. Again, a dictum from Deng Xiaoping is crucial here: "Keep a low profile; never take the lead." Therefore, when we say that no nation has grown as fast as long as China, we should quickly add that no nation has more single-mindedly pursued policies designed to power an economy through the structural transformation required to reach "modernization." In order to make economic growth a reality, Chinese leaders subordinated nearly everything to the mobilization of resources for the growth process.

The relative priority given to growth is so consistent that it is often seen as simply reflecting Chinese "pragmatism," as if there were no implicit trade-offs involved. But in fact it is not so much that Chinese policymakers are pragmatic, as that it is virtually impossible to find a "revealed value" that competes with growth itself. A simple example that exemplifies the argument is China's overwhelming dependence on coal for energy (almost 70 percent of consumption, far higher than any other country). At first glance, this seems to be simply another case of Chinese pragmatism, since coal is abundant, cheap, and relatively widespread. But in fact China has never been able to mobilize sufficient technology and capital resources to allow state enterprises to produce enough coal, so in order to take advantage of coal's abundance, China has allowed entry into this sector by small-scale township and village enterprises and private firms. In 2005, for example, over 10 percent of output by value came from private firms, and over a third from other small-scale firms. This has been a consistent part of China's development approach for the past thirty years.

Yet this simple outcome is possible only because Chinese policymakers are willing to override at least three potentially competing principles. First, China's mineral resources are owned by the national government, and we might expect the government to closely guard these valuable resources, just as it closely guards other strategic monopolies.[1] But in fact, China has consistently allowed new entrants to appropriate natural resource rents that theoretically belong to the state. Second, China's mines produce an enormous output of extremely low-quality coal, heavy to transport and laced with impurities that are pumped into the air and water. While Chinese policymakers have repeatedly recognized the enormous environmental costs, they have never significantly restricted the use of low-quality coal. Third, small mines operate with appalling disregard for safety and work conditions. As a result, coal mines are deadly, killing over six thousand miners annually until the early 2000s (SAWS Annual)—this compares to twenty-two deaths in coal mines in the United States in 2005. In fact, a recent study sponsored by Greenpeace and carried out by reputable Chinese economists concluded that coal use imposed an annual cost on China equal to 7 percent of gross domestic product (GDP). Each ton of coal—which sells for 300–400 yuan—causes an additional 150 yuan of costs in terms of environmental and health damage. These unpriced negative externalities are not accounted for in any decision-making (Mao, Sheng, and Yang 2008). We would normally expect to see the Chinese government carry out regulatory, natural resource, and pricing policies that internalize the cost of some of these externalities, or prevent their emergence in the first place. This would balance to some extent the trade-offs between highly desirable economic growth and other goods, such as safety and environmental quality. Yet until the recent shift in declared development objectives—discussed later—we see little effort and no successful efforts in this direction.

Broadening the discussion, we can ask in which strategic policy arenas do policymakers decide the most important developmental outcomes? That is, what are the broad policy areas in which policymakers must balance growth with other social and political objectives? In the Chinese context, we can identify three strategic policy arenas that are most crucial for shaping economic growth, while also inevitably shaping other aspect of society's evolution. I call these three transition strategy, industrial development strategy, and the repurposing of the Communist Party hierarchy. In all three of these we see the privileging of rapid economic growth above other considerations.

Transition Strategy

Given the prominence of rapid economic growth among policymakers' objectives, rapid "big bang" scenarios of transition were rejected. It was never conceivable that China would willingly sacrifice a year or two of growth in order to complete a rapid and thorough transition to a market economy, as reformers in Poland, for example, envisaged. Instead, Chinese policymakers adopted measures that would increase growth in the short run, by lowering entry barriers, encouraging the growth of markets alongside the plan, strengthening incentives for increased output, and so on. This has already been well covered in the transition literature. Not only have specific measures of economic reform repeatedly been judged on the basis of their contribution to growth (Heilmann 2008), the entire strategy of reform can be seen as subordinate to the quest for growth.

Industrial Development Strategy

China's development strategy has been an aggregation of multiple industrial policies. In the cases of Japan and Korea we can describe clearly the focus of industrial policies in certain eras, and reasonably trace the impact those policies had on developmental outcomes. Thus, industrial policy in the late 1970s accelerated Korea's transition to heavy and chemical industries. Efforts in Taiwan in the 1980s to promote the semiconductor and related industries are plausibly related to Taiwan's emergence as a high-tech hub in the 1990s. It is virtually impossible to make similar judgments about China. There are many cases where government industrial promotion policies are associated with successful subsequent development, but just as many cases where industrial promotion was an abject failure (Murakawa 2000; 2001). More crucially, it is not clear that industrial policies targeted at specific sectors do not simply cancel each other out, as preferences and priorities given for one type of investment cancel out those given to another. Chinese industrial policy reflects fragmented policy formulation and multiple, inconsistent interests at play, and end up hit and miss.

However, all of the various industrial policies tend to promote investment. Tax breaks, subsidized land development and public utilities all serve to subsidize investment. While the sectoral impact of industrial policy may be ambiguous, the net impact in tilting priorities toward industrial and infrastructure investment is quite strong. The diversity of industrial policies may be the natural outcome of an enormous and diverse economy like China; diverse and competing national and regional policies might even be an efficient solution, as long as competition washes out the least effective policies. The point is that a congeries of inconsistent industrial policies adds up to a consistent policy priority to industrial and infrastructure investment, at the expense of other objectives.

Repurposing the Communist Party Hierarchy

The most fundamental thing that a communist party does is manage personnel. A communist party is a human resources department that, in an economy with a large state presence, manages the allocation and reward of personnel throughout the economy. Since China entered the reform era, it has not left this personnel system unchanged. Rather, the entire personnel system has been regularized, given much stronger incentives, and focused on the objective of economic growth. Since the early 1980s, national "cadre responsibility systems" have provided for systematic evaluation of government officials at all levels through a system of success indicators (*kaohe zhibiao* 考核指标) and their reward with year-end bonuses. Cadres are annually assigned points for performance in several different policy arenas, and the total score determines the cadre's annual bonus. A large bonus can easily double a cadre's annual income. Crucially, for general government officials, indicators directly related to economic growth—GDP growth, tax collections, and industrial output—typically accounted for 60–65 points out of the 100 total possible (Edin 2000, 125–40; Whiting 2001; Whiting 2004; Zhuang Guobo 2007). As a result, government officials at all levels are strongly "incentivized" to support specific progrowth policies.[2]

Combining transition strategy, development strategy, and the manner in which incentives are built into the political system, it is clear that proinvestment and progrowth policies are built into the Chinese system in an extremely profound way. Indeed, a progrowth bias is integral to the functioning of the system as a whole. To be sure, China may be uniquely well positioned to generate rapid growth and, as mentioned above, China is in the midst of the highest-growth phase of the development process. But on top of these structural factors, the policy and systemic features of China over the past thirty years have been clearly focused on promoting precisely the outcome of maximum speed growth.

There is nothing irrational or misconceived about China's ranking of economic growth above other objectives. No country as poor as China was in the 1980s could hope for international respect or ever attain objectives that were in competition with other, more powerful nations. Nor could a rich and satisfying life for its people be attained without economic development. Elevating economic growth to the top of a poor country's objectives is entirely reasonable. But emphasizing the implicit choices behind the growth strategy reminds us that no strategy is inevitable or immutable. Moreover, any choice, no matter how reasonable, involves costs as well as benefits. A choice that seemed overwhelmingly obvious at one time may gradually become less compelling, and over time, the balance among different objectives will gradually shift. That is particularly true as countries move from one set of developmental conditions to another.

The Concomitants of China's Growth Strategy

The commitment to rapid growth has in practice meant an enormous mobilization of resources for investment. China's investment rate—fixed investment as a share of GDP—is higher than any other country has achieved on a sustained basis.[3] China's investment rate was already as high as any other country in the ten-year period from 1993 to 2002, and it then rose over 40 percent during the five-year growth surge from 2003–2008 (figure 4.1). Moreover, as discussed later, the investment rate jumped even higher in 2009 in the wake of the global financial crisis. In addition, figure 4.1 shows that China has run a consistent large trade surplus since 2004 (peaking at 8.9 percent of GDP in 2007) that stands in marked contrast to the modest surpluses and occasional deficits that China generated before 2004. These numbers show that China's growth pattern is certainly "unbalanced," in the sense that it has been accompanied by extremely high levels of investment, and extraordinarily large international imbalances as well.

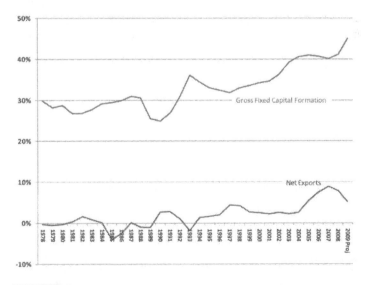

FIGURE 4.1
Investment and Net Exports (Share of GDP)

The huge effort expended on investment and exporting inevitably implies that consumption—and particularly household consumption—is a correspondingly small part of the Chinese economy. As figure 4.2 shows, the consumption share of GDP declined dramatically after 2003, corresponding to the surge in investment and net exports in that period. It is worth tracing the roots of this dramatic decline by reading figure 4.2 from left to right. As Chinese households began to emerge from the planned economy in 1978, they consumed less than 50 percent of GDP. However, successful rural and urban reforms put more money into the hands of households, and rapid growth of household income pushed consumption expenditures significantly above 50 percent of expenditure-side GDP by the mid-1980s. But after 1989, China's economic structure began to swing back to earlier patterns. The mid-1990s brought a surge of investment, such that household consumption dropped to around 45 percent of GDP and then stabilized. During the new millennium, though, household consumption as a share of GDP dropped again, to just above 35 percent of GDP in 2008, much lower than it had been during the Maoist period. Again, this is internationally unprecedented. US household consumption was about 62 percent of GDP from the 1950s through the early 1980s (Parker 1999). US household consumption rose to exceed 70 percent of GDP after 2001, but this reflected the unsustainable housing and financial bubbles in the United States in those years. In any case, the consumption-dominated economy of the United States is something of an outlier, and the more relevant comparison may be with Japan in the early 1970s. Between 1970 and 1973, Japan devoted 49 percent of its GDP to household consumption, and 37 percent to fixed capital formation. Net exports were only 2 percent of GDP, and government consumption was 11 percent of GDP, compared to China's 13–16 percent (World Bank). Generally speaking, these macrostructural figures tell us that China in the 1980s and 1990s was quite similar to Japan in the early 1970s, as both economies pumped a comparatively high level of resources into investment and enjoyed rapid growth. However, China's experience in the 2000s has diverged from Japan's earlier experience. In Japan, the early 1970s were the final years of the high growth era, and subsequently investment declined, while growth dropped off markedly. In China, however, investment, net exports, and economic growth all reached more extreme values, and surpassed all historical precedent.

The huge volume of resources devoted to new investment created a very powerful process of transformation that included exceptionally rapid structural change. During the period of maximum structural change, the benefits to a high investment policy are also arguably at a peak. Each worker who leaves agriculture for a nonagricultural job creates a demand for new fixed capital for productive machinery, housing, and urban infrastructure. At the same time, the productivity

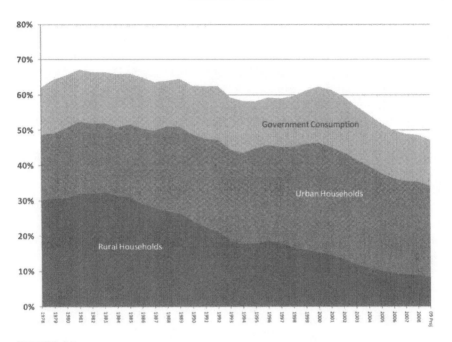

FIGURE 4.2
Consumption as a Share of GDP

of that new investment is high because it enables a previously underemployed agricultural worker to perform much more productive tasks. Figure 4.3 shows that rapid structural change in employment has followed on high investment. There are numerous problems with the official labor data, but the pattern they portray is so strong that it would survive any plausible data revision. During three periods, agricultural workers have left the farms in large numbers. From 1983 through 1988, following the success of rural reforms and the growth of township and village enterprises; from 1991 through 1996, as the economy surged back from the post-Tiananmen recession; and again from 2002 through 2007. During this last five-year growth surge, the agricultural labor force declined from 369 million to 314 million, a net decrease of 55 million people. Since the natural increase in the agricultural labor force over this period would have been at least 4 million per year, a total of 75 million people—about 10 percent of the total labor force—left the farm sector in the past five years. As these people move from low productivity farm jobs to higher productivity urban jobs—even at the margins of the urban economy—they provide a huge impetus to the growth process.

Given China's size, and the fact that few farmers leave the land after age thirty-five, mass rural-urban migration will probably slow down before the

agricultural labor force sinks below 30 percent of the labor force, with the re-
mainder of the transformation taking place more slowly as the labor force ages.
In any case, the process of transformation today is certainly not exhausted, but
the bulk of it has passed astonishingly rapidly. In the Yangtze Delta, with a total
population approaching 150 million, less than 20 percent of the labor force is
left in agriculture; in Guangdong—with 94.9 million people in 2007, China's
most populous province (!)—only 29 percent of the labor force is in agriculture.[4] These nation-sized entities have transformed into middle-income economies, like Korea and Taiwan in the 1980s. However, figure 4.3 tells an additional
story as well. After each surge of structural change, the economy has suffered a
setback that temporarily brought structural change to a halt, and even threw it
into reverse for a period. Another of these temporary phases of recoil took place
in 2008–2009, but appears to have lasted for only one year.

China's high investment rate relies on a financial system that mobilizes resources into investment. The banking and fiscal systems play a large role in this
outcome, and they have been extensively studied. State-run banks channel
household saving into new investment. The crucial role of the fiscal system was
temporarily occluded by the crisis of state capacity that appeared immediately
after the Tiananmen debacle, but has come back strongly in fifteen years since
fiscal reforms were enacted at the end of 1993. The additional piece of the system that needs to be emphasized is the importance of retained profits, particularly within the industrial system. Proproducer policies have succeeded in stabi-

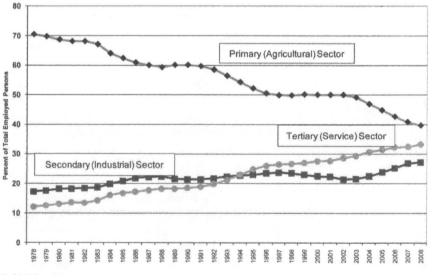

FIGURE 4.3
Structural Change in Employment

lizing the state-run industrial sector and in boosting the profits of industrial enterprises, whether state-owned or not. As figure 4.4 shows, the turnaround has been particularly striking since 2002. The surge in profitability of the industrial sector was the proximate source of the increase in the investment share after 2003. Flush with cash, industrial enterprises channeled funds into expansion, feeding the great Chinese boom of 2003–2008. Only after midyear 2008 did the growth of profits stall with the onset of the global crisis.

For China as a society, these patterns lead directly to the disproportionate power of the corporate and government sectors as compared to the household sector. Resources are concentrated in large organizations, often state-owned and staffed by the Communist Party. Access to a position in the large-scale sector is an important determinant of wealth as well as status. Access can come through entrepreneurship and cultivation of personal networks, as well as through political power and influence. The system is thus dramatically different from the old Maoist system, under which only political power provided meaningful access to resources. But it is still a system in which access is selective and control over resources is highly concentrated. These disproportions support corruption and breed resentment among the general population. Society, especially rural society, is low powered.

More indirectly, the high growth system contributes to high levels of income inequality across the board in society. Despite high levels of rural to urban migration, the income gap between urban and rural households has hardly shrunk, and may even have widened. High rates of investment equip

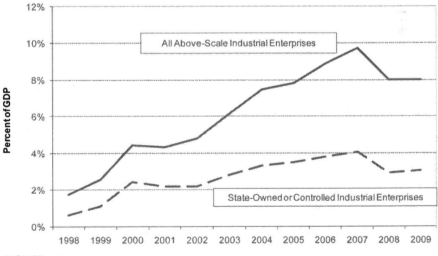

FIGURE 4.4
Industrial Profits (Share of GDP)

the new urban immigrant with fixed capital, but also increase the capital that existing urbanites dispose of, and raise their income directly and indirectly. Urban economies—especially coastal cities—continue to surge ahead of rural areas. China's income inequality, as measured by the Gini coefficient, has increased from its low point below .3 in the early 1980s (after successful rural reforms) to .45 in 2002, according to Ravallion and Chen (2007; see chapter 5 for a discussion of these trends). These household survey-based calculations do not capture the extremes of power and income inequality referred to in the previous paragraph. Both kinds of inequality breed resentment and, under certain circumstances, can lead to lower returns to investment in human capital among those at the lower end of the income scale (Chauduri and Ravallion 2006; Li et al. 2005).

China's growth strategy also has huge environmental costs. In part this is simply because in any given decision process, environmental factors will almost always play a secondary role compared to the overriding goal of economic growth. The utilization of coal, as discussed above, is the most obvious case of repeated subordination of environmental considerations to the growth imperative. The environmental costs of China's development are also high simply because the high investment strategy inevitably implies that demand for energy-intensive and often polluting heavy industrial products is large. China's limited progress in continuing to improve energy efficiency over the past five years has been largely due to the remarkable growth of energy-using heavy industry (Rosen and Houser 2007). Finally, the concentration of the governmental incentive system on the pursuit of economic growth—so useful in adapting the Communist hierarchy to the needs of a market economy—stands in the way of increasing the weight of environmental considerations in decision making. Even if the center declares its support for a given environmental outcome, the officials on the ground charged with implementing that decision still find their incentives shaped by a system that prioritizes growth above anything else. In other words, this is a system that has been tuned up; it is optimized for supporting growth policies. As a result, policies designed to achieve other objectives typically get short shrift, and are weakly implemented by a system that is not really set up to deliver those goods.

The Shift from Growth to a "Harmonious Society"

Chinese policymakers are acutely aware of the problems sketched out in the previous paragraphs. Since the Hu Jintao–Wen Jiabao administration assumed power at the end of 2002, policy has shifted in numerous areas. Government policymakers have adopted a broad array of policies designed to improve social security, protect the disadvantaged, improve living conditions in rural areas, and improve the overall environment (Naughton 2008b). Ambitious goals have been laid out in general programmatic documents, including the Eleventh Five Year Plan (Naughton 2005). Concrete policy measures have been successively implemented. The most dramatic set of policies, and the most successful, have been those policies by which the central government has assumed budgetary responsibility for core social programs in rural areas. Central government budget transfers have begun to fund primary education in most of rural China, and have made significant contributions to the new rural health insurance program.[5] These have been combined with the abolition of the agricultural tax and the institution of direct subsidies to grain growers to significantly increase the profitability of farming.

In fact, it is fair to ask a very general question: which of the social problems spawned by China's rapid economic growth have been addressed by new policies in China in the last five years? The answer is clear, but may be surprising: all of them. The sheer range of issue areas in which new policy initiatives have emerged over the past five years is staggering: in rural areas, along with the income-related policies mentioned above, new land policies seek to strengthen farmers' rights to control, buy and sell, and lease their land. Policies toward rural-to-urban migrants have shifted markedly, with government increasingly recognizing the huge contribution such migrants make to development. Local areas now often provide premigration training classes to prepare departing young people for the challenges of urban life. The State Council has issued a series of documents designed to establish the rights of migrants: migrants have a right to live and work in cities; cities have a responsibility to educate migrant children; and migrants should not be subjected to exorbitant fees or police harassment.

In the urban workplace, enormous effort is now going into the support of worker rights. The number of members of the government-run union, the All China Federation of Trade Unions (ACFTU) has gone from 87 million in 1999 (the recent low), to 193 million in 2007 (NBS 2008a, 875). The new Labor Law that came into effect on January 1, 2008, gives workers the right to a labor contract, and the right to a clearly specified severance pay, calculated according to a simple formula (one month of pay per year of seniority). A major effort to improve workplace safety has been put into effect, with a special focus on coal mines. The coal mine death toll has been brought down by more than half, falling below three thousand in 2009 (SAWS Annual).

In the area of environment, enormous steps have been taken in principle, steps that are only beginning to have an effect. The Eleventh Five Year Plan was followed by an ambitious programmatic document drafted at the Chinese Academy of Sciences, declaring that China had to sidestep further deterioration of the environment as implied by an environmental Kuznets curve. Again, looking to coal for evidence of implementation, we find that several thousand small coal mines have been shut down in the last two years, as a process of inspection and licensing finally begins to come into effect (SAWS 2007). The government has finally acknowledged that pure automobilization on the American model is not feasible in the Chinese context, and State Council [2005] article 46 decreed that cities must quickly give priority to public transport in allocation of street space, and urged cities to proceed with the construction of mass transport systems for the medium to long run. There is no area of Chinese policymaking that has not been affected by the new thinking, and the push for a more harmonious and scientific growth path.

And yet, seen from thirty thousand feet, the Chinese growth path reveals absolutely no impact from this apparent change of course. It is relatively easy to see why not: while the government has made important new allocations of resources around the margins of the existing system, and while institutions have been tinkered with to address new needs, all of the core elements of the existing growth engine are still in place. The resource allocation decisions involving really large sums of money are still made on the same basis; the incentive structure rewards the same types of behavior and decision making; and the opportunities for rapid development are still enticing. Given that the basics of the high investment growth pattern were still in place, the early and modest efforts toward a more "balanced" and higher quality society were simply swamped by a cyclical intensification of the old pattern.

By 2004, Chinese economists and planners had begun to seriously worry about an overheated economy. But continued productivity improvements kept a lid on costs and macroeconomic policy adjustments prevented the imbalances from erupting into sustained open inflation. Instead, China pulled into a sustained boom, led by investment and a steadily growing trade surplus. Although China let the value of its currency drift upward slowly after mid-2005, the currency remained distinctly undervalued. Only at the end of 2007, as new inflationary pressures emerged, did China allow the currency to appreciate significantly. In the meantime, sustained productivity growth drove a steady increase in exports, and China's homegrown heavy industries increasingly substituted for imports of heavy and machinery industry products. Demand for investment goods fueled additional new investment, which fed into a virtuous growth cycle. But in the process, all of the core imbalances of the economy became more pronounced (Lardy 2008). Moreover, China became, willy-nilly, more dependent on external demand than it had ever been before. It was in this context—as Chinese policymakers struggled with their own ambivalence and with their limited success in taming their overheated and unbalanced economy—that the global financial crisis arrived in China with unexpected force.

The Crisis and China's Response

China's growth turned down sharply after August 2008. Chinese policymakers hesitated only a few months as they digested the magnitude of the internal and external economic challenges they faced. Then, in early November 2008, policymakers launched an economic stimulus program of enormous scale. Planners laid out a two-year program of government infrastructure investment with a total value of about 4 percent of GDP. Crucially, the leadership then used the hierarchical political system to send a message to local leaders: initiate work immediately on your most urgent local investment projects; submit lists of "shovel-ready" projects to the central government; get started as soon as possible. Policymakers then opened the spigots of the state-owned banking system. Beginning in January 2009 a massive flood of credit flowed to support investment by local governments and (primarily) state-owned enterprises. The flood of liquidity into the system was more than enough to offset the decline in profits in the industrial system in 2008–2009 (shown in figure 4.4). Bank credit grew an average of 9.2 percent during the first half of the years 2002 through 2008. By that standard, "normal" credit growth in 2009 would have been about 2.8 trillion RMB. Instead, credit surged more than twice that much, jumping to 7.4 trillion RMB. That part of 2009 credit growth that was *above normal*—4.6 trillion RMB—was equal to 14 percent of annual GDP, giving an indication of the huge stimulus provided the economy in this way. Finally, the government rolled out measures to stimulate consumption as well, providing tax breaks and rebates to a range of goods from small autos to electronics products in the countryside (Naughton 2009).

This vigorous program had the desired effect. China's response was one of the most "Keynesian" of all the national responses to the global crisis, in that it combined size and speed, with increased activity in the real economy evident within ninety days of the policy's birth (by February 2009). In addition, the government infrastructure investment program was fairly well targeted, with a focus on transportation and rural infrastructure. Of course, the flood of funding from bank credits far exceeded the needs of the initial infrastructure investment program, and could not possibly have been so precisely targeted. By the second quarter of 2009, economic growth had stabilized and began to increase. Virtually all the impetus to growth in the first half of 2009 came from the expansion of government investment. While consumption grew as well, it was barely enough to offset the decline in net exports. China rode a surge of government investment out of the global financial crisis.

Figures 4.1 and 4.2 include a projection of 2009 data based on data through the first three quarters of the year. While preliminary, the figures show a striking fact. In response to the crisis, the Chinese economy has become even more unbalanced than it ever was before. By conservative estimate, the Chinese investment rate will soar to 45 percent of GDP in 2009 (as figure 4.1 shows). Household consumption, despite turning in a solid growth performance, will continue to erode as a share of GDP, dropping below 35 percent of GDP for the first time (figure 4.2). Net exports (the trade surplus) do show a trend toward "rebalancing," as the surplus will decline to just over 5 percent of GDP. This is still a large surplus, but down significantly from its peak two years earlier. Even more than in the past—and more than any economy in history— China is dependent on domestic investment to drive growth.

In brief, China has responded to the crisis by reinstating its existing growth model. Ironically, the unprecedented economic crisis has caused a reversion to old habits. But in the successful response to the crisis, we have also seen China's existing growth model display its most characteristic features. The concentration of power allowed decision makers to be extremely decisive in changing policy in November 2008. The growth-compatible incentives in place throughout the hierarchical system facilitated an extraordinarily rapid implementation of the policy turn. Direct government influence over the banking system elicited a flood of credit, quickly. Most important, the ever-present demand for new investment and new growth-supporting measures implied that decision makers at all levels jumped at the opportunity to roll out new projects, and thus supported the recovery of final demand. Not surprisingly, Chinese leaders during 2009 began to display a degree of pride about their success in dealing with the crisis, the achievements of their economic and political system, and their newly prominent place among the leading nations of the world as well.

The Future

China appears to have successfully sidestepped the worst of the global financial crisis. In this, we see a recapitulation of one of the most striking aspects of China's growth experience over the past thirty years. One of the most surprising things about China's economic growth since 1978 has been the virtual absence of crisis. The political crisis around Tiananmen in 1989 shook the political system to the core, it is true, but the political recovery was quick and fairly predictable—circle the wagons and hang together—and the economic recovery was even swifter. But ever since Tiananmen, people have been predicting crisis for China. All these predictions have proved wrong, whether they came from China pessimists or from China optimists. Given this background, it would be foolhardy to predict a crisis for the Chinese economy in the immediate future, and this chapter does not make any such prediction. However, we cannot neglect the fact that a newly complex mix of economic challenges currently faces China.

While China has been able to reinstate growth and its old growth model, it is unlikely that this will lead to a smooth return to precrisis growth levels. China's dramatic expansion of exports is likely to slow permanently, given the long-term reductions in the purchasing power of American consumers, who lay behind so much of the global boom of 2003–2008. Government investment simply cannot keep expanding at the rates it grew during 2009. Overall, then, China probably has no choice but to adjust to a somewhat slower overall pace of economic growth, reliant to a larger extent on domestic consumption growth. The problem here is that consumption is such a small share of China's GDP that even large increases in consumption will not be enough to restore very rapid growth. The transition to moderately fast growth in the 8 percent range (down from the 10–12 percent range in the five-year growth surge) is probably unavoidable.

Beyond this stabilization of growth, China will soon be facing the shift to a different kind of growth strategy as discussed at the beginning of this chapter. The shift has been temporarily deferred by the expansionary policies of 2009, but cannot be put off indefinitely. With structural change ongoing in 2009, the abundant labor surplus in the rural areas is already beginning to face exhaustion. Labor force growth is beginning to slow down, and will reach zero growth by around 2015. To be sure, China has taken many steps that may position it well to make the transition to a "higher quality" growth path. Education standards have risen dramatically in the past five years. New industries have been created that may play a role in future environmental cleanup. Consumer living standards have increased and an urban middle class is growing. There is nothing in economic theory that tells us that such a transition cannot be smoothly made (Holz 2008).

However, past experience of rapidly growing East Asian economies tells us that such transitions are rarely entirely smooth. Japan grew at 10.4 percent per year between 1950 and 1973, raising its investment effort to a peak in the last three years of the period. But after the first global energy shock, Japan's growth rate dropped sharply, and after 1974 Japan never grew more than 6 percent in a single year. Korea, Thailand, and Malaysia made their largest investment efforts in the early 1990s and enjoyed very rapid growth. But after the East Asian financial crisis in 1997–1998, investment and growth dropped sharply and has never fully recovered to precrisis levels. The transition in Taiwan was less dramatic, perhaps because of the opportunity to transplant export networks to the China mainland, but eventually led to a similar growth slowdown. Looking backward, it is obvious that crisis punctuates—and punctures—long-run trends, marking turning points or sudden shifts from one apparently stable long-run path to another. These crises often appear inevitable in retrospect, yet hardly anybody predicted them beforehand, and even fewer were those who adapted their behavior beforehand to the brewing storm. As the crisis recedes—having been dealt with effectively or not—many find that their behavior has adapted to something new, that things don't ever return to the way they were, and that the crisis has marked the beginning of a new era. There are crises; they don't disappear; they are very difficult to predict; and then they end up changing everything.

We can predict with a fairly high degree of confidence that by around 2015—that is, within five years of this writing—that China will be undergoing a transition to a slower but higher quality growth path. We are on the threshold of a new era, and the extraordinary growth bonus that China reaped in the early part of this century is either over or will soon be over. The one certainty is that the China that develops from this different growth model will be quite different from the China we know today: it will be more sophisticated, more prosperous, with an older population, and a much more desirable living environment. How the transition to that new era happens is hard to predict, even more so in the wake of the uncertainties caused by the global financial crisis. Perhaps China will indeed experience an acute short-run crisis, if stimulus measures ultimately fail to revive high-speed growth and a "W-shaped" recovery emerges in 2010–2011. It is also possible that China will be forced into a painful and protracted shift of economic growth model, struggling to find a new set of economic relationships that work. Yet it is also possible that China will move aggressively, in the immediate future, to increase consumption, democratize its economy, and spread the benefits of growth more widely. In that case, slower growth might be smoothly achieved, along with rapid increases in well-being. In that case, China will have surprised us again with its ability to avoid crisis.

References

Chaudhuri, Shubham, and Martin Ravallion. 2006. "Partially Awakened Giants: Uneven Growth in China and India." Policy Research Working Paper 4069. Washington, DC: World Bank, November.

Edin, Maria. 2000. *Market Forces and Communist Power: Local Political Institutions and Economic Development in China* (Uppsala: Uppsala University Printers).

Heilmann, Sebastian. 2008. "Policy Experimentation in China's Economic Rise." *Studies in Comparative International Development* 43, no. 1 (March): 1–26.

Holz, Carsten. 2008. "China's Economic Growth 1978–2025: What We Know Today About China's Economic Growth Tomorrow." *World Development* 36, no. 10: 1665–91.

Lardy, Nicholas R. 2008. "Sustaining Economic Growth in China." In C. Fred Bergsten, Charles Freeman, Nicholas R. Lardy, and Derek. J. Mitchell, *China's Rise: Challenges and Opportunities*, chap 6. Washington, DC: Peterson Institute for International Economics.

Li Rongrong. 2009. *Fully Implement the Perspective of Scientific Development to Raise the Quality of State Enterprise Growth*, December 24, 2009. www.sasac.gov.cn/n1180/n1566/n259730/n264153/6870745.html (accessed December 30, 2009).

Li Shi, Bai Nansheng, et al. 2005. *China Human Development Report*. Beijing: UNDP and China Development Research Foundation.

Mao Yushi, Sheng Hong, and Yang Fuqiang. 2008. *The True Costs of Coal*. Greenpeace. act.greenpeace.org.cn/coal/report/TCOC-Final-EN.pdf.

Marukawa, Tomoo, ed. 2000. *Iko-ki Chugoku no Sangyo Seiasaku* [China's industrial policy in transition]. Chiba: Institute of Developing Economies.

———. 2001. "WTO, Industrial Policy and China's Industrial Development." In Ippei Yamazawa and Ken-ichi Imai, eds., *China Enters WTO: Pursuing Symbiosis with the Global Economy*. Chiba: Institute of Developing Economies.

National Bureau of Statistics (NBS). 2008a. *China Statistical Yearbook*. Beijing: Zhongguo Tongji.

———. 2008b. *Zhongguo Fazhan Baogao* [China development report]. Beijing: Zhongguo Tongji.

———. 2009. "Industrial Profit Shot Up from January to November." December 29. www.stats.gov.cn/enGliSH/newsandcomingevents/t20091229_402610800.htm (accessed December 30, 2009).

Naughton, Barry. 2005. "The New Common Economic Program: China's Eleventh Five Year Plan and What It Means." *China Leadership Monitor*, no. 16 (Fall 2005). www.hoover.org/publications/clm/issues/2898936.html.

———. 2008a. "Market Economy, Hierarchy and Single Party Rule." In Janos Kornai and Yingyi Qian, eds., *Market and Socialism Reconsidered (with Particular Reference to China and Vietnam)*, 135–61. London: Macmillan, for the International Economic Association.

———. 2008b. "China's Left Tilt: Pendulum Swing or Mid-course Correction?" In Cheng Li, ed., *China's Changing Political Landscape: Prospects for Democracy*, 142–58. Washington, DC: Brookings Institution Press.

———. 2009. "Understanding the Chinese Stimulus Package." *China Leadership Monitor*, no. 28 (Spring). www.hoover.org/publications/clm/issues/44613157.html.

Parker, Jonathan. 1999. "Spendthrift in America? On Two Decades of Decline in the U.S. Saving Rate." *NBER Macroeconomics Annual* 14: 317–70.

Ravallion, Martin, and Chen Shaohua. 2007. "China's (Uneven) Progress against Poverty." *Journal of Development Economics* 82, no. 1: 1–42.

Rosen, Daniel, and Trevor Houser. 2007. "China Energy: A Guide for the Perplexed." The China Balance Sheet: A Joint Project by the Center for Strategic and International Studies and the Peterson Institute for International Economics. Washington, DC: Peterson Institute for International Economics.

SASAC. 2006. "Guanyu tuijin Guoyou Ziban tiaozheng he guoyou qiye zhongzu de zhidao yijian" [Guiding opinions on advancing the readjustment of state capital and the reor-

ganization of state-owned enterprises]. www.sasac.gov.cn/2006rdzt/2006rdzt_0021/
gzw/03/200702050217.htm.

———. 2009. "General Operating Conditions of Central Enterprises in 2008." September 18, 2009. www.sasac.gov.cn/n1180/n1566/n258203/n258329/6649463.html
(accessed December 30, 2009).

State Administration of Work Safety (SAWS). Annual. "Annual Statistical Analysis
Page." www.chinasafety.gov.cn/newpage/aqfx/aqfx_ndtjfx.htm (accessed December
19, 2009). [Contains safety reports for most years since 2000.]

———. 2007. "State Administration of Work Safety Announcement No. 15 on Closure of Unsafe Coal Mines in 2007." www.chinasafety.gov.cn/2007-09/19/
content_260837.htm (accessed December 19, 2009).

Whiting, Susan H. 2001. *Power and Wealth in Rural China: The Political Economy of
Institutional Change.* New York: Cambridge University Press.

———. 2004. "The Cadre Evaluation System at the Grass Roots: The Paradox of Party
Rule." In Barry Naughton and Dali Yang, eds., *Holding China Together: Diversity and
National Integration in the Post-Deng Era*, 101–19. New York: Cambridge University
Press.

World Bank. Annual. World Development Indicators (WDI). web.worldbank.org/
WBSITE/EXTERNAL/DATASTATISTICS/0,,menuPK:232599~pagePK:64133170~
piPK:64133498~theSitePK:239419,00.html.

Xinhua. 2006. "Guoziwei: Guoyou jingji ying baochi qige hangye de juedui kongzhili"
[SASAC: The state-owned economy ought to maintain absolute control over seven
sectors]. December 18, 2006. www.gov.cn/jrzg/2006-12/18/content_472256.htm
(accessed December 19, 2009).

Zhuang Guobo. 2007. *Lingdao ganbu zhengji pingjia de lilun yu shijian* [Theory and
practice of evaluation of political performance by leadership cadres]. Beijing:
Zhongguo jingji.

5

Inequality

Overcoming the Great Divide

Carl Riskin

THE STUDY OF ECONOMIC INEQUALITY IN China has become a cottage industry.[1] The obvious reason is that, along with much else in China over the
past thirty years, inequality has been changing rapidly. What was once a fairly
egalitarian society, at least in terms of measured income, is now among the
more unequal in the world. The United Nations Development Programme's
(UNDP) 2006 Human Development Report (HDR) showed only 30 countries
out of 177 with greater income inequality than China's (Young 2007). The
2008 HDR gives the most recently calculated Gini coefficients for China and
seven of its Asian neighbors, with China the most unequal (table 5.1).

Yet inequality is a complex concept with many possible dimensions and
implications. There are many ways to view it. On the one hand, Meng et al.
(2005) measure the degree to which rising inequality has retarded poverty
reduction. They show that the elasticity of the poverty rate with respect to the
Gini coefficient is almost 3: specifically, a 10 percent increase in inequality is
associated with a 28.4 percent increase in income poverty. This is almost as
high as the negative income elasticity of poverty (3.13), meaning that equal
proportionate increases in income and inequality will almost cancel each
other out, leaving poverty unchanged.[2] Moreover, as one voluminous writer
on Chinese inequality has put it, "It is found that inequality is harmful to
growth no matter what time horizon . . . is considered."[3] Thus, growing inequality makes poverty alleviation more difficult and hinders growth itself.
This is a hopeful conclusion, in that it encourages the search for ways to make
growth more equalizing when it has been highly disequalizing, not only be-

TABLE 5.1
Income Inequality in Asia

Country	Year	Gini
Japan	1993	21.9
Korea	1998	31.6
Vietnam	2004	34.4
India	2004-05	36.8
Sri Lanka	2002	40.2
Singapore	1998	42.5
Philippines	2003	44.5
China	2004	46.9

cause this is right in principle, but also on the instrumental ground that it is progrowth.

On the other hand, the conclusion that inequality and growth are in contradiction is evidently not shared by Luo and Zhu (2008), who propose that increasing income inequality in China is the product of a "race to the top," in which everyone is better off, but some much more so than others. This, they argue, is a "normal process of development at a certain stage" and "desirable to some extent as it unleashes competitive pressure and creates incentives for investment in skills."[4] There is an implicit commitment to the Kuznets curve in this argument, in that it presupposes a turnaround toward reduced inequality at a higher stage of development. I recently considered the evidence for a Kuznets curve in the behavior of urban and rural income inequality between 1988 and 2002 (Riskin 2007). The conclusion was that, although intra-rural and intra-urban inequality appears to have been tempered in the latter half of that period, having risen sharply in the first half, this pattern appears to be largely the result of policy changes in urban China and possibly in rural China, as well. The apparent change from exacerbated to alleviated inequality did not obviously stem from automatic market forces, as the common interpretation of the Kuznets curve predicts.[5]

Forrest Zhang (2008) reminds us that one must pay attention to the particular kind of inequality that is of concern. He argues that increasing inequality of land use in one province (Zhejiang) has been a means by which poorer villagers trade land for off-farm income, leading to increased inequality of farm income but reduced inequality of total income. This is a reminder also of what development economists have long believed, that markets can be equalizing if the original distribution of assets is equal, as they certainly were in post–land reform China.[6] It also raises the question of what happens to these villagers during an economic downturn in which they lose their off-farm jobs but can no longer return to their farms for subsistence.

Of the many dimensions of economic inequality (consumption vs. income, urban-rural, intra-urban, intra-rural, coastal-interior, interprovincial, inequality of income types such as wages, and so on) perhaps the two most prominently discussed are the urban-rural gap and inequality between the eastern and western regions, or the coastal-interior gap. In both cases inequality has grown considerably over the entire period of reform and transformation. These two dimensions of inequality turn out to be linked to each other in interesting ways. Overall urban-rural inequality has been shaped by the different changes in urban-rural inequality within the three macroregions. Moreover, in the cases of both urban-rural and coastal-interior inequality, a potentially countervailing force has existed in the form of massive rural-urban and west-east migration. Migration raises average income in the source region and reduces it in the target region and thus should reduce inequality. Migration can also be an engine of growth working to enhance the dynamism of the target areas and thus further raise incomes there, thus maintaining or increasing inequality. On balance, however, one would expect that the amount of labor mobility implicit in two decades of massive rural-urban migration should have had some dampening impact on the urban-rural differential. Yet this gap still registered as greater than 3:1 in the early 2000s, which is extremely high by international comparative standards.[7] The gap manifests itself in other ways besides income. For instance, average life expectancy in the countryside is six years below that in the cities and town. This gap varies regionally, surpassing eight years in the ten less developed western provinces. Indeed, the gap in rural life expectancy between the poor provinces of Tibet, Guizhou, and Yunnan, on one hand, and Hainan and Jiangsu, on the other, is more than nine years. With regard to education, the 2000 census revealed that while 14 percent of the urban population had received no more than a primary education, the figure was 39 percent for the rural population (UNDP 2005, 8–9). A similar gap manifests itself in public health and in the kinds of diseases contracted by the two groups.

This urban-rural gap was of course a product of China's immediately pre-transition history, when the urban and rural populations were walled off from each other by means of a rigid system of population registration (*hukou* 户口), together with food rationing that made evasion of controls almost impossible. In this bifurcated system, urban residents enjoyed full employment at wages much higher than average farm incomes, as well as social benefits (pensions, health care, subsidized housing) not available to rural residents. The urban-rural disparity, after falling in the early 1980s as early reforms focused on the countryside, began rising again when an urban-biased coastal development

strategy was adopted in the mid-1980s. Yet that very strategy provoked a countervailing response in the form of massive rural-urban migration from the
countryside to the coastal cities, a response made possible by the relaxation of
the *hukou* system and the end of food rationing. Why did not such massive labor
mobility have a greater equalizing effect on urban-rural income differences?

This issue is dealt with in depth by Sicular et al. (2008), who try very hard to
measure the urban-rural income gap accurately. As they point out, most estimates are biased for a number of reasons, among which the most important are
faulty measures of income, lack of correction for regional price differences, and
neglect of rural-urban migrants. They attempt to correct for these weaknesses,
first by using a measure of income that is closer to international standard practice, especially in including imputed rental value of owned housing. Second,
they adjust for regional differences in cost of living by applying a set of spatial
price indexes developed by Brandt and Holz (2006). Finally, to overcome the
omission of rural-urban migrants in previous surveys, they make use of a special China Household Income Project (CHIP) 2002 survey of migrant households in urban areas to include migrants in the urban sample for that year.[8]

The results of the latter two efforts are instructive (table 5.2). First, adjusting
for regional price differences alone reduces the urban-rural gap by 28 percent in
1995 and by 29 percent in 2002, and essentially eliminates its increase between
the two years. However (as Sicular et al. point out) while the ratio of urban to
rural income rises only minimally, the absolute gap between them grows by 64
percent from 2,360 yuan to 3,687 yuan in constant 1995 prices. Thus the urban-
rural gap continues to grow in absolute if not in relative terms.

Including migrants in the urban population reduces the gap by another 7
percent from its price adjusted 2002 value without migrants. Together, these
two adjustments reduce the urban-rural gap by one-third, bringing it from an
extraordinarily high value of 3.18 to 2.12 in 2002.[9] This value is still at the high
end of Asian countries (see Eastwood and Lipton 2004), but is less of an extreme outlier in comparative international experience and it thus eliminates
the improbable story that China's urban-rural disparity remains much greater
than practically anywhere else, even after decades of migration of unprecedented scale. Nonetheless, it is interesting that it is regional price differentials,
not migration, that is responsible for the bulk of this correction. Evidently the
gap was smaller than generally thought, when measured in prices of roughly
equal purchasing power, at least as far back as 1995. Perhaps migration had
already effectively reduced the gap by then or perhaps, properly measured, the
gap was never as large as it appeared.

What is likely to happen to the urban-rural gap over the coming years? A clue
might emerge from interpreting a cross section of macro regions as pointing the
way to longitudinal change. Of the three macro regions, east, west, and central,

TABLE 5.2
Ratio of Urban to Rural Household Disposable per Capita Income,
Adjusting for Regional Price Differences and Rural-Urban Migration

1995	
Unadjusted for regional price differences	3.11
PPP (adjusted for regional price differences)	2.24
2002	
Unadjusted for regional price differences	3.18
PPP (adjusted for regional price differences, and in 1995 prices)	2.27
Unadjusted for regional price differences, migrants included in urban population	2.97
Adjusted for regional price differences, migrants included in urban population	2.12

Source: Sicular et al. (2008).

the east had the smallest price-adjusted urban-rural income ratio in 2002, of 1.89; the central region's ratio was 2.29 and that of the west was 3.49 (Sicular et al. 2008, 39). Moreover, the gap actually increased where it was already largest, in the central and western regions between 1995 and 2002, and fell in the east where it was already lowest. The urban-rural gap in 2002 was responsible for over half of total income inequality in the west, over one-third in the central region, and less than a quarter in the east. This suggests that a key to reducing the gap for China as a whole is to reverse this centrifugal tendency among macro regions. Urban development in the poorer parts of the country has not been sufficient to pull the rural population into its orbit as has already been happening in the east. Development in the central and western regions spurred by investment in both physical and human capital infrastructure, and giving rise to a proliferation of industries and sectors offering nonagricultural jobs, is a likely roadmap for reducing urban-rural inequalities in China.

On regional inequality there is a vast literature[10] containing many diagnoses of the problem, with some authors finding a trend of convergence among provinces, others divergence, and still others convergence among some groups of provinces and divergence among others. From 1949 to the start of the reform period there was absolute divergence but relative convergence among the provinces in provincial average per capita output. Between 1952 and 1979, for instance, there was a trebling of the ratio of the per capita industrial output of the most industrialized to that of the least industrialized province, while the coefficient of variation of provincial industrial output per capita fell by a fifth (Riskin 1987). This was not only an arithmetic effect of the extremely small bases from which the least industrialized provinces began, but

also a product of conscious government efforts to achieve the spread of industrialization, promoted in part by highly redistributive central plans and fiscal
policies. The widening of absolute inequality in this period despite fairly
strenuous efforts to reduce it was a symptom of the persistence of early Kuznets curve forces, of the urban bias of policy despite reigning ideology, and
perhaps of the "comparative advantage defying" nature of central investment
in the interior,[11] which greatly limited spread effects to the local economy.

With regard to the period of reform and opening, much of the literature on
regional inequality generally agrees with Lin et al. (1997) that, as measured by
provincial GDP per capita, such inequality probably lessened during the early
years of the reform period, roughly from 1979 to the late 1980s, but that thereafter it increased again. Even the early convergence is in doubt, however, as
Naughton (2002) shows that much of it disappears when province-specific
deflators are used. Moreover, at least until 1995, provincial personal income
per capita behaved rather differently than GDP per capita, converging only
briefly between 1979 and 1982, and then steadily diverging.

Khan and Riskin (2005) unexpectedly detected a small decline in inequality
of both rural and urban personal disposable income between 1988 and 1995.
In both instances, an important contributing factor was a decline in regional
inequality: the coefficient of variation of provincial income per capita fell for
both rural and urban samples. From 1988 to 1995, the coefficient of variation
of rural provincial per capita disposable income had grown by two-thirds, but
from 1995 to 2002 it fell by about 11 percent. For urban per capita disposable
income, the coefficient of variation of provincial averages rose by 24 percent
during the first period and fell by 20 percent during the second.[12] Indeed,
Khan and Riskin (2005) offer one of the few less pessimistic recent discussions
of China's income inequality.

Naughton (2002) takes a skeptical view of the likelihood of regional convergence in the near future because the forces that had produced it in the past,
such as a heavily redistributive public finance system and the ability to raise
agricultural prices to enhance farm incomes, are no longer available. His one
more hopeful factor is the possibility that market forces themselves will begin
to favor interior development, a possibility that he urges should be abetted
with appropriate supportive public investment. Naughton (2004) discounts
the likelihood that the much-touted western development program, begun in
the late 1990s to offset the recessionary impact of the Asian financial crisis,
will significantly counteract the tendency toward wider regional disparities.
He points out that China's further plunge into the global market after World
Trade Organization (WTO) accession in fact promised to exacerbate this tendency. That such indeed has been the case is argued by Wan et al. (2008). One
discussion, which tries explicitly to build spatial dimensions into its analysis

in confluence with the "new economic geography" arguments of Paul Krugman and others, arrives at a similarly pessimistic conclusion that China faces increasing regional polarization: "Especially the strong probability of the rich staying rich and the poor staying poor may sustain this trend, resulting in long-lasting regional income disparities between the core and the periphery regions . . . in the presence of high interregional transportation costs" (Aroca et al. 2008).

A rather different view of China's regional disparities is that of Justin Lin, as put forth in general form in his 2007 Marshall Lectures at Cambridge University (Lin 2009) and applied specifically to the regional inequality issue in Lin and Liu (2008). This view is that China's large regional disparities are "endogenously determined by its long-term economic development strategy." The strategy in question is identified as a capital-intensive "leap forward" strategy in which industries were established whose technologies conflicted with China's factor proportions and were thus "comparative advantage defying (CAD)." Although reforms began to change this picture in 1978, much of the former strategy was nevertheless retained in poorer central and western interior regions. For instance, prices of raw materials and natural resources, coming largely from the poorer western regions, were suppressed to favor state enterprises in the east. Western regions thus subsidized eastern industrialization and, in turn, they themselves had to be subsidized more directly in order to survive, which sustained and worsened their soft budget constraint and weakened efficiency. Moreover, the internal regions entered the transition period already laden with a heavy burden of CAD enterprises established earlier. These were nonviable without government support and had little or no technology transfer potential toward the capital-scarce surrounding local economy. Nor did they create many employment opportunities either for surrounding low-income farmers or for better-educated workers from the more developed east. An econometric exercise is used by Lin and Liu to buttress the argument that adoption of a CAD industrial development strategy has hindered a province's GDP growth, and that the central and western provinces have tended to follow such a strategy more closely than the eastern provinces have. Thus, they conclude that implementation of a misguided industrial development strategy in the central and western regions was at least partly responsible for the widening of regional disparities after 1978.

Lin's view of the effect of WTO accession on China's regional disparities is more optimistic than Wan's cited above. Lin argues that WTO membership has limited the ability of the government to subsidize a CAD strategy in the interior, and has already led the Chinese government formally to favor the principle of comparative advantage in China's development strategy. He accordingly expresses the belief that China's immersion in the global market, by inducing it to accept a development strategy for the interior that has more positive potential, will eventually work to bring down regional differences in China.

A common feature of virtually all the views summarized above is that the two most distinguishing features of income inequality in China—the urban-rural gap and the east-west disparity—are highly policy dependent. That is, while there are certainly geographic and historical bases for regional and urban-rural differences, there is nothing inevitable about their widening—or for that matter their failure to narrow—in the course of economic development. It follows that the future course of regional and urban-rural inequality in China depends upon the kinds of policies adopted by the government and the resources put into implementing these policies. Of course, it was already clear from international experience that there is no necessary relation between rate of economic growth and degree of income inequality, and that rapid growth is consistent with many different distributions of income. The discussion of income inequality in China by scholars with a variety of points of view merely corroborates this general truth in its specific application to China.

Thus, implicit in the findings of Sicular et al. (2008), that taking account of rural-urban migration reduces the size of the urban-rural gap, is the importance of the *hukou* system in widening this gap in the first place. It follows that encouraging labor mobility and investing in human capital formation in the source regions will work to increase incomes there in two ways: by raising labor productivity directly and by providing an additional source of income in the form of remittances from out-migrant family members. Indeed, the *hukou* system itself is but one manifestation of the long-standing posture of urban bias in China's development strategy. Policy changes that have occurred since the accession to power of Hu Jintao and Wen Jiabao indicate a rethinking of that strategy, with potential positive consequences for the urban-rural gap.

Khan and Riskin (2005), as already mentioned, using a comprehensive measure of income closer than China's official measure to the international definition, find small declines in the inequality of intra-rural and intra-urban personal household per capita income between 1995 and 2002. Inequality of the distribution of rural income fell by almost 10 percent as measured by the Gini ratio; this reduction was the product of a decline in both interprovincial and intraprovincial inequality in most of the provinces. There was an improvement in the distribution of farm income and wage income and a reduction in the regressivity of net taxes. The improved equality of wage income was largely due to a better regional balance in the access of the rural population to wage employment, which might have been a product of the creation of many wage earning jobs in poorer regions by domestic stimulus spending on infrastructure during the Asian crisis (Riskin 2007). Inequality of the distribution of urban income fell by 4 percent, mostly the product of a decline in interprovincial inequality. From the perspective of what happened to individual components of income, the increased equality of urban income distribution stemmed mainly from reform of housing and of public finance. Housing rent subsidies, which had been disproportionately enjoyed by better-off households, were sharply reduced between 1995 and 2002. As housing reform spread home ownership widely through the urban population, its benefits, in the form of imputed rental income of owned housing, became more broad-based and less disequalizing.

In addition, the elasticity of per capita personal consumption with respect to per capita GDP rose sharply from 0.63 in the pre-1995 period to 0.98 in the 1995–2002 period. A much higher incremental share of GDP accrued to households in the latter period than before, presumably as a direct result of government efforts to prop up domestic demand as a substitute for declining growth of external demand after the Asian crisis.

Thus, in discussing the forces behind the apparent decline in intra-rural and intra-urban inequality between 1995 and 2002, Khan and Riskin (2005) find that policy changes regarding housing, net taxes, and government domestic stimulus spending were all involved. They also suggest that diminution of the urban-rural gap through further improvement of rural income is likely to depend on three kinds of policies: those that improve factor productivity in agriculture, promote rural nonfarm employment opportunities, and facilitate the continued flow of labor out of rural areas.

Justin Lin, as we have seen, argues that the widening of regional gaps was the result of adoption of a CAD industrialization strategy and its perpetuation in the poorer interior regions, and that changing this strategy will create the conditions for faster development of those regions, which will in turn discourage the widening of regional disparities. Inherent in this "get the prices right" argument is that the government should continue to eliminate the privileges granted eastern regions as part of the coastal development strategy, such as suppression of the interior's resource prices in order to subsidize coastal industries. Even the more skeptical views of Naughton and of Aroca et al., regarding the likelihood of a near-term diminution of regional inequalities, allow for the possibility that effective policies could reduce regional disparities in comparison with what they would become without such policies. So the future of income inequality in China would seem to depend in no small degree on whether the government puts progressive, inequality-reducing policies in place, and, if so, on its capacity to implement them.

Other major features of the Chinese growth model that have promoted income inequality include its growing reliance on exports, which increased through 2007 and until the global downturn, and which favors already advantaged coastal regions; also, a bureaucratic and economic incentive system that promotes hyperinvestment-led growth and shuns all competing values, including equity and protection of the environment. The urban-rural divide and associated *hukou* system likewise breed inequality between city and countryside. Finally, a capital-intensive mode of industrialization, promoted by artificially cheap capital as well as the lack of access to credit of small and medium enterprises, creates too few jobs, generates high corporate profits, and represses wages and consumption.

These problems have been recognized by the government, which has made inequality a target of policy. Hence the proposed new development paradigm emphasizing the building of a "harmonious society" with more balanced development across regions and sectors. The government has also committed to "rebalancing" economic growth by moving from investment- and export-led growth to growth that is based more heavily on domestic consumption, a change that implies reduced inequality, especially between export-dependent coastal provinces and inland regions. Indeed, the rhetoric of government pronouncements since the current Chinese administration took office in 2002–2003 has certainly heightened expectations for such policies, such that the China Human Development Report 2007/08 can state baldly that "the bridging of development gaps between urban and rural areas; among the eastern, central and western regions; and among social groups is now one of the highest priority public policy objectives" (UNDP 2008, 69).

Indeed, the government has stepped up spending on various pro-poor programs, greatly increased transfers to poorer regions of the country, and taken steps to reform public services and public sector performance. Taxes in rural China have become far less regressive than they were. The agricultural tax was reduced and then eliminated between 2004 and 2007.[13] The threshold for income to be subject to the income tax was raised 250 percent between 2006 and 2008. The central government has encouraged faster increases in local minimum wages, greatly expanded coverage of social insurance programs, in part through an 80 percent increase in its spending on health, education, social security, and unemployment programs from 2004 to 2007. Between those years, the number of workers covered by a basic pension grew by 23 percent (and numbered 219 million in 2008); the number of workers receiving basic health insurance grew by 80 percent (317 million in 2008); coverage by workers compensation increased by 78 percent (138 million in 2008); and coverage by unemployment insurance increased by 10 percent (124 million in 2008).

However, despite these accomplishments, the architecture of China's growth and the structure of public expenditures have not changed much, and to some degree have deteriorated. For instance, not only did the growth rate accelerate still further after 2002, exceeding 10 percent in all of the years 2004 through 2007, in contradistinction to the moderation that was explicitly part of the "balanced growth" objective; but exports grew faster, consumption fell as a proportion of GDP, and the investment rate reached new and unprecedented heights. Moreover, the substantial increases in progressive spending by the central government were dwarfed by the stagnation of social spending at the local level, where over 90 percent of such spending occurs, and where the "rebalancing" objectives of the center were evidently not shared. Thus, overall spending on social insurance and safety net programs, as a fraction of GDP, rose only half a percentage point between 2002 and 2007 and household disposable income hardly benefited from the cuts in taxes on rural and urban incomes and the increased minimum wage levels (Lardy 2008).

The basic reason for the failure of the harmonious society and rebalancing objectives to make more progress is simple: the incentives that drive local government behavior are tied first and foremost to the expansion of local revenue by means of rapid growth. No other policy objective is competitive against this one. Both local fiscal power and prospects for bureaucratic promotion depend almost exclusively on achieving growth. Complementary to this explanation is a weak and flawed public finance and governance system that leaves the central government unable to get its policies implemented at the local level, where the great bulk of relevant spending takes place.

Thus, a longtime student of China's fiscal structure, Christine Wong (2007a; 2007b; 2009), is skeptical that China will succeed in the near future in building an economic governance system capable of achieving a more equitable and well-regulated economic outcome. She traces the problems of poor governance, growing inequality, and regulatory failure to the fiscal retrenchment of the 1980s and 1990s and the various ad hoc arrangements that grew up simultaneously, giving rise to a distorted set of incentives facing public institutions:

> At present, the capacity of the central government to direct economic and social change is constrained by: 1) a broken intergovernmental fiscal system that is unable to support national policy implementation, 2) accountability mechanisms that have been severely eroded by long periods of inadequate finance, so that local governments and public institutions could not be held accountable for results; 3) an information system that is very weak from disuse; 4) a bloated bureaucracy where authorities are fragmented, where the transmission of policies and resources are complex and unreliable. Most of all, government is hobbled— through the whole administrative set-up, by agents whose revenue-hunger dominates decision-making. (Wong 2009, 27–28)

Unless the incentive structure is "fundamentally altered," she writes, the public sector reforms that the center has been trying to implement "will likely have only limited effect."

Analyzing inequality in 2005, a group of Chinese scholars proposed the following ten broad policy objectives for making development more equitable (UNDP 2005, 4):

Allocating public resources to promote human development
Unifying the labor market and promoting informal sector development
Improving rural infrastructure and living environments
Investing in public education and promoting people's capabilities for development
Strengthening public health and improving basic health care
Improving the social security system
Eliminating social discriminative barriers and promoting social harmony and mutual assistance
Improving the rule of law and transparency
Reforming the taxation and fiscal systems for equitable distribution
Promoting government reform and improving governing capacity

Several of these themes were taken up again three years later in the most recent China Human Development Report (CHDR) 2007/08, whose theme is the provision of basic public services to the entire population. An important component of the effort to overcome both urban-rural and regional inequality is to implement basic safety net, social welfare, and social security programs that greatly improve the living conditions and opportunities of rural people and residents of poor areas. CHDR 2007/08 urges early implementation of these programs, arguing that China has reached a level of development at which they are affordable. Table 5.3 presents its estimates of the annual cost of implementing the most important programs: universal free compulsory nine-year education, universal basic medical coverage, basic social security for "flexibly employed workers" (mostly farmers), and a minimum living subsidy for the rural population. These rough estimates add up to about 370 yuan (in 2005 prices), or 7.5 percent of budget revenues. Although the assumptions (given in the table's notes) make it clear that the standards for benefits are very low, they would make a beginning and could be upgraded as economic (and political) conditions permit.

Prima facie economic feasibility is a necessary condition for progressive government action but not a sufficient one. Also critical is the political economy that influences the way government wields its resources. By the mid-1990s, measured net central transfers of revenues among provinces had fallen from almost 5 percent of GDP in 1986 to only 1 percent, following the similar trend in discretionary central revenues. According to Wong (2009), "the collapse of transfers was far more drastic than that depicted in [these numbers]," since measured transfers were only a fraction of the actual redistribution that occurred before

Table 5.3
Cost of Basic Social Welfare Programs

	Annual cost (bills 2005 yuan)
Free compulsory nine-year education	60
Basic medical coverage[a]	180
Basic old-age insurance for "flexibly employed" workers[b]	65
Minimum living standard (*dibao*) subsidy allowance [c]	65
Total	370

Source: UNDP (2008, 72).
[a] Assumes individuals bear 25 percent of medical costs.
[b] Assumes 400 million people were flexibly employed and all participated in a basic old-age insurance for flexibly employed workers, that each contributes 5 percent of the rural per capita net income to the program, and that the government matches this amount.
[c] Assumes a *dibao* standard of $0.50 per day in purchasing power parity (PPP) terms.

the tax reform. Under the Tax Sharing System instituted by the reform, central and local governments all had designated revenues of their own, and transfers became explicit. But the great bulk of transfers went back to the provinces where the revenues originated, and very few were redistributed to poorer regions. Moreover, the fiscal decline up to the mid-1990s meant that early efforts to increase spending on education, health, poverty alleviation, and other public welfare concerns petered out. Budgetary spending on education, for instance, fell to 1.5 percent of GDP in 1995. Although there has been a recovery in the wake of the recentralization of revenues after the mid-1990s, China's expenditures on social services remain low relative to GDP, compared to either other Asian countries or to middle-income countries as a whole. Starved local governments, especially in poorer areas, have responded to the lack of budgetary support by imposing user charges on public services. As a result, the share of public funding in total spending on public services fell continually until 2000 and then began rising slowly. In recent years, budget allocations have paid for only about half of public services, the rest coming from user fees and other sources:

> Passing along costs to users and charging for services is so universal that in a 2004 field visit to one of China's poorest villages in the Southwest, I was astonished to find that not a single public service was offered free of charge to the residents, not schooling, health care, or even policy services. (Wong 2009, 16)[14]

As a result of this system, social services are available in much greater quantity and quality in richer regions, as both their local governments and their populations can afford to spend more on them. Shanghai in 2004 spent nine times as much per student on primary education as did China's poorest province, Guizhou, and Shanghai's advantage was about the same in both public and private contributions to total spending. This gives an impression of the difficulties faced by China's progressive-sounding leaders in reengineering the public finance system into one that will combat inequality by channeling resources to poorer regions and sections of the population.

Yet there has been progress. The central government policy of "two frees, one subsidy" (*liang mian yi bu*, 两免一补), which eliminates school fees and provides boarding allowances for poor students during their nine years of compulsory education, has penetrated at least part of the countryside and made a difference to many poor students. Introduced in 1998 on a trial basis, it was formally launched in 2001 and its funding has increased greatly since. In 2005, more than 34 million rural students in central and western China received free textbooks and 32 million had school fees waived. Six million received a living allowance. Beginning in 2006, the state began paying for school and textbook fees for all rural students in thirteen western provinces, and in 2007 this policy was extended to all provinces (Chang 2006). Of course, the policy applies only to primary school education, falling far short of giving children the means to compete in a global economy. Yet merely achieving universal nine-year education for virtually all rural children would be a major accomplishment, and would surely lead to the demand that the policy be extended to the secondary level.

On the health front, a long-awaited plan for reform of the health system was released in draft form in October 2008 and a final, revised plan is due for release by the end of 2010. The draft, which has been in the works for several years, promises a "safe, effective, convenient and affordable" healthcare system that will cover all urban and rural residents by 2020. It promises to correct the inequities of the current system and stress the dominant responsibility of government to provide public health and basic medical care. However, it remains vague as to details, including the level of public funding to be provided.[15]

The global economic recession beginning in 2008 is likely to affect the prospects for a more equitable development model for China. To the extent that job creation is pushed to the top of the priority list of the government, other objectives such as rebalancing, greater equity, environmental protection, and so forth, may be pushed to its bottom. The government could fall back on its tried and true formula of promoting investment-led growth first and foremost. Indeed, without reforms that would make growth less employment-averse, the greater the felt need for job creation the higher the target growth rate and the less likely that "rebalancing" policies will be taken seriously. Moreover, redistributive policies are much easier to implement in a régime of high growth, using the growth premium progressively and avoiding actual losses for anyone. Yet even during the 2002–2007 period, when growth was barreling along at over 10 percent per year, China managed to increase the ratio of total spending on social insurance and safety net programs to GDP by only half a percentage point. Is it likely to be able to do better than that, or even as well, when growth founders and redistribution implies real losses for some? The massive stimulus package announced in March 2009 contains many progressive elements, including public housing, rural infrastructure, increased *dibao* 低保 (urban poverty alleviation) stipends, higher farm prices and farm subsidies, and so on. Yet the scanty information available about its implementation is mixed. Several speakers at the National People's Congress in March 2009 criticized the current implementation of the program for benefiting mainly large-scale capital-intensive industries and thus failing to create enough jobs per yuan spent.

The future of inequality in China is tied closely to the outcome of the tension between the equity-oriented reforms of the present and recent past, on the one hand, and the systemic and structural impediments to changing the real distribution of income through effective public policy, on the other. It is easy to identify these impediments and to be persuaded by them that the barriers to change are overwhelming. Yet the consequences of failure are also great, and they take the form most feared by the leadership: political instability. This fear creates a strong incentive to move and shake the system until something more than marginal change has occurred. Some of China's most pressing economic problems would be eased by the evolution to a less inegalitarian system that provides health, education, social security, and other social services reliably to the entire population. Chinese economic growth would be tied less closely to the vagaries of foreign demand as citizens, no longer having to save such high proportions of their incomes, both become more willing to spend and have more to spend. Even the trade imbalance with the United States would benefit from the emergence of a Chinese population that felt freer to spend its money. The seriousness with which education reform has been implemented, and even the early indications, discussed above, that policies may have indeed begun to ameliorate income inequality within the rural and urban populations, testify to the strength of the positive incentives for change. Were they to prevail, income inequality (and, one hopes, other more organic forms of inequality, such as in nutrition, literacy, etc.) in China could decline to levels more normal in its region of the world. If not, forces widening inequality could continue to prevail, at the cost of growing challenges to equity, the global and local environment, and even to stability.

References

Aroca, P. A., D. Guo, et al. 2008. "Spatial Convergence in China, 1952–99." In G. Wan, ed., *Inequality and Growth in Modern China*. Oxford and New York: Oxford University Press.

Brandt, L., and C. Holz. 2006. "Spatial Price Differences in China: Estimates and Implications." *Economic Development and Cultural Change* 55, no. 1: 43–86.

Chang, T. 2006. "Rural Education: Subsidies Provide Palliative, But Not Panacea." China Development Brief.

Eastwood, R., and M. Lipton. 2004. "Rural and Urban Income Inequality and Poverty: Does Convergence between Sectors Offset Divergence within Them?" In G. A. Cornia, ed., *Inequality, Growth and Poverty in an Era of Liberalization and Globalization*. Oxford: Oxford University Press for UNU-WIDER.

Khan, A. R. 2004. "Growth, Inequality and Poverty in China: A Comparative Study of the Experience in the Periods Before and After the Asian Crisis." International Labour Organization (ILO), Issues in Employment and Poverty, Discussion Paper (15).

Khan, A. R., and C. Riskin. 2005. "China's Household Income and Its Distribution, 1995 and 2002." *China Quarterly* (June).

Kuznets, S. 1955. "Economic Growth and Income Inequality." *American Economic Review* 45.

Lardy, N. R. 2008. "Sustaining Economic Growth in China." In C. Fred Bergsten, Charles Freeman, Nicholas R. Lardy, and Derek J. Mitchell, *China's Rise: Challenges and Opportunities*. Washington DC: Peterson Institute for International Economics.

Li, S., C. Luo, et al. 2007. "Appendix: The 1995 and 2002 Household Surveys, Sampling Methods and Data Description." In B. Gustafsson, S. Li, and T. Sicular, *Inequality and Public Policy in China*. New York: Cambridge University Press.

Lin, J. Y. 2009. *Economic Development and Transition: Thought, Strategy, and Viability*. Cambridge and New York: Cambridge University Press.

Lin, J. Y., F. Cai, et al. 1997. "Social Consequences of Economic Reform in China: An Analysis of Regional Disparity in the Transition Period." Beijing: UNDP.

Lin, J. Y., and P. Liu. 2008. "Development Strategies and Regional Income Disparities in China." In G. Wan, *Inequality and Growth in Modern China*. Oxford and New York: Oxford University Press.

Luo, X., and N. Zhu. 2008. "Rising Income Inequality in China: A Race to the Top." Policy Research Working Paper 4700, East Asia and Pacific Region, Poverty Reduction and Economic Management Department. Washington, DC: World Bank.

Meng, X., R. G. Gregory, et al. 2005. "Poverty, Inequality, and Growth in Urban China, 1986–2000." *Journal of Comparative Economics* 33, no. 4: 710–29.

Naughton, B. 2002. "Provincial Economic Growth in China: Causes and Consequences of Regional Differentiation." In M.-F. Renard, ed., *China and Its Regions*. Northampton, MA: Edward Elgar.

Naughton, B. J. 2004. "The Western Development Program." In B. J. Naughton and D. L. Yang, eds., *Holding China Together*. Cambridge and London: Cambridge University Press.

Ravallion, M., and S. Chen. 2004. "Understanding China's (Uneven) Progress against Poverty." *Finance & Development* (December).

Renard, M.-F., ed. 2002. *China and Its Regions: Economic Growth and Reform in Chinese Provinces*. Northampton, MA: Edward Elgar.

Riskin, C. 1987. *China's Political Economy: The Quest for Development since 1949*. Oxford and New York: Oxford University Press.

———. 2007. "Has China Reached the Top of the Kuznets Curve?" In V. Shue and C. Wong, eds., *Paying for Progress in China*. London and New York: Routledge.

Shue, V., and C. Wong. 2007. *Paying for Progress in China: Public Finance, Human Welfare and Changing Patterns of Inequality*. London and New York: Routledge.

Sicular, T., X. Yue, et al. 2008. "The Urban-Rural Gap and Income Inequality." In G. Wan, ed., *Understanding Inequality and Poverty in China: Methods and Applications*. Basingstoke, Hampshire: Palgrave Macmillan.

UNDP. 2005. "China Human Development Report 2005: Development with Equity." Beijing: China Development Research Foundation (for UNDP).

———. 2008. "China Human Development Report 2007/08: Access for All, Basic Public Services for 1.3 Billion People." Beijing: China Publishing Group Corp. (for UNDP).

Wan, G. 2007, ed. "Inequality and Poverty in China." Special issue, *Review of Income and Wealth* 53, no. 1.

———. 2008a. "Regional Income Inequality in Rural China, 1985–2002: Trends, Causes and Policy Implications." In *Understanding Inequality and Poverty in China*.

———, ed. 2008b. *Understanding Inequality and Poverty in China: Methods and Applications*. Basingstoke, Hampshire: Palgrave Macmillan.

Wan, G., M. Lu, et al. 2008. "Globalization and Regional Income Inequality: Empirical Evidence from Within China." In *Understanding Inequality and Poverty in China*.

Wong, C. 2007a. "Can the Retreat from Equality Be Reversed? An Assessment of Redistributive Fiscal Policies from Deng Xiaoping to Wen Jiabao." In V. Shue and C. Wong, eds., *Paying for Progress in China*. London and New York: Routledge.

———. 2007b. "Fiscal Management for a Harmonious Society: Assessing the Central Government's Capacity to Implement National Policies." Workshop on China's Institutional Design, Manchester, England.

———. 2009. "Rebuilding Government for the 21st Century: Can China Incrementally Reform the Public Sector?" *China Quarterly* 200: 929–52.

Xie, Y., and X. Wu. 2008. "Danwei Profitability and Earnings Inequality in Urban China." *China Quarterly* 195.

Young, N. 2007. "How Much Inequality Can China Stand?" China Development Brief.

Zhang, Q. F. 2008. "Retreat from Equality or Advance towards Efficiency? Land Markets and Inequality in Rural Zhejiang." *China Quarterly* 195.

Zhou, Y., H. Hua, et al. 2008. "From Labour to Capital: Intra-Village Inequality in Rural China, 1988–2006." *China Quarterly* 195.

6

Economic Governance

Authoritarian Upgrading and Innovative Potential

Sebastian Heilmann

THIS CHAPTER QUESTIONS CERTAIN analytical and normative predispositions that dominate the Western debate about the future of economic governance. I argue that China, due to its distinctive processes of economic policy-making, may be rather well positioned to deal with the novel structural and contextual challenges of the twenty-first century. I hold that the key to understanding the adaptability of China's political economy over the past few decades lies in the *unusual combination of extensive policy experimentation with long-term policy prioritization* that has been practiced under the shadow of a hierarchical authority structure. Therefore, China's economic governance represents a case of authoritarian upgrading that challenges traditional assumptions about the economic and institutional superiority of Western governance models.

The main focus of my analysis are the *processes* of crafting policies and institutions that advance economic change. A static institutional focus will not help to understand developmental dynamics since the setup of China's economic institutions and economic administration has been in constant flux for most of the PRC's history. In such a rapidly shifting context, the informational content and explanatory power of institutions should not be overrated. I also doubt the usefulness of reproducing the usual GDP and income growth statistics that may look impressive but are often misleading as national average data in a highly heterogeneous economic space and as the products of China's heavily politicized statistics administration. So as to avoid the pitfalls of institutional and statistical analysis and still obtain general insights into the mechanisms that have driven China's economic transformation, I rely on an explicitly process-oriented political economy perspective that is focused on shifting modes of interaction, communication, coordination, and feedback in economic policymaking, planning, and experimentation.

One important caveat has to be made from the start when analyzing China's record of adaptiveness and inferring the potential for future innovation from past experience. The hardest test for systemic adaptive capacity arrives with disruptive developmental fractures, that is, domestically or externally induced systemic crises, in which not only economic and social learning but also political-institutional responsiveness and societal support for the political system and the incumbent government are stretched to their limit. China, as well as other political systems, may have to face such a crisis in the coming years. And it remains to be seen how China's government, beyond the creative economic policy process that has been so productive in times of normal politics, will respond to a developmental fracture that hits economic growth, social cohesion, and political authority at the same time.

In this chapter, I proceed in four steps. First, I clarify what I mean by "authoritarian upgrading" and "innovative potential." Second, I present core findings on the intriguing interplay between development planning and policy experimentation in China's economic governance. These two core mechanisms in China's overall policy process are much too often ignored, since they don't fit well into standard models of market-based political economies. Third, I suggest that planning and experimentation, if constantly refined and refocused, may also have the potential to promote China's innovative potential tremendously over the next decades. This hypothesis is not just based on past achievements and experiences, but rather on the assumption that the coming decades will be shaped by technological, environmental, and sociodemographic contextual factors that will be starkly different from previous decades. Powerful nontraditional forces will be at work in the twenty-first century, and these new forces will privilege modes of governance that are substantially different from governance modes that have been successful in the past. In my fourth and concluding step, I will deal with the possible advent of a type of governance that I call, as a shorthand for a rather complex phenomenon, "techno-authoritarianism."

The Significance of "Authoritarian Upgrading"

The term "authoritarian upgrading" was coined by Steven Heydemann in a paper for the Brookings Institution that deals with political and economic modernization in the Arab world. In his analysis, Heydemann focuses on how autocratic rulers in resource-rich political economies try to contain and deflect the forces of political liberalization. He explains the selective and limited institutional and policy adjustments made by Arab rulers as a series of ad hoc responses to pressures for political reform and to Western democracy promotion strategies. As a result, politically "upgraded" authoritarian regimes appear smarter and more complex than in the past while autocratic rulers avoid ceding any of their substantive authority.[1]

In order to adapt Heydemann's authoritarian upgrading model to the East Asian, and especially the Chinese, experience with the political management of economic and social modernization, I reformulate and add a number of distinctive governance features that can be found in the East Asian context. Authoritarian upgrading thereby is depicted as a more proactive, foresighted, and broad-based enterprise and trajectory (instead of being just a reactive, evasive, and elitist effort) than is usually assumed from a normative democratization perspective (see table 6.1).

Though political competition and opposition still have no legitimate role in this variant of authoritarian governance, striking unconventional elements can be seen in the much more consultative, pluralistic, and globally integrated policy process that makes upgraded authoritarianism much smarter than its precursors in the twentieth century and much more challenging to established democracies and market economies.

TABLE 6.1
Core Features of Authoritarian Upgrading in the Early Twenty-first Century

- *Making the political economy more inclusive*: spreading the benefits of economic reforms beyond the state elite to broader segments of the population.
- *Engaging in consultative policymaking*: precluding open conflict through systematic consultation of important interest groups before issuing major regulatory/redistributive policies.
- *Appropriating civil society*: integrating civic organizations as gongos (government organized nongovernmental organizations) into the official system; absorbing, warping, or deflecting the language of democracy and the rule of law.
- *Cultivating a split public sphere*: upholding a strict delimitation between a tightly controlled official public sphere and an unofficial, volatile, fragmented, and therefore rarely politically threatening, blogosphere (thereby nurturing a systemic collective action deficit).
- *Maintaining direct state control over core parts of the economy*: fostering powerful and profitable government-linked companies in oligopoly areas of the national economy.
- *Fostering a national innovation system* through massive acquisition of technology and organizational know-how, while simultaneously building up the indigenous foundations for technological innovation.
- *Promoting international outreach*: increasing international linkages, establishing economic bridgeheads in strategic locations of the global economy; making key players in the world economy dependent on capital and/or resource flows from authoritarian upgraders.

The term "innovative potential" in the title of this chapter points to processes and mechanisms that are conducive to the incessant generation of new knowledge and technologies that can be put to work in diverse parts of the economy, society, and public administration. The Organisation for Economic Co-operation and Development (OECD) defines a national "innovation system" as the "purposeful combination of market and non-market mechanisms to optimise the production, deployment and use of new knowledge for sustainable growth, through institutionalised processes in the public and private sector."[2] According to the OECD and a growing body of scholarly literature, it is a creative combination of market and nonmarket, public and private forces that produces the strongest capacity for innovation in modern political economies.

China is dealing with these requirements of "mixed governance" in a very ambitious way. The Chinese leadership defined crafting an innovation-driven nation as one top priority in 2006 when a Long-term Plan for the Development of Science and Technology (2006–20) was issued. Hu Jintao outlined strategic objectives for propelling China onto a "new path of innovation with Chinese characteristics" and formulated four general guidelines, each in a four-character slogan, aiming at: indigenous innovation (*zizhu chuangxin*自主创新), leapfrogging in key areas (*zhongdian kuayue*重点跨越), science and technology supporting economic and social development (*zhicheng fazhan*支撑发展), and science and technology leading the future (*yinling weilai*引领未来). According to the strategic plan's prescriptions, China is supposed to become a leading global science and technology power by the middle of the twenty-first century. Technological innovation is intended to become the central pillar of upgrading China's economic, social, and political order.

Distinctive Features of China's Economic Governance

Though the Chinese government and Chinese academia since the 1990s increasingly came to use Western concepts to describe their approach to economic governance, there are many misnomers and misunderstandings in this effort due to the very different political, legal, social, and cultural-linguistic context that China provides for making these concepts work. Even China's basic policy cycle, including agenda-setting, formulation, implementation, and revision of policies, is essentially different from the Western experience that dominates social scientists' and legal scholars' discussions.

The Chinese polity is not dominated by the rhythm of election campaigns with their inherent shifting policy priorities and their often abrupt leadership changes in key executive positions. Beyond short-term crisis management, economic policymaking in China is instead still dominated by the rhythm of programs that are drafted with a much longer time horizon in mind than in most other political economies. In China, policy priorities are not supposed to shift quickly. Remarkably, the regular five-year planning periods are not synchronized with the turnovers in party and state leadership. Incoming new leaders remain bound to the previous plan for three full years and thus cannot openly discard the policy goals that had been laid down by their predecessors. In effect, policy priorities really do not shift quickly in the Chinese polity. This feature of "long-termism" (as opposed to the "short-termism" built into global capital markets and also into electoral cycles), has given China comparative advantages in pursuing economic modernization and may also provide advantages in dealing with certain future challenges.

Key components of China's policymaking approach to economic growth and restructuring in the past thirty years are summarized in table 6.2. Beyond the growth imperative, no preconceived and sweeping reform strategy (such as "privatization" or "marketization") was laid down. The means to achieve economic growth and efficiency gains were largely left open to broad-based explorative efforts and policy experimentation. Since Chinese policymakers, in the context of an authoritarian polity, do not have to face organized opposition and electoral competition they can afford to wait for newly emerging elements in the political economy to "outgrow" the old ones over an extended period. The comparatively stable position and extended time horizon of top policymakers thus facilitated "institutional displacement" and "institutional layering."[3] Moreover, the protracted process of policy learning was made possible by the massive growth in nonstate economic activity that lessened the pressure for immediate structural reform in the public sector and thereby provided Chinese policymakers with an unusually opportune environment for learning and adaptation over an extended period of time.

It must be emphasized here that China's reform experience cannot be characterized sweepingly as "gradualist" or "incrementalist" across the board. Major reform breakthroughs such as those in 1992–1993 (program for market-oriented restructuring as a response to the collapse of socialism in the Soviet Union and Eastern Europe), 1997–1998 (state-owned enterprise, SOE, reform under the shocking impression of the Asian financial crisis), and 2001–2002 (foreign trade liberalization as a result of WTO accession negotiations) clearly went beyond cautious incremental adjustments. Big reform pushes such as these should be seen as instances of "political lightning"[4] or, in Chinese political jargon, as "assaults against fortified positions" (*gongjian*攻 坚) that can only be achieved in extraordinary periods when top-level policymakers are facing intense, unifying decision pressures.[5]

TABLE 6.2
China's Economic Governance: Core Processual Features, 1978–2008

Strategic Orientations

- Embracing an *open-ended design* to economic reform: Western standard recipes such as the "marketization-cum-privatization" paradigm were never fully accepted and therefore effectively shunned or warped by Chinese policymakers; beyond the growth imperative, no preconceived reform strategy and no clear vision of the resulting economic "system" were laid down; the means to achieve economic growth were generated in an open-ended, experimental process.
- Promoting a *fixation with national growth, wealth, and power* while neglecting the social and ecological consequences of economic expansion (1978–2003).

Development Planning

- Setting *policy priorities and goals* through refocused development *planning*: from socialistic "planning as a *substitute* for markets" to "planning *with* and *for* markets."
- Initiating recurrent *big pushes in infrastructure, manpower, technology*.

Experimentation

- Searching for suitable *policy instruments* through *experimentation*: decentralized policy experimentation (including illicit policy initiatives) stimulated/tolerated by national policymakers.
- *Experience first, lawmaking later*: local policy experiments seen by decision makers as successful and acceptable were selectively expanded "from point to surface" in official pilot programs. Major economic legislation usually came only as a result of extended experimental programs.

Learning from Abroad

- Selective learning from "advanced *foreign experience*"; translating these experiences into reforms that serve China's "national situation."
- Employing *foreign investment*, foreign firms, and foreign technology to advance economic modernization while keeping foreign business on a leash through regulatory discrimination.
- *Playing two-level games*: policymakers play two-level games in economic diplomacy (e.g., WTO negotiations) to intensify transnational adaptive pressures and accelerate economic restructuring.

Institutional Layering

- Longer time horizon of policymakers facilitates *institutional layering/displacement* over an extended period (*"dual track"*: new system can outgrow old system).
- Working with *transitional and hybrid institutions*: economic institutions constantly recombined in unconventional ways resulting in an uneasy, yet flexible and often productive, shifting mix of state and market, centralized and decentralized coordination.

Authoritarian Safeguards

- Sustaining the *state's capacity to intervene* by administrative means in core branches of the economy and to curtail private and foreign businesses.
- *Communist Party reserve capacities in economic administration*: in "periods of extraordinary politics" (1992–1993, 1997–1998, 2001–2002, 2008–2009) when big reform pushes were undertaken by the center, top-level initiatives and institutional reorganization were imposed through the party hierarchy.

Development Planning and Innovation

In characterizations of China's reform period, there is much talk about the "demise of the plan," the "dismantling of the state planning apparatus," and the "transition from plan to market."[6] In a recently published state-of-the-art volume on China's economic rise, coordination through state planning is mentioned in passing only.[7] From a comparativist perspective, influential economists edited books with titles such as *The Collapse of Development Planning* in which the contributors told readers why national governments, including China's government, would have to retreat, why economic planning would necessarily result in underdevelopment, and why markets would regulate themselves and guide economic activities in an efficient way in developing countries.[8] So as to make China's success story fit into Western marketization narratives and models, coordination through plans has rarely been allowed to play a role in standard explanations. Instead, to make China's achievements intelligible to Western preconceptions, it is widely assumed that markets *must* have taken over and *must* have pushed back incompetent state bureaucrats.

Contrary to the sweeping mainstream logic that takes the demise of the plan for granted, institutionalized planning can be found in almost every policy domain in China to the present day, though it has undergone substantial reorganization in terms of content, process, and methods since the mid-1990s.[9] An inventory of the wide range of recent and current government plans and programs makes it clear that the very essence of state development planning—*ex ante coordination and proactive prioritization of a government's economic activity, instead of ad hoc or reactive intervention through individual policies, laws and funding schemes*—is still being preserved in China's polity, with particularly profound ambitions in the realm of the "national innovation system" (i.e., complementary industrial, technology, and research programs).[10] Long-term, mid-term, and short-term plans can be found in every single policy sector. And beyond the rather general national Five Year Plans (FYP), detailed and partly mandatory Special Program Plans (专项规划) are designed to steer the economic behavior of firms, households, and individuals "through scientific forecasting, clearly defined objectives, government policies, and public goods provision." Special Program Plans deal with key areas of public policy and include not only policy objectives and quantitative targets, but frequently also a catalogue of concrete measures and funding arrangements.[11]

It is not surprising that the Chinese government continues to draft and implement plans for certain key industries, technology, education, and the environment since mid- to long-term planning exercises are made in these policy areas even by the most market-oriented governments in the West. Yet in China, we find multiyear as well as annual, national as well as subnational plans in domains ranging from human resources, lawmaking, and social security to tourism and national morality. Even for managing insolvencies in the state sector in a phased manner, a National Plan for Enterprise Closures and Insolvencies was drafted for the 2005–2008 period. And this plan was carried out in a rather consistent way.[12]

All these examples make it clear that China still is a *planning polity* that is committed to guiding economic, social, and technological development through state coordination and from a longer-term perspective. Among China's policymakers we rarely find an inclination to move to an ad hoc mode or "bystander and fireguard mode" of economic policymaking that had become so prevalent in the governance of Western political economies since the late 1970s.

From 1994 on, the functions of planning were redefined fundamentally to give room to market coordination while preserving overall state "macro-control." The "new-style development planning system" was supposed to move away from fixing a huge number of quantitative targets and control figures to focusing on macro, strategic, and policy issues.[13] While planning had been used as a *substitute for markets* in the Maoist era, Chinese administrators were now charged with the task to "take markets as the foundation" (*yi shichang wei jichu* 以市场为基础), that is, to *plan with and for markets*, to absorb major trends in domestic and global markets into mid- and long-term government programs. By 2004, plan formulation had moved from the traditional *model of closed, intrastate bargaining* (often punctuated by interference from top policymakers) to a *multiple advocacy model* that is based on consultation of state, nonstate, and even foreign economic actors and on much more regularized administrative procedures that are supposed to support "scientific" policymaking.

The effects of this departure from traditional socialistic planning on administrative practice and economic performance have proven to be very uneven. Table 6.3 provides a matrix of governance modes that are all based on detailed, formal Special Program Plans, yet reveal strong variation across policy sectors.

We find policy sectors in which public and social goods (such as railroad infrastructure, anti-poverty programs, environmental protection) are supposed to be provided through *mandatory planning* that includes direct allocation of funding and administrative oversight (see table 6.3, column I). This type of planning has driven the spectacular expansion of China's physical infrastructure since the 1990s. The Railway Ministry and the Transport Ministry in particular have demonstrated that they are capable of launching and implementing very "big pushes" to top-priority sectors of national development. Yet, big pushes can only be initiated from the center if the ministries in charge

TABLE 6.3
The Governance of Development Planning in China (2006-2010)

	I **Mandatory Planning** *(administrative and SOE-based provision of public/social goods)*	II **Contractual Planning** *(central-regional and government-enterprise cooperation)*	III **Indicative Planning** *(government-induced market activities)*
Allocative-Promotional	railway construction	technology policy	"going global" program (outbound investment)
Redistributive	anti-poverty programs	rural health services	rural income generation
Regulatory	environmental policy	energy industry restructuring	private/SME sector restructuring

Note: Typology based on range of "Special Programs/Plans" (专项规划/计划) under Eleventh FYP (2006-2010).

provide generous funding and can rely on an integrated administrative apparatus. That is why the Railway Ministry has been exceptionally effective in directing the massive infrastructural buildup in its sector, while policy coordination has been much more fragmented, for instance, in the realms of energy production/electricity supply and alleviation of regional disparities.

Generally, China's efforts at development planning display a fundamental weakness in pursuing redistributive goals (improving the development potential of disadvantaged regions and population groups) that are at the heart of the western and northeastern development programs and also at the heart of rural healthcare reform. Mandatory environmental and energy conservation targets that have been part of many recent long-term plans have failed even more obviously, according to official evaluation of these programs. Mandatory planning appears to work best if focused on narrow policy targets that avoid redistributive battles, add value on top of an already profitable (i.e., usually monopolistic) sector, and can be pursued by well-integrated, financially strong administrative "agencies-cum-investors," such as the Railway Ministry with its affiliate corporate vehicles.

Besides classical mandatory planning, Chinese planners have increasingly employed nonstandardized forms of *contract-based planning* to guarantee implementation of their policy goals by lower-level agents (see table 6.3, column II). Targets and funding arrangements are written into formal contracts that are concluded between, for instance, a central ministry and a provincial government, or a provincial government department and major enterprises that take part in implementing state plans. Plan implementation through contractual targets is most visible in technology zones, energy production, and marketing reforms (e.g., for rural or cultural products) for which government organs need the collaboration of major market participants.

In the top-priority realm of technology policy, striking achievements based on long-term planning have been diagnosed in a comprehensive OECD report that states that Chinese innovation policies are "characterised by the strong legacy of the planned economy, as the programmes—literally 'plans' in Chinese—are the main instruments for addressing policy priorities."[14] While the OECD judges Chinese technology planning as successful in comparison to many other economies, numerous policy advisors and academics in China and abroad question the overall effectiveness of government-sponsored, centrally coordinated innovation policies. They point to the failures and misallocations that have accompanied state technology planning and stress the potential of decentralized, market-driven innovation that has not been fully utilized in China yet.

In addition to mandatory and contractual planning, we find a plethora of less binding forms of *indicative planning*, that is based on government forecasting (e.g., statements that attest growth potential to certain industries), signalling (e.g., announcements about substantial, step-by-step cuts of rural taxes or about preferential policies for small and medium-sized enterprises, SMEs), and indirect incentives (e.g., improved access to bank credits and domestic/overseas markets) to stimulate market activities and resource mobilization in sectors that are identified by the government as having development potential (see table 6.3, column III).

Considering the mix of coordination mechanisms, the variation in the effectiveness and credibility of planning efforts across policy sectors, and the scores of special plans that have been evaluated officially as failing (most notably in environmental and energy conservation), one can hardly speak of integrated national planning in China. Development planning in China confirms one core lesson of policy studies: political economies should be disaggregated into policy subsystems, each of which is characterized by very different dynamics.[15] Thus, we will find effective plan implementation in certain policy areas, while finding persistent blockades or outright failures of plan-based coordination in other policy realms. Due to such crass variation, it is imperative to exercise restraint on generalizing across policy subsystems and refrain from jumping to sweeping hypotheses (e.g., "China even makes planning work" or "Chinese planning is a complete failure and has to make way for markets") about the entire planning system.

Beyond its patchy role in economic coordination, development planning serves crucial integrating functions in China's polity that are regularly overlooked. The formulation of comprehensive, long- and mid-term plans and programs provides top policymakers with an extraordinary opportunity to set the agenda, define new priorities, influence the direction, and coin new slogans for communication and coordination across all levels of China's administration. Lower-level administrators may prefer to ignore novel policy priorities and high-minded goals defined by the central government. But they are still compelled to pick up national policy conceptions and regularly spend considerable time with formulating and justifying local development plans that must not contradict nationally defined priorities. Across administrative levels, plan-making thus amounts to a strategic exercise in administrative communication that includes a formal demonstration of compliance with the national leadership. Development planning thus fulfills important, and possibly indispensable, functions for integrating China's vast, fragmented administrative apparatus and legitimating the Communist Party's central leadership.

The planning system has also served unintended functions and provided useful policy instruments for the stimulus programs that China's government launched in 2008 and 2009 to counter the global economic downturn. Several Special Program Plans that included detailed investment schemes, policy packages, and administrative coordination mechanisms for boosting infrastructural buildup in western China, had already been drafted before the onslaught of global economic downturn. When Chinese policymakers needed swift action to counter economic contraction, they could literally download these plans from the government server, squeeze them into an accelerated schedule for implementation, and thereby had readymade policy packages for boosting investment and creating employment at their disposal.

Overall, the functions of "new style development planning" for policy prioritization and administrative integration may be more important than the concrete allocative, redistributive, and regulatory functions of most planning exercises. Planning that defines long-term development priorities yet remains incoherent in implementation provides space for a governance technique that has arguably been the most powerful driving mechanism behind institutional and policy innovation from 1978 to 2008: broad-based, decentralized policy experimentation.

Policy Experimentation and Innovation

Whereas planning is about setting policy *goals* and clarifying policy *priorities* for the longer term, experimentation is about finding the policy *instruments* to meet the goals and priorities defined in the government's programs. Policy experimentation in China consists of a process in which central policymakers encourage local officials to try out new ways of problem solving and then feed the local experiences back into national policy formulation. This processual pattern, as depicted in figure 6.1, has been a pervasive feature in China's economic

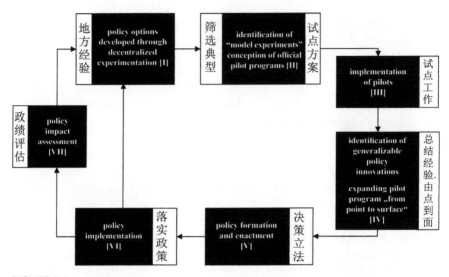

FIGURE 6.1
China's Experimentation-Based Policy Cycle. Note: For more details on this policy
cycle, see Sebastian Heilmann, "Policy Experimentation in China's Economic Rise,"
Studies in Comparative International Development 43, no.1 (March 2008): 1–26.

transformation. This experimental cycle has decisively shaped the making of
policies in areas ranging from rural decollectivization, foreign economic opening, and promotion of private business to state sector restructuring.

A striking example of the experimental approach to economic restructuring is the introduction of stock markets in China, since these had to be
"squeezed into an economy still based on state planning and the absence of
private ownership."[16] Chinese stock market history is marked by a series of
experimental schemes. Limited experiments with share issuance and trading
had already been approved by the central government and undertaken locally
during the 1980s. Larger-scale experiments were promoted with the repackag-
ing of SOEs into listed shareholding companies (early 1990s), selected transfers of legal person shares to new owners (1992), Hong Kong listings of SOEs
(1993), the creation of "national champions" (from the second half of the
1990s), and several attempts at reducing the holdings of state shares (1999,
2001, and 2005). The two stock exchanges in Shanghai and Shenzhen themselves were classified as "experimental points" from 1990 to 1997. Remarkably,
giving stock exchanges a try was supported even by otherwise staunch sceptics
of capitalist methods since this experiment was designed to open new channels for SOE financing without relinquishing state control over the listed entities. The introduction of exchanges produced the volatile dynamics of equity

trade and speculation, while private property and equity rights were still ill-defined and hardly protected. The Shanghai and Shenzhen stock exchanges were under the supervision of the respective municipal governments in the early to mid 1990s. Only after 1997, responding to a series of domestic scandals and to the Asian financial crisis, did the central government bring the stock exchanges under its control, affirm their legitimate role in a "socialist market economy," and make them serve the purposes of national industrial policy and SOE restructuring.

Chinese-style experimentation comes in three main forms as (1) experimental points (pilot projects in a specific policy domain, such as the Shanghai and Shenzhen stock exchanges in the 1990–1997 period), (2) experimental zones (local jurisdictions with broad discretionary powers, such as the special economic zones), and (3) experimental regulation (provisional rules made for trial implementation).[17] These experimental policy tools are regularly used for pioneering reforms that belong to the top of the policy agenda.

In China, experimentation implies a policy process in which experimenting units try out a variety of methods and processes to find imaginative solutions to *predefined tasks* and to *new challenges that emerge during experimental activity*. Policy experimentation leaves a lot of room for decentralized tinkering and creative ad hoc solutions that can best be found by actors on the ground who are in command of the necessary local knowledge, as opposed to central policymakers who lack this knowledge, yet can benefit from it. Thus, unexpected, random policy fixes seem to have shaped China's economic transformation to a considerable extent. Yet, in the context of China's hierarchical polity, experimentation is not equivalent to freewheeling trial and error or spontaneous policy diffusion. It is a purposeful activity geared to producing novel policy options that are injected into official policymaking and then replicated on a larger scale, or even formally incorporated into national law. It is precisely the dialectical interplay between dispersed local initiative and central policymaking that has made China's economic governance so adaptive and innovative from 1978 to 2008.

In many social science analyses of China's reforms, the effectiveness of experiment-based policy-crafting tends to be underestimated. But it is this particular approach to policymaking that has helped to facilitate policy and institutional adaptation. A type of governance that I tend to characterize as *experimentation under the shadow of hierarchy*,[18] stimulated policy learning and economic expansion effectively in those sectors in which political elites could benefit from supporting new types of economic activity. And it has served as a powerful correcting mechanism to grand technocratic modernization schemes that are often part of state planning.

Combining Planning and Experimentation

In generating capacities for "indigenous innovation," as demanded by the Chinese government, a plethora of mutually complementary plans containing industrial, technology, and science policies as well as educational and infrastructural components have come to be one major focus of state activity in recent years. Yet, China's "national innovation system" does not rest exclusively on plans and industrial policy, but is combined with myriads of local-level implementation experiments that are concentrated in special zones and industrial parks. National policies are thus combined with bottom-up initiatives sponsored by local authorities that oftentimes go beyond, or run ahead of, national plans, in constructing an innovation-driven economy. Though capacities for technological innovation are still confined to a limited number of special zones with "limited synergies between them and . . . limited spillovers beyond them," China has "excelled in mobilising resources for science and technology on an unprecedented scale and with exceptional speed,"[19] thanks to a combination of planning with experimentation in this crucial arena of state-promoted modernization.

China's planning process constitutes a strategic exercise in communicating national priorities and demonstrating political unity and common purpose across administrative levels. It thus bolsters the national government's claim to be in control of economic administration though this claim may appear as predominantly symbolic with a view to administrative practice that often ignores centrally defined goals. For realigning state and market activity, decentralized policy tinkering fulfills vital functions by facilitating creative problem solving and policy innovation on the ground. While the recurring planning exercises thus serve as an integrating mechanism for China's fragmented administration, experimentation provides the policy agility that makes a bureaucratic polity work for and adapt to economic change.

Government Interventionism in the
Twenty-first Century: Nontraditional Forces at Work

Most studies of present-day China focus on traditional forces of discontinuity that may bring change or collapse to the present political system: social, ethnic, religious, economic, financial, and political contradictions and upheaval. Though these forces are clearly important and hotly debated, I want to focus on a new class of nontraditional factors that may work for authoritarian upgrading, not for systemic collapse or democratization, in China and elsewhere. There are a number of novel macrotrends under way that may compel us to redefine some basic assumptions about successful modes of governance for the future. The following points are a consciously one-sided extrapolation from these trends and are put together exclusively for analytical purposes. Thus, please note, the following paragraphs do not reflect the normative preferences of the author of this chapter.

As to *domestic and global markets*, we have entered a *new cycle of economic ideology* that is moving away from the discredited "market fundamentalism" of the last two decades to a kind of "neo-etatism" that will be based on tighter economic regulation to avoid the investment bubbles of the recent past and will be oriented toward more social redistribution in order to counter growing social inequity and resulting political instability. Globalization of trade and capital flows has possibly passed its peak. National and regional protectionism is on the rise. Nation-states will try to establish stricter oversight over domestic and transnational economic activity. The resulting losses in growth potential will be accepted by most people, as long as they feel protected against market risks and social insecurity by the state. Against this background, the Chinese complementary view of state control and market coordination in the economy will appear modern and up-to-date in the transformed ideological and regulatory context of the early twenty-first century.

As to domestic politics, *big and interventionist government* will be accepted in most societies to counter market volatility, security threats, social instability, and environmental degradation. Democratic decision making may come to be seen as slow and costly in a world of fast-changing technological, social, and environmental challenges.[20] Overall, due to a massive concern with economic, social, and environmental stability, the legitimacy of governments will increasingly be judged by performance (output and crisis management) criteria, whereas procedural legitimation will loose the understanding and attention of many citizens. Present-day China is the major protagonist of such an output-based polity.

Regarding *political values and the public sphere,* modern societies will become more and more technology- and media-driven. Beyond short-term attention cycles (e.g., during electoral campaigns, political scandals, single-issue protests, etc.), public interest and trust in both markets and democracy will decline considerably. As long as personal security and consumption are not threatened, political apathy will grow along with pronounced consumerist attitudes. The media will be less and less independent, either commercialized as subdivisions of huge corporations or directly controlled by the state. Cyberspace will result in an extreme fragmentation of the public sphere that will be split into myriads of minigroups that communicate in quasi-sectarian online communities without being able to act collectively. China has already moved quite some way into this direction.

With a view to *social development*, we are entering a period of increasing *demographic pressures* in the aging societies of Europe and East Asia. The growing proportion of elderly people will challenge the previous generational contract and possibly delegitimize the democratic welfare state. The cost explosion in health care, the redistributive burden to the younger generation, and the ethical requirements of caring for the elderly in an appropriate way will become a huge strain for any political system that has to manage it. China will have to face the impact of a rapidly aging society already from the end of the next decade. Yet its authoritarian system may be in a position to deal with the demographic challenge by way of longer-term anticipatory policymaking and accumulation of old-age reserve funds so as to contain politically divisive and ethically destructive generational conflict in the future.

Concerning *resources and technology*, becoming more independent from oil and gas imports, finding alternative technologies for producing and saving energy, as well as minimizing environmental damage will move to the center of economic innovation. This will give rise to a new class of technology-driven political economies and "techno-states." Technological innovation and leadership will determine the status of a nation-state in the global power distribution. Governments will become obsessed with technological innovation. China is already working hard for achieving technological leadership as soon as possible.

As to the *environment*, ecological pressures will move to the center of national and global policy agendas. Disaster control will require extensive government interventions. Various types of "eco-reformism" and "eco-authoritarianism" will emerge. The state-primacy theory in green thinking[21] will supersede the market-primacy thinking of the late twentieth century and therefore bolster the emergence of big government and authoritative interventions in markets and societies.

In sum, we are witnessing changes in our environment, demography, technology, and in communicative interaction that provide a political, economic, and social playing field that will be rather different from what we have seen in the nineteenth and twentieth centuries. And this is what may propel authoritarian upgrading in China and possibly elsewhere.

The Advent of "Techno-Authoritarianism"

In such a changing macrocontext, what kind of comparative advantages does China have to outperform other political economies? The prerequisites to a planning and experimenting "techno-authoritarianism" are strong. During the last three decades, China's political economy has proven to be highly innovative in finding policies and institutions to master the complex challenges of large-scale economic, social, and international change while avoiding systemic breakdown. China's economic transition has been facilitated by an unusual adaptive capacity. This adaptive capacity entails institutions and processes that, despite ubiquitous uncertainties, enable a society to try out alternative approaches to overcome long-standing impediments to development, tackle newly emerging challenges, and grasp opportunities when they open up.[22]

State coordination for the longer term will be essential in dealing with the gigantic challenges of environmental degradation and the massive increase in the proportion of elderly people in China's demography. Markets won't help of their own accord to contain the impact and prevent the worst in dealing with these megachallenges. Long-term policy prioritization, at least in part at the expense of economic growth and free markets, will be in very strong demand. It will be one general core challenge for future policymaking to overcome the short-termism that most societies have become used to over the twentieth century. China, with its refocused planning capacities and its government-initiated rush for environmental technology, appears to be quite well equipped to make the transition from "red authoritarianism" to "green authoritarianism," as some commentators called it,[23] in the next two decades.

Beyond the capacity for long-term policy prioritization, it is another crucial challenge of the twenty-first century that we do not yet know the policy instruments and policy combinations that may help to master the many new tasks that we are facing. Here the entrenched Chinese technique of institutional and policy experimentation comes into play. In a rapidly aging society, for example, conventional ways of organizing and funding social welfare will not work anymore. In addition, due to a constantly changing demography, a welfare system that may have been useful in the past or in the present may become rapidly outdated and overburdened within a few years. This will require constant institutional and policy adaptation. China's experience with extensive experimentation under the shadow of hierarchy may serve as a powerful mechanism of innovation in such a context.

Overall, China's unorthodox approach to policymaking that can be paraphrased in a short formula as "foresighted maximum tinkering"—that is, pursuing priorities defined in long-term programs while constantly searching for and experimenting with novel policy instruments—may become a huge processual advantage in the years to come, if this variant of steady, yet flexible governance is being maintained and adapted in creative ways.

Therefore, I suggest that China's mode of governance may become instrumental in dealing with the novel environment of the twenty-first century. China is in a position to be at the forefront of "neo-etatist" trends that are already under way. The scenario that I depict here is one of a highly diversified techno-authoritarianism that is partly "welfarist" and partly "green" out of necessity. It will be a variant of authoritarian governance that is obsessed with technological innovation, yet must balance the traditional growth imperative with powerful social, political, and ecological constraints.

There are many counterarguments to be made against this scenario. There clearly also exists a strong potential for traditional movements (e.g., social protests and political divisions) and for nontraditional developments (e.g., new activist political values emerging from the cybersphere; environmentally or technologically induced systemic disasters; all sorts of random events and disruptions) that may work against a further upgrading of China's authoritarian governance. There even may be new human value systems emerging globally over the next few decades that leave the old growth and consumption paradigm behind. But as I tried to demonstrate: the conditions for economic governance are currently shifting in fundamental ways, and the possibility of authoritarian upgrading should therefore be taken seriously.

III

THREE: POLITICS

7

Foreign Direct Investment

Diaspora Networks and Economic Reform

Min Ye

IN DECEMBER 1978, THE INAUGURATION of the Third Plenum of the Eleventh National Party Congress formally ushered in China's economic reform. No one at the time predicted China today—a vibrant capitalist economy with considerable impact on its 1.3 billion residents as well as many in other regions. When the Chinese central government authorized four experimental special economic zones in southern China in 1980, no one at the time expected that China would emerge to be the largest recipient of foreign direct investment (FDI) in the developing world and the second largest such recipient in the world. Today, not only southern China is home to foreign investors, foreign-invested firms (FIFs) are ubiquitous throughout the mainland.

Foreign direct investment has been China's dominant means of integration into global capitalism. The widely acclaimed export success in the PRC has also been achieved through FIFs. How did China join the world through FDI since 1980? How was the PRC's openness policy being implemented and why was it so successful?

Previous studies have offered rich insights in probing these questions. They have focused on the top leadership and argued that individual leaders such as Deng Xiaoping engineered China's openness through fiat. Related to this approach, China's single-party authoritarian system is also an important condition for China's economic reform.[1] Still others argue that the local governments play an entrepreneurial role in initiating China's economic reform.[2]

The present study builds on these previous insights and tries to address three questions unanswered in the literature. First, if individual leaders were responsible for initiating new economic policies, where and how did those leaders receive information of the policy and how did they mobilize resources to support it? Second, if local governments were the main agents of change, how and why? Why only some of them? How did they gather favorable information and resources? Third, why would the openness strategy be so endurable and expansive?

To answer these questions, I introduce a sociological framework on studying innovative diffusion.[3] As FDI was new to China before its opening, the introduction and expansion of various liberal FDI policies have similar dynamics as adopting other innovative practices or ideas. Diffusion analysis presumes that decision makers adopting a new policy or individuals adopting a new practice are embedded in their social relations that provide distinct information and resources. As information about a new policy or practice is typically from outside of the jurisdiction, it is the external networks of individuals that supply such information. This process of external agents transferring new information to individual decision makers through their social ties is called persuasion.

The effectiveness of persuasion depends on two factors: first, the superiority of the external information perceived by individual actors; second, the quality of ties between external agents and domestic actors. Ideas passed through external agents with a high degree of homophily—indicated by shared physiological traits, language, and ancestry—are likely to be seen as trustworthy but also seen as superior, especially the external agents that are associated with more resources and efficiency in achieving tasks that the domestic actors aspire to achieve.[4]

The social network analysis of innovative diffusion also emphasizes the *process* of diffusion, that is, successful diffusion starts with a few actors with better ties to external agents and then spills over to other actors. The speed and scope of diffusion are dependent on another important development: the early adopters demonstrate "observable" success. As new innovation is usually at odds with old practices in place, entrenched interests are likely to resist the adoption of a new policy that jeopardizes their advantages. Observable success is critical for supporters of the new policy to expand their coalition, reduce resistant forces, and co-opt more social actors.

Following these sociological logics, I emphasize one particular type of external networks in China—diaspora networks. Diasporas share physiological attributes as well as linguistic and social norms with Chinese actors; their communication with Chinese domestic actors is smooth. As they achieved economic success from the 1950s to 1970s through manufacturing and international trade, they were eager to access the Chinese market when the mainland leaders and local chiefs sought new solutions to their economic plight in the end of 1970s. Ideas and resources from the diaspora communities helped initiate external openness to FDI. Thanks to diasporas' information and resources, a liberal, yet limited FDI policy produced quick returns to the Chinese economy in the experimental stage. The policy permitted in selected small areas thus rapidly expanded to broader regions in China. With every successful expansion was the dynamic presence of diaspora investors in China.

This social network approach differs from previous studies of China's reform in that all the other studies see policy changes as driven primarily by internal dynamics: individual leaders, political institutions, and local governments. This chapter emphasizes the *interactive* nature between external networks and domestic forces—how external ideas helped some domestic agents initiate liberalization and how external resources facilitated the durability and diffusion of liberalization in the domestic context.

The process of diaspora-induced openness is captured in figure 7.1. In step 1, diaspora's impact is important and direct. They transfer ideas favorable to openness to local governments and central actors that are prone to reform. Local governments, driven by incentives provided by potential diaspora investment, ask for the national government's approval to experiment with openness. As the central government, as a whole, is interested in economic growth, as well as building local support, it is likely to sanction openness in a limited fashion (step 2), because the new practice is quite different from the existing institutional environment.

Because of this difference, new policy faces challenges from vested interests in the existing environment, which comprises opposition groups (step 3). In overcoming the opposition challenges, diaspora communities are again im-

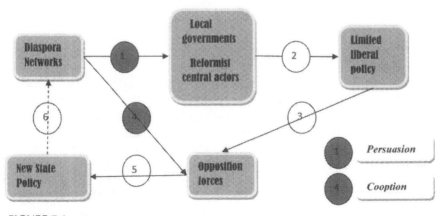

FIGURE 7.1
Diffusion of FDI Policymaking in China

portant. On the one hand, capital and technology inflows from diaspora investors help to produce early success in the areas that are open to FDI, thus increasing the appeal of the new practice. On the other, diasporas interact with opposition groups and coopt part of the opposition (step 4). Now that opposition forces are reduced and the new policy appears successful, the central government, especially the reformist actors within the government, expands the new policy (step 5). As the nation is more open to external investment, the strength of diaspora networks increases as well (step 6). The policy role of diaspora communities is demonstrated in step 1 and step 4 in particular. In step 1, diasporas persuade reformist groups. In step 4, diasporas coopt opposition groups.

Although this model stresses the role of diasporas, domestic actors are important in the diffusion process, and local actors often play quite proactive policy roles. Local governments, for example, took initiative to seek diaspora networks for advice and material inputs. They also proactively lobby central leadership for favorable policy change. Yet these domestic actors' activism has been conditioned by the presence of strong diaspora networks. To use a simple analogy, local governments in northeastern China will not have the same activism as those in southern China, due to their lack of access to diaspora communities. Central leadership is also an important condition in the diffusion model. It is important to note that the reformist leadership after 1978 was permissive of local experiments and willing to change national policies in light of local development. However, the central support for FDI was conditioned on favorable information on FDI and observable success in the early openness to FDI, both being facilitated by the PRC's overseas business networks.

1978–1980: Formation of Special Economic Zones

When Mao Zedong passed away in 1976, the new government gained momentum for economic development. In the following two years, lively policy debates took place in Beijing, and there was concerted effort to learn from abroad. Although openness to FDI, as an industrialization strategy, was presented to the central government, political leaders preferred and implemented other alternative strategies, as documented later. Yet in 1980, Beijing passed the legislation on special economic zones (SEZs) that offered favorable conditions to foreign direct investment. How did this transition happen? The following analysis demonstrates the important and transformative role played by Chinese diaspora communities.

In 1977–1978, Beijing was eager to learn from abroad, and many senior leaders visited foreign countries and gathered successful development experiences that might be relevant for China. These visits intensified China's determination to catch up—with their own eyes the leaders saw how behind China had lagged other countries in its neighborhood and faraway.[5] These visits and the reports produced by the delegations served as the basis for the Central Committee Work Meeting of November 11–December 15, 1978. The policy options discussed are summarized in table 7.1.

From the wording of the reports and records of discussions at the meeting, it was clear that Chinese leaders preferred the first option. FDI liberalization was the least desirable. The report on socialist adjustment—option 1—was the longest and in its conclusion it used the strongest Chinese word for learning (*xuexi* 学习). The second model, from Japan, was appealing to the leadership too, and the lessons could be borrowed (*jiejian* 借鉴). FDI-led development was said to be worthwhile to study (*yanjiu* 研究), a phrase with an unusually unimpressive connotation. Indeed, many senior leaders believed that economies like Hong Kong were too small to serve as a model for China. Liberal FDI policy that worked for Hong Kong was not applicable for China.

Although Deng Xiaoping was receptive to all kinds of developmental experience, his visits to Japan had the strongest economic mission. During his visit in late 1978, he expressed strong desire for closer economic cooperation with Japan. With intense interest, Deng dined with business representatives, rode *shinkansen* (high-speed railway), and toured the Nissan factory in Kanagawa and the Matsushita factory in Osaka.[6]

TABLE 7.1
China's Policy Options in 1978

	Models for China	Policy Suggestions
Option #1	Yugoslavia, and other socialist countries	(1) adjust state-owned companies (2) transfer advanced technology (3) stress domestic saving and production
Option #2	Japan, France, and Germany	(1) transfer technology (2) use foreign capital (3) use foreign loans
Option #3	Hong Kong and Macao	(1) use foreign capital (2) exploit cheap labor (3) develop special economic areas in Shenzhen (4) decentralize trade, currency regulation, personnel, tax, and so on

Source: Original data is from publications in *jingji yanjiu cankao* [Economic Research Internal Reviews], 1979. Specific titles include Deng Liqun, "jiangjiang wode xuexi tihui" [On my thoughts]; "zhong guo cai zheng jing ji kao cha tuan fan wen bao gao" [Report from visits to Yugoslavia and Romania]; "dong ou ge guo gong ye guan li qing kuang" [Industrial management in East Europe]; "ri ben jing ji zhuan jia zuo tan yi jian" [Japanese Economists' Workshop Report]; Ma Hong, "zhen yang li yong xiang gang wei wo guo si ge xian dai hua fu wu" [How to take advantage of Hong Kong economy].

The role of diaspora Chinese in influencing FDI policies in China is more direct than demonstration through success. The ties between diasporas and top leaders and those between diasporas and local governments were critical for the initiation of SEZs in 1979–1980. Those ties served as channels not only for information but also for resources. Resources flown from diasporas, such as capital, equipments, and purchasing orders, were critical to change incentives at a local level and were also important for later success in those zones.

By the late 1970s, Hong Kong had become one of the four Asian tigers that achieved remarkable industrial and commercial success. When the mainland was deliberating economic reform, Hong Kong capitalists viewed it as an opportunity for them. Indeed, Hong Kong businessmen accumulated substantial capital, manufacturing skills, and global trade networks, yet production costs in Hong Kong rose rapidly in the 1970s, making manufacturers eager to look for alternative sites. Nowhere offered as conducive a site as southern China, across a narrow river from Hong Kong. Most of Hong Kong's residents claimed ancestry from this region and continued to speak the same local dialect. In this area, compared to Hong Kong, the wage level was only a fraction of Hong Kong's standard, and land was practically free.

Hong Kong's strong interest in the mainland was clear in 1977, when business representatives from Hong Kong held a huge celebration for the Chinese National Holiday in both Hong Kong and Beijing. On both occasions, the Hong Kong business world networked with political elites in the mainland. While prominent Hong Kong businessmen such as Lee Kashing, Henry Fork, Gordon Wu, and Y. K. Pao fostered ties to Beijing leaders, they were also conscious of building ties to local governments in southern China, where these businessmen's ancestors were from. Thus, with Hong Kong acting as a pivotal node, a pro-openness network linking Hong Kong, southern China, and Beijing was formed. With the Hong Kong business world serving as information and resource supplier, the network was quite effective in shifting Beijing's policy toward foreign capital.

The first SEZ was established before the central endorsement was given. In January 1979, the head of the Hong Kong Merchants' Group, Yuan Geng, helped initiate the SEZ project. Yuan proposed establishing an export processing zone in Shekou (part of today's Shenzhen) to the Guangdong government and the Ministry of Transportation (*jiaotong bu* 交通部) in Beijing. In this zone, Hong Kong would serve as the source of materials, technologies, and market. Driven by foreseeable economic returns, Guangdong officials enthusiastically lobbied central leaders. The Guangdong-born minister of transportation showed his support for economic development in the province and asked central leaders for favorable consideration.[7] This process is demonstrated in figure 7.2.

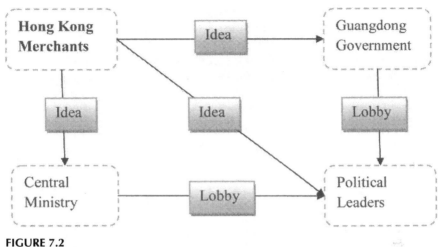

FIGURE 7.2
Network Chart: Shekou Industrial Export Zone, Guangdong, January 1979.

In early 1979, businessmen in Hong Kong suggested that the Shekou zone be expanded to encompass property development and tourism and suggested the name "Special Economic Zone" to reflect the broader scope (Ho 1984, 49). In the zone, a 15 percent corporate tax rate was applied to match the tax rate in Hong Kong (Sung 1991, 13). The business world in Hong Kong provided ideas on how to run a SEZ and also promised capital and technology transfers to the zone. In Shenzhen, for example, in 1979 and 1980, practically all the investment in infrastructure came from overseas investment.[8]

The SEZ policy also received positive response from central leaders in Beijing, including Deng Xiaoping. Ye Jianying, head of the state at the time, and Yang Shangkun, Guangdong vice governor and military chief, were also influential. Zhao Ziyang, who became the premier in 1980, was a former party boss of Guangdong. These top leaders were sympathetic with Guangdong's underdevelopment in comparison to Hong Kong and favorably inclined toward the local government's request for special open policies.

In July 1979, the Equity Joint Venture Law, the first one that legitimized FDI in China, was inaugurated. In August 1980, the National People's Congress approved the Guangdong government's SEZ proposal, which included extensive and detailed incentives for diaspora investors.[9] Yet, before the official decision on SEZs, Hong Kong investors had already contracted one hundred merchandise assembly projects with the Guangdong government for a total investment of $33.5 million (Xiao 2005).

Hong Kong businessmen's early involvement in the SEZ process contrasted sharply to nondiaspora investors. China's cheap labor and potentially huge market also appealed to Western corporations and Japanese capital. Those actors, however, were cautious about investing in China in the early period. They were unfamiliar with realities on the ground, despite their contacts with senior leaders in Beijing. The Japanese companies, for example, were seriously courted by Beijing and yet remained reluctant to invest directly in the mainland. Not until the 1990s did Japanese investment come in substantial measure. Without Hong Kong investment in the early stage, it is unlikely that FDI liberalization in southern China would have been so successful that it stimulated a diffusion process of openness to broader China.[10]

1982–1983: Anti-Bourgeois Pollution Campaign

Despite the dense diaspora networks, FDI created political, social, and economic challenges to China's existing system. Domestic resistance, based on both interest and ideology, persisted in the period 1980 to 1984 (Schram 1984). In 1981, the CCP Propaganda Department promoted a rectification campaign in response to a growing sense of "ideological dissolution" (Dittmer 1982, 39). Furthermore, growing corruption and other economic crimes became a serious concern in China.

Under the above pressure, Beijing adopted a more cautious approach to FDI in the period 1982–1984. The Propaganda Department, led by Deng Liqun, launched the "anti-spiritual-pollution campaign" targeted at the SEZ policy. Deng Xiaoping also shifted toward the left in order to appease his critics within the military (Dittmer 1982, 43). Overall, Beijing pursued a somewhat more conservative policy and focused on the danger of "bourgeois liberalization" (Lieberthal 1983, 25). Although a general focus on economic development remained, there was a clear recentralization trend within the central government (Lieberthal 1983). By 1983, ideological debates and political turmoil once again obstructed China's modernization (Kallgren 1984).

In the period 1982–1984, Western investors became more cautious and adopted a wait-and-see approach. If not for the locally rooted diaspora business networks, the downward trend may have lasted longer. Through 1984, these networks remained strong, and diaspora investment continued to flow in. Indeed, as production costs rose further in Hong Kong in the early 1980s, Hong Kong producers' desire to relocate to China grew. Diaspora investors' interests resonated with the preferences of local governments. Thus, as the conservatives in Beijing attacked SEZs, local governments continued to embrace FDI. As China and Britain were on the verge of reaching an agreement on Hong Kong's reversion, it made sense to Deng Xiaoping also to deepen economic ties across the Pearl River.

Under this context, Deng Xiaoping and other senior leaders visited the special economic zones in early 1984. This tour was accompanied by local officials and business representatives in southern China. It lasted twenty-seven days and was highly publicized in China. Deng's pictures were taken alongside brand-new trade centers, businesses, factories, hotels, industrial parks, power stations, and homes of ordinary citizens. The economic success of SEZs was compelling. On one occasion, Deng was informed that the average monthly income for villagers in Guangdong was RMB500 (equivalent to $250). He reportedly replied that the villagers made more money than he did.

With the results of development so visible, Chinese political leaders became convinced that continuing to open to the outside world would serve the Chinese national interest.[11] Deng Xiaoping was no exception. During the visit, he listened and watched carefully. Only when he was impressed and convinced of the utility of openness to China did he endorse SEZs personally.

More importantly, with Deng Xiaoping's visit, the success of SEZs was demonstrated to the rest of China. Local governments in coastal China were eager to replicate the development marvels in Guangdong and Fujian. They began to court Hong Kong investment and asked the central government for similar open policy. The tip of balance shifted in favor of pro-FDI interests in China. The fourteen open coastal cities were a response to this new dynamic unleashed in 1984.

The fourteen coastal cities were a diverse set with different infrastructures and labor skills.[12] However, most of the cities had linkages with external actors and their external relations grew between 1979 and 1984.[13] In 1984, the SEZs in southern China were also greatly expanded.

Upon inauguration, a Symposium on Investing in China's open cities was held in Hong Kong, which was attended by diaspora investors, as well as Chinese companies, financial institutions, local governments, and ministerial officials.[14] Business contacts were fostered, and investment plans were drawn.[15]

The spillover effect from SEZs to other localities was an important part of the diffusion. Although Beijing was complicated by ideology debates and power struggle in the late 1980s, township and village enterprises (TVEs) in southern China took off. All the counties in the inner Pearl River Delta had export-processing factories that imported primary inputs from Hong Kong and shipped finished products back to Hong Kong to be sold on world markets (Vogel 1989). These factories were typically not located in centrally licensed areas. Localities outside the SEZs and open coastal cities (OCCs) also established their footholds in southern China, hoping to take advantage of the networks to Hong Kong's business world. By 1987, twenty-seven of China's twenty-nine provinces and many municipalities had established offices, as well as their own provincial guest houses, in Shenzhen (Vogel 1989, 141).

Some twenty-five different central government ministries established over two thousand "domestic link" ventures under Shenzhen offices.

1989 Tiananmen Crisis and 1992 Southern Tour

Despite the success of openness and support of FDI at the local level, the upset of the Tiananmen crisis left the future of China's FDI policy uncertain. After the crisis, domestic resistance to openness was strong in China. The conservative faction of the CCP blamed the openness policy for "bourgeois pollution." Moderate reformers became wary of the uncontrollable consequences of FDI and the penetration of Western capital. To them, foreign-invested firms (FIFs) not only created income gaps among workers but also aggravated unemployment and undermined the state sector in general. Both income inequality and unemployment arguably contributed to the growing social unrest leading up to the events of June 1989 (Fewsmith 2001).

When speaking to the Japanese media, the State Council claimed that China's socialist reform should and would stay on the course of socialism.[16] Communist theorists suggested that the purpose of China's reform was to solidify socialism, not to move toward capitalism. Economic liberalization advocated by the West was "peaceful evolution" (*heping yanbian* 和平演变) in disguise.[17] The party newspaper, *Renmin ribao* [People's Daily], published a series of articles entitled "Only Socialism Can Develop China," which argued for the supremacy of the plan versus the market.[18]

The conservatives attacked and silenced reformist members of the government. Zhao Ziyang—a key advocate of openness—was under house arrest, and officials associated with him were removed. In Beijing, even Deng Xiaoping was on the defensive, and his recommendations went unheeded. Western observers were pessimistic about the durability of China's open policy after the Tiananmen crisis.[19] In 1991, confronted with the collapse of the Soviet Union and Eastern Europe, Beijing became even more cautious in implementing economic reforms (Shambaugh 1992).

Unexpectedly, a major shift was about to take place. In January 1992, Deng visited five southern cities and rallied proliberalization coalitions incorporating local officials and diaspora investors. Beijing's media did not report on the Southern Tour in the beginning. When overseas Chinese rallied behind Deng's push for economic liberalization, the debates in Beijing shifted.[20] As policy debates shifted favorably toward the proliberalization coalition, the central government expanded openness to FDI in 1992, incorporating more regions and more sectors. By the end of 1992, any doubt about China's economic reform was dispelled. These developments were the direct result of external liberalization in the 1980s.

First, China's economy had been opened to the point that significant domestic groups became vested in FDI liberalization. From 1979 to 1988, China's foreign trade increased by five times, rising from $20.6 billion to $102.8 billion, and its share of global trade rose from 0.75 percent to 1.57 percent.[21] In 1979, foreign capital in China was negligible. In 1988, foreign capital comprised substantial international loans, portfolio investments, and direct investments, which together amounted to $16 billion. Also by 1989, more than six thousand FIFs operated in China.[22]

Areas open to FDI had expanded from four SEZs, with total land of less than 400 km^2, to fourteen open cities along the coast, plus Guangdong, Fujian, and Hainan provinces, three delta regions, and various border areas, which covered a total area of 320,000 km^2 and boasted a population of 200 million.[23] All of these open areas experienced significant improvements in industrial output, infrastructure, and living standards. The local governments became much richer and gained more bargaining leverage with the central authority. Much of their revenue came from FDI in their localities (see table 7.2).

Second, local governments launched proactive campaigns to support continued liberalization. They used impressive statistics and graphics in official media to showcase the phenomenal economic achievements in their areas. Fujian, for example, contrasted its industrial backwardness in 1978 with a new image of a vibrant manufacturing hub in the *People's Daily*. Statistics demonstrated that from 1978 to 1986 industrial output in Fujian increased sevenfold, GDP increased sixfold, and saving increased by fourteen times, which correlated with rising trade and increased foreign investment. Guangdong showcased its "golden era" of economic development in the *People's Daily* in Sep-

TABLE 7.2
The Significance of FDI in Select Local Economies, 1992

Regions FDI as % of	GDP	Exports	Tax
OCC and SEZs	12.6	34.5	N/A
NTDZs	59.0[a]	33.5	N/A
Beijing	11.0	13.0	12.0
Shanghai	17.0	22.0	16.0[a]
Fujian	33.0	45.0	16.0
Guangdong	19.0	28.6	13.3
Zhejiang	16.0[b]	12.0	2.7

Source: *China Statistical Yearbook 1993, zhongguo duiwai maoyi nianjian* [China's statistics yearbook of foreign trade], 1993; and supplementary materials.
[a] 1993 figures
[b] Fixed Assets Investment

tember 1989. From 1978 to 1989, Guangdong's GDP increased by 312.2 percent, its industrial output by 422.0 percent, and its governmental revenue by 172.8 percent at the same time foreign investment and trade rose by 578.7 percent and 432.2 percent respectively.[24] In Shenzhen, GDP grew forty-two times over from 1979. This growth again was attributed to growing foreign trade, investment, and the number of foreign-invested firms.

Economic statistics were persuasive, and local governments also assured central leaders that FDI strengthened socialist society and facilitated the national "reunification" (*tongyi daye* 统一大业) of China. Guangzhou advertised itself as the "smiling city" in service to the people (*fuwu renmin* 服务人民). It was noted that overseas Chinese not only set up factories, but also built universities, hospitals, kindergartens, and nursing homes, as well as roads, bridges, buildings, dams, and power plants. The slogan "socialism is progressing" (*shehui zhuyi shiye zai qianjin* 社会主义事业在前进) marked the core theme of their lobby effort.

Finally, the strength of diaspora networks had increased substantially by the 1990s. The Hong Kong business community maintained strong economic, social, and political ties to Beijing. Hong Kong representative, Stanley Ho, for example, served as a standing member of the National People's Congress in China and was directly involved in the legislation over Hong Kong's reversion and postreversion institutions. The Hong Kong and mainland economies were deeply interdependent. Hong Kong's exports to and from the mainland together increased sevenfold, making the two economies more intertwined than ever. [25] Increased tourism from diaspora regions to the mainland accompanied deepening economic ties. Visitors from Hong Kong, Macao, and Taiwan increased from 5.14 million in 1980 to 25.6 million in 1990. After the ban on travel across the Taiwan Strait was lifted in late 1987, more than 55,000 Taiwanese visited Fujian in 1988.

Diaspora capital was important for sustaining China's economic liberalization also because it did not decline between 1989 and 1992. Despite a decline in foreign loans from Western countries and international organizations, FDI, originating primarily from diaspora investors, grew. For example, US investment in Guangdong declined from $306.7 million in 1989 to $64 million in 1991, while Hong Kong investment in Guangdong increased from $1.8 billion to $4.2 billion in the two years. Taiwanese investment in the province also doubled.[26]

Overall, foreign investment was more important to China's industrialization at the end of the 1980s than it was in the early part of the decade. In 1983, for example, the share of fixed assets comprised by foreign investment was 1.68 percent. In 1989, the share had jumped to 6.63 percent.[27] Then, again, the majority of foreign direct investment originated from diaspora communities.

From 1979 to 1993, for example, Hong Kong supplied 73 percent of registered foreign capital in China. Taiwan provided more than 9 percent. Macao and Singapore's investment constituted 3 percent and more than 2 percent respectively. In contrast, the United States offered less than 6 percent, and Japan less than 4 percent.[28]

New Dynamics after 1992

With rapid inflows of FDI in the 1990s, China achieved remarkable economic success. GDP increased almost fivefold, central revenue more than sevenfold, exports quadrupled, and the ordinary Chinese income multiplied in the decade. International observers also acclaimed China's economic success based on external openness. Surprisingly, within China, the debates on openness were more heated than ever, and policy liberalization changed from substantial opening to streamlining FDI in the decade. How shall we explain this paradox? How did the FDI liberalization endure this wave of opposition?

In the 1990s, as diaspora investors reached broader China, their ideational superiority lost in the eyes of many Chinese, who were now more exposed to Western ideas. They realized that diasporas did not necessarily bring in more advanced technology than what China had. Furthermore, the preferential policies given to FDI created competition to both inefficient SOEs and growing private firms in China. Due to these two developments, some Chinese elites became intolerant of the open and favorable policies granted to foreign investors.

Under these torrents, a statist trend became powerful in Beijing. This trend aimed to strengthen the power of the central state and domestic industry, while aiming at reducing favorable policies toward FDI. Chen Yuan, an influential economist and the son of conservative political leader Chen Yun, was a main advocate of "new centralization." He admired the Japanese/Korean model and argued that a strong state was indispensible for late industrialization (Chen 1991). Chen claimed, whereas China participated in the international division of labor and economic exchanges, "China must develop as an economic great power not dependent on any other country or group of countries." China must have a complete and advanced industrial system (Chen 1991).

Following Chen Yuan, Hu Angang and Wang Shaoguang, two American-trained scholars, advocated a strong central state in China. They especially criticized the special economic zones. In 1994, Hu raised the issue in an internal report to Beijing and later expanded his views in writing to the Hong Kong newspaper *Ming Bao*. Hu also published in Singapore about his disapproval of SEZs, arguing that local authorities should not have the right to reduce or waive central tax levies or to enjoy any extralegal economic privileges and that the present FDI policies led to vested local interest groups (Zhang 2000). Hu and Wang's arguments had appeal in Beijing. Prime Minister Zhu Rongji told visiting Singaporean Prime Minister Goh Chok Tong in 1996 that, although the basic policies would remain unchanged, "some adjustment and improvement" were needed (Fewsmith 2001).

However, in this period, the ties between diasporas and local governments ran deeper and broader than before, effectively overcoming anti-FDI rhetoric in Beijing. After Hong Kong, Taiwan became a substantial source of investment, information, and resources. When first allowed to visit the mainland in 1987, Taiwanese visited their birthplaces and worshiped at their ancestors' graves. Through these social interactions, ethnic ties were reestablished and evolved into business ties. Some prominent economic figures in Taiwan had close ties to the Yangtze River Delta region. Business representatives, including Xu You-yang, Wu Shun-wen, and Jiang Jing-yi were from Jiangsu. Wen Da-ming, Yin Zhi-hao, Zhang Min-yu, Xu Zhi-feng, and Zu Zhi-qin, were from Zhejiang. The well-known chairman of Thompson Inc, Tang Jun-nian, was from Shanghai.[29]

Despite turbulent debates over FDI in Beijing, local governments in Zhejiang, Jiangsu, and Shanghai actively facilitated entries of Taiwanese investment. The first high-tech export processing zone in China, modeled directly after Taiwan's high-tech export zones such as Xinzhu and Nanzhi, was established in Kunshan, Jiangsu Province. It took Beijing several years to approve this zone, and the authorization came only in 2000. Yet, before obtaining central endorsement, Kunshan export zone had already begun operation. In the 1990s, more than 60 percent of hotel guests in Kunshan were business travelers from Taiwan.[30] By 2000, Kunshan had received one-tenth of Taiwanese investment in China and served as a critical manufacturing site for computer peripheries. Kunshan has today emerged as the major IT manufacturing and export hub in the PRC, thanks to substantial investment from Taiwan's IT companies.

A similar process was undertaken in Suzhou (also in Jiangsu Province) and Ningbo (in Zhejiang Province). In Suzhou, major Taiwanese companies such as Benq, Asus, Mitac, Yageo, and Umax established their presence. The Suzhou New Industry Park ran special daily tours for Taiwanese business delegations.[31] In Shanghai, Taiwanese extensively engaged in service sectors. In 2000, Taiwanese owned an estimated 10,000 to 20,000 businesses in Shanghai. Estimates of the number of residents ranged from 200,000 to 900,000.[32]

Wealthy Taiwan businessmen helped build Pudong, Shanghai, which was typically known for the pervasive presence of Western multinational corporations (MNCs). In reality, however, diaspora capital was more significant in the early period, supplying more than 73 percent of total foreign capital.[33] Taiwan's Thompson Group arrived in Shanghai in 1991, and within one year, contracted billions of dollars of investment in twelve projects. In 1993, Thompson simultaneously launched a financial center in Shanghai's hottest financial district, a trade center near the Customs, a commercial center in downtown, 230 mansions in Shanghai's green zones, massive factories, and residential buildings in industrial districts. It also built the first five-star luxury hotel in Pudong.[34]

In the latter half of the 1990s, Taiwan investors invested heavily in technology-intensive manufacturing, such as computers, pharmaceuticals, chemicals, and electronics, and they used their mainland sites mainly to manufacture for the global market. By 1999, 28 percent of Taiwan-branded PCs has been made in China; a year later the share rose to 42 percent.[35] In 2000, China replaced Taiwan to become the world's third-largest producer of IT hardware—after the United States and Japan—and Taiwan-invested firms accounted for 72 percent of China's $25.5 billion in production (Lardy 2002).

Hong Kong, after years of involvement in China's economic reform and openness, had a more special role to play in the 1990s. Many Chinese companies, both state-owned and private, used this city as their base for global expansion and capital accumulation. They were listed in the Hong Kong Stock Exchange (HKSE). Meanwhile, Hong Kong business reached broader regions and more sectors on the mainland. The Wharf Ltd., run by Y. K. Pao's son-in-law, expanded aggressively into central China. Lee Ka-shing's Cheung Kong Holdings likewise sprawled their reach in China.

In this period, as Chinese new private sectors grew, their linkage with diaspora business was important. Sanguang, for example, a precision machine--tools producer in Suzhou, formed a joint venture with Hong Kong–based trading company COSMOS Machinery International in order to secure funding for expansion.[36] Kelon, a major appliance company, built itself using Hong Kong connections as well. It was listed on the HKSE in 1996, and a year later, Hong Kong investors held almost half of Kelon's equity shares.

As China was implementing SOE reform, many local governments sought to sell bankrupt SOEs to diaspora buyers. Quanzhou in Fujian Province, for example, sold almost all its SOEs to the Hong Kong–based China Strategy Co. Tai Fook Ltd. from Taiwan also bought many SOEs in 1997 and successfully turned them into profitable companies. By 1998, Tai Fook had built the largest chain of paper mills in China.[37] These diaspora buyouts were publicized in mainstream newspapers as successful examples of SOE reforms, leading many local governments to emulate.

The networks between diaspora capital and local governments have arguably influenced the SOE reform in the PRC. No wonder when Beijing criticized FDI, local officials defended FDI.[38] Pan Huanyou, a local official in Zhejiang Province, went on public media in 1995 to discuss FDI's role in the SOE reform. He listed specific SOEs in Zhejiang that used FDI to transform themselves from loss-making companies to globally competitive producers.[39] His positions were echoed by local officials in other areas.

These efforts gradually paid off. Views in Beijing were slowly yet surely swayed. A government-sponsored research team reached a compromise position in 1997. In general, it argued that foreign affiliates of MNCs in China had to satisfy the global strategy of their parent companies and thus their operations may not necessarily be conducive to Chinese development. In reality, however, China needed FDI to help alleviate the SOE burden. Thus, the team suggested that the central government analyze individual cases of FDI-SOE partnership, while emphasizing the strategy of "grabbing the big and letting go the small (*zhuada fangxiao* 抓大放小)."[40] The Fifteenth Party Congress in September 1997 affirmed the importance of FDI in China.[41]

The Future of China's Liberalization

Economic liberalization in the PRC has come a long way. Its entry to the WTO has shown significant impact on itself as well as the rest of the world. In recent years, globalization faced lively debates, and doubts remain as to whether China can continue the liberal trend. Pei Minxin (2006) argues that China's economic transition may well have been "trapped." Some unsettling trends during the Hu Jintao administration also signal that we cannot take liberalization in China for granted (Fewsmith 2008).

However, the factors that sustained China's openness in the 1990s are likely to continue. First, foreign-invested firms and export sectors constitute the main growth in China. In 2004, the trade to GDP ratio in China was almost 80 percent, FDI stocks over $60 billion, and more than half of exports from China were made by foreign-invested firms. Second, local governments remain the primary economic actors in their localities. They will continue to welcome foreign investment that promises additional government revenue and local employment. Third, domestic industries are deeply embedded in openness. Even state companies have used international information, technology, market, and institutions extensively. Aspiring private companies likewise see foreign collaboration as pivotal to their growth and expansion.

The Future of Diaspora Networks

As China has been fully incorporated in the global system, the role of diaspora investors from Hong Kong and Taiwan as information providers and bridges to international markets has become less prominent. It seems that these diasporas ideational superiority over domestic companies has largely diminished. Compared to the PRC's substantial horde of material wealth, these diasporas' advantage in resources is also in decline. The diaspora community as a source of capital is much less important than before.

Nevertheless, as of 2005, Hong Kong and Taiwan investment flows together accounted for 34 percent of actually used FDI in China, much higher than Japan and the United States combined. As an indispensible part of a global production network centering on the PRC, these diaspora-invested companies remain formidable and significant for the PRC's continual development. Indeed, these companies accounted for the majority of high-tech exports from mainland China, as pointed out before. At the local level, diaspora investors continue to play significant policy roles, integrating more localities in openness to FDI. Local governments, with the exception of major municipalities in the mainland, continue to look for additional capital and technology input. These localities have fewer ties to Western actors and institutions. Typically, their call for external ideas and resources is met by diaspora investors.

Diaspora capitalist networks can potentially play a more salient role in partnering with private enterprises in China. In previous periods, diaspora networks concentrated on collaboration with local governments in coastal China and SOEs. As these prioritized economic actors now have access to global capital and information, diaspora networks—as sources of information and resources—are waning. Private enterprises, in contrast, have been disadvantaged by current Chinese institutions and have had difficulty gathering capital, technology, and international linkages on their own. To these enterprises, diaspora networks can be rather complementary. Different from managers at major SOEs who are versed in Western norms and socialization, private entrepreneurs typically grow from the grassroots level and feel much more comfortable dealing with diaspora partners who speak the same language and share some social norms.

Beyond diaspora communities in Hong Kong, Taiwan, and Southeast Asia—the focus group here—overseas Chinese who have been trained and gained work credentials in the United States Japan, and European countries, are expected to play a growing role in China. The trend has shown itself in technology sectors and higher education. As the Chinese government increasingly prioritizes quality growth, it begins to tap into the vast talents in the external environment. China has one of the largest overseas populations that trained in the best institutions in the world. Lured by the government's policy and ever-improving conditions in China, more and more overseas Chinese expertise has returned to China in recent years, and the trend is deepening rapidly. How these diaspora networks influence China's development in the new century remains understudied and underappreciated.

References

Chen, Y. 1991. "Wo guo jing ji wen ti de shen chen wen ti he xuan zhe." *Jing ji yan jiu* 4: 18–26.

DiMaggio, P, and P. Powell. 1991. *The New Institutionalism in Organizational Analysis.* Chicago: The University of Chicago Press.

Dittmer, L. 1982. "China in 1981: Reform, Readjustment, Rectification." *Asian Survey* 22: 33–46.

———. 1990. "China in 1989: The Crisis of Incomplete Reform." *Asian Survey* 30: 25–41.

Donnithorne, A. 1972. *The Budget and the Plan in China: Central-Local Economic Relations.* Canberra, Australia: National University Press.

———. 1994. *Dilemmas of Reform in China: Political Conflict and Economic Debate.* Armonk, NY: M.E. Sharpe.

Fewsmith, J. 2001. *China since Tiananmen: The Politics of Transition.* New York: Cambridge University Press.

———. 2008. *China since Tiananmen,* 2nd ed. New York: Cambridge University Press.

Granovetter, M. 1985. "Economic Action and Social Structure: The Problem of Embeddedness." *American Journal of Sociology* 91: 481–510.

Granovetter, M. S. 1973. "The Strength of Weak Ties." *The American Journal of Sociology* 78: 1360–80.

Harding, H. 1987. *China's Second Revolution: Reform after Mao.* Washington, DC: Brookings Institution.

Ho, S. 1984. *China's Open Door Policy.* Vancouver: University of British Columbia Press.

Huang, Y. 2003. *Selling China: Foreign Direct Investment during the Reform Era.* New York: Cambridge University Press.

Johnton, A. 2008. *Social States: China in International Institutions, 1980–2000.* Princeton, NJ: Princeton University Press.

Kallgren, J. 1984. "China in 1983: The Turmoil of Modernization." *Asian Survey* 24: 60–80.

Khanna, T. 2007. *Billions of Entrepreneurs.* Cambridge, MA: Harvard Business School Press.

Lardy, N. 2002. *Integrating China into the Global Economy.* Washington, DC: The Brookings Institution.

Lieberthal, K. 1983. "China in 1982: A Middling Course for the Middle Kingdom." *Asian Survey* 23: 26–37.

Lieberthal, K., Michael Oksenberg, and David Lampton. 1992. *Bureaucracy, Politics, and Decision Making in Post-Mao China.* Berkeley: University of California Press.

Pei, M. 2006. *China's Trapped Transition: The Limits of Developmental Autocracy.* Cambridge, MA: Harvard University Press.

Rogers, E. M. 1995. *Diffusion of Innovations.* New York: Free Press.

Schram, S. R. 1984. "Economics in Command? Ideology and Policy since the Third Plenum, 1978–84." *China Quarterly* 99: 417–61.

Shambaugh, D. 1992. "China in 1991: Living Cautiously." *Asian Survey* 32: 19–31.

Shirk, S. 1994. *How China Opened Its Door: The Political Success of the PRC's Foreign Trade and Investment Reforms.* Washington, DC: Brookings Institution.

Shue, V. 1988. *The Reach of the State: Sketches of the Chinese Body Politics.* Stanford: Stanford University Press.

Sung, Y-W. 1991. *The China-Hong Kong Connection: The Key to China's Open Door Policy (Trade and Development).* New York: Cambridge University Press.

Vogel, E. 1989. *One Step Ahead in China: Guangdong under Reform.* Cambridge, MA: Harvard University Press.

Walker, J. 1969. "The Diffusion of Innovations among the American States." *American Political Science Review* 63, no. 3: 880–99.

White, L. 1998. *Unstately Power.* Armonk, NY: M.E. Sharpe.

Xiao, D. 2005. "1978–1984 nian zhongguo jinji tizhi gaige silu de yanjin" [Reformist thinking of China's economic system, 1978–1984]. In *Deng Xiaoping yu gaige kaifang* [Deng Xiaoping and China's reform and openness]. Beijing: CCP History Publisher.

Zhang, X. 2000. *Zhong guo gao chen zhi nang (I)* [Chinese top level advisors to policymaking]. Beijing: jing hua chu ban she.

Zweig, D. 2002. *Integrating China: Domestic Interest and International Linkage.* Ithaca, NY: Cornell University Press.

8

Elite Politics

The Struggle for Normality

Joseph Fewsmith

TODAY, THE "RISE OF CHINA" IS ON EVERYBODY'S lips and books on the
subject are published with regularity.[1] By the end of 2009, China was the
third-largest economy in the world and set to become the second largest,
and it had amassed over $2 trillion in foreign exchange reserves. The mod-
ernization of its military has provoked both analysis and concern, and
China's two-decade-old pursuit of "comprehensive national power" seems
well on its way to being realized.

When one looks back three decades, this sudden rise seems unlikely and
indeed, improbable. In 1978, at the time of the watershed Third Plenary Session of the Eleventh Central Committee, which inaugurated the policies of
economic reform and opening to the outside world, China's national income
was only 310 billion yuan (about $150 billion at the then prevailing exchange
rate), its foreign trade stood at a very modest $20.6 billion, the per capita in-
come of its urban residents was 316 yuan, while the per capita income of its
rural residents was only 134 yuan, making China one of the poorest countries
in the world. Over one-quarter of China's rural population had an annual
income of less than 50 yuan.[2] Chen Yun, the senior economic specialist in the
party, famously warned that if the livelihood of the peasants did not improve,
party secretaries would lead them into the cities to demand food.[3]

The rise of China is, of course, an economic story, one that has been told
very well by Barry Naughton and other economists,[4] but it is just as much a
political story. Having recovered in the early 1950s from years of foreign and
civil war, China's economic growth then stagnated between the launch of the

Great Leap Forward in 1958 and the end of the Cultural Revolution in 1976 as China was repeatedly torn apart by political and ideological conflicts. As much as the poverty China faced in 1978, this legacy of political struggle, which had percolated through China's twentieth-century history, suggested that China would have a difficult time achieving the political stability and policy prescience that would allow the economy to take off.

Explaining the change from a legacy of political instability to one of at least relative stability is by no means easy. Political science is not generally well equipped as a discipline to explain political change and the changing dynamics of power in nondemocratic systems. One place to start is the relationship between formal and informal power, an issue raised pointedly by William Riker many years ago:

> Every time I convince myself that I have found an instance in which constitutional forms do make a difference for liberty, my discovery comes apart in my hand. It is, of course, all a matter of the direction of causality. Professor Ostrom believes that at least part of the reason we are a free people is that we have certain constitutional forms; but it may just as easily be the case that the reason we have these constitutional forms is that we are a free people. The question is: Does constitutional structure cause a political condition and a state of public opinion or does the political condition and state of public opinion cause the constitutional structure?[5]

Although William Riker was speaking in terms of democratic institutions, his comments can just as easily, perhaps more easily, be applied to nondemocratic settings. If we understand the Cultural Revolution, in part, as a radical breakdown in the relation between formal institutions—the state constitution, the party charter, and the various written prescriptions on the fora in which political decisions were to be made—and the informal rules of the game, in which internalized understandings of power played an important role, then it is difficult to explain why, in the years after 1978, the formal rules of the game came, gradually and uncertainly, to play a greater role in the Chinese political system. Had the formal rules gained greater credence with the passing of Mao and the end of the Cultural Revolution? If so, why, and to what extent? Had informal understandings of the rules of the game changed? These questions are important not only for the understanding of the emergence of reform, but also for comprehending the peaceful transfer of political power from one leader to another, something nondemocratic systems are not generally noted for, and for our best guesses of how the exercise of political power is likely to evolve in future decades.

Part of the answer lies in the organizational response of the party following the chaos of the Cultural Revolution. As Frederick Teiwes has argued, norms did develop within the Chinese Communist Party, even if those norms were increasingly violated by Mao's high-handed leadership style, particularly in the years following the 1959 Lushan Plenum.[6] Much as the Communist Party of the Soviet Union following the death of Stalin took organizational measures to ensure that no leader would again dominate the party the way Stalin had, the CCP began taking steps to restore "normal" inner-party life.[7] Those measures began with the "Guiding Principles for Political Life within the Party," were followed by the 1982 Constitution, and increasingly became meaningful as the party began to implement rules governing retirement.[8] The convocation of the Twelfth Party Congress in 1982, five years after the Eleventh Party Congress, was the first time that the party had followed the rules in the party charter to convene party congresses every five years—and the CCP has managed to adhere to that schedule, regardless of whatever political conflicts and upheavals it has undergone, from that time to the present.

There was much reason to be optimistic about the progress made in the 1980s. The state began withdrawing from society. For the first time since the founding of the PRC a process of depoliticization set in; private life was restored and citizens engaged once again in leisure activities.[9] With the implementation of the Household Responsibility System, agricultural production not only revived but accelerated to the point that grain overflowed storage capacity. Industrial reform started more slowly, but gained rapidly from mid-decade. And China's new attitude toward opening to the outside world, as detailed in chapter 7, drove the growth of foreign trade and foreign investment in China. At least as important, China's relations with foreign countries, frozen by the radicalism of the Cultural Revolution, eased and then warmed as China pursued a policy of "peace and development," which might be understood as development through peace. Intellectual life revived. Ideology faded (but did not disappear).

Nevertheless, China's reforms set off tensions that ultimately could not be contained by the political system. Although reformers talked about "crossing the river by feeling the stones," conservatives were wedded by ideology, interest, and the structure of the PRC system to their understanding of "socialism." Conservatives were indeed distraught by Maoist radicalism, but they nevertheless believed that the planned economy, Marxist ideology, and party organization could pave the way for a viable socialist system. Introduction of market forces, opening to Western ideas, and generational change challenged their ideas and unbalanced their plans; economic decentralization eroded the power of the center. Inflation, corruption, and new interpretations of Marxism fed into increasingly contentious debates over whether reform was "enlivening" the society and the economy or threatening socialism and the unity of China.[10]

The details of the spring 1989 demonstrations and subsequent crackdown have been explored in many books and articles. What is important for our purposes was the apparent reversion to politics as a game of "win all, lose all."[11] In his speech to the Fourth Plenary Session of the Thirteenth Central Committee, which took place in June following the suppression of the student movement and which fixed blame for the movement on General Secretary Zhao Ziyang, Premier Li Peng talked about the demands of the student movement as being irreconcilable with the continuation of party rule. As he put it:

> All participants maintained that if they admit that there are "mistakes" in the *Renmin ribao* editorial [of April 26, 1989, which accused the students of "opposing socialism"], and recognize the student movement as a patriotic democratic movement, they will necessarily force the party and government to accept their erroneous and even reactionary political programs, and to recognize all illegal student organizations as legal ones. They will make further efforts to set up other illegal organizations, including opposition factions, and opposition parties. They will try to establish a multiparty government, force the Communist Party to step down, and subvert the socialist People's Republic. This is their objective, and they will not stop until they reach this objective.[12]

The political implication of this was that Zhao Ziyang, who had suggested compromising with the student movement in order to resolve the situation peacefully, had to step down. Although not at the same level as Mao Zedong's purge of Liu Shaoqi in the Cultural Revolution, this clash was clearly a battle over succession. Deng Xiaoping and Chen Yun were getting old; the question was whether "conservatives" or "reformers" would inherit the leadership mantle. And it was a contest in which neither side was willing to compromise.

The dynamic of the 1980s and the tensions that built up—and exploded—in the CCP comport very well with Kenneth Jowitt's understanding of Leninist regimes. Leninist regimes begin as "exclusionary" systems that are bent on remaking society in their own image. As revolutionary fervor fades and economic difficulties mount, Leninist systems embark on reforms that make them more "inclusionary." But the process of inclusion—recognizing the legitimacy of societal forces—conflicts with the Leninist organization of the party, generating tension and eventually collapse.[13] Jowitt's analysis works well in explaining the collapse of the Soviet Union and other socialist regimes, and it provides a useful framework for understanding China in the 1980s. The problem, of course, is the CCP did not collapse. Indeed, two decades after Tiananmen, the CCP is perhaps more securely in power than at any time since 1949. The economy has been doing extremely well, China's diplomatic position has never been stronger, and decentralization of state revenues, a major problem in the 1980s, has been reversed. Although many social problems remain—and burst out in frequent mass incidents—the vast majority of the people seem to accept the legitimacy of the CCP despite, or perhaps because of, its policies of cooptation.[14] In short, since 1989 the CCP has remade the political system in ways that have, to date at least, contained political conflict and appear to have paved the way for the CCP to remain in power for many years to come. How did this come about?

Putting the System Back Together

The immediate post-Tiananmen situation did not appear to bode well for the long-term future of the PRC: the political tensions within the CCP remained high, the economy stagnated under the anti-inflationary measures adopted by Li Peng, interenterprise debt escalated as efforts were made to strengthen the planned economy, intellectuals were cowed and dispirited, and the newly named general secretary, Jiang Zemin, did not appear to have the political heft to remain in power. Western newspapers regularly compared him to Hua Guofeng, the ineffectual leader who took over after Mao's death only to yield power to Deng Xiaoping. And Jiang's caution did not help. Yielding to the conservative leaders who dominated the post-Tiananmen political scene, Jiang eventually managed to frustrate Deng to the point that Deng seriously considered removing him.

Angered that his vision of reform was being put aside and that he himself was being ignored or worse (Deng allegedly fumed that the "*People's Daily* wants to comprehensively criticize Deng Xiaoping"[15]), Deng went to the Shenzhen Special Economic Zone in the south of China and launched a broadside of criticism against conservative leaders.[16] Convinced that Jiang would, at last, loyally uphold reform and opening (and that the political cost of removing Jiang was prohibitively high), Deng engineered a change in the political atmosphere that culminated in the Fourteenth Party Congress in the fall of 1992. Conservative leaders—most notably Yao Yilin, Song Ping, and Li Ximing—fell from power and the Congress's political report called for the creation of a "socialist market economy," employing that previously taboo word "market" for the first time in an authoritative party document. Just as important, immediately following the close of the Congress, Deng engineered the ouster of Yang Baibing as vice chairman of the Central Military Commission (CMC) and set off a major purge of followers of Yang and his half brother, Yang Shangkun. The Yang brothers had not shown any deference to Jiang, who had been named chairman of the Central Military Commission in September 1989, thus setting up the possibility that following Deng's demise the People's Liberation Army (PLA) would not accept the leadership of Jiang.

Fearing the sort of conflict Mao had bequeathed to the party fifteen years earlier, Deng oversaw a shakeup of the military that would ensure Jiang's ability to continue to lead China in the years ahead.[17] Contributing to Deng's efforts to pave the way for a smooth transition following his death were the actuarial tables that caught up with the most senior conservative leaders before Deng's own passing: Vice President Li Xiannian, one of Jiang's strongest supporters, died in June 1992, ideologue Hu Qiaomu followed in September 1992, and senior economic specialist Chen Yun passed in April 1995 (Deng died in February 1997).

So the first answer to the question of how the CCP put its political system back together is that Deng Xiaoping lived long enough to remove the political obstacles for Jiang Zemin to take over, and those who might have dominated the political scene in the absence of Deng died before they had a chance to. Design and luck both helped. There is an irony in this: if we think of post-Tiananmen politics as a period in which stronger institutions were created, then one of the keys to this institution building was the efforts of Deng Xiaoping, who operated largely outside the bounds of institutions. Of course, it is also important to bear in mind that part of what Deng was doing was not building institutions, or not just building institutions, but rather balancing political forces in a way that would support his agenda and provide political stability—which gets one back to Riker's question about the relationship between institution building and the informal distribution of power.

As actuarial realities thinned the ranks of senior leaders, major generational change was taking place. This generational change was not simply the passing of power from one generation to another, but more importantly, the passing of the revolutionary generation to a decidedly postrevolutionary generation. The revolutionary generation (and Deng Xiaoping was clearly one of the revolutionary generation despite his reference to himself as the core of the "second" generation) was one that had risen through the violence and chaos of China's civil and foreign wars and had survived the internecine conflict that engulfed that generation after the founding of the PRC. There was nothing modest about this generation. They were fighters and organizers, propagandists and mobilizers. Typically this generation had worked in many of the systems (*xitong* 系统) of the Chinese Communist Party and thus had understandings of a wide variety of different functions and friends (and, no doubt, enemies) throughout the system. These were people who in their youth set off to "overturn heaven and earth," and they dominated Chinese politics for nearly half a century. As revolutionaries, they did not have the incremental visions of bureaucrats and more modest reformers. Mao Zedong unleashed the Great Leap Forward and the Cultural Revolution without fear that he could not rein in the forces that he had unleashed. And Deng Xiaoping embarked on market-oriented reforms without worrying that he could not control the consequences.

The postrevolutionary generation of Jiang Zemin, Li Peng, and others had fundamentally different career paths than their revolutionary elders. Most of the leaders that came to the fore in this generation were trained as engineers. Engineers tended to have fewer political problems coming out of the Cultural Revolution than those trained in the humanities and the social sciences, and thus it was easier for elders to agree on their promotion in the 1980s as China was seeking younger leadership following the Cultural Revolution. Engineers by training tend to be problem solvers rather than visionaries. Moreover, the career tracks of this generation tended to be in a single field. This generation climbed the bureaucratic ladder step by step, suggesting just how much their personalities, vision, and experience differed from those of their revolutionary elders. In addition, having stayed in narrower career tracks suggested that their ability to forge personal links across systems (*xitong*) would be limited; they would have to depend more on institutional linkages than their elders had. Perhaps more important, it was less clear what they would do with such extensive personal networks if they did have them. Securing power was one thing, and they certainly used personal relationships to achieve that goal, but they and their generation did not have the overarching political agendas of Mao Zedong with his antibureaucratic passion for permanent revolution or Deng Xiaoping with his desire to normalize political life and embark on market-oriented reform. The times had changed along with the generations, and there was little choice but to pursue an agenda of economic growth, political stability, and a peaceful international environment.

Generational transition also inevitably raised questions about procedure. Whereas those of the revolutionary generation could legitimize their positions by pointing to their contribution to the revolution, successors (and successors to successors) would have a more difficult time doing that. Questions would increasingly be raised (implicitly or explicitly) about why one person rather than another was promoted. And such questions led to a desire to enunciate such criteria as age, education, and experience, which the party has increasingly done. Thus, we see positions in the Central Committee being allocated to those holding specific government, military, or party jobs rather than simply to loyal individuals. Such procedures do not eliminate favoritism or factionalism—patrons can and do plan years in advance to promote the career of their protégés—but it does constrain the way competition can be pursued.

At the Fifteenth Party Congress in September 1997, Jiang Zemin called for "holding high the banner of Deng Xiaoping Theory," lauding the thinking of the recently deceased "architect" of reform and opening. But even as Jiang was praising Deng Xiaoping's thinking, it was evident that a new, or at least modified, approach to ideology was coming into being. Whereas the 1980s had been dominated by debates between reformers and conservatives, the trauma of Tiananmen and the collapse of the Soviet Union had revealed both the impossibility of returning to orthodox Marxism and the political unacceptability of radical reform. What emerged in the 1990s as Jiang began to consolidate his position would be a "neoconservative" approach that was, on the one hand, not intellectually satisfying—it did not articulate any political or social ideal to which people could aspire—but was, on the other hand, both pragmatic and conservative. It was conservative in the sense that it upheld the absolute primacy of the party-state against any real or perceived challenge (such as the founding of the China Democracy Party in 1998[18]), and it was pragmatic in that it accepted the absolute need for economic growth. In contrast to the immediate post-Tiananmen efforts, both ideological and practical, to shore up the old planned economy, the neoconservative approach accepted both the continued growth of the private economy and the rapid expansion of foreign trade even as it sought to revive a leaner, meaner state sector. Neoconservatism was reflected in both the new statism of the Jiang period (the tax reform of 1994 would usher in a period that continues to the present, in which the growth of central revenues outpace the growth of GDP) and the shedding of some two hundred thousand state-owned enterprises and perhaps as many as 50 million workers from state rolls.

Neoconservatism was never articulated as a formal ideology because it was primarily a pragmatic response to the exigencies of the day, but its emergence as the dominant approach to governance serves as a marker of the ideological distance that China had traveled in the two decades since Mao died. Deng Liqun, the conservative ideologue who in the 1980s became the *bête noire* of liberal reformers, tells of preparing himself for the post-Mao era by reading and rereading the Marxist classics, including the works of Mao Zedong.[19] Although Deng Liqun would be far more ideological than the pragmatic Deng Xiaoping who led the reform movement, his mastery of Marxist ideology reflects the importance of ideology and ideational manipulation in the reform movement and in moving away from Maoist ideology. A decade later, no one would think of preparing for high office by painstakingly studying the Marxist classics (indeed, no one has thought of Ding Guan'gen or Li Changchun, who have been responsible for ideological issues from the 1990s to the present, as particularly knowledgeable Marxists). Neoconservatism was not inspirational but it served as a marker of the de-ideologicalization of the Chinese political system.

The passing of the revolutionary generation, the rise of a technocratic leadership, the increasing emphasis on procedure, the decline in the importance of ideological issues in favor of practical solutions, and the adoption of neoconservative approaches to governance all point to the gradual, incomplete, but nevertheless important emergence of formal institutions as constraints on political competition, something that had been absent in China at least since the fall of the Qing. But to see post-Tiananmen China as the incremental emergence of institutionalized politics misses important dimensions of the period. First, the decline of ideology, while beneficial for the growth of the private economy, for bringing more intellectuals into the party and for the pragmatic adoption of public policies, was not good for the organizational integrity of the party or for public values. Public intellectuals on both the left and right lamented the loss of an idealism that could bind a large and diverse nation like China together.[20] And membership and promotion in the party seemed to be even more a matter of opportunism, corruption, and personal loyalty than ever. The outright sale of office became a major problem.[21] Such issues made the building of governance difficult and the provision of public goods anemic, and those issues would, in turn, become bases for social protest and criticisms of reform—but now we are getting ahead of ourselves.

It was too much to expect that the nascent institutions being forged in the 1980s and 1990s would be strong enough to provide a solid basis for exercising political power; personal relationships remained too much a part of Chinese public life for that to happen quickly. Certainly Jiang Zemin, even as he called for the "rule of law" and for "regularization, standardization, and proceduralization" (*zhiduhua* 制度化, *guifanhua* 规范化, *chengxuhua* 程序化),[22] built his political power and indeed a good bit of his development strategy on the promotion of close associates from Shanghai, who were inevitably dubbed the "Shanghai gang." Similarly, as the Yang brothers were being purged from the PLA, new leadership was sought from the thinning ranks of the former Third Field Army, the army that had been based in East China and to which Jiang Zemin's martyred uncle had belonged. The PLA was itself becoming more professional in this period, but personal relations between the head of the party and top PLA generals nevertheless remained important.[23] In other words, even as there were signs that political life was indeed being institutionalized and regularized, there was the simultaneous existence and arguably growth of personalism and perhaps even factionalism. Factionalism has existed throughout the history of the PRC, but the political system has never been a factional system. Indeed, the party has had strong injunctions against factionalism, and that has been a factor both in the centralization of power in the CCP and in the sometimes harsh conflict between leaders.[24] Factions may be more important in contemporary China than they were in the Dengist period or before, but they have not (at least not yet) come to define the political system. Rather, like the institutionalization that has emerged and the cooptation of societal interest, they stand in tension with the still Leninist structure of the party.

Hu Jintao and the Call for a "Harmonious Society"

The pattern of a gradual leadership transition that Jiang Zemin etched, being named as general secretary in 1989 and consolidating power (if one can ever define a point in time) only at the Fourth Plenary Session of the Fourteenth Central Committee in September 1995, was followed when Hu Jintao succeeded Jiang at the Sixteenth Party Congress in November 2002. This leadership transition was not as smooth as frequently depicted, and it raised important questions about institutionalization, but it was, nevertheless, successful. Deng Xiaoping, like the Daoist strategist Zhuge Liang in the classic novel *Romance of the Three Kingdoms,* influenced events even after his death by engineering Hu Jintao's eventual succession to power even as he helped Jiang consolidate his power (it was Deng who had appointed Hu to the Politburo Standing Committee in 1992, putting him in position for succession). Unwilling to let go of the reins of power quickly or easily, Jiang expanded the size of the Politburo Standing Committee (from seven to nine) in 2002 and arranged for several of his close colleagues to sit on it, apparently to maintain watch over Hu.[25] Jiang himself held onto the critical position of head of the Central Military Commission for an additional two years, just as Deng Xiaoping had held onto that position after retiring from the Politburo at the Thirteenth Party Congress in 1987.

The personnel arrangements reflected both the limitations on the degree of institutionalization that had occurred over the previous decade and more as well as the uneasiness in relations between Jiang's followers and those of Hu Jintao. Jiang, as mentioned above, drew his closest followers from his political base in Shanghai, while Hu, who had spent much of his career in China's poor interior drew his followers from the interior and from the Communist Youth League (CYL), which he had once headed. Jiang's coastal orientation would be—and continues to be—in tension with Hu's greater emphasis on the interior and the need for balanced development.[26] The tensions evident in this transition were by no means debilitating, but they did reflect the continuing need to carefully balance institutional rules and norms with the informal balance of power.

To an even greater degree than Jiang before him, Hu emphasized the importance of institutions and following the rules. Hu's first public appearance after being named general secretary was to deliver a speech on the twentieth anniversary of the promulgation of China's 1982 constitution. Hu declared that "no organization or individual can be permitted the special privilege of going outside the constitution and the law."[27] Hu also emphasized such procedures as having the Politburo formally report to the Central Committee during plenary sessions, conducting collective study sessions of the Politburo in an effort to reach common understandings and policy consensus, and developing "inner-Party democracy" in an effort to regularize party processes. Although such measures point in the direction of further institution building, it must be emphasized that they remain very preliminary as yet.

In addition, Hu began to shift China's official rhetoric in a more populist direction, emphasizing the need to build a "people-centered" society, implement his "scientific development concept," and create a "harmonious society." These ideological tropes, which began to eclipse Jiang Zemin's preferred theory of the Three Represents as Hu began to consolidate power, reflected Hu's different policy emphases. Whereas Jiang had stressed China's rapid economic development, Hu and premier Wen Jiabao began to emphasize social justice issues—the problems left unaddressed as China, or more precisely the urban east coast of China, barreled headlong forward in pursuit of higher GDP.[28]

This change in official rhetoric is politically interesting for two reasons. First, the populist rhetoric of the Hu-Wen administration was joined by a rising tide of "New Left" criticism, directed against the policies of reform and opening up initiated by Deng and furthered by Jiang, and the Hu-Wen rhetoric, intentionally or unintentionally, seems to have encouraged further criticism. This populist upswell became quite heated, particularly over the issues of management buyouts (MBOs) and the protection of property rights, and the debates between "mainstream" (that is, market-oriented) economists and "nonmainstream" (leftist critics) became so heated that both Hu Jintao and Wen Jiabao were compelled to give strong statements reaffirming their commitment to reform and opening up in the spring of 2006.[29] The issues of how to reform, who should (or could) benefit from reform, the provision of public goods, and the direction of reform were all sensitive and foci of heated discussions among intellectuals. Public voices were playing a greater role in politics, and the issue of how the political system would or could respond to them became important. Democratization was not on the table, but issues of responsiveness were.

Second, the raising of different issues and the implicit criticism of the previous administration for neglecting these issues raised the question of how the Chinese political system could process political disputes. Those close to Jiang felt that unless Hu's populist rhetoric could be reined in, it could destabilize the political system and severely harm reform and opening. The way this issue was handled was to change the rules governing party congresses once again to allow greater "inner-party democracy." Whether through the expression of genuine feelings or through the mobilization of personal ties, this process resulted in the selection of Xi Jinping as heir apparent (though no official announcement has yet been made), leaving Hu Jintao's favorite, Li Keqiang, as the probable next premier. Moreover, although the congress accepted Hu's scientific development viewpoint, it relegated Hu's theme of harmonious society to a secondary position. In short, the congress reached compromise but only by constraining Hu Jintao.[30] In this instance, informal politics were at least as important as any institutional rules governing leadership selection.

As the working through of these issues suggest, Chinese politics in the contemporary period is composed of a complex interplay between the more populist forces that support Hu Jintao and his "people-centered" approach to governance and the elitist developmental approach associated with former general secretary Jiang Zemin. The difference between the two approaches should not be exaggerated. Despite some of the harsh language posted on the web by New Left intellectuals, it is difficult to imagine Hu Jintao, who is anything if not cautious, adopting the more radical, highly nationalistic policies urged by some in the New Left. Rather Hu Jintao's policies tend to address the concerns of the New Left, emphasizing the need to deliver better health care to the rural areas, working to build social security for the poor, and reflecting economic nationalism in keeping foreign investment out of some sectors, but without adopting the populism being urged upon him. Indeed, there is little in Hu Jintao's program that would increase popular involvement in the political process, especially with regard to national policies.

Similarly, those who emphasize the need for economic growth acknowledge the need to address social justice issues. Where they differ from the New Left is first in their basic acceptance of economic theory as it is understood in the West. While China's economists have never accepted market fundamentalism, they have appreciated the value of markets and competition in the allocation of resources, decreasing the ability to engage in arbitrage, and stimulating growth. In their view, there is no need to articulate a unique Beijing consensus in contradistinction to an alleged Washington consensus. Mainstream economists also differ from their New Left critics in believing that social justice issues can only be addressed over a long period of time. Given the size of China's population and the enormity of its social needs, the ability to provide public goods can only be built over time as the overall economy grows. China, in other words, has no choice but to outgrow its problems over time. Diverting scarce resources in an effort to address social needs in the short term can only disrupt China's long-term growth.[31]

Politically these different views and emphases coexist and reach compromise because of the way in which the Chinese elite turns over. In contrast to democratic systems in which one administration ends and another, with a separate agenda and different personnel, takes over, China has a revolving elite. It now seems that the model for the transfer of power is that the senior, outgoing leader, will stay around, both by holding onto a senior portfolio (it has been the critical position of head of the CMC so far) and by surrounding the incoming party head with close associates who both constrain the new party head and perhaps provide policy bridges with the former leader. At the same time, the membership of the Central Committee turns over gradually. On average, about half of the membership of the Central Committee retires at each party congress.[32] Of the newly appointed members, about two-thirds are promoted from the ranks of Alternate Members of the previous Central Committee, and about one-third are newly appointed. This suggests a conscious effort to mix people who have worked their way up the system with newcomers who "helicopter" onto the Central Committee—but not into top-ranked positions. In short, the newly appointed party head has the opportunity, but only over time, of weeding out his predecessor's associates and building a party leadership contingent more in line with his own preferences, but only in time for his own retirement—at which time he can hover over *his* successor.

This is a process which, all other things being equal, is biased toward the old leadership, not the new leadership. For instance, the critical decisions on the makeup of the Politburo that emerged from the Seventeenth Party Congress in 2007 were actually made at a Central Committee meeting on June 25, 2007. That is, the decisions on China's new leadership were not made by the incoming Seventeenth Central Committee (as the party charter appears to prescribe) but rather by the outgoing Central Committee—on which the supporters of Jiang Zemin would have been more numerous.

What Type of System Is This?

My argument is that after three decades of reform and opening, elite politics have been transformed in important ways. Rules governing retirement, qualification for higher position, and selection of new leaders have become fairly well institutionalized. There has been a remarkable transition to civilian control over the military, and the military itself seems to participate less and less in nonmilitary political issues (though 20 percent of the seats in the Central Committee are still occupied by the PLA). However, there is still a substantial amount of room in the political system for informal politics to play themselves out. Every five years the rules governing retirement or leadership selection change somewhat, and there are periodic arrests of political opponents on corruption charges that might be better understood as crimes of *lèse majesté*. That the rules governing leadership selection are not changed more radically than they are suggests that the institutional framework does constrain the pursuit of power to an important degree; that they are nevertheless changed in important ways suggests that the informal balance of power remains important to the operation of the political system. That the rules are never committed to paper and publicized suggests that the leaders understand the continuing importance of informal politics and do not want to (or believe they can) further restrain political behavior through the use of institutions.

I have taken to calling such a situation "quasi-formalized." Such a concept is not useful if it suggests either intellectual surrender (it is a "mixed system") or a temporal oddity (it is in transition to something more identifiable), but it might be a useful concept if by it we can understand a particular interplay between formal and informal rules, such that each is seen as complementary to the other. That is to say, if we view elite politics in China as not institutionalized in important ways but also that the informal politics do not so overwhelm the formal rules as to render the latter meaningless. Quasi-formalization could thus be seen as describing a situation in which formal rules had indeed gained institutional traction, circumscribing the scope of informal rules, but that informal rules filled out the empty spaces not defined by the formal rules and indeed pushed against the formal institutions and importantly against the further formalization of the rules. Importantly, quasi-formalization implies that there is no third-party enforcement, including recourse either to an independent judiciary or the opinion of voters. Most important, if a concept of quasi-formalization is to make any sense, is the idea that it is not "halfway" between informal and formal, transiting in one direction or the other, but rather that it is a reasonably stable situation that can exist for a prolonged period of time. It is a deliberate blurring of the lines between formal and informal in a way that prevents formal institutions from emerging full blown and yet prevents informal political balances from overwhelming institutionalized rules.

Implications for the Future

If the concept of quasi-formalization is an adequate description of the present state of elite politics in China, then we must ask what the implications for the future are. As with all things in the future, caveats are in order. First, we see that while there are many reasons to believe that the current order seems likely to continue, there clearly will be challenges. For years, the greatest challenge to the political order has appeared to be a prolonged setback to continued economic growth. Now, with the world financial crisis, that possibility seems real, even if the Chinese economy has responded remarkably well to this challenge. We know that there have been continual challenges to the status quo in the form of "mass incidents," which grew from 8,700 in 1993 to 87,000 in 2005. If quasi-formalization works well enough as a framework in which political conflict can be mediated at the elite level, there are other arenas that simply do not accept such a framework. It is possible, if prolonged economic stagnation would result from the current global economic crisis (which does not seem likely) or from other causes, that local protests could escalate to the point that they either bring about systemic change or they bring down the whole system. Bringing down the current system seems unlikely—the government has many resources to prevent such an outcome—but the challenges presented by such protests could lead, over time, to systemic changes, such as real elections or the establishment of an independent judiciary, that would jolt China out of the current quasi-formalized setting into the realm of political contestation through formal institutional arrangements. Alternatively, the continuation of protests could exacerbate policy differences within the elite in ways that cannot be contained by quasi-formalization. Such an outcome would reflect a breakdown in the balance between the formal rules of the game and the informal balance of power, possibly triggering the sort of "game to win all" from which China has suffered so much over the past century.

Such outcomes do not seem likely to me. On the contrary, the pliability of the current system, which allows institutional rules to be stretched but not broken and thus accommodates conflict while upholding a fundamentally hierarchical order, seems sustainable over a prolonged period of time. Though this chapter has explored the development of quasi-formal arrangements at the elite level, I believe that patterns of governance at the local level are also evolving in this direction: New interests are being accommodated by a variety of quasi-formal linkages to the local state without recognition of their separate legitimacy. New developments in law could challenge these arrangements, but quasi-formalization seems to possess durability.

If the current political arrangements do continue into the future, they augur not only for continuity in policy but also for only incremental change. The political status quo mixes different economic, political, and geographic interests and is designed to maintain a balance among diverse elements, turning political power over only incrementally and incompletely. The upside of such a political arrangement is that it is basically conservative and predictable. The downside is that it may not be able to respond quickly to crises, and crises are a normal feature of political life—as the SARS epidemic, the Asian financial crisis, the Sichuan earthquake, the bombing of the Chinese embassy in Belgrade, and the EP-3 incident all suggest. So far, China has contained the political fallout from each of these crises, but that does not mean it will continue to be able to do so. China has not yet earned high marks for crisis management, yet such skills are likely to become more important in the future.

The other problem with a political arrangement that permits only incremental change is that it can allow problems to mount. As the rising number of mass incidents suggest, China has not yet mounted an effective political response.

China has certainly talked about and experimented with political reforms at the local level, but to date these have been limited. They have been limited because more extensive political reforms would challenge the hierarchical, authoritarian nature of the political system, and that would set off political changes that would be as far-reaching as they would be unpredictable.

The pliability of China's quasi-formal arrangements could be challenged, however, by slower economic growth (see chapter 4 on the change from quantitative to qualitative growth), by increased competition within the political system, or by a continued diversification of developmental goals to include environmental protection, health care, social security, and so forth, as is already happening. Such changes, singly or in combination, would put strains on China's political economy in ways that might bring very discontinuous change. Some such scenarios are pursued in the conclusion to this volume.

9

Local Elections

The Elusive Quest for Choice

Yawei Liu

A Low-key Celebration and Subsequent Loud Questions

ON THE DAY THAT AMERICA WENT TO THE POLLS to decide who would be the next president, and the whole world was holding its breath to see if an African American could be voted into the White House, a group of Chinese officials gathered together in a small meeting room in the cavernous Great Hall of the People to celebrate the tenth anniversary of the promulgation of the *Organic Law of Villager Committees of the People's Republic of China* (hereafter the Organic Law). It is this law that made direct village committee elections mandatory. The same law also fermented the hope that China's long-overdue democratization through grassroots elections would eventually move from the village level upward to higher echelons of the Chinese government. The media report of the event was entitled "Ten Years of Villager Self-government: 900 Million Chinese Farmers' Real Democratic Exercise."[1]

According to this report, as of December 2007, there were 610,000 villager committees in a nation where 2.41 million village committee members were directly elected by the voters. Minister of Civil Affairs, Li Xueju, who guides and supervises this largest election in the world, declared that in the past ten years there were three great accomplishments. First, provincial governments have supplemented the national law with provincial ordinances guaranteeing farmers' democratic rights. Second, under the strong leadership of village party branches, three rounds of elections were held and 85 percent of the villager committees have set up villager representative assemblies. Third, village democracy has established a solid foundation for the political development of Chinese characteristics delineated by the Seventeenth National Congress of the Chinese Communist Party. It was also made public during the celebration that the revision of the Organic Law would be listed in the five-year legislative agenda of the Standing Committee of the National People's Congress.[2]

No prominent leader from the party or the government appeared at this occasion and the rhetoric from both Minister Li Xueju and the media seemed to be drastically subdued from what was said about this so-called silent revolution back in 1998 when the provisional Organic Law became official. It was even more hushed than it was in 1987 when Peng Zhen tried to convince a suspicious Standing Committee of the National People's Congress (NPC) to adopt the Organic Law on a provisional basis.[3]

What is the current status of village elections in China? Are they still meaningful? Do Chinese leaders and the elite still believe in elections as a way to launch political reform, reinvent the Chinese Communist Party's (CCP) legitimacy, curtail corruption, and introduce a new governance of choice and accountability? Has the top Chinese leadership decided not to delve into electoral reform, but to adhere to the old method of increasing moral purity and erecting a new behavioral and decision-making standard (the scientific concept of development) in order to move China forward to jostle for global leadership with the United States and other democracies in the world?

"The Great Leap Forward": 1998–2004

Arguably, the period between 1998 and 2004 was the most exciting time during which efforts were made to replicate what was limited only to the village elections for township administrative position elections and people's congress deputy elections at the district/county level. In November 1998, the Shenzhen People's Congress sent a request to the Standing Committee of the NPC via the Guangdong People's Congress to experiment with direct election of township/town magistrates. The request was denied by the NPC although the details of this significant rejection remain secret to today. Despite this rejection, there were almost simultaneous movements in Sichuan, Guangdong, and Shanxi provinces. These extraordinary experiments culminated in the direct election of a township magistrate in Buyun Township, Suining Municipality, Sichuan Province, on December 31, 1998. This election not only triggered enormous excitement among reform-oriented scholars and officials within China, but also captured the imagination of Westerners who had been looking for signs to buttress the claim that village elections were indeed the first steps toward direct elections at higher levels of the government.[4]

The outcome of the Buyun election was determined to be unconstitutional by the Standing Committee of the NPC, stifling reformers who had declared that Buyun was the political equivalent of Xiaogang Village in Fengyang, Anhui.[5] In 2001, before the new round of township/town people's deputy elections were to take place, the NPC issued a circular through the General Office of the CCP Central Committee, which specifically banned any elections of the Buyun type. Leaders in Suining defied this ban through a procedural change. The change was to have the voters directly elect two final candidates as township magistrate instead of selecting the final appointment for the magistrate.

At the same time, in Buyun, Tan Xiaoqiu, who won the election three years ago, was reelected.[6] There was not much controversy this second time around and there was no media frenzy. Tan Xiaoqiu was no longer the media darling and the talk of Buyun being the "political Xiaogang" had disappeared altogether. Yet the impact of Buyun was clearly felt and gave birth to much political imagination among reform-oriented officials in different provinces.

In August and September 2002, Jingshan County, Hubei Province, conducted a pilot election project to directly elect the party secretary as well as the magistrate in the town of Yangji. It was the first time that both town-level leadership positions were opened up to a popular nomination process. The Yangji experiment, according to media reports, was aimed to increase both intraparty democracy and grassroots democracy at the town level.[7] Yangji has a population of fifteen thousand. Eighteen candidates vied for the position of party secretary and seventeen for town magistrate. Final candidates were determined through a popular opinion survey. Although both incumbents were reelected, this was quite different from the past when candidates were selected by the county-level party organization apparatus.[8] The decisions by the Jingshan leaders to introduce such an experiment was partially due to a poll conducted by the county among residents on how to best select village and town leaders. Of 2,200 residents polled, 1,613 believed that candidates should be nominated directly by the voters.[9] It was rumored that the Yangji experiment was endorsed by Zeng Qinghong, a member of the Standing Committee of the CCP Politburo in charge of organization work.[10] Although there was no evidence proving Zeng's involvement, scholars from Central China Normal University were invited by government officials to observe and record the entirety of the pilot procedures.[11]

In August 2003, Wei Shengduo, the party secretary of Pingba Town, Chengkou County, Chongqing Municipality, planned a direct election of both town party secretary and magistrate. He made a grave error by not seeking approval from the higher up. On the election eve, the County Party Committee put the brakes on his bold experiment and Wei Shengduo was put under "house arrest" for fifteen days. He was later stripped of his titles as party secretary and county people's congress deputy.[12] Wei was later demoted to run the county supply and sales operation and has been fighting to reverse what he considers a wrongful action by the County Party Committee. Wei told a reporter from *Nanfengchuan* (a weekly published in Guangzhou) in early 2008 that he believed there was nothing wrong with what he did in the summer of 2003. The only mistake he made was not to consult the county Party Committee in advance. But the Party Discipline Committee of Chongqing still refuses to overturn the disciplinary action against him.[13]

In April 2004, Honghe Prefecture in Yunnan Province experimented with direct nomination and direct election of township/town magistrates in seven townships and towns in Shiping County under the leadership of Prefecture Party Secretary Luo Chongmin. Over a hundred thousand voters were involved. The entire experiment was conducted in secrecy and was not reported by the Xinhua News Agency journal *Banyuetan* [Bimonthly forum] until six months later. According to the report, these direct elections, which began in February 2004, could be characterized by being open, competitive, fair, and transparent. According to Luo Chongmin, the officials were keenly aware of the constitutional arrangement of having township/town people's congress deputies elect township/town magistrates and the popular desire to get involved in the electoral process. He claimed that what Honghe had done fell completely into the letter and spirit of the Political Report of the Sixteenth Party Congress on expanding grassroots democracy. He also said that introducing reform measures meant daring to take risks. Reporters from Xinhua found out from the residents that directly elected officials were much more polite and responsive to residents' needs. He also said that to introduce direct nomination and election on a large scale required political vision and courage. Luo stated: "As a prefectural Party secretary, I feel obligated to be innovative and explore new ways to advance political civilization and enhance the capability to govern."[14]

In April 2005, in the same city where Wei Shengduo could not find any moral support for his bold attempt, the direct election of a township magistrate took place. Details of the election in Zhangguan, Yubei District, Chongqing Municipality, are scarce. According to a report filed by the *Chongqing Shibao* dated April 4, 2005, there were initially twelve candidates. There was a preliminary selection process by a small group of electors. They trimmed the pool of candidates to five. Then, the plenary session of the Yubei District Party Committee chose three final candidates. On April 2, 2005, 2,400 voters went to the polls to choose their next magistrate. There was a report as to who won and by how many votes.[15]

In addition to these innovative and exciting experiments at the township/town level, 2003 saw the limited but still unprecedented competitiveness at district people's congress deputy elections in Beijing and Shenzhen respectively. The Carter Center's website on Chinese elections and governance (www.chinaelections.org) followed these elections very closely and convened a meeting at Shenzhen University attended by leading democracy scholars from various universities in China.[16] In both cities, there were independent candidates who succeeded in winning the nomination. They all campaigned diligently. Shu Kexin, a Beijing homeowner and resident scholar at Renmin University of China, even organized a campaign staffed by volunteers and planned to raise funds for his campaign. He lost because local election officials manipulated the process and doomed his chance from the very beginning.

Yuan Dayi, a professor of the Beijing Municipal Party School, wrote an article about how he lost his nomination to a candidate who received fewer votes. Before the Chinese *Newsweek* published his article, officials from his school tried to persuade him to withdraw his piece. He refused and the article appeared on December 8, 2003. In the article, he complained about the opaque centralization process through which he lost his candidacy in an inexplicable way. Yuan later met with the municipal people's congress official in charge of elections. The official told him that he was famous in Beijing because he challenged the openness of the electoral process. He was concerned about retribution against him but nothing happened.[17]

It was during this period that a few Chinese scholars began to publish research on China's elections. The most notable scholarly accomplishment was a series of books edited by Bai Gang and authored or coauthored by Shi Weimin. Both Bai Gang and Shi Weimin are researchers at the Institute of Political Science at the Chinese Academy of Social Sciences.[18] Cai Dingjian, a former NPC official turned constitutional law professor at the Chinese University of Political Science and Law, edited the first ever report on the status of elections in China. The book contains three parts, including an objective election status report, an examination of the voters' psychology and behavior, and a procedural design for future elections. The media also created a blitz about the book. There were numerous interviews with Cai and rave reviews of the book.[19]

This was also the period when Western organizations were warmly invited to observe Chinese elections, provide assistance and advice in standardizing election procedures, and offer funding for field research. The International Republican Institute, the Carter Center and the Duke University China Election Study Group, UNDP, the European Union (EU), and other bilateral agencies were all involved in these activities.

The "Color Revolution" and the Big Chill

By 2005, following the change of regimes in Central Asian countries and the Bush administration's call to support democratization in Asia, a big chill descended upon the Chinese leadership. Chinese reporters and scholars began to warn that the wave of the so-called color revolution would expand to China. An April 4, 2005, article by the *Liaowang News Weekly*, entitled "'Color Revolution' Reveals America's Change of Strategy" warned that Washington was using democracy as a weapon to justify its legitimacy as a global leader and that it planned to work with Japan and South Korea to intensify the democratization assault on Asia.[20]

In the summer of 2005, residents of Taishi Village on the suburbs of Guangzhou initiated a recall of their villager committee chairman Chen Jinsheng, whom they elected back in April. The cause of the recall was that several plots of village land were graded for business development and most of the villagers had no clue when the deals were struck and who approved them. They filed a complaint with the Panyu District government but saw no action taken. They then invoked the Organic Law and launched a petition to recall Chen Jinsheng. On August 29, a month after the petition was filed, the district government claimed that the signatures were forged and rejected it. The villagers began a hunger strike and surrounded the villager committee office to prevent any accounting records from being taken away. On September 12, armed police were then dispatched and high-pressure water cannons were used to disperse the crowd, mostly old women from the village.[21]

On September 15, an article appeared in the *People's Daily*, praising the Taishi villagers' heroic efforts to recall their leader, calling it democracy on a pile of rocks. This is a reference to Feng Qiusheng, leader of the recall effort, reading clauses from the Organic Law on a pile of rocks at the entrance to the village to villagers who participated in the recall and the blockade of the villager committee office. The article said that after the district government rejected the first petition request with four hundred signatures, five villager representatives came back with a new petition that had eight hundred signatures. When civil affairs officials went down to the village to verify signatures, hundreds of villagers went to the place where the verification was going to take place, including an old woman more than one hundred years old.[22] In an earlier article in the now shut-down website "yannan," the author, who was believed to be observing the villagers' agitation in Taishi, called the Taishi recall the Xiaogang of democratization in China. This article cited five characteristics of the Taishi agitation. First, it was a combination of obeying the law, defending rights, and protecting the constitution. Second, it used the practice of civil disobedience. Third, the hunger strike of limited scale but unlimited time could be used in the future as an effective weapon against an indifferent regime. Fourth, it was not just the pursuit of economic rights that united the villagers; they were pursuing their political rights that were guaranteed by the law of the nation. Fifth, the initial success of the Taishi recall was due to the intersection of the small cohesive village with the society at large.[23]

There were outsiders in Taishi. One of them was Lü Banglie, a fired people's congress deputy from Hubei who was looking for a job in Guangdong. He heard of the recall in Taishi and went there to provide advice. Guo Feixiong and Yao Lifa were also there. It became a battleground where societal forces and government control clashed. Western reporters learned of the recall and also showed up. One, a reporter from the *Guardian* went to Taishi in a car with Lü Banglie. They were pulled out by a bunch of people of unknown identity. Lü Banglie was severely beaten. The reporter filed a story of Lü having been beaten to death. However, this account was incorrect—Lü was badly injured but survived.[24]

On September 18, Panyu District government held a briefing meeting, claiming that a small ring of thugs instigated the Taishi unlawful recall efforts. Due to the unlawful and disruptive behavior of the villagers, the government took action on September 12 to clear out the villagers who participated in the sit-in outside the villager committee office. At the same briefing, an official accused "outside organizations and financial corps of secretly funding the agitation."[25] A satire entitled "The Bush Administration Is Manipulating the Taishi Village Election" appeared in the famous Chinese social critique website www.cat898.com on September 20, 2005. Having learned of the Panyu official accusation that Western agents were involved in the Taishi recall, the author said he could certainly understand why evil Americans had chosen Taishi— Taishi is a village in Panyu; Panyu is a district in Guangzhou; Guangzhou is the capital city of Guangdong; Guangdong is a province of China. Taishi is located in the Pearl River Delta, a strategic location guarding China's southern gate. A Dongfeng missile deployed here could hit Australia; Australia is a good ally of Great Britain; Great Britain enjoys good relations with the United States. If one reverses the sequence, the control of Taishi by the United States will easily lead to the American control of China.[26]

In the same month, an international conference of lawyers was held in Beijing. Both Hu Jintao and Wen Jiabao met with foreign participants. Both talked about China's determination to pursue democratization in China. Hu talked about four democracies: democratic elections, democratic decision making, democratic management, and democratic supervision. Wen was more specific, indicating a few years after villagers managed to run their villages they would learn how to manage a township. The system would eventually move upward.[27]

On August 30, 2006, in an article that appeared in *Seeking Truth*, the mouthpiece of the party's theory apparatus, Sheng Huaren, secretary general of the Standing Committee of the NPC, made the warning of the "color revolution" official and linked it with China's own elections. According to Sheng,

"Internationally, the enemy from the West is intensifying its strategic scheme to Westernize and divide China. They make a big fuss on 'democracy' and 'human rights' and attempt to penetrate China through grassroots elections. These are new issues and new problems that are out there, unavoidable, that should not be neglected and must be dealt with utmost attention." He asked leaders at all levels to promote voters' participation and to prevent all outside interference. In section 6 of the article, Sheng specifically declared that no popular nomination of candidates for township/town magistrates would be tolerated. They must be nominated by the presidium of the township/town people's congress or by deputies freely associated. In the previous two rounds of elections, there were areas where township/town magistrates were popularly elected. Although they were attempted as democratic experiments, they violated the constitution and other relevant laws. In the upcoming elections, such practices should be strictly prohibited.[28]

With Sheng's article circulated as a mandatory order from the central government, all innovative practices ceased. A big chill descended and elections came and went, causing no domestic excitement or international attention. Programming and activities by international organizations, particularly those based in the United States were unilaterally terminated by their Chinese partners. There was the typical *waisong neijin* 外松内劲 (loose behavior on the outside and tight control from the inside) in China. This was best reflected by the trip memorandum written by John Thornton after his visit to China in late October 2006. Thornton reported that during a seventy-five-minute conversation with Wen Jiabao, he saw the looming emergence of "democracy with Chinese characteristics." In Wen's scheme, China's democracy has three important components: "elections, judicial independence, and supervision based on checks and balances." Thornton described Wen's vision as follows:

> He could foresee the direct elections currently held at the village level, if successful, gradually moving up to towns, counties, and even provinces. What happens beyond that was left unsaid. As for a judicial system riddled with corruption, Wen emphasized the urgent need for reform in order to assure the judiciary's "dignity, justice, and independence." He explained that the purpose of "supervision"—a commonly used term in China that is better translated as "ensuring accountability"—is to restrain official power: "Absolute power, without supervision, corrupts absolutely." Wen called for checks and balances within the Party itself and for greater government accountability to the people. In his view, the media and even the 110 million Internet users in China should also participate "as appropriate" in supervision of the government.[29]

Wen's description of the path of China's political reform seemed to be designed purely for foreign consumption. At the Sixteenth Party Congress, Jiang

Zemin referred to the four democracies as part of China's overall political reform efforts. He also said that expanding grassroots elections is fundamental to the development of socialist democracy in China. Toward the end of the section on political reform, Jiang talked about maintaining social stability.[30] Five years later, at the Seventeenth National Congress of the CCP, Hu Jintao spent more time talking about how democracy should be introduced but less on specifics. The most revealing paragraph is as follows:

In deepening political restructuring, we must keep to the correct political orientation. On the basis of ensuring the people's position as masters of the country, we will expand socialist democracy, build a socialist country under the rule of law and develop socialist political civilization to enhance the vitality of the Party and the state and arouse the initiative of the people. We must uphold the Party's role as the core of leadership in directing the overall situation and coordinating the efforts of all quarters, and improve its capacity for scientific, democratic and law-based governance to ensure that the Party leads the people in effectively governing the country. We must ensure that all power of the state belongs to the people, expand the citizens' orderly participation in political affairs at each level and in every field, and mobilize and organize the people as extensively as possible to manage state and social affairs as well as economic and cultural programs in accordance with the law.[31]

Hu did say more about grassroots democracy than Jiang Zemin but focused little on how China was going to move fully into a new phase of political reform.[32] There is a very dire lack of vision for political reform and no mention of using elections to deepen such reform. There was a section in Hu's report entitled "Comprehensively Carrying Forward the Great New Undertaking to Build the Party in a Spirit of Reform and Innovation." According to Hu, building up the party requires intraparty democracy and one of the methods recommended by him was to introduce a new personnel selection system. Hu said:

Adhering to the principle that the Party is in charge of cadre management, we will establish a scientific mechanism for selecting and appointing cadres on the basis of democracy, openness, competition and merit. We will standardize the cadre nomination system, perfect the cadre assessment system in accordance with the requirements of the Scientific Outlook on Development and a correct view on evaluating cadres' performances, and improve the procedures for open selection, competition for positions and multi-candidate election. We will expand democracy in the work related to cadres and make democratic recommendation and assessment more scientific and authentic. We must enforce stricter oversight over the whole process of selecting and appointing cadres.[33]

A year has passed since Hu's call for innovative measures to democratize the party. How much has happened? Is the CCP seriously pursuing opening leadership selection at various levels?

Democratization Has to Begin from the CCP:
From the Qingxian Model to the Guiyang Experiment

Qingxian is under Cangzhou City in Hebei Province. Since 2002, a series of governance and electoral experiments were introduced and selectively adopted. These innovative measures gradually became know as the Qingxian model. In the words of its former party secretary, Zhao Chaoying, the Qingxian model is made up of four components: restructuring village governance, enhancing party leadership, expanding democracy, and standardizing village governance in accordance with the law.[34] The current Qingxian model was, to a certain extent, coopted and remodeled to fit the party's requirement. Back when the Qingxian experiment was first noticed by the Ministry of Civil Affairs, it was largely seen as a way to resolve the growing tension between the villager committee and the party branch at the village level. Zhao Chaoying once summarized what he was trying to do as "let the Party be in charge of big issues and let the villager committee be responsible for concrete things." When asked to define "big issues" and "concrete things," Zhao said, "big issues" referred to recruiting members and member education and "concrete things" were related to village governance. Zhao's scheme of sidelining the party at the village level was quickly seen by the officials from the organization apparatus and they began to put tremendous pressure on him.[35]

If one peels away all the rhetoric regarding the Qingxian model and looks at its core, it is easy to see it is indeed a bold effort to subject the party to some sort of checks and balances in a way that will not offend the party. What Zhao Chaoying was trying to do was to restructure the party branch–villager committee relationship through adding a villager representative assembly (VRA). The VRA is not a new development in China's countryside. What is new in Qingxian is that the incumbent party branch secretary runs for the speaker position of the VRA as well as the chairperson of the villager committee. If the party secretary loses in the race, he or she will have to resign and a new party branch election will be held. To many scholars, the Qingxian model, if implemented nationwide, could possibly resolve the party branch–villager committee tension and turn village governance into something truly participatory and democratic. Others question the legality of the VRA since the Organic Law did not make it a legal entity at the village level. Zhao Chaoying himself also said there were three seemingly insurmountable challenges to the Qingxian model. First, there is no legal foundation for the VRA chairmanship. Second, there are not clearly defined VRA member electoral procedures and responsibilities. Third, there will be inevitable conflict between Qingxian regulations and national laws. Many doubt its usefulness in actual governance. They believe the party will never surrender its decision-making supremacy through chairing the VRA. However, Cao Yesong from the Central Party School sees unlimited significance to the Qingxian model. There are 345 villages in Qingxian and more than 600,000 villages in China. Cao believes that if this model could be applied to all villages there would be a vast system of accountability in place. If the system is to be applied at higher levels, it may lead to a new kind of democracy in China.[36] The Qingxian model began long before the Seventeenth Party Congress but it does fit into Hu's framework of intraparty democratization at the local level.

On May 28, 2008, the Party Committee of Guiyang Municipality made the decision to introduce a new method to "appoint" the next party secretaries for four county-level positions, in Xiaohe District, Huaxi District, Xifeng County, and Xiuwen County. On July 23, all four positions were filled after a very elaborate process, fascinating those who have been waiting for China to launch its political reform.[37] Li Jun, Guiyang party boss, said at the end of the Guiyang pilot that what happened in Guiyang was only a small test. Bigger and more difficult exams lie ahead. He thanked the eighty-one candidates who tried to win the four open offices and particularly commended the four final candidates who lost to their opponents during the last procedure, a vote among forty-eight members of the Municipal Party Committee.[38] During his June 30 mobilization speech, Li Jun mentioned the Tian Fengshan and Han Guizhi (both found guilty of corruption) case in Heilongjiang. He said of several hundred government officials involved in the case, none was chosen through open, transparent, and competitive procedures. "To let power operate under the sunshine is effective in preventing the abuse of and mistaken use of power."[39]

The Guiyang experiment was called *gongtui jinggang* 公推竞岗, or open nomination and competitive selection. After the decision to open the process, a total of eighty-two candidates meeting the initial requirements (a candidate must be at the rank of deputy county magistrate or deputy party secretary position) were nominated or self-nominated. An initial screening disqualified one candidate. The second procedure was to trim eighty-one candidates to five per county through a small-scale primary. There were 275 electors. Except 19 that were ordinary party members, the rest were all movers and shakers in the Guiyang officialdom: leading officials from the Municipal Party Committee, municipal government, municipal people's congress and municipal political consultative conference, and delegates to the national and provincial party congresses. It is not clear how these electors got to know candidates or if they were told to vote for a particular set of candidates. After the votes were processed, the pool was trimmed to twenty candidates.[40]

The third phase was known as "getting to know the place." Each candidate was assigned a district and county and went to talk to the officials working in that district or county for three days. They would then write a governance report in two days and submit it to the Gongtui Jinggang Leadership Commission for evaluation. Each report would receive a score to be added to the total points. On July 14, all twenty candidates faced a nine-member panel and the same group of electors to defend their governance reports. To avoid any potential conflict of interest, all nine members came from outside Guiyang. One of the members was from the Organization Department of the CCP Central Committee. The defense was televised and transmitted live through the Guiyang television network and the Internet. Following their presentation, the electors would vote again (a procedure that was not made clear by media reports).

On July 15, all candidates took a leadership capability test on the computer. There were twenty-five multiple-choice questions designed by the CCP Organization Committee. The weight for the five procedures was determined to be 2:2:2:3:1 respectively. Based on the final scoring, the top two vote getters for each position became the final candidates and the other three were dropped from the roster. On July 23, the final eight candidates each delivered a campaign speech to the forty-eight members of the Municipal Party Committee. Although the point difference between the final two candidates for each position was quite small, the vote outcome in four races was shockingly lopsided. In each of the appointments, the winner won by a huge percentage of the vote. In Xiaohe, 39:9; in Huaxi, 42:6; in Xiuwen, 46:2; and in Xifeng, 47:1. It is hard to believe that the final two candidates for each appointment were so far apart from each other, but we are not certain if this outcome is the result of the Organization Department officials manipulating the committee members' votes.[41]

The Guiyang experiment triggered a flurry of media reports in China, and in Guiyang, a winner told the reporter from *Liaowang*, the new greeting is "Have you studied today?" This is a reference to the fact that if one does not have enough knowledge there is no way for him or her to win in the race to be promoted. The same winner also said, "We have made our pledges in front of a big audience through television. We will be scolded if we do not deliver."[42] *Study Times*, a publication of the Central Party School, ran an article entitled "A Political Science Interpretation of Open Nomination and Open Election." According to the author, similar elections were also conducted in Nanjing but the open positions were for the government, not for the party. Both the Nanjing model and the Guiyang model reflect the supremacy of the CCP in leadership and governing in that the final procedure is the vote by the members of the Municipal Party Committee. This approach does not contradict the current ironclad arrangement of the party making all personnel decisions, but creates a huge space for meaningful democracy within the party to flourish. Although the party controls the entirety of the procedures, it cannot overtly dictate and manipulate the final outcome. This is what democracy is all about. It transforms rule by men into rule by procedures.[43]

Reform via Elections a Dead End

This review of what happened in the past decade concerning elections leads us to a few tentative conclusions:

1. Competitive village elections created a groundswell and led many reform-minded officials to try to adopt similar measures into the election of officials at higher levels of the government. If the top leadership of the CCP had vision and courage, following the bold Buyun direct election in 1998, they could have done what Deng Xiaoping, Wan Li, Hu Yaobang, and Zhao Ziyang did after they saw the Xiaogang experiment and moved China to a new path of political reform. Not only did top leaders back away from it, officials at the lower level, who may see competitive elections as a threat to their comfortable positions, managed to convince them it was unconstitutional and illegal.

2. The initial prediction that China had made a plan to begin direct and competitive elections at the bottom and slowly move elections up the chain was wrong. What Peng Zhen said in the mid-1980s and what Wen Jiabao has repeated more recently are not backed up by any tangible plan. If what Peng Zhen said was meant to convince suspicious members of the Standing Committee of the NPC to approve the Organic Law on a provisional basis, Wen made similar remarks only to please Western ears. Wen may be sincere in drawing the trajectory but we have to see the leadership as a whole produce a timetable and an action plan.

3. The fear of Western political penetration into China through grassroots elections did not begin with Hu Jintao and Wen Jiabao. As early as 2001, Jiang Zemin voiced the concern that Westerners' interest in village elections in China was probably underlined by an attempt to force China to adopt Western-style democracy wholesale.[44] Hu and Wen have an even deeper fear of such penetration because of what happened in Central Asian countries and the Bush administration's worldwide effort to promote democratization. The tragic consequence of this linkage is that by seeing a black hand behind genuine Chinese efforts at reform, the leadership is blind to the fact that Chinese people and many Chinese officials are reform oriented and want to promote competitive elections within the framework of the Chinese law. The anti-West argument also serves the need of many corrupt and incompetent officials who can avoid being held accountable by associating social agitation and political protests with Western conspiracies.

4. Village elections have completed their mission of maintaining social and political stability and helping the township/town government to collect

taxes and fees and implement policies of the central government. To continue to bill it as a useful and indispensible democratic exercise is a delay tactic to elevate such direct elections to higher levels. At the same time, it does not appear village elections are still high on the radar screen of the top leadership. There are much more urgent developments in rural areas that warrant their attention. Migration, declining income, breakdown of rural communities, deterioration of environment, and lack of health care and social security are factors that are turning China's countryside into a powder keg. None of these problems can be effectively dealt with unless there is choice and accountability at higher levels of the government.

5. Due to China's relative economic strength, its quick response to the Sichuan earthquake, and the successful 2008 Summer Olympic Games, there is a growing consensus among Chinese elite that there is indeed such a thing called Chinese exceptionalism, that is, China does not need to have a liberal democracy in order to provide public goods to the people and maintain government efficiency and effectiveness. There is no end to history and the Beijing Consensus is now a shining beacon. The party chief of the Beijing Daily Corps wrote in an article that Western-style elections are all about money. High cost has turned elections into caged birds. Since the 1980s, China has slowly built an organically cohesive democratic system buttressed by three pillars: the supremacy of the CCP, the rule of law, and allowing Chinese people to be their own masters through representation at different levels of the government.[45]

6. It is also wrong to say that China will be at a total standstill regarding democratization. China will collapse one way or the other if it does not adopt measures to curtail corruption, reduce popular anger, enhance its legitimacy, and make people feel happy about life and politics. Nationalism can only fill these voids for a certain period of time. Heavy-handedness can control a certain number of people. Neither can work all the time on all the people. No measures are as effective and as fast as open and transparent election or selection of government and party leaders. Given what we know now, without first resolving the issue of party supremacy it is hard to make elections at any level meaningful. In this context, both the Qingxian model and the Guiyang experiment seem to be a good and feasible way to move forward. The Qingxian model does not appear to have any legal foundation and its applicability is also questionable. With Zhao Chaoying's recent transfer, the model seems to have collapsed already. The Guiyang experiment in the wake of the Weng'an riot seems to be more significant and necessary. The best

way is to figure out problems, standardize procedures, and selectively adopt the system in multiple places throughout the country.

7. Following intraparty democratization, which may take a decade or more to accomplish, it will then be time to make direct elections of township/town people's congress deputy elections open, competitive, and transparent. China will be much more democratic if people's congress deputies can elect government officials at the same levels and people's congress deputies to higher levels. Though China does not need to use Western-style democracy, China needs to trust her people and allow them to elect whom they are entitled to elect in accordance with the law. The omnipotent party must not continue to retreat, prepare, and train its candidates, and then manipulate and control the electoral procedures.

10

Ideology

Its Role in Reform and Opening

Ren Jiantao

C HINA'S REFORM AND OPENING UP OVER the past thirty years were initiated under an atmosphere dominated by the ideology of Leninism and Stalinism.[1] Between 1949 and 1978 the typical Chinese form of Leninism and Stalinism—Mao Zedong Thought—absolutely dominated China's social and political life.[2] At the end of 1978, at the Third Plenary Session of the Eleventh Central Committee, there was a reconsideration of the circumstances of China's sociopolitical life as constricted by Mao Zedong Thought, and thus the beginnings of China's startling journey of reform and opening up.[3] However, in the not overly long course of reform and opening up, reform ideology and traditional revolutionary ideology increasingly reflect the tense circumstance of direct confrontation. Because of this, China's reform and opening have exhibited a twisting path of progress and reversal. Looking to the future, it is uncertain what type of impact ideology will have on China's deep reform.

The Utilitarian Nature of Reform Ideology

In order to understand the function of ideology in reform and opening up, it is necessary to describe briefly the general situation of ideology prior to reform. In ideological terms 1949–1976 was a period in which China absolutely chose Stalinism, and the form that Stalinism took in practice was Leninism. The Marxist image of the utopic ideal society took another step forward in China and became transformed into an ideology of pursuing comprehensive control of state power. Lenin's plan to have comprehensive control over a state's resources made the modern nation-state generate a substitute form of the state, namely, the party-state. In the party-state not only was the goal of the state continuously subordinated to the goals of the party, the party that occupied the system of state power also sought to dominate all spiritual, political, economic, cultural, and daily aspects of life in the country. In addition, Lenin believed that the ideology of a political party had the function of bringing into full play the ideology of the state. This implied that the party's ideology, while pursuing its own survival, would not tolerate any alien ideologies, including ideologies of reform. Only when the ideology of the political party could not sustain itself and could only draw on the resources of other modern ideologies to uphold the legitimacy of its own ideology would the ideology of the political party loosen up. This loosening, then, became the motive force and symbol of the reform of the Leninist state.[4] In 1976, after Mao Zedong died, the successor he had personally chosen, whether from the perspective of his psychological leanings or his political adaptability, naturally chose to maintain the political circumstances that had already been established. This choice was manifested in ideological terms as the "two whatevers": "Whatever Chairman Mao decided we must resolutely uphold; whatever Chairman Mao instructed, we must follow without wavering."[5] The appearance of the two whatevers was the equivalent of announcing that it was impossible to adjust the state's development. It was not until the Chinese Communist Party (CCP) convened the Third Plenary Session of the Eleventh Central Committee in 1978 that the CCP could set to rights the Cultural Revolution, correct extreme leftism, and adopt rational development.

Beginning in 1978, China launched onto its contemporary journey of ideology. On the one hand, the traditional Leninist ideology continued to play the fundamental role of integrating the state's strength. On the other hand, reformist ideology, especially liberal economic and political functions began to take the stage. The overlapping functions of these two ideologies formed a unique combination: extreme leftist ideology and rightist ideology simultaneously acted on the state's fundamental policy choices. However, the pallor of the structure of reformist ideology led it from the beginning into the awkward position of being reliant on Leninism. Perhaps this is why some scholars say bluntly that China's market economy is not a form of a modern, regularized market economy but really takes the form of "market Leninism."[6]

The process by which reformist ideology came about was really not smooth. Even though Deng Xiaoping was the "general architect of reform and opening," he had no plan for reform and opening at the beginning. At first he was still conservative—his attitudes toward settling accounts with the Cultural Revolution, dealing with Mao's revolutionary legacy, and even with regard to the Tiananmen incident were all inclined toward avoidance. Even later when Chen Yun and Hu Yaobang were struggling over political leadership in the party, Deng finally forcefully advocated liberating thought. The CCP's inauguration of reform and opening up was precisely based on this sort of coincidence and had no blueprint.[7] Comprehensively promoting reform and opening up in the 1980s was really adopting a reformist experimental orientation of taking one step and then looking before taking another step—"crossing the river by feeling the stones." However, it was precisely the reform orientation that forced the rigid constraints of Leninist-Stalinist ideology to continuously loosen. Reform itself gradually replaced Leninist-Stalinist ideology to become the ideology integrating the state's force.

However, reform ideology was not a true modern ideology constructed on a basis of a complete philosophy. The utilitarian principal of "it doesn't matter whether the cat is black or white, the cat that catches the mouse is a good cat" already determined that it could not possibly establish a complete philosophical system. Because reform lacked the resources to prove that it was a legitimate ideology, it could not replace Leninist-Stalinist ideology; on the contrary, it still mistakenly sought to borrow Stalinist ideology to defend the real political measures of reform and opening up. This sort of an awkward circumstance meant that reform ideology could only adopt an attitude of avoidance with regard to ideological disputes, and it reflected as well the dilemma of a completely utilitarian ideology in the process of reform. This position was unfavorable to reform ideology, but when Deng Xiaoping restarted reform in his 1992 talks while inspecting the south the best he could do was to call for "not arguing." This condemned reform ideology to be weak and lacking in strength.

The Rebuilding of Revolutionary Ideology

Indeed, as stated above, China's ideology at the commencement of reform was ultraleftist revolutionary ideology—Leninist-Stalinist and its Chinese form, Mao Zedong Thought. In the thirty years in which China has been engaged in reform and opening up, the traditional ultraleftist form of revolutionary ideology (the "old left") has been replaced by a modern ultraleftist form (the "new left"), but both have continuously blocked reformist ideology from playing its role and have successfully constructed a "critical" ideology in this period that has had the function of resisting China's transition.[8]

The criticism of reform and opening coming from the Old Left's revolutionary ideology was extremely harsh. They believed that no matter how low the production efficiency is under the state ownership system, if there was any reform of state-owned property rights, then that was the same as falling into the chasm of capitalism. Because of this they took guaranteeing the socialist nature of reform as the sole criterion for judging whether or not to reform a given economic mechanism.[9] This sort of simple, politicized judgment was the fundamental train of thought in Chinese politics for the thirty years before reform and opening up. The Old Left also used political movements to continuously obstruct the deepening of reform. In 1983 they used the campaign against spiritual pollution to attack the idealistic reform spirit and to reorganize the ultraleft.[10] In 1986–1987 and again in 1989–1992, they used opposition to bourgeois liberalization to obstruct people from deepening the design of reform and pushing reform forward substantively. Particularly the antibourgeois liberalization movement of 1989 not only severely limited the continuation of reform, it also fiercely restricted the space that romantic reform had created in the 1980s, causing problems that urgently needed to be reformed to be stifled by political correctness.[11] In 1996, under the pull of ultraleftist ideology, the ideological struggle between public and private politicized the question of property rights and became an obstacle to property rights reform. In 2004–2006, the third settling of accounts with reform and opening up caused the social acceptance of reform to decline. From this we can see that the Old Left maintains a high level of awareness of anything that might affect the interests of the Chinese Communist Party in the least, and this leads people to refuse to take another step forward in reform.[12]

However, the Old Left's rejection of reformist themes has limited influence. This is closely related to their extremely ossified attitude in upholding the ultraleftist position and the fact that they are distanced from the discourse the contemporary age has chosen. In contrast, the New Left choice of a flexible political attitude has a much more intimate feel. Moreover, the New Left's harsh critiques of the leftover problems of the planned economy and the newly emerging problems of the market economy, as well as its use of peoples' nostalgic mood to link up with their sentiment toward the Cultural Revolution, all bring together those who are unsatisfied with reform or who have lost out in the course of reform.[13] The New Left also uses equality and justice as a moral appeal. They use ideals to inscribe a picture of a completely equal society that comport with the nationalistic mood of Chinese who want to resist Western values and system, and even more use a so-called democratic social system design to suggest their well-intentioned plans to resist autocracy. Because of this, there is no doubt that the New Left has the ability to incite society and influence the lower strata.

The relationship between the Old Left and the New Left is fairly complicated. The Old Left can be called the left with power because it is easy to see that they have the support of power holders behind them.[14] The New Left can be called the academic left that has no support from power holders. Most of them are academics and artists, and they primarily rely on the emotions of literature and art to denounce things.[15] There is really a gap between the power logic of the former and the literary thinking of the latter, but, despite this, the New Left and the Old Left indeed together create a mainstream trend of social thought and political trends that oppose modernization. The Old Left from within the centers of power resist the deepening of reform, continuously using the threat of the extinction of the party and state to bring together all those within the party who oppose reform. The New Left then uses ideological thought to start up a wave of opposition to reform and uses a complete theoretical system to establish a critical theory that seeks to overthrow the present order.[16] The New and Old Left are completely united in their nostalgia for socialist fundamentalism and revolutionary vistas. At the same time, they win over those people who have been frustrated in their daily lives and who lack the basic abilities to think about politics and therefore resist reform, and thereby form a social psychology with a substantial mass base that is opposed to reform. The social psychological resources that underlie reform are thus obviously undermined and eroded. This is the leftist ideological foundation that has made it difficult for modern China to generate a reformist consensus.

The Permeation Effect of Liberal Ideology

The New and Old Left have judged that reform and opening had already remade China as a liberal (*ziyou zhuyi* 自由主义) country.[17] This pronouncement caused the liberal direction of China's reforms to become the subject of far-ranging discussions. In form, China's economic market-oriented reforms really do seem to share some of liberalism's profound respect for market economics. But in reality, the state's strong control over the economic structure means that these reforms are certainly not regularized market economic reforms, but are merely market activities under the control of the state. Any Chinese even without any modern economic sense can still recognize the state capitalism—all important market resources are completely controlled in the hands of the state. From this it can be seen that China can still not be considered a place in which a real market has appeared, one in which the state and market play an equal role in a national system of a market economy. As for being a liberal constitutional democracy, China still doesn't even have the form.

From the perspective of the political leadership's subjective intentions to manipulate state ideology, liberalism is certainly viewed by them as the opposition. However, they cannot help but recognize that mainstream liberal ideas are in some respects effective in curing the "Chinese disease." Liberalism is certainly something that the architects of China's reform and opening up could not reject completely, particularly the so-called liberal orientation in the economic arena has always caught people's eye. Despite this, liberalism must always play its role "under the stage" of Chinese politics; on the stage it is continuously attacked and criticized. Because of this, those who express the state's stance on ideology have never given liberal ideology any political space. Not only do state leaders criticize and reject contemporary mainstream ideologies, scholars who think that they represent the state's ideology carry out political criticism of liberal ideology.[18] But even though it is like this, the critics all recognize that neoliberalism is something that China needs to use for reference. This perhaps reveals that the China that is trying to make the transition to a modern state needs to take a relaxed attitude toward liberalism.

The situation of liberalism is somewhat more favorable among the people than it is in official circles. On the one hand, this is related to the relaxed attitude officials take toward liberal ideology, while, on the other hand, it is because society has imported and discussed liberalism.[19] Since 1998, when scholars raised the idea that "liberalism floats to the top of the water," the theory of Chinese liberalism finally began to take off.[20] The publication of *Res Publica* provided a rather stable platform for liberal scholars. However, expressions of liberalism were still crippled. This was primarily because scholars discussing liberalism had serious problems in their understanding of liberalism. This was especially the case with regard to the artificial separation of "economic liberalism" and "political liberalism," which further tore apart the extremely rare spiritual resources behind liberalism, although those spiritual resources cannot themselves openly prove the legitimacy of liberalism. In Western society no matter whether John Locke or Adam Smith in classic liberalism's founding age or neoliberals like Friedrich von Hayek and John Rawls—all took both economics and politics as something liberalism addressed in common. This reflected the theoretical route demanded by the thorough-going and comprehensive nature of liberalism. However, scholars who addressed liberalism in Chinese, especially those who advocated so-called political liberalism, under the conditions of recognizing the New Left's criticism that economic liberalism had brought about polarization in China, sought to draw a clear distinction between political liberalism and economic liberalism. This is a manifestation of the immaturity of Chinese liberalism.

If one judges that China has already successfully established a market economy governed by law and a constitutional democratic state, then that is completely rash. If you judge that in the last thirty years China has practiced an extremely weak form of liberal ideology, then even that is at variance with reality. The stubbornness of China's state ideology far exceeds the imagination of most people. At the same time that it is constantly changing the circumstances of its own existence, it is continuously concentrating the most important resources in support of state ideology. Not only does this deprive other modern ideologies of the basic resources needed to mature, it also makes it completely impossible for other ideologies to compete with state ideology. Because of this, to imagine that there is an intuitive relationship between China's reform and opening up and liberalism is something that only an extremely imaginative scholar could do.

Remaking Ideology with "Core Values"

Given that there is no fundamental change in the state structure, the evolution of China's ideology over the thirty years of reform and opening shows that there is no way to replace the leading position of the existing state ideology; nevertheless, there are three challenges that force the articulators of China's state ideology to continuously change the way in which state ideology is explained and to incrementally drop some of the classical propositions of Leninism-Stalinism and gradually establish "socialism with Chinese characteristics."

The first challenge is the effective development of the economy. This challenge has remade the rigid state planned economy into a so-called socialist market economy, which is composed of socialist state power and a market economic form, and which has released enormous economic vitality. But whether Marxist ideology can digest the new economic structure of the market economy is absolutely something that will continue to be tested by China's reform and opening. The second challenge is that of the state's effective governance. First, the CCP must change from a revolutionary party into a ruling party, but this is not an easy matter. Mao Zedong's "theory of continuous revolution under the dictatorship of the proletariat" guided the Cultural Revolution. The ten years of the Cultural Revolution obviously eroded the reputation of CCP rule, and there was no other choice in 1978 but to try changing Mao Zedong's rigid war thinking toward thinking in terms of a ruling party. However, the revolutionary ideals of a revolutionary party not only made it a stranger to the policies necessary for a state to rule but even to reject such policies in their hearts. Moreover, changing the unique political habits of a political party that had grown to enjoy state power was even more difficult. In addition, because it had fallen into the experience of war from which it could not rescue itself, the Chinese government for a long time relied on using the state structure to rule the country and would not flinch from paying any price to realize its ruling objectives. In the Cultural Revolution and before, to consolidate the ruling position of the CCP, and to concentrate all power, material, and loyalty to "prepare for war, prepare for natural disasters, and [serve] the people" reflected the special characteristics of a wartime administration under extraordinary circumstances. Only when this type of structure was on the edge of bankruptcy could reform be initiated. How to establish limited and effective government became a difficult governmental and administrative question in the course of reform and opening. From 1978 until now, people remain obviously unsatisfied with the way this task has been completed.

The third challenge is that of the ideological battle over state identity. As the Leninist-Stalinist state ideology of China has been challenged and has been shaken by economic reform, a wide variety of ideologies have mounted the stage and become a live drama. Since 1978, democracy, constitutionalism, nationalism, statism, conservatism, liberalism, and feminism have all stirred commotion in Chinese society. At present, Chinese ideology is generally composed of the three parts of New Left, liberalism, and conservatism. These three types of ideology have gradually received the support of fixed groups, and have raised a basket of policies that lie outside of Marxism for solving China's problems. This, no doubt, increases the sense of crisis on the part of those trying to build China's state ideology.

Sensing the urgency of the need for constructing a state ideology, the ruling CCP in the past three years has clearly accelerated steps toward rebuilding party and state ideology. In 2006, the CCP raised the issue of building socialist core values. This not only implied that the absence of core values had already led to a crisis in the state's rule, but also that it still remained to be determined what values could become state values. A question that had incomparable clarity prior to reform and opening up had now become foggy, and the debate over state core values became ever more heated. This debate not only thoroughly demolished the reform consensus, it also raised sharply the issue of leadership authority over state ideology, which then completely politicized the question of constructing state ideology. Responding to this, the ruling CCP could only handle the matter by putting forth the even murkier idea of building a socialist harmonious society, but there was obviously a huge gap between the exposure of contradictions and the goal during the transition period.

In 2007, the Seventeenth Party Congress tried to escape from this dilemma. On the one hand, the CCP diluted the decisive position of Marxism-Leninism and Mao Zedong Thought, adopting a position of further rejecting ossified party-state ideology. On the other hand, it clearly raised "theoretical system of socialism with Chinese characteristics" as the leading thought for China's contemporary development. The hidden intention to replace the leading ideology and the cool treatment of Mao Zedong Thought are two interrelated aspects.[21] There was one further aspect, namely, the Congress defined the content of socialism with Chinese characteristics as "continuing to liberate thought, resolutely upholding reform and opening up, promoting sustainable development, and advancing social harmony," which has strengthened the legitimacy and justness of reform ideology itself. However, this slogan contained many possibilities and so has not calmed the debates over state ideology. Thus, the debate over universal values broke out in 2007 and 2008.

Premier Wen Jiabao's expressions toward ideology are really worth paying attention to. In one essay, he strongly pointed out: "Science, democracy, law, freedom, human rights are not the sole possession of capitalism, but are the result of a common pursuit of values through a long historical process common and the civilizational products produced [by mankind] in common.... The objective existence of a pluralistic world culture is not determined by the subjective views of any people. It is precisely this common existence of many types of culture, and their interaction and integration, that has promoted the progress of humankind. We must recognize the multiplicity of world cultures, and different cultures must not exhibit prejudice, enmity, or rejection [of each other] but must respect each other and learn from each other, they should draw on the strengths of others to make up for their own deficiencies, and work together to form a harmonious and varied human civilization."[22] This statement can be said to be the clearest expression of the CCP leadership's recognition of universal values, and it is also an expression of the CCP leadership's perception that state ideology cannot follow the road of exceptionalism. However, for the CCP—this ruling party that has not yet been able to say farewell to the way of thinking of a revolutionary party—it is not easy to escape from the position of Marxist ideology being so high above everything. Chen Kuiyuan, who is president of the Chinese Academy of Social Sciences (CASS), which the CCP has designated as its think tank, carried out a political criticism of universal values that spared no feelings. He argued, "In the past Christianity touted its values as universal values; now Western discourse loudly proclaims that 'democracy,' 'human rights,' the free market, and so forth are universal values. China, too, has some people who follow [the West] like a shadow and boast about converging on 'universal values.' We research important, practical questions that affect the party's line, orientation, and policies. On such important theoretical and strategic issues, we must be clear headed."[23] The political coloration of this expression is obvious.

In order to give space to reformist ideology and to calm the debates within the party over universal values, Hu Jintao, in his "Talk Commemorating the Thirtieth Anniversary of the Third Plenary Session of the Eleventh Central Committee" on December 19, 2008, emphasized the "three noes" ("no shaking, no laxness, and no deviating") very clearly. The three noes are a double-edged sword: they can cut against the attacks of dogmatic Leninism-Stalinism on utilitarian reformist ideology, and they can cut against those designing a Chinese constitutional, democratic polity. In general, however, its goal is to quiet the interference that ideological debates cause the CCP's leadership of reform and opening.

From this it can be seen that the difficulty of constructing China's state ideology and the future of China's reform and opening up are bound tightly together. The successful transformation of the state's ideology has already been combined with the modernization of the state. But has the difficult dilemma of transforming state ideology over the past thirty years already clearly predicted the difficulty in transforming the state's modernization? We are still searching for the answer.

IV

FOUR: SYSTEMIC CONSTRAINTS

11

Central-Local Relations

The Power to Dominate

Yongnian Zheng

Defining Central-Local Relations

CHINA DOES NOT HAVE A FEDERALIST SYSTEM of government—it has neither the constitutional division of power among different levels of government nor the separation of power within the branches of government. Nevertheless, with deepening reform and openness, China's political system in terms of central-local relations is functioning more and more on federalist lines. This chapter defines China's existing political system as de facto federalism. In my earlier works on China's central-local relations,[1] I defined de facto federalism as follows:

A relatively institutionalized pattern which involves an explicit or implicit bargain between the center and the provinces, allowing the provinces to receive certain institutionalized or *ad hoc* benefits in return for guarantees by provincial officials that they will behave in certain ways on behalf of the center.

More concretely, China's central-local relationship is defined as de facto federalism because it satisfies the following conditions:

1. A hierarchical political system in which the activities of government are divided between the provinces and the center in such a way that each level of government makes final decisions in certain fields.
2. Intergovernmental decentralization is institutionalized to such a degree that it is increasingly becoming difficult, if not impossible, for the cen-

tral government to unilaterally impose its will on the provinces and alter the distribution of authority between levels of government.

3. The provinces have primary responsibility over the economy and, to some extent, politics within their jurisdictions.

In China's system of central-local relations, power is divided between the central government and the provinces. Some areas such as foreign policy, national defense, and population planning are controlled exclusively by the central government, and it is very difficult for the local governments to have a say in the formulation of policy in these fields. Notwithstanding, some matters are exclusively dictated by the local governments, such as local public security, road construction, and school building. Most economic matters are exclusively handled by the local governments while others are shared by the central government and the provinces, such as policies that are made by the central government but implemented by the local governments. The central government also has to consult local governments in the formulation of certain policies.

De facto federalism was a product of intergovernmental decentralization. The de facto institutional arrangement has greatly contributed to China's high economic performance.[2] However, it has also become a major institu-

TABLE 11.1
Two Stages of Decentralization

Decentralization	Stage I Intergovernmental	Stage II State-Society (enterprise)
Economic	Central-Local	State-Enterprises
	Outcomes: • Local or regional property rights • Jurisdictional competition • Limited marketization • Local intervention • Local protectionism, etc.	Outcomes: • Private property rights • Privatization • Marketization • Competition among individual enterprises • Less or no government intervention, etc.
Political	Central-Local	State-Society
	Outcomes: • Local democracy • Perforated sovereignty and de facto federalism • Limited individual rights, etc. • Governmental NGOs	Outcomes: • Democratization • Popular sovereignty and individual rights • Political participation • NGOs and civil society, etc.

Source: Compiled by the author.

tional barrier for meaningful nationwide reforms that have implications for both the central government and the provinces. The central government tends to be increasingly defensive politically in economic regions, recentralizing many aspects of power. While all recentralization measures have enabled the central government to sustain its domination over the provinces, they have actually discouraged changes at the provincial level. Although some provinces are economically powerful, their political power has been greatly constrained by these recentralization measures. Consequently, rich provinces are economically powerful enough to resist central policy initiatives while poor ones are economically too weak to implement central policy initiatives. They are also politically too weak to initiate any meaningful reforms within the provinces.

This chapter explains how such an institutional arrangement of central-local relationship has increasingly constrained China's reform process. First, it will briefly review the evolution of central-local relations and discuss how the transition from intergovernmental decentralization to intergovernmental recentralization has taken place. Second, it will use two cases to show how such a central-local relationship has constrained China's reforms. And finally, the chapter will draw some policy implications.

Intergovernmental Decentralization and High Economic Performance

In the era of reform and openness, China's de facto federalism has been driven by intergovernmental decentralization. Decentralization has been widely used as a reform strategy by political leaders in communist and postcommunist states to resolve economic and political problems resulting from overcentralization in the old planning economy. Different ways of decentralization lead to rather different outcomes. Table 11.1 outlines two main types of decentralization and four major dimensions of decentralization. The Chinese leadership focused on intergovernmental decentralization. I will argue that while intergovernmental decentralization has led to high economic performance, the central government will have to shift its focus from intergovernmental decentralization to state-society decentralization to increase its capacity to enforce meaningful reforms in the provinces and in central-local relations.

Intergovernmental Economic Decentralization

Although China's reforms are said to be market-oriented, there have been few serious attempts at providing the central features of private markets, or a system of securing private property rights. Commercial law and an independent court system are virtually nonexistent. So, how did China achieve high economic performance without any of these factors assumed to be essential for economic growth elsewhere? This is largely due to what I call de facto federalism, or market-persevering federalism, as suggested by Montinola, Qian, Weingast, and others.[3] Central to de facto federalism and market-persevering federalism is intergovernmental decentralization.

After China began its economic reform in 1979 and before the recentralization efforts in the mid-1990s, the leadership under Deng Xiaoping repeatedly emphasized devolution of authority from the central to local governments. Intergovernmental decentralization provided an important set of limits on the behavior of all levels of government, which was in favor of economic growth. As Montinola, Qian, and Weingast point out, "By design, decentralization directly limits the central government's control over the economy. It also induces competition among local governments, serving both to constrain their behavior and to provide them with a range of positive incentives to foster local economic prosperity."[4] Intergovernmental decentralization rules out the possibility of a single government monopolizing control over the economy. "If many regions can choose policies for themselves, all can compare the results, including those which do not wish to initiate reform policies."[5]

Intergovernmental decentralization also provides great market incentives. Efficient markets require two related sets of initiatives for credible commitment by the state—"positive" market incentives that reward economic success, and "negative" market incentives that punish economic failure. According to Qian et al., the two main features of China's political economic system—decentralization of information and authority and interjurisdiction competition—provide credible commitment to securing economic rights and preserving markets. During the process of economic reform, China's central government deliberately limited its access to certain information in order to prevent the center from repeating the pernicious behavior of the previous reform period. For instance, the center allowed local governments to maintain various "extrabudget" and "off-budget" accounts. Limited knowledge of these budgets ensured that the central government could not tax them. This in turn encouraged local governments to generate prosperity and revenue.

The effect of decentralized allocation of information and authority in achieving credible commitment helps to explain why many local government–owned enterprises, such as local township and village enterprises (TVEs), perform better than state-owned ones. These local government–owned enterprises have a different governance structure from state-owned enterprises (SOEs) and thus face better positive and negative incentives. By fully controlling the assets of TVEs, the local governments have access to information not available to the central government, and are thus able to resist state revenue predation in a credible way.

Competition among jurisdictions also forces local governments to represent citizen interests and to preserve markets. Jurisdictional competition among local governments increases efficiency through sorting and matching. It also serves as a disciplinary device to punish inappropriate market intervention by lower government officials. It further helps limit the government's predatory behavior. Mobile resources quickly flee jurisdictions that practice inappropriate behavior. Competition for mobile sources of revenue prevents local political leaders from imposing debilitating taxes or regulations.

Intergovernmental Political Decentralization

Unlike other communist political institutions, China's political system is flexible, thus offering opportunities for policy innovation. Top leaders in China's political hierarchy have not, as is commonly assumed, always dictated economic decisions. Rather, provincial officials have had an important say in decision making at the central level.

Intergovernmental decentralization has produced what Susan Shirk called "reciprocal accountability,"[6] a type of power relationship between top leaders and other Chinese Communist Party (CCP) cadres. According to Shirk,

> The relationship between party leaders and subordinate officials is not a pure hierarchy: according to the party rules, the Central Committee has the authority to choose party leaders, and the Central Committee consists of party, government, and military officials appointed by party leaders. The leaders appoint the officials and the officials in the Central Committee choose (or at least ratify the choice of) the leaders. Government officials are both the agents and the constituents of central leaders; local officials are both the agents and the constituents of central leaders. Officials hold their positions at the pleasure of the party leadership, but party leaders hold their positions at the pleasure of the officials in the selectorate (e,g., the Central Committee). The lines of accountability run in both directions, turning a hierarchical relationship into one of "reciprocal accountability."[7]

Given the fact that officials from the provinces (e.g., provincial party secretaries and governors) are the largest bloc in the selectorate, the relationship between the center and the provinces is more reciprocally accountable than any other types of relations in China's political system. The relationship of "reciprocal accountability" matters for China's economic performance. It helps the formation of the reform coalition between the central reformist leadership and local governments. On the one hand, since provincial officials seek to be promoted in the Chinese political hierarchy, the central authorities could "play to the provinces" to gain the political support of provincial officials by providing them with political incentives through the appointment system or the central *nomenklatura*. Playing to the provinces became an important strategy of the reformist leadership to mobilize local support for the reforms. On the other hand, provincial officials could also "play to the center" because they form the majority of the selectorate and their votes are important to any top leader's political legitimacy. Once the provincial representatives in the Central Committee put the weight of the party behind the reforms, they are capable of forcing the central leadership into implementing economic reforms in favor of local economic growth. By playing to the center, provincial officials were able to maintain the reform momentum in favor of local growth.

The Centralized Political Structure

Despite decentralization elements in intergovernmental relations, the centralized structure is maintained. This structure also matters for high economic performance since it helps overcome resistance and opposition from the administrative hierarchy itself. Compared to Russia, China's political system has been able to exploit the "positive" effects of decentralization while overcoming the "negative" effects. An obvious example is that the local governments in China have actively contributed to the growth of new firms, while the local governments in Russia have typically stood in the way.

While China's central-local institutional arrangements endow local governments with considerable operational autonomy, local officials are agents of the central government (the principal). Chinese central authorities have retained a firm grip over the vital aspects of personnel allocation such as selection, promotion, and dismissal. According to Yasheng Huang, two institutional factors have contributed to this. First, the party's principle of management stresses ideological conformity and gives the CCP dominant procedural control over appointment decisions. Second, cadre management is centralized. Though considerable changes have taken place in the cadre management system, the reach of the center is both extensive and deep. Control over personnel allocation is the ultimate trump card that the center wields over the provinces. It is a fundamental constraint faced by all Chinese local officials.[8]

According to Olivier Blanchard and Andrei Shleifer, this type of centralized structure is a precondition for the transition to succeed.[9] While neoclassical political economy literature tends to focus on market competition in the rewarding of "good" behavior and punishing of the "bad" behavior, the market mechanism alone is not enough to explain China's transition from a planned economy to a market one. China's transition has taken place under the tight control of the CCP. The central government has been in a strong position either to reward or punish local administrations. By contrast, Russia's transition came with the emergence of a partly dysfunctional democracy. The Chinese central government has been strong enough to neither impose its views, nor set clear rules on the sharing of the proceeds of growth. As a result, local governments have encountered few disincentives either to resist or rein in competition for rents.

The CCP has utilized the power to appoint and fire governors to support governors whose regions have performed well economically, and to discipline those who have failed to follow its economic policies. Without such a structure, the incentives to pursue regionalist policies are too high, a tendency that cannot be eliminated solely through clever economic and fiscal arrangements. This is evident in Russia's case, where governors are elected, not appointed. As a result, the ability of the central government to reward or penalize governors through administrative and electoral support has been limited.

Intergovernmental Decentralization and Its Consequences

Intergovernmental decentralization has been very successful in achieving high economic performance, but this comes with costs and contradictions within the administrative hierarchy. Although the centralized structure remains, the cost of maintaining this structure becomes increasingly high. Even though rapid intergovernmental decentralization did not lead to the breakup of China as it did with the Soviet Union, localism or regionalism often became uncontrollable and posed increasingly serious challenges to the central power.

Under intergovernmental decentralization, economic power shifted from the central state to local governments at different levels. For example, central revenue shrunk from 40.5 percent of the total revenue in 1984 to 22 percent in 1994 while central expenditure declined from 52.5 percent to 28.3 percent during the same period (figure 11.1). With their economic power, the provinces began to resist new fiscal policies initiated by the central government. When the central government wants to increase its taxes, resistance from the rich provinces has been strong.

Rapid economic decentralization also widened the income gap among provinces and regions. In coastal areas such as Guangdong, Zhejiang, Jiangsu, and Shandong, local officials have developed very strong nonstate sectors including collectives, private economies, and joint ventures, which are very profitable and beyond the control of the central government. In inland provinces, owing to various factors such as the lack of financial resources and skilled personnel, local governments have difficulty pushing local growth.

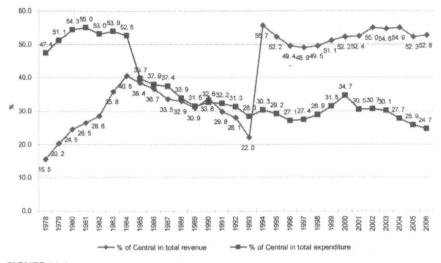

FIGURE 11.1
Central Government in Total Revenue and Expenditure (percentage). Source: *China Statistical Yearbook,* various years.

Consequently, some provincial governments achieved a high capacity to lead local development and improve local residents' living standards, while others did not. Due to an increase in local diversity, the central government finds it difficult to implement unified policies to lead and constrain local governments while local officials could easily nullify central policies.

The decline of central power prevented the central government from coordinating local economic activities effectively. Rich provinces were reluctant to cooperate with one another when they could plan local development independently. Poor and rich provinces were also reluctant to cooperate. Besides the presence of a similar industrial structure, the psychology of being victimized by rich provinces among the local officials in poor provinces was also important. The lack of coordination in regional development on the part of the central government is the key factor driving widening income disparities among regions.

It is important to note that economic decentralization from the very beginning was accompanied and indeed facilitated by China's globalization. These two developments resulted in a relatively greater increase in interdependence between the Chinese provinces and the outside world, and a surprising decrease in interprovincial interdependence. According to a study by the World Bank, as of the early 1990s, internal trade as a percentage of GDP among the Chinese provinces was 22 percent, which was lower than the then European Community's 28 percent and the 27 percent among the republics of the former Soviet Union. The World Bank thus warned that individual provinces had the tendency to behave like independent countries, increasing external (overseas) trade and reducing trade flows with each other.[10]

This trend led to the development of a discourse on recentralization that emphasized the importance of state capacity in regulating the national economy and maintaining the country as a united state. Scholars such as Wang Shaoguang and many others presented strong arguments in favor of recentralization. These scholars concentrated on how economic decentralization had weakened central power. For example, the fear of Wang Shaoguang and Hu Angang of a possible breakdown of the Chinese nation-state was supported by their comparison of China with other former communist states, especially former Yugoslavia.[11] Like many others, they believed that radical intergovernmental decentralization had become a major barrier to the formation of an integrated national market economy. They also argued that a highly centralized state was not necessarily totalitarian or authoritarian. Instead, to build a strong democratic China, the country had to have a centralized state. Wang and Hu published their coauthored book on state capacity (in terms of central fiscal power) in 1994.[12] The book was widely circulated in the academic circles and among government officials. In the same year, the central government started to initiate a recentralization movement by implementing a new taxation system called the tax-division system. The Wang-Hu report undoubtedly justified the efforts of the central government in recentralizing the country's fiscal power.

Selective Recentralization

Around the mid-1990s, the Chinese leadership began its recentralization efforts. Recentralization does not mean that the leadership intends to reverse the reform process and go back to the old system. What the leadership did was to selectively recentralize certain aspects of power, powers that were vital to the survival of the administrative hierarchy. In the economic realm, selective centralization was initially concentrated on two major reforms—taxation reform and central banking system reform. Since the early 2000s, recentralization has taken place in a wider range of policy areas such as environment, consumer/product safety, labor, land, and so on, as the central government began to make greater attempts at establishing an effective regulatory frame.

Taxation Reform

In 1994, the central government began to implement a new taxation system, a tax-division system or a federal-style taxation system. Before this system, the center did not have its own institutions to collect taxes. All taxes from the provinces were collected by provincial governments first before they were divided between the center and the individual provinces through bargaining.

With the reformed taxation system, taxes are divided into three categories—central, local, and shared. Central taxes would go to the central coffer, local taxes would go to local budgets, and shared taxes would be divided between the center and the provinces according to previously established agreements. Moreover, tax administration is centralized. Instead of authorizing local tax offices to collect virtually all the taxes, the center now collects taxes through its own institutions independent of the provinces, meaning that the center has established its own revenue collection agency—the national tax service. The new system also recognizes independent provincial power, that is, provincial authorities and lower governments can collect several types of taxes without interference from above. There are now two parallel and independent systems for tax administration—a national system for central taxes and a local one for local taxes. Shared taxes were collected by the central government first, and then divided between the center and the provinces.[13]

These institutional changes shifted fiscal power from the provinces to the center. Total government revenue has increased quite dramatically as a result. The proportion of central collection has increased from lower than 30 percent to around 50 percent after the implementation of this reform (see figure 11.1). If the locally collected revenues that local governments are obligated to remit to the central coffer are included, the central government's share would constitute about two-thirds of total government revenue. Since most revenues are now collected and redistributed by the center, the fiscal dependence of the provinces on the central government has increased substantially. Before the taxation reform, the central government had to rely heavily on coastal provinces for revenue contribution. The reform has reversed this trend.[14]

Central Banking System Reform

Similar efforts have been made to reform the central banking system. Before the reform, China's central banking system was highly decentralized. The central bank, People's Bank, had branches in every province. Local branches were often exposed to the political influence of local governments since the personnel of local branches were appointed and their welfare provided for by the local governments. This frequently led to local branches ignoring orders from the central bank and subordinating themselves to local influences. While local branches of the central bank often became an effective instrument for local governments to promote local economic growth, rapid local growth was achieved at the expense of the stability of the national economy. The decentralized central banking system eventually led to the crisis of macroeconomic management after Deng's southern tour in 1992. After a new government with Zhu Rongji as China's new premier was established in 1998, the central government implemented a most daring measure to reform China's financial system: all provincial branches of the central bank were eliminated and nine cross-provincial or regional branches established. This reform has made local interferences into the central banking system impossible.[15]

Political Recentralization

Most important are efforts in recentralizing political power. Initial political recentralization took place immediately after the crackdown on the prodemocracy movement in 1989 and the collapse of the Soviet Union in the early 1990s. The central government restrengthened the old *nomenklatura* system, a traditional method for communists to control local party cadres and government officials.[16] It reinforced the system of "party management of cadres" (*dang guan ganbu* 党管干部), one of the most important organizational principles. This system gives the central government a dominant say over personnel decisions at the provincial and city level.[17] The central government also reemphasized the cadre transfer system or the cadre exchange system (*ganbu jiaoliu zhidu* 干部交流制度), which enables the center to tighten control over local cadres.[18]

Selective recentralization has been intensified recently in the central leadership's attempts to change the development model. During the Jiang Zemin era (1989–2002), the leadership gave highest priority to rapid economic development. But the old model was inefficient, caused greater social divides, income disparities, and environmental degradation on a colossal scale, and lacked industrial innovation. All these factors impacted negatively on the sustainability of China's development. The Hu Jintao-Wen Jiabao leadership since 2002 has made great efforts to develop a new model that places emphasis on "scientific development" (namely, balanced development), and "harmonious society." This shift in emphasis is proving to be extremely difficult. Vested interests under the old model have resisted a drastic policy shift. According to one official survey conducted in 2006, the overwhelming majority (86 percent) of the respondents (no. 4,531) believed that power was too decentralized, and it is now time to recentralize.[19] To overcome local resistance, the central government is recentralizing in key areas, including quality control, auditing, environment, land management, statistics, and industrial safety. The rationale behind these recentralization efforts is to transform the Chinese state into a regulatory one.[20]

Political recentralization has been effective in constraining the influence of local officials in policymaking at the central level. It is true that some regions

TABLE 11.2
Distribution of Home Provinces of Central Committee Members

	17th Central Committee		16th Central Committee		15th Central Committee	
	Freq.	Percent	Freq.	Percent	Freq.	Percent
North						
Beijing	6	1.63	10	2.81	6	1.74
Tianjin	5	1.36	7	1.97	9	2.62
Hebei	41	11.11	26	7.30	16	4.65
Shanxi	17	4.61	10	2.81	13	3.78
Inner Mongolia	7	1.90	3	0.84	2	0.58
subtotal	76	20.61	56	15.73	46	13.37
Northeast						
Liaoning	19	5.15	17	4.78	25	7.27
Jilin	9	2.44	8	2.25	18	5.23
Heilongjiang	11	2.98	8	2.25	6	1.74
subtotal	39	10.57	33	9.28	49	14.24
East						
Shanghai	7	1.90	9	2.53	6	1.74
Jiangsu	31	8.40	46	12.92	50	14.53
Zhejiang	23	6.23	24	6.74	22	6.40
Anhui	17	4.61	16	4.49	17	4.94
Fujian	10	2.71	5	1.40	7	2.03
Shandong	42	11.38	42	11.80	46	13.37
Taiwan	1	0.27	1	0.28	1	0.29
subtotal	131	35.50	143	40.16	149	43.30
Central						
Jiangxi	8	2.17	9	2.53	10	2.91
Henan	19	5.15	16	4.49	12	3.49
Hubei	18	4.88	16	4.49	8	2.33
Hunan	13	3.52	18	5.06	18	5.23
subtotal	58	15.72	59	16.57	48	13.96
South						
Guangdong	5	1.36	8	2.25	8	2.33
Guangxi	7	1.90	4	1.12	3	0.87
Hainan	1	0.27	1	0.28	1	0.29
Hong Kong	0	0.00	0	0.00	0	0.00
Macao	0	0.00	0	0.00	0	0.00
subtotal	13	3.53	13	3.65	12	3.49
Southwest						
Sichuan	7	1.90	7	1.97	10	2.91
Chongqing	6	1.63	5	1.40	2	0.58
Guizhou	5	1.36	5	1.40	4	1.16
Yunnan	3	0.81	4	1.12	4	1.16
Tibet	3	0.81	3	0.84	3	0.87
subtotal	24	6.51	24	6.73	23	6.68

TABLE 11.2
Distribution of Home Provinces of Central Committee Members

	17th Central Committee		16th Central Committee		15th Central Committee	
	Freq.	Percent	Freq.	Percent	Freq.	Percent
Northwest						
Shaanxi	16	4.34	15	4.21	10	2.91
Gansu	5	1.36	5	1.40	1	0.29
Qinghai	1	0.27	1	0.28	1	0.29
Ningxia	2	0.54	3	0.84	1	0.29
Xinjiang	4	1.08	4	1.12	4	1.16
subtotal	28	7.59	28	7.85	17	4.94
Total	369	100.00	356	100.00	344	99.98*

Source: Data collected by Bo Zhiyue.
*The total is not 100 due to rounding.

are always more powerful than other regions in economic terms. In general, the more economically developed regions are also the more politically powerful regions, as demonstrated in table 11.2. However, the power of economic regions does not guarantee their political power. Take the Seventeenth Central Committee as an example. In terms of regional distributions, the East Region is dominant with 131 members (35.5 percent), the North Region is second with 75 members (20.6 percent), while the South Region is last with the least representation of only 13 members (3.5 percent). Unlike previous central committees, members of the Seventeenth Central Committee come from across the regions. The share of the East Region declined from 43.3 percent of the Fifteenth Central Committee to 40.2 percent of the Sixteenth Central Committee to 35.5 percent of the Seventeenth Central Committee. The North Region climbed up to the number two spot, from 13.4 percent of the Fifteenth Central Committee to 15.7 percent of the Sixteenth to 20.6 percent of the Seventeenth Central Committee.

"Strong economy and weak politics" is particularly true of provinces that are often regarded as being capable of imposing power challenges to the central government. Guangdong and Shanghai are two cases in point. Guangdong has the largest economy in China, but it failed to be dominant at the Seventeenth Central Committee. Only five Central Committee members are from Guangdong Province, down from eight in both the Sixteenth and Fifteenth Central Committees. Seven members of the Seventeenth Central Committee have Shanghai as their home province, but none of them are qualified to be a member of the so-called Shanghai Gang formed under Jiang.

Both Guangdong and Shanghai are economically significant for China. Their economic significance can be transformed into political influence. Nevertheless, once the central government feels threatened by their political influence, the former will make efforts to constrain the latter's political influence. Take two examples. During his tenure in Guangdong, Zhang Dejiang took great initiatives to develop a development program, namely, the "9 plus 2." The program aimed to integrate the economies of nine Chinese provinces surrounding the Pearl River Delta and those of Hong Kong and Macao. Given that Zhang was a member of the Politburo, he was able to coordinate these provinces and Hong Kong and Macao.[21] Nevertheless, this program was regarded as unjustifiable to the interest of the national economy. At the Seventeenth Party Congress in 2007, Zhang retained his membership in the Politburo and was promoted to Beijing, but played an insignificant role as a vice premier. Indeed, ever since the establishment of the People's Republic, Guangdong has struggled for more political influence in the central government. Guangdong, however, has never been successful since such efforts have been identified as localism, which the central government is against.[22] In the case of Shanghai, it was extremely powerful during the era of Jiang Zemin, as reflected in the existence of the Shanghai Gang. The political power of the Shanghai Gang was evident when its party secretary, Chen Liangyu, challenged the power of the Hu Jintao-Wen Jiabao leadership. However, prior to the Seventeenth Party Congress, Chen was removed and jailed for alleged corruption.

State Incapacity

All these measures of recentralization have drastically increased state capacity, be it fiscal power (as Wang Shaoguang would argue) or personnel appointment (as Huang Yasheng would argue). Recentralization and state capacity, however, are hardly identical. These measures have enabled the central government to accumulate its power resources vis-à-vis the province. The capacity of the central state has been in decline. It has failed to produce any significant changes in the provinces. Examples are ample. While its revenue has increased rapidly in the past decades, the central government has not been able to reduce income disparities of various forms. It has yet to provide sufficient public goods such as health care, social security, education, and environmental improvements. While fiscal recentralization does not generate expected results, it has led to unexpected consequences. For example, while fiscal centralization has drastically reduced revenues of local governments, it has also encouraged corruption of various forms at local levels. As shown in table 11.3, while the central government has accumulated an increasingly large amount of revenues over the years, local governments are in serious deficits, which have contributed to widespread corruption at local levels.[23]

TABLE 11.3
Deficits of Central and Local Governments (billion yuan)

	Total	Central	Local
1953	-0.60	1.49	-2.10
1960	-7.14	-13.85	6.44
1965	1.33	-12.81	14.15
1970	1.35	-19.94	21.30
1975	-0.53	-31.28	30.75
1976	-2.96	-27.87	24.91
1977	3.10	-27.98	31.08
1978	1.02	-35.63	36.65
1979	-13.54	-42.38	28.83
1980	-6.89	-38.23	31.35
1981	3.74	-31.46	35.19
1982	-1.77	-30.50	28.73
1983	-4.25	-26.96	22.70
1984	-5.81	-22.78	16.97
1985	0.05	-2.57	2.62
1986	-8.29	-5.80	-4.30
1987	-6.28	-10.93	4.65
1988	-13.40	-7.02	-6.37
1989	-15.89	-6.63	-9.26
1990	-14.65	-1.21	-13.44
1991	-23.71	-15.25	-8.46
1992	-25.88	-19.09	-6.79
1993	-29.33	-35.46	6.12
1994	-57.45	115.21	-172.66
1995	-58.15	126.12	-184.27
1996	-52.96	150.98	-203.94
1997	-58.25	169.44	-227.69
1998	-92.22	176.64	-268.86
1999	-174.36	169.69	-344.04
2000	-249.93	147.18	-485.08
2001	-247.30	282.40	-529.70
2002	-314.96	361.69	-676.65
2003	-293.47	444.52	-737.99
2004	-209.04	660.90	-869.94
2005	-228.10	777.26	-1005.36
2006	-166.25	1046.52	-1212.78

Source: *China Statistical Yearbook*, various years.

A full description of state incapacity and its consequences is not appropriate here. As such, this chapter only presents two cases, one economic, and the other political, to show why recentralization has become an increasingly serious constraint on China's further reforms. The economic case, namely, the state-owned enterprise (SOE) reform, attempts to demonstrate how recentralization has discouraged the central government from achieving what it had planned. The SOE reform was to restructure the economy and provide an institutional foundation for the development of small and medium-sized enterprises (SMEs). It, however, turned out that the reform has created an institutional setting for state monopoly, which is a major barrier for sustainable development. The political case, namely, the rise of social forces and bottom-up political participation, shows that recentralization has constrained the social initiatives of political development.

The SOE Reform

The SOE reform has been the core of China's economic reform for almost three decades. The reform has achieved great success in improving the productivity and efficiency of state-owned enterprises. Although China began SOE reforms in the 1980s, radical reforms only took place after Deng's southern tour in 1992. It was heavily debated whether China should adopt a market economy approach until 1992 when the Fourteenth National Congress of the CCP clearly stated that China's economic reform was to establish a socialist market economy. The pursuit of "market economy" status provided the necessary conditions for China to begin large-scale economic decentralization. Since then the SOE reform has gone through two phases: the strategy of "grasping the big and letting go of the small" under the previous premier Zhu Rongji and the management by State-Owned Assets Supervision and Administration Council under the current premier Wen Jiabao.

The Zhu Rongji Initiative

In the mid-1990s, Zhu Rongji formulated a new strategy for the SOE reform called *zhuada fangxiao* 抓大放小 (grasping the big and letting go of the small). It was officially established as China's new economic reform strategy at the Fifteenth Party Congress in 1997. This strategy gave the SOE reform a clear direction, especially in the case of the large SOEs. "Grasping the big" means developing large, strong, and competitive enterprises and enterprise groups into cross-regional, cross-sectional, multiownership, and multinational big firms. "Letting go of the small" implies that the government allows small and medium-sized SOEs to face market forces. The government would actively support SMEs, especially technology companies, to develop and become "specialized, lean, unique and innovative." The government would use various realistic methods, such as joint ventures, mergers and acquisitions, leasing, contracting, shareholding, and selling-off, to deregulate and invigorate SMEs. The ultimate goal of this strategy was to privatize most of the SMEs and control only a limited number of large central and local SOEs. The latest policy on big SOEs issued by the Chinese government focuses on seven key areas and industries related to national security and economic lifelines, including military industry, electricity and the electrical grid, oil and the petrochemical industry, telecommunications, coal, civil aviation, and shipping.[24]

When the Zhu administration initiated and implemented the policy of grasping the big and letting go of the small, it had an ambitious strategic perspective. Most industrialized countries have successfully developed many large enterprise groups. As a big country, China certainly needs to establish enterprise giants to form the pillar of the national economy and to enhance its international economic competitiveness. More importantly, the existence of such large enterprise groups in the critical areas will also provide strong support to national economic security. In designing such a strategy, the Zhu government aimed to follow the path taken previously by Japan and South Korea.[25]

Privatizing state-owned SMEs was also a rational choice for the Chinese government. A large number of state-owned SMEs were inefficient and unprofitable. They were not competitive in the market and often became heavy financial burdens on all levels of government. Their ambiguous property rights more often than not caused serious managerial agency problems. Privatization could be an effective means to restructuring these SOEs, thus improving the efficiency of the whole economy. Moreover, privatizing SMEs was also socially and politically significant. SMEs could play a highly important role in the provision of employment opportunities and the rationalization of income distribution.

The policy of grasping the big and letting go of the small was carried out too hastily in many ways. In its implementation, grasping the big was exaggerated ruthlessly by all levels of government. Government officials tried to use political and administrative means to merge enterprises in order to create giant monopolies, simply for the sake of appearing to be "big," disregarding other economic and social considerations. With the implementation of this policy, various positive aspects of big enterprises, such as the capacity for innovation, efficiency, and competitiveness, did not develop as initially expected. Many Chinese SOEs have become internationally famous for their huge size, but their large assets are often assembled by the state in various ways other than from the profit of their ventures. Further, these giant SOEs are often monopolies that control the upstream supply market for the entire industrial chain. Therefore, they earn hefty monopoly profits at the expense of consumers.

In industrialized countries, privatization has improved industrial efficiency and kept a balanced public service sector in many cases, such as the United Kingdom in the 1980s and 1990s. However, the Chinese local governments did not have a systematic and effective plan for the privatization process. They simply "let go" of the state-owned SMEs to the market. Consequently, sizable state-owned assets were lost due to inappropriate administration and regulations. Enormous numbers of employees were laid off during the process, causing social unrest and even conflicts between the government and the public.

The aim of privatization is to improve the efficiency of the economy, provide better services to the public, and ultimately increase consumers' overall utilities. However, in China local governments used administrative power to enforce privatization in favor of the capital owner rather than the public—the taxpayers. Many SMEs, after being privatized, struggle to survive. Since they do not enjoy a supportive financial, legal, and policy environment, their development has been greatly constrained.

The number of SOEs and employees has decreased dramatically since the "grasping the big and letting go of the small" policy was put into force. The Chinese government has often claimed that the SOEs' economic efficiency and competitiveness are improving and the quality of state-owned assets enhanced. However, these assessments, which are based on numerical evidence, have to be regarded with caution. The overall improvement of the SOEs' profitability is very likely due to the exclusion of many badly performing SMEs under the "letting go of the small" policy, and not due to higher efficiency among existing firms. Also, the increase in SOEs' profits very likely comes from the monopolistic income of those newly merged large firms under the "grasping the big" policy, rather than from SOEs' better performance in the market.

The Wen Jiabao Initiative

At the Sixteenth National Congress of the CCP in 2002, the direction of SOE reform was further readjusted by the newly appointed Hu-Wen leadership. The government continued to make efforts to restructure the state-owned economy and reform the state assets management system. According to the new policy initiatives, except for a handful of SOEs to be run solely by the state, the government would implement a diversified ownership structure in the majority of the SOEs and control only the important enterprises. Governments at the central, provincial, and municipal levels were required to set up special institutes to represent the state as performing investors' responsibilities.

In 2003, the State-owned Assets Supervision and Administration Council (SASAC) of the State Council was established. SASAC supervised 196 central SOEs and RMB 6.9 trillion (US$ 0.9 trillion) state-owned net assets.[26] Since then, local SASACs have been gradually established. This arrangement was intended to solve three key problems concerning the implementation of property right liabilities. First, vertically, it clearly defined the property right liabilities among governments at different levels. Second, horizontally, responsibility was localized, which was not the case while many government departments had administrative authority over the enterprises. Investors' rights were centralized to the SASAC from various departments, including the Ministry of Finance, the Central Work Commission of Enterprises, the Financial Work Commission, the State Economic and Trade Committee, the National Development and Reform Commission, and the Ministry of Labor and Social Security. Third, the government's executive power and the SOEs' ownership rights would no longer affect each other. These were the major breakthroughs in the institutionalization of the SASAC system. Currently there are 159 central SOEs supervised by the SASAC, down from 196 in 2003. SASAC is aiming to further reduce the number of SOEs to between 80 and 100 by 2010.

According to the official definition, besides being an investor, SASAC is also responsible for guiding the reform and restructuring the SOEs, forming the board of supervisors in large SOEs on behalf of the state, supervising and managing state-owned assets by statistical and audit means, and developing relevant regulations and laws.[27] The establishment of SASAC indicates that the Chinese government is aware of the significance of inefficient and asset-losing SOEs.

An important part of the reform directed by SASAC is the personnel system reform as an essential part of building modern corporate governance of SOEs. Managerial positions would be filled through open competition rather than by administrative appointments. The new system also emphasizes the value of talent in an enterprise. From 2003 to 2006, eighty-one senior posts in seventy-eight central SOEs were openly advertised and recruited and twenty deputy senior posts in ten central SOEs were recruited through internal competition.[28]

The core issue for SOEs is the problem of soft budget constraints. On one hand, SOE managers do not have the incentive to cut costs and to maximize profit simply because the enterprises are owned by the state. On the other hand, if the SOEs perform badly, the state cannot simply let them be eliminated by market competition. Rather, it will find ways such as the provision of financial subsidies and creation of a monopoly environment to bring the SOEs out of their predicament. For SOE managers, it is much easier to plead for support from the state than to build the business in the competitive market. Therefore, there is no reason to expect these managers to improve the efficiency of firms.

In such cases, SOEs rely on the state for survival and often become a heavy burden on public finance. The establishment of the SASAC and the related institutional adjustments by the State Council have transferred the task of state-owned assets management from several government departments into one, hopefully reducing the inefficiency caused by the bureaucracy. However, greater efforts are needed to solve the problem of soft budget constraints.

SOE Monopoly and Its Discontents

After years of reform efforts, the number of SOEs in the whole economy has decreased significantly and SOEs' strength has increased. By the end of 2006, the number of central SOEs supervised by the central SASAC had decreased to 159 while their total assets reached RMB 12.27 trillion (US$ 1.59 trillion), a 16.2 percent rise from the previous year. Their sales, realized profits, tax payment, and net assets have strong yearly growths of 20.1 percent, 18.2 percent, 20 percent, and 15.2 percent, respectively.[29] The 1,031 SOEs supervised by the local SASACs also achieved similar outstanding performance.[30] Furthermore, SOEs, especially large SOE groups, are concentrating on monopoly industries. Sectors such as oil and gas, telecommunication and other information transmission services are occupied predominantly by state-owned or state-holding enterprises. Some other sectors, such as electricity, heat production and supply, coal mining and washing, transport and transportation equipment manufacture, which are the key industries related to the national economic lifeline, are mostly shared by the SOEs. At local levels, SOEs that are owned by different levels of government monopolize most profitable sectors without any justification.

The obvious result of such a situation is an enhancement of the profitability of SOEs. One might think that the high profitability of the SOEs would benefit the country's fiscal revenue through taxation. However, this does not seem to be so. While SOEs are increasing their tax contribution to the state, the negative effects of the excessive concentration of SOEs in monopoly areas are greater. Due to their low efficiency, SOEs do not have comparative advantages, especially in competitive industries. Therefore, SOEs are being moved from competitive sectors to monopoly sectors. These SOEs subsequently claim, proudly, that they are turning losses into profit. This is especially true for SOEs supervised by local SASACs. While the monopoly of central SOEs are justifiable for national strategic reasons, local SOEs often exercise monopoly wherever it is profitable. The increase in profits does not stem from an improvement in firm efficiency, but from the benefits of monopoly. SOEs have been strengthening their control of upstream resources of industrial chains. Their extra profits come at the expense of the general public.

Usually, a firm's profitability comes from effective management and an increase in efficiency. In China, there might be a slight improvement in the management and efficiency in SOEs when they become monopolies. However, what firms actually seek in becoming monopolies is the monopoly price, which brings them the extra monopoly profit. In other words, the profitability of the monopoly sector is not due to its efficiency, but to the benefits of the monopoly.

Monopolies cause unfair competition in the market. Employees in the monopoly sectors earn extraordinarily high incomes, and this has become a major source of China's widening income gap and rising social tensions. In their own closed-market setting, these conglomerates operate according to their own rules and not to market principles. Prices are often inflated to feed the needs of the employees of these monopolies. For example, a graduate in a major coastal city earns an average of about 2,000 RMB per month, but a highway toll collector working for a monopoly earns as much as 8,000 RMB per month. An investigation by the Guangdong provincial government shows that in 2006, although many big SOEs in the province were making losses, the wages of their employees continued to increase.

The growing trend of monopoly also amplifies inefficient economic expansion in China. A vivid example is the world's top five hundred Chinese firms. They are basically monopolies and fundamentally different from multinational firms of industrialized countries as they do not have strong market competitiveness even though they are physically large.

Ten years ago, China's SOEs struggled to control their expenditure to pay their employees' salary. The Chinese government then tried to "revitalize" and "save" SOEs. But today, the topics associated with SOEs are "high salary," "huge profits," and "dividends sharing." Price inflation in SOEs has generated enormous popular dissatisfaction.[31] To deal with these issues, a series of new policies are being put into practice. SASAC, together with labor and social security, finance, and audit departments, has tried to put a check on the salary of employees in monopoly sectors.[32] Li Rongrong, director of SASAC, revealed that from 2007 SOEs would be required to pay dividends to the state treasury again, twelve years after the suspension of this policy in 1994.[33] However, this policy also led to the concern that it would justify SOEs' monopoly behavior since the SOEs concerned would argue that their dividend payments contributed directly to the state's fiscal revenue. Furthermore, if there is no well-designed channel for the government to systematically use this income, for example to subsidize SMEs or to spend on education and social security funds, then this dividend payment to the government would not fulfill the purpose of income redistribution.

Due to various institutional defects, corruption is often prevalent in SOEs. In SOEs, the unjustifiable corporate power structure and unclear statutory responsibilities and duties prevent the development of an effective system for keeping power in balance. Poor law enforcement and low opportunity cost provide insiders with strong incentives for corruption, which results in the huge loss of state assets. Corruption in SOEs bears two characteristics: the majority of individuals implicated are senior managers, and the amount of money and assets involved is massive.[34] Senior managers in SOEs normally have unsupervised power over everything within the firm. Consequently, they abuse this power for their own benefits. The Chinese government has also found that monopoly industries have the highest incidences of corruption and bribery. In recent years, the government has targeted the monopoly SOEs in its anticorruption drive.[35] However, no matter how effective the law enforcement departments are in fighting corruption, their actions are merely palliatives if there is no institutional reform alongside. To eliminate corruption in SOEs, the Chinese government will have to reform the SOE system and break the administrative monopolies.

Another controversial issue closely related to SOE reform is its impact on the survival and development of SMEs, particularly private ones. SMEs currently contribute about 60 percent of China's gross domestic product and 50 percent of the country's tax revenue, and provide over 75 percent of total urban employment opportunities. SMEs are responsible for about 65 percent of inventions and patents and over 80 percent of new product development.[36] Nevertheless, China's industrial and financial policies at different levels of government have long favored state-owned and large firms.

Before its reform, China's state-owned banking sector simply took orders from the government to allocate financial resources to the SOEs, while denying the same resources to China's most efficient private SMEs. Official statistics show that although over 99 percent of the firms in China were SMEs in 2005, they shared only 16 percent of total bank loans, the dominant means of external finance for Chinese firms.[37] The majority of SMEs in China are private firms. With the banking reform, state-owned banks (SOBs) have become increasingly commercialized. They could make rational business decisions independent of the government. However, due to information asymmetry in the market and in traditional bank relations, SOBs still prefer to lend to large SOEs, not SMEs. SMEs are also discriminated against in terms of access to external funding, market opportunity, property rights protection, and taxation. The latter two were given some relief when China's new *Property Law* and *Corporate Income Tax Law* were put into effect on October 1, 2007, and January 1, 2008, respectively.

In China's transitional economy, if the government "lets go of the small" and puts them entirely at the mercy of the market, the country would be at risk of losing its most efficient SMEs to foreign and domestic competitors when China becomes a fully open economy according to its WTO obligations. On the other hand, if China ruthlessly pursues the policy of "grasping the big," it may use its limited financial resources to subsidize and invest heavily in its inefficient large SOE sector, even at the cost of providing necessary public goods. Consequently, resources would be seriously misallocated. If this becomes the case, China's economic development could not be sustained, leading to social instability.

In fact, SASAC itself has also been criticized for the ambiguity between its own administrative function and its market activities. SASAC specifies its responsibilities as safeguarding the rights and interests of owners and preventing the loss of state-owned assets. On the one hand, as a government agent it fulfils the duty of managing state assets, and as an investor it operates the firms and leads the restructuring of SOEs. On the other hand, as a quasi-governmental body, it is responsible for market regulation and control on behalf of the government; SASAC has been given the dual rights of an investor and a supervisor.

Power has a logic of self-inflation. SASAC has repeatedly emphasized the importance of the growth of central SOEs' profit. This mode of economic development raises doubts over whether SASAC intends to further strengthen the current monopoly profit model of SOEs or that it might use its administrative power to benefit various interest groups in the course of conducting market operations.

The Chinese government has been endeavoring to optimize the SOE sector, but with little success. The monopoly status did not increase the productivity of the SOEs; neither did the monopoly profits benefit the majority of the taxpayers, creating, instead, income disparity. The reform so far has improved the situation of the SOEs in the short term, but hurt the unfavored SMEs. Yet, if SOEs' monopoly status continues to be tolerated or even encouraged, the economic recourses will shift from the more productive sectors and firms to these monopolists, hampering China's growth in the long term. The Chinese leadership does not seem to have a clear direction of how SOEs should be further reformed.

Political Participation from Below

Participation from below does not mean that the central government does not play an important role in this process. Indeed, without political support from the central government, no bottom-up participation initiative would have been possible. To highlight participation from below, this chapter emphasizes that there is an increasingly high demand for political participation from the society, but centralization has served as an effective political and legal constraint on bottom-up initiatives. In the case of the SOE reform, centralization does not enable the central government to fulfill its planned policy mission since the policy is manipulated, reinterpreted, and modified during the implementation process. The case of political participation seems to have backfired too since it is centralization that has nullified local initiatives. While there is a wide range of areas where participation from below has taken place, this discussion focuses on the development of local semi-competitive elections and nongovernmental organizations (NGOs).

Semi-Competitive Local Elections

This refers to rural village elections for village committees since the late 1980s, and township elections for the heads of townships since the 1990s. The rural election system was formally introduced in the late 1980s after it was practiced by rural residents in some provinces. In the late 1970s, China initiated the rural reform, which was characterized by radical decentralization based on the Household Responsibility System. The popularity of this system soon led to the collapse of the old system of governance, that is, the production brigade system, and eventually the collapse of the commune system. In 1987, the National People's Congress (NPC) passed the Village Committee Organic Law of the PRC (Experimental). According to the law, "village committees should be established in China's rural areas in order to safeguard farmers' opportunities and rights of political participation. The control over village cadres by farmers and the level of villagers' self-government will be improved through direct election of the directors, deputy directors and members of the villagers' committees, thus upgrading the quality of farmers' political participation."[38] Since the mid-1990s, the election system has developed rather impressively. According to the Ministry of Civil Affairs, which has been tasked with the implementation of this election system, more than 80 percent of China's 930,000 villages had conducted at least one round of relatively democratic elections by early 1997. By 2001, this system was widely adopted by the whole country.

The fact that the central government nationalized this bottom-up initiative did not mean in any sense that the CCP was to give up its rule in the countryside; instead, it was aimed at strengthening the rule of the party in rural areas by accommodating democratic elements.[39] So, while the village committee was elected by villagers, the CCP committee continued to exist. The rapid spread of rural democracy, however, soon created contradictions between the elected body and the party branch in the same village. While the elected village committee can draw its legitimacy from villagers, the party branch often faced challenges in dealing with the former. To eliminate this contradiction, many provinces have developed a system of "two-ballots" in which the party secretary in a village is subject to a popular vote, meaning that in these places both committees are elected.[40] The parallel system of the party and the village branch continues, but their relations with each other are transformed.

Reformist leaders in the central government have also allowed direct elections at the township level—the basic level of administration—on an experimental basis. In the mid-1990s, China experienced its first cases of township elections for key township officials. Since then, the new election practices have been adopted in many townships in many counties of a number of provinces. The positions open to the elections have been extended from township vice mayors to township mayors, and sometimes even township party secretaries. The number of cases increased from a dozen in the mid-1990s, to several hundred in the late 1990s, and to several thousand by the early 2000s. Compared to village elections, township elections are more constrained by various factors, thus earning their name of "semi-competitive elections"[41] as coined by the scholarly community.

Township elections were policy products, not legal ones. As a matter of fact, township elections have not been justified in Chinese laws, and remain controversial even though they are now widespread. For example, in August 2006, Sheng Huaren, then vice chairman of the NPC Standing Committee, reiterated that direct elections of township government leaders were illegal and warned that evil foreigners were using the tool of human rights and democracy against China.[42] The political support from the leadership, both at the central and local level, is the key factor that has facilitated the implementation of this system.[43] Apparently, once such political support disappears, there is no way for local democracy to spread to the whole nation and extend to higher levels of government.

Besides village and township elections, China today is experimenting with different kinds of democratic elements such as the election of urban community committees, inclusion of independent candidates running for local people's congresses, emergence of what China called "rights-democracy," and social movements.[44] But certainly, the government has cracked down on many of such "rights-democracy" movements by disgruntled social groups such as farmers, migrant workers, and urban poor.

The Growth of NGOs

The development of nongovernmental organizations (NGOs) has been a major part of state-to-society decentralization.[45] This is especially true since the early 2000s after the leadership began to place an emphasis on social reforms. Reforms have led not only to a relaxation of state control over society, but also to the active establishment and sponsoring of NGOs by the state to offload certain state functions to them. Chinese NGOs have increased steadily in numbers over the years. The statistics of the Ministry of Civil Affairs (MCA), which is in charge of NGO registration, show that before 1978 there were only about 100 national social organizations in China. By the end of 2003 this number had reached 1,736. Meanwhile the number of local-level social organizations grew from 6,000 to 142,121. The number of private non-enterprise organizations (PNEOs), which did not exist before the reforms, reached 124,491. By the end of 2005, there were 168,000 social organizations, 146,000 PNEOs, and 999 foundations. However, scholars found that a large number of associations had been left uncounted. By adding different types of nonregistered NGOs, Wang Shaoguang believed that the total number of civil organizations had reached 8.8 million by 2003.[46] Despite its rapid develop-ment, scholars have argued that NGOs in China are still underdeveloped. For example, the number of civil organizations per ten thousand people in China is 1.45, but the same number in France is 110.45, United States is 51.79, Brazil is 12.66, India is 10.21, and Egypt is 2.44.[47]

In the West, an NGO is autonomous and independent from the govern-ment. In China, however, the autonomy of NGOs depends on their relations with and thus their political "distance" from the government. Government regulations stipulate that any social organization must be approved by and registered with the civil affairs departments at the county level or above, while foundations (e.g., charity organizations) must be approved at the provincial or central government level. Any civil organizations that do not register with the Ministry of Civil Affairs are outlawed. Government regulations require every social organization to find a "professional management unit" (*yewu zhuguan danwei* 业务主管单位) to act as its sponsoring agency. Only after obtaining the approval of its sponsor can an NGO apply for registration with civil affairs departments. The sponsor must be a state organ above the county level or an organization authorized by such an organ. It must also be "rele-vant" to the activities proposed by the NGO, that is, it must have responsi-bilities in the same field in which the NGO operates. Regulations also disallow NGOs with similar missions to coexist in the same geographic area.

As a result of these strict rules, many grassroots NGOs were unable to reg-ister, either because they failed to find government agencies that are willing to act as their professional management units, or because other NGOs with similar missions had already been registered in the sites where they intend to base their operations. In order to exist legally, some NGOs registered with industry and commerce bureaus as businesses instead, even though they en-gage in public-benefit activities and are non-profit-making. There are also unregistered, hence illegal, organizations that nevertheless carry out activities openly and that have been left alone by the government instead of being banned according to the regulations.

Nevertheless, the registration requirement does not apply to eight big national social organizations that are often referred to more specifically as "people's organizations" (*renmin tuanti* 人民团体) or "mass organizations" (*qunzhong tuanti* 群众团体), such as All China Federation of Trade Unions, the All-China Women's Federation, and the Communist Youth League. These social organizations were created by the party-state and perform administrative functions on its behalf. Indeed, they are independent organizations, and are not under civil affairs' supervision. Their heads are appointed by the top leadership of the CCP. Government regulations also exempt from the registration requirement "organizations formed within administrative agencies, social organizations, enterprises, or service units which are approved by these organizations and which only carry out activities internally."[48] University student unions fall under this category since they do not need to be approved by and registered with the civil affairs departments as long as they have been approved by their universities. Some grassroots organizations are not required to register with the civil affairs departments, such as property owners' committees (*yezhu weiyuanhui* 业主委员会) that are formed by owners of apartments in the same housing compound and urban community-based organizations, for example, leisure activity groups formed by residents in the same neighborhood.

Moreover, the development of NGOs in different functionaries has been uneven. In the economic sphere, the government has attempted to reduce its direct management role by establishing intermediary organizations such as trade associations and chambers of commerce to perform sectoral coordination and regulatory functions. In the social welfare sphere, the government wants to foster NGOs onto which it can offload some of the burden of service provision. In the social development sphere, the government wants NGOs to mobilize societal resources to supplement its own spending.[49] These NGOs will have to perform their role according to the party line—they will be "helping hands" rather than independent organizations.

The political influences of China's NGOs also vary widely across different areas and as well as between different NGOs. In some areas such as poverty reduction, charity, and environmental issues, NGOs are being encouraged to play a greater role. But in other areas such as religious issues, ethnicity, and human rights, the influence of NGOs is much weaker. Also, some NGOs are more powerful than others. Most commercial organizations are extremely powerful in influencing the government's policymaking process. It is not difficult to find business people sitting in the People's Congress and the Chinese People's Political Consultative Conference at different levels of the government. But workers and farmers are not allowed to organize themselves, and thus do not have any effective mechanisms to articulate and aggregate their interests. In fact, the decline of workers and peasants in the total membership of the party implies their weakness in China's political system.

When powerful social groups organize themselves, they become ever more powerful. There is no effective means for weak social groups such as workers and farmers to promote their own causes. As long as the party-state does not allow these weak social groups to organize themselves or to be organized, they are unlikely to have a say in the decision-making process or gain equal citizenship rights as other social groups. The fear of their organizational power has justified all measures of centralization by the party-state in exercising tight political control over social forces. Needless to say, centralization serves as an effective means to contain participation and democracy from below.

State-Society Decentralization: A Solution

Intergovernmental decentralization has served as an effective means for China to achieve high economic performance. It was effectively implemented due to great incentives from both the central government and the provinces. The rationale for the central government, especially the reformist leadership, was that rapid economic development would enable the party-state to deliver economic goods to the people and thus maintain its political legitimacy. This is also true for the provinces. Rapid local economic development would not only bring wealth to local officials, but also help in their political career since local economic growth was the most important indicator for their promotion in the hierarchy of the party-state. Therefore, intergovernmental decentralization was a win-win game for both the central government and the provinces.

Nevertheless, both the nature and rules of the game changed at a later stage. With intergovernmental decentralization, economic decision-making power shifted to the provinces. Instead of privatization, property rights were decentralized to the local governments rather than to individual enterprises or entrepreneurs. Local governments became de facto owners of state enterprises. Understandably, even though the central government gradually withdrew from the economic affairs of individual enterprises, local governments became highly interventionist. Generally speaking, intergovernmental decentralization created an institutional setting and legitimacy for local governments to intervene in economic activities within their jurisdictions. Intergovernmental decentralization does not necessarily deny marketization. In fact, marketization was encouraged due to intense competition among different jurisdictions and enterprises with different forms of ownership. Local protectionism existed at the early stages of economic reforms; however, with the growth of market mechanisms, it was constrained. All these factors contributed to high local economic performance.

Intergovernmental decentralization empowered local governments and made them more efficient in responding to social demands and changing socioeconomic circumstances. It thus changed the interaction pattern between the central government and the provinces. With an increase in local responsibilities, central-local relations became interdependent. While in principle the central government still held great power over local governments, cooperation from the provinces became essential. The provinces developed and strengthened their own power bases and created incentives for the central government to adjust its relations with the provinces. The provinces had the power to not only deal with local affairs but also influence decision making at the central level.

Intergovernmental decentralization also empowered local governments in their interaction with society. The focus of intergovernmental decentralization was power shifts not between the state and society, but between the center and the provinces. The central leadership did not want to decentralize political power to the society; instead, it believed that political participation should be constrained and that mass mobilization would not help in the transition to an efficient government. With intergovernmental political decentralization, the political spaces for free expression and collective actions by individuals and social groups were extended; however, limited political participation from below took place, as in the case of the development of semi-competitive local elections, as social forces remain weak. In actuality, intergovernmental decentralization has produced local regimes of dictatorship, and local high economic performance has been associated with serious human rights violation on the part of the local governments.

Therefore, selective recentralization, as described in this chapter, is justifiable. Selective recentralization was able to not only change the interdependency between the central government and the provinces, but to regain the domination of the central government over the provinces. More importantly, it was to engage state-society decentralization. In order to implement state-society decentralization, the central government has to recentralize power first since intergovernmental decentralization empowered local governments, and powerful local governments often become a barrier to state-society decentralization.

While selective recentralization enabled the central government to regain its domination over the provinces, it did not empower the central government in terms of policy implementation (get things done in the provinces). Why? Among others, a key factor is that state-society decentralization has been greatly constrained by both the central government and the provinces. Without state-society decentralization, the central government does not have a level of legitimacy that would enable it to establish its power over the provinces while society is not empowered to establish its power over both the central government and the provinces.

So, the game of power continues to be played between the central government and the provinces. Without the participation of social forces, the central government still lacks the infrastructural power to dictate to the provinces, meaning that the central government is not able to ask the provinces to do what it wanted them to do. While the central government maintains its official domination over the provinces and has de jure power to veto initiatives by the provinces, the provinces also have de facto power to veto policy initiatives by the central government. When a party has the power to nullify decisions by another party, a policy deadlock becomes inevitable. This characterizes China's central-local relations today. As long as such a situation prevails, it is unlikely for both the central government and the provinces to engage in any major meaningful reforms.

To avoid such a situation, state-society decentralization is inevitable. In other words, the society must be empowered. Only when its power is mandated by the whole society can the central government gain power over the provinces. When the society becomes an active actor in the game, local dictatorships can be constrained and avoided. It is unfair to say that the central leadership is unaware of the importance of state-society decentralization. As discussed in this chapter, the purpose of the SOE reform under Zhu Rongji was to empower the SMEs, especially in the private sector. Similarly, many measures of social reforms by the Hu Jintao-Wen Jiabao government were to empower society as in the case of the development of NGOs and local semi-competitive elections. All these measures of empowering society, however, were either too reluctant or too cautious. Social changes have forced the party-state to open its process to social forces, as in the admission of capitalists into the ruling party. The party-state, as a well-entrenched vested interest, continues to be resistant to social forces. Before the political process is opened wide to social forces, the game between the central government and the provinces will not lead to drastic political changes in China.

12

Energy Governance

Fueling the Miracle

Edward A. Cunningham

Overturning a World Energy Order: China as Number One

T HE RISE OF CHINA'S ECONOMIC SYSTEM is commonly understood to be one of the pivotal developments of the late twentieth century. The rise of China's energy system, upon which such economic growth has depended, remains much less understood. Little is known about how the nation's natural resources were marshaled to support such rapid and sustained economic growth. Yet the decisions of Chinese energy firms and energy regulators have already begun to influence significantly world energy markets, climate change patterns, and international climate negotiations. Understanding China's model of energy governance is central to understanding the ways in which the role of the state in China has, and has not, changed through the reform period, as well as how the state's capacity to govern this critical sector will evolve in the near to medium term. The implications of this national model of governance are increasingly international in nature, and are shaping many of the most intractable public policy challenges facing the global community.

In 2009 China replaced the United States as the world's largest primary energy producer, a position the United States had enjoyed for well over a century.[1] In that same year, China managed to provide over 94 percent of its primary energy demand domestically. As figure 12.1 illustrates, this ratio represents a rather remarkable feat in comparative terms. China's energy self-sufficiency is high relative to that of large developed economies, such as the United States and

Japan, but also high relative to large developing countries, such as India. This large-scale utilization of domestic resources is particularly remarkable in the context of the Chinese central state's historical lack of capital and energy technology, splintered energy regulatory institutions, and rapid economic growth during the past three decades of reform. This chapter explains the development of China's modern energy system, its industrial structure, its mode of governance, and the implications of such governance for larger questions of energy security, efficiency, and environmental sustainability.

From Producer to Consumer

The rise of China's energy market has shifted the landscape of global energy production, and, increasingly, consumption. China's share of world primary energy consumption has risen from a mere 4.8 percent in 1965 to 16.8 percent in 2007, to become the second largest in the world. The US share has dropped from 33.6 percent to 21.3 percent in the same period.[2] Between 2000 and 2007, China accounted for 77.1 percent of total growth in world coal consumption, 37.2 percent of world growth in oil consumption, and 28.2 percent of nuclear energy consumption growth.[3] As a result, in this eight-year period China accounted for an astounding 50 percent of global growth in primary energy consumption.[4] The International Energy Agency (IEA) estimates that

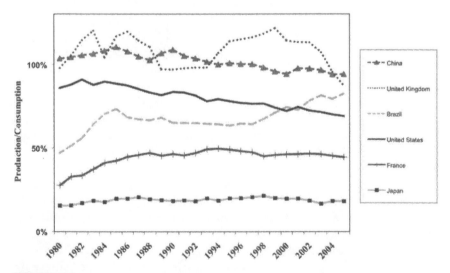

FIGURE 12.1
Comparative Primary Energy Self-Sufficiency Ratios. Source: British Petroleum (BP), *Statistical Review of World Energy*, 2008.

China will likely become the world's largest energy market in 2010.[5] Such rapid expansion earned China its position as the world's leading emitter of greenhouse gas emissions, vaulting ahead of the United States between 2006 and 2007.[6]

The magnitude of this change has driven a powerful conceptual shift away from China as the "world's largest producer" of manufactured goods and natural resources such as coal, to China as the "world's largest consumer" of nearly all strategic resources necessary to sustain industrial growth.[7] This shift has been fueled by perceptions that China is already highly dependent on the volatile international energy market (and therefore increasingly without strategic energy options), and dependent on inefficient energy firms that are largely owned and guided by an interventionist central state. Many observers view China's energy system in the following terms:

> Unlike most sectors of China's economy, the energy sector remains subject to a high degree of state control and of state ownership. Despite periodic reorganizations of both government agencies and of state energy companies, the close relationship between the energy companies and the government is loosening only very gradually. [8]

Many experts argue that China's energy sector is therefore the least open to change because it is the least reformed, least flexible, and most centralized sector of the economy. Studies and media reports relating to China's energy system have grown increasingly alarmist as China's energy market has grown increasingly global in scale. Observers often argue that China is the "sinner" of the energy world, responsible for rising global commodity prices and greenhouse gas emissions that have resulted from a system largely insulated from price signals and dominated by state cartels.

This chapter argues that China's energy governance apparatus is instead fragmented and contentious, that the bulk of its energy market (coal and electricity generation) is also fragmented, and that this dual fragmentation at the levels of government and industry has enabled China to meet the majority of its considerable energy needs.[9] Such variation in state ownership, state investment, and market concentration in these industries is the result of a successful "portfolio approach" to energy governance adopted by core central governmental actors beginning in the early 1980s. This approach treated Chinese energy firms as a portfolio of assets in which central state ownership could be strengthened during periods of energy surplus and weakened during periods of energy shortage. This periodic devolution of investment and ownership to non-state firms has remained limited in the oil and gas sector but has proven significant in the industries that provide the majority of Chinese energy supply: coal and electric power generation.

Meeting Demand

The growth of China's energy system in the past three decades has depended primarily on rapid capacity increases in coal and electric power production. This increase in capacity in turn depended on the devolution of investment and ownership rights, evident during periods of energy shortage, from the central government to firms and authorities at the provincial and local level.[10] In the case of the coal industry, collectively owned mines at the township and village level served as a form of "shock absorber" when rapid economic growth led to stress on national energy supplies. These mines grew from providing 9 percent of the 354 million tons of coal produced in 1970 to 46 percent of the 1.30 billion tons produced in 1995 to 38 percent of the 2.33 billion tons produced in 2006. The production of local collective mines in 2006 equaled about three-quarters of total US production that year. In electricity generation, power plants owned and financed by provincial and municipal governments, foreign firms, and private domestic firms served a similar purpose. These plants grew from providing zero percent of the 23.8 GW of generating capacity in 1970 to 57 percent of the 718.9 GW capacity in 2007. This capacity is equal to about three times the national generating capacity of India or four times that of the United Kingdom that year, or the size of China's entire national generating capacity as recently as 2004. One of the leading observers of China's energy system, Philip Andrews-Speed, recognized the success of such an approach, arguing that "the electrical power sector has been the most successful of the Chinese energy industries in investing in domestic capacity and delivering additional energy to consumers."[11]

The devolution of finance and delegation of responsibilities to build energy production capacity in part solved immediate fiscal challenges for the central government that emerged in the early 1980s when economic growth began to accelerate. These local firms in coal and electric power also served as a source of system flexibility when energy demand fluctuated, in the late 1990s during the Asian financial crisis, and excess capacity required shuttering.[12] Writing about the electric power generation industry, Chi Zhang and Thomas Heller noted this pattern, arguing that "during the period of surplus supply, political controversies sprang up over which plants would be dispatched; the central government used these controversies to reassert authority and also to initiate planning for further organization reform."[13] As 81 percent of electricity generation is fueled by coal, such electricity growth would have been impossible without major success in coal reforms as well. Despite intermittent coal and electric power bottlenecks over the years, China has successfully met the majority of its domestic needs for electric power and, importantly, served as a major net exporter of coal (see figure 12.2).

The Wizard, Revealed—Who is Regulating?

National energy systems are characterized by high levels of capital intensity (oil refining), long-cycle investments with extended payback periods (oil exploration and production), natural monopolies (electric grid transmission), and high levels of risk that result from the combination of these attributes. Energy flows also carry the added complexity of perceived national security externalities, such as sole supplier risk. The role of government in such an industry is therefore of critical concern, both in theoretical and empirical terms. This chapter begins with a historical review of energy governance in China that reveals the persistently fragmented nature of such governance over time.

Repeated Attempts at Administrative Centralization (1953–1982)

The most recent creation of the National Energy Commission in early 2008 is the latest in a long line of centralization efforts, and precedent suggests that the lifetime of such an institution in China may be quite short. China's regulatory entities have been, and continue to be, characterized by overlapping jurisdictions and waves of centralization and decentralization. Analysis of four key centralization initiatives conveys the consistently splintered nature of such governance.[14] Tellingly, Beijing's first attempt to centralize energy oversight proved short-lived. Between 1953 and 1955, the newly founded central gov-

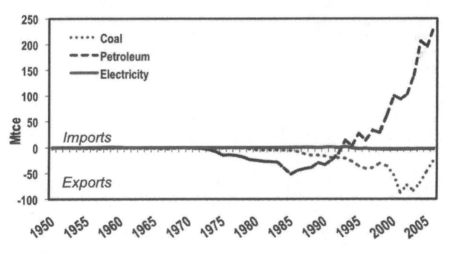

FIGURE 12.2
Net Trade in Petroleum, Coal, and Electricity. *Source:* LBNL, *China Energy Databook,* **2008.**

ernment created the Ministry of Fossil Fuels (MFF) to combine the coal, electricity, and petroleum industries into one entity for energy policymaking, allocation, planning, and development. By 1955 the need for management specialization and heightened growth of energy demand from 6 percent to over 15 percent quickly led to the abolishment of the MFF and the formation of separate ministries for coal and petroleum.

A second administrative consolidation trend emerged in 1960, when the disastrous results of the Great Leap Forward and the withdrawal of Soviet advisers led to economic growth plummeting from slightly under 9 percent the previous year to negative 0.3 percent. Coordination was strengthened among the Ministry of Electric Power (MOEP), Ministry of Coal Industry (MCI), and Ministry of Petroleum Industry (MPI) while reduced demand required the shuttering of many plants and refineries. This consolidation then moderated with the decentralization trends unleashed by the Cultural Revolution mid-decade. The markedly lower growth rates in 1971 coincided with a partial reconsolidation effort, whereby the MOEP and the Ministry of Water Resources Utilization were combined to form the Ministry of Water Resources and Electric Power, and the Ministry of Petroleum Industry merged with the Coal and Chemical ministries to form the Ministry of Fuels and Chemicals.

By mid-1980 the economy's growth rate began to drop, reaching a mere 5 percent the following year. The central government launched a third wave of attempted administrative centralization that led to the creation of the State Energy Commission (SEC), which, however, never received dedicated staff, an independent base of operations, or funding, and whose creation qualified "as one of the major non-events of 1980."[15] Previously existing agencies continued to operate as before, and the commission dissolved two years later amid 9 to 10 percent economic growth rates and a proven inability to raise the capital necessary to support sufficient power generation for the burgeoning national economy. As Victor Shih notes: "The planners' tight grip on the economy was first loosened when growth far exceeded the plan in 1982 and in 1983. Deng responded by sending a series of political signals to members of his factions in the provinces to increase investment and to take their own initiatives."[16] Shih also argues that in early 1984 the economic figures from 1983 revealed "continual economic vigor and a thirst for capital from the grassroots level . . . [and] in late April 1984 . . . the *Meeting for Some Coastal Cities* . . . had a strong agenda to devolve investment and lending power to the localities."[17] The growth of the early 1980s provided an opportunity for the new, reform-oriented leadership to begin the process of removing government from commercial enterprise work and the business of controlling energy production.

Decentralization I: Rise of Corporations (1982–1998)

This need for capital and technology acquisition, most immediately for the electric power generation necessary to the industrial growth that China's leaders were encouraging, led to 1986 policy changes that allowed the entrance of new investors upstream into coal, electric power, and oil production. Provincial, municipal, and local governments, as well as private domestic and foreign firms were encouraged to invest in coal mines, power plants, and a range of oil refining and production activities. In order to facilitate this step-change in energy production, energy assets were also corporatized. During this decade major energy firms were established such as China National Petroleum (Group) Corporation (CNPC), China Petrochemical (Group) Corporation (Sinopec), and China National Offshore Oil Corporation (CNOOC) in the oil industry as well as Huaneng Group in electricity generation. In 1988 the ministries of Petroleum, Water Conservancy and Power, and Coal Industries were abolished, and many of their regulatory responsibilities were transferred to the new corporations.

Such a combination of trends necessitated, in the eyes of many conservative leaders, a movement to reassert Beijing's authority in the form of a centralized Ministry of Energy (MOE). The ministry was launched in June of 1988, as economic growth began to dip, reaching 4 percent the following year, and was designed as a fourth attempt to provide central oversight over the newly complex set of actors in the energy sector. The ministry never integrated well with the much more powerful State Planning Commission (SPC). This gap in coordination was perhaps best illustrated in the major disparity between energy demand estimates that the SPC and MOE calculated for the Eighth Five Year Plan. The 1991 SPC estimate for total required electric power build-out for the 1991–1995 period equalled 83.6 GW, only 70 percent of the 121.7 GW estimate of the MOE.[18] This new "supra-ministry" soon followed in the footsteps of its predecessors, however, suffering from internal competition and dissension, and was disbanded less than five years later, in March 1993. As one scholar wrote: "Unfortunately, the MOE was little more than a collection of the same vested interests within one umbrella organization, the same personnel, the same allegiance, and the same entrenched interests. . . . The MOE was never able to function as a cohesive group."[19]

The creation of energy corporations in the mid-1980s marked an important break from past governance patterns, and represented a new model of both interacting with the rapidly evolving global energy market outside China's borders and also attracting the financing and technology necessary to harness the energy potential within the country. This need was articulated in numerous official documents, including a September 10, 1993, MOEP instruction: "Foreign investment in the nation's electric power industry not only supplements inadequate domestic construction funds and ability to manufacture power generating equipment, moreover the technology and management experiences that foreign investment will bring, as well as the economic efficiency created, will be good. . . . In the past 10 years alone foreign investment constitutes 11 percent of electric power construction investment."[20] A 1994 Ministry of Electric Power plan reiterates this need: "China can fulfil about three-quarters of the new business [which includes rehabilitation programs for existing plants] internally, leaving $25 billion for foreign suppliers; such help will be welcomed, provided it is accompanied by foreign finance."[21] The emergence of corporations also marked a critical step in the "marketization" of China's infrastructure. As one scholar has noted, corporate involvement "fundamentally changed expectations about electricity—power was now regarded as a commodity to be bought and sold on the market, rather than allocated by government."[22]

In addition, the corporation emerged in part as a means of organizing productive assets and property rights. The proliferating government entities discussed above claimed ownership over financial stakes in SOEs that overlapped and that were often illegitimate and at odds with one another. The logic of corporatization[23] stemmed from "its ability to specify ownership rights and to legally separate enterprise from state administration."[24] The "Company Law," which was passed on December 29, 1993, served as the primary legal framework to identify claims over liabilities and assets of the rapidly diversifying economy, and to regulate formal decision-making powers at the firm level in an effort to make firms more independent of political influence. In fact, articles 3 and 4 clearly state that the liability and rights of shareholders of a firm are in proportion to their capital contribution to the firm. Moreover, article 7 explicitly states that SOEs under reorganization to corporation status must "identify and verify" the firm's assets and "determine the respective owners of the property rights therein, and settle its creditor's rights and liabilities."[25] The law therefore provided an opportunity both to reevaluate the nest of outstanding claims against many SOEs in the energy sector and to at least begin the process of removing party political actors from the daily management of firms.

By the mid-1990s the central administration of the energy sector was again performed by disparate entities, many of which had been reinstated, as well as the rising energy corporations that were increasingly straddling commercial and regulatory functions. This array of government actors included, but was not limited to, the State Development and Planning Commission (SDPC), the State Economic and Trade Commission (SETC), the Ministry of Petroleum Industry, the Ministry of Geology and Mineral Resources, the Ministry of

Electric Power, the Ministry of Land and Natural Resources, and the Ministry of Coal Industry. In 1998, as part of a government-wide restructuring of industrial policy in the "pillar industries" of energy, transportation, and telecommunications, the Ministry of Coal Industry and Ministry of Electric Power Industry (MEPI) were abolished and the State Administration of Coal Industry (SACI) was formed under the SETC, granting provincial governments operational management over coal mining enterprises and larger-scale electric power projects. Much of the operational authority for the electricity industry was transferred to the newly established State Power Corporation of China (SPCC).

Decentralization II: Rise of Multiple Agencies (1998–2008)

The pluralization of corporations during the 1980s and 1990s led to a major set of industrial and institutional reforms in 1998 that significantly reduced central government capacity in the form of personnel, dedicated funding, and institutional structure. Despite the mobilization of corporate resources, the central state did not initially redeploy its resources to guide energy investments at the firm level. Philip Andrews-Speed captures this process well, observing:

> In the past, the leaders of the major state-owned energy companies were able to play a major role in determining the policies and plans for their individual industries. Progressive corporatization of these companies has reduced the power of these executives to influence national policy to a great extent, but the capacity of government to lead has not been enhanced in a commensurate way. Indeed, with more players in the sector, the government's ability to manage the energy sector has actually diminished.[26]

Barry Naughton has also recognized the migration of energy decisions to the firm level, writing:

> Particularly following the revival of state sector profitability, some of these organizations are extremely rich and powerful. The state companies under central SASAC's [State-owned Assets Supervision and Administration Commission] purview include, for example, the State Electricity Grid and the big electric power–generation companies. . . . This middle layer of the state economy is the least transparent . . . in between the fully corporatized and often listed companies, and the national government.[27]

In March of 1998 the NPC approved a wide-ranging plan that had been designed by the Politburo the year before to consolidate the central government apparatus and state-owned industry. The forty ministries overseeing China's growth were reduced to twenty-nine, with many employees transferred to SOEs, research institutes, quasi-private firms, or simply laid off. The reforms affected over 33,000 central government personnel and within two years more than 4 million government employees had been laid off.[28] In the energy sector, power struggles between the SDPC and the SETC ensued, and by February 2001 the SACI and coal, power, and other administrations under the SETC were closed, as were most of their provincial, prefectural, and county counterparts. In March 2003, the SETC itself was abolished and the majority of its functions transferred to the SDPC, subsequently renamed the National Development and Reform Commission (NDRC). Immediately prior to this major realignment, the nation's first independent regulator for the power industry was established: the State Electricity Regulatory Commission (SERC). The emergence of this unprecedented, arm's-length body heralded what many scholars have termed a new era of the "regulatory state" in energy.[29] Others, such as Margaret Pearson, argue that such restructuring is another attempt to strengthen state control but one that continues to be plagued by historical institutional fragmentation. She writes: "The most recent round of bureaucratic restructuring in March 2003 strengthened the state's efforts to maintain authority over strategic assets."[30]

However, while some degree of consolidation under the NDRC did take place by the early 2000s, a range of new entities, like SERC, began to proliferate and become linked to the energy sector. At the central level, the State-owned Assets Supervision and Administration Commission (SASAC), established in 2003, claims ownership rights over, and bears responsibility for, the management and disposal of certain state-owned assets (including merger and acquisition approval and other energy asset restructuring). The commission also has input into personnel movements concerning individuals of vice ministerial rank and below. The State Environmental Protection Agency (SEPA) was recently raised to ministerial rank to become the Ministry of Environmental Protection (MEP), and enforces environmental standards and compliance by energy firms, while resource extraction rights, operation management, and conflict resolution responsibilities are largely shared by the Ministry of Land and Resources (MOLAR), the Ministry of Water Resources (MWR), and the State Administration of Coal Mine Safety (SACMS). The interests of these entities, of course, do not always align. SERC and the pricing bureau of the NDRC seek to strengthen competition by maintaining higher numbers of energy firms in industries such as power generation. In contrast, other central agencies, such a SASAC, aim to maximize returns on assets by encouraging the consolidation of existing firms.

This fractured system of energy governance in China is reflected in the energy industry's fractured structure. The following section will address the market structure of China's oil and gas, coal, and electric power industries in an effort to illustrate the significant differences between the concentrated oil and gas on the one hand and fragmented coal and electric power on the other. While much of the relevant literature is concerned with reforms in the Chinese oil and gas industry and the rise of such firms, the vast bulk of national energy production relies on coal and electric power—markets as fragmented as the authorities attempting to regulate them.

China's Energy Structure: An Overview

Oil and Gas

Scholarly and political analyses of China's energy system often focus primarily on the oil and gas industry, motivated by (1) the perceived strategic nature of these hydrocarbons; (2) China's relatively recent emergence as a net oil product importer and net crude oil importer in 1993 and 1996 respectively; and (3) the increasingly global investment activities of Chinese oil and gas firms since the late 1990s.[31] This attention has reinforced the view that China's energy sector is heavily concentrated and dominated by a handful of large incumbent firms, financed largely by the central government, and therefore resistant to major change, institutional or otherwise.[32] Unlike analyses of the private or quasi-private sector in China, which frame state involvement as a largely "helping hand" model of development,[33] analysis of the energy sector often characterizes Beijing as an interventionist state actor pursuing regressive pricing and finance policies.[34] These perspectives argue that barriers to market entry for nonincumbent firms are high, incentives to support protectionism by incumbent firms are many, financial resources for non-central-state actors are limited, and political pressure to subsidize prices dominates the political economy landscape.

This analytical framework is influential and its implications significant, because it implies that forces for change—technological, financial, or regulatory—are greatly weakened in China's energy sector. Indeed, much of the data culled from subsectors that are most exposed to international markets (and therefore most "visible" to international observers) support this characterization. The oil and natural gas industries have remained cartelized in structure despite the introduction of significant institutional reforms in the late 1990s and various reforms related to WTO compliance in the early 2000s. China's three major oil and gas firms traditionally functioned as separate segments of the supply chain. CNPC was created in 1988 to manage China's oil and gas exploration and production onshore, both domestically and internationally.

Sinopec was established in 1983 to build and operate China's refining capacity downstream and petrochemical production. CNOOC was created in 1982 to specialize in the exploration, development, and production of oil and gas in China's territorial waters (with a depth over five meters).

However, this corporate separation of upstream exploration and production of crude from downstream refining of product proved difficult to maintain once upstream price reforms were designed to stimulate production. Partial liberalization of crude oil prices by the mid-1980s through the mid-1990s rendered CNPC's onshore exploration and production activities upstream increasingly profitable. Such liberalization did not occur downstream in the oil product market. Heavily regulated downstream retail prices for oil products such as diesel and gasoline increased losses for the refining activities of Sinopec. For example, in 1983 the central government introduced a three-track pricing system. A fixed annual quota of output was determined, and over two-thirds of that output was sold at a first, low price of RMB100/ton ($5.60/ton), while over one-quarter was sold at a second, higher price of RMB555/ton ($31.00/ton). Above-quota production (6 percent of total production that year) could be sold at a negotiated price on the market. The low price was abolished by 1993, at which time over two-thirds of crude oil was sold at negotiated prices. In refining, foreign companies had begun to enter oil storage, product importation, and third-party processing, as did provincial and local companies.[35]

Rising imports (leading to China's switch to net importer status of oil product that year) led to a focus on managing oil consumption and by 1994 the oil pricing market was dismantled. All crude and product prices returned to being fixed by the central government. In April all import rights were abolished. As Andrews-Speed has written: "Thus, having introduced an oil-pricing system which was evolving rapidly towards being an open market, the government has made a rapid retreat. Prices are now tightly controlled and respond only sluggishly to the international markets. . . . In one step the government reversed ten years of reform."[36]

The wide-ranging industrial and governmental reforms introduced in 1998 sought to improve the competitiveness of these three firms by vertically integrating them, with particular focus on the two largest (CNPC and Sinopec). After the reforms, Sinopec held both upstream and downstream assets in China's southern and eastern regions while CNPC held upstream and downstream assets in the north and western regions. To deepen commercial reforms and separate regulatory function and corporate management, all three firms listed portions of their assets on foreign exchanges through newly established subsidiary firms.

Yet, despite these considerable attempts to reform the structure of the oil and gas market, much remained the same. Peter Nolan captures this stagnation well, and highlights remaining unresolved questions relating to the continuing influence of the central government and competition between the firms, writing: "The relationship between the floated company and the parent remains unresolved. While the floated 'children' [subsidiary firms listed on international stock markets] may wish for prosperous independence from their 'parents,' the 'parents' (CNPC and Sinopec) have responsibility for a total of 1.5 million employees and several million family members."[37] He concludes that the "Chinese oil and petrochemical industry is still highly protected."[38]

Indeed, a review of oil and gas production figures since the 1998 reforms reveals little significant change in ownership structure. Barriers to significant market entry have remained high. As table 12.1 illustrates, one firm—CNPC—accounts for over one-half of China's crude oil production and nearly three-quarters of its natural gas supply. CNPC has actually consolidated its dominance in gas over time and the lack of significant domestic market structure change in crude oil is also apparent. Andrews-Speed highlights the continuing obstacles to competition in the industry, arguing: "The issue which does not seem to have been addressed is whether one oil company may invest and conduct exploration, production, refining or distribution in the other's territory. . . . The longer the period of [regulatory] ambiguity, the stronger the position of the companies. One glaring deficiency in the legal framework is the absence of a petroleum law."[39] Given the reform challenges present in the oil and gas industry, it is understandable how analysis of China's energy market, particularly when viewed through this prism, would support a bias privileging a more monolithic status quo.

Coal and Electric Power

Despite the concentration of actors in China's oil and gas industry, it is important to note that the term "fragmented authoritarianism," which accurately

TABLE 12.1
Market Concentration of Energy Subsectors, Post-1998 Reform

Top Firm	Share of Production in Respective Industry (%)		
	1998	**2003**	**2009**
CNPC (Crude Oil)	67.3	64.5	60.4
CNPC (Natural Gas)	70.8	72.9	71.1
Huaneng (Electricity)	2.4	9.7	11.5
Shenhua (Coal)	0.6	5.1	6.9

Sources: NBS, *China Energy Yearbook*, various years; NBS, *China Electricity Yearbook*, various years; China Economy Supervision Center, ed., *China's Industrial Map: Energy* (Beijing: Social Sciences Academic Press, 2006, 49, 134; INNET, *China's Energy Outlook*, 2004, 11; LBNL, *China Energy Databook*, 2008; Company annual reports, 2009; Author's estimates.

and persuasively framed the political economy of a reform-era China, emerged first from a study of China's electric power system.[40] Returning to table 12.1 the coal and electricity statistics reveal these markets to be considerably less concentrated in structure than their crude oil and natural gas counterparts. Shenhua Group, China's leading coal supplier, has only recently neared 7 percent of national production. In contrast, its American counterpart, Peabody Energy, commands over 20 percent of the US coal market. In 2005 China's top four coal firms produced 16.5 percent of China's coal and the top eight firms produced 24.4 percent. Comparable US figures are 44.8 percent and 59.8 percent.[41] Huaneng Group, the largest power producer in China and until recently led by former Premier Li Peng's son Li Xiaopeng, produces 11.5 percent of national generation.

Perhaps most important, oil and gas combined contribute only 15 percent of China's national primary energy production. As table 12.2 illustrates, the nation's coal industry forms the backbone of the sector, consistently accounting for three-quarters of China's national primary energy production. However, in contrast to the oil and gas markets, the structure of the coal and electricity industries, upon which China's economic growth is based, have been anything but static.

Ownership and Price Reforms

Coal Industry

Unlike the situation in the oil and gas industries, twin processes of ownership and investment diversification have penetrated extensively upstream, in the coal market. Coal fuels over two-thirds of primary energy consumption in China and dominates the electric power industry, contributing 81.1 percent of total electricity production in 2008.[42] This most vital foundation of China's energy supply has relied significantly on mines owned and operated by firms at the provincial or local level. At the outset of the Cultural Revolution in 1966, approximately 80 percent of China's coal was produced by "state key

TABLE 12.2
Dominance of Coal: Primary Energy Production (percent)

	1976	1986	1996	2006
Coal	68.8	72.4	74.9	75.7
Oil and Gas	27.5	23.3	18.9	15.3
Other	3.7	4.3	6.2	9.0

Source: LBNL, *China Energy Databook*, 2008. Data normalized (EJ) and percentages calculated.

mines" owned and operated by the central government. In the beginning of the reform period in 1978 this ratio had been reduced to slightly above 55 percent. By 1995 these central state mines contributed 37 percent of output.

Much of this variation in ownership over time is the result of limited central state capacity to increase supply through SOE mines administered by the central and local governments during periods of rapid economic growth and resulting energy shortage. This shortage led to the promulgation of policies that encouraged local non-state mines (LNSM) to grow to fill the gap in production. This cycle is evident in figure 12.3, which illustrates the greater volatility of LNSM in comparison to mines owned by the central and local state. The figure also illustrates the greater time sensitivity of LNSM production rates. These mines were able to stop and start production in a much more timely fashion and in step with economic growth, while state-owned mines at the central and local level display both growth rates clearly lagging economic growth and displaying lower values than LNSM.

Responding to the high economic growth of 1978–1979 and then again of 1982–1985, LNSM grew at rates that were at times multiples of the central state-owned mines (CSM) and local state-owned mines (LSM), and well higher than GDP growth rates. LNSM growth averaged 22.5 percent during the boom of 1982–1985. Subsequently, during the economic slowdown of the

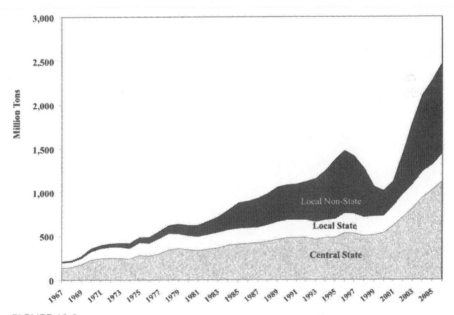

FIGURE 12.3
China's Coal Production by Ownership. *Source:* LBNL, *China Energy Databook*, 2008.

late 1980s, the growth of LNSM dropped precipitously to rates lower than the central state mines. LNSM growth returned during the boom of 1992–1995, averaging 13.8 percent in comparison to a meagre 0.1 percent for CSM and 1.2 percent for LSM. By the end of 1997 the combination of a slowing economy and central government rhetoric regarding the enforcement of regulation closing down LNSM led to significant declines in LNSM growth.[43] The overall pattern is clear: LNSM growth rates far exceed CSM and LSM growth rates during periods of high economic growth, while LNSM growth rates fall dramatically (often below CSM and LSM rates) in periods of lower and moderating economic growth.

As a result of such growth patterns, the overall share of output contributed by LNS mines increased from 14.1 percent in 1978 to 38.3 percent in 2006. By 2006 more than half (52.0 percent) of China's coal was produced by firms owned by actors outside of the central government. As Elspeth Thomson has documented:

> By the late 1970s the government had recognized that the fastest output growth was being achieved by the LNS mines and that their continued existence was vital to the economy. It therefore adopted a policy of spending the limited capital

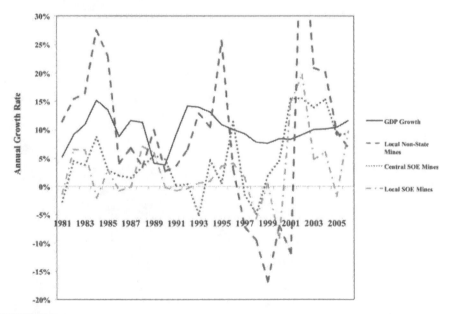

FIGURE 12.4
GDP Growth and Mine Growth by Ownership. *Source:* **LBNL,** *China Energy Databook,* **2008.**

resources available on a few key large mines and infrastructure projects too large and capital-intensive for the peasants to undertake. Operators of local mines were encouraged to open mines using whatever resources they could find.[44]

Even during the most recent period of high economic growth since 2002, during which CSM did begin to increase output rapidly, non-state mine growth rates exceeded that of mines owned by the central and local state (see figure 12.4).

Financial data for these coal firms highlights both their economic importance and their ownership diversity. Recent sales income figures, which distinguish between private, joint shareholding, collective, and foreign-invested firms, reveal the range of non-state actors that is obscured by aggregate national statistics. As seen in figure 12.5, 47.5 percent of total sales income for the coal industry in 2005 was earned by firms without controlling stakes owned by the central or local government.

Much of this decentralization of ownership and investment resulted from the gradual liberalization of coal pricing. Coal prices were partially liberalized in

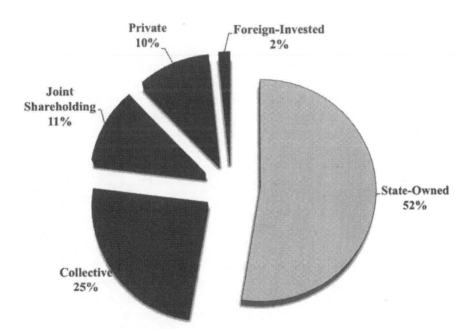

FIGURE 12.5
Breakdown of Total Sales Income by Firm Type, 2005. *Source:* China Economy Supervision Center, ed. *China's Industrial Map: Energy* (Beijing: Social Sciences Academic Press, 2006), 203.

1984, immediately preceding the 1986 regulation allowing sub-central government actors and firms to invest in electric power generation, discussed at length below.[45] Coal prices were reformed to account for coal quality differences in the early 1980s, and in 1984 a dual track system of prices was introduced, as it had been earlier in agriculture, to create incentives for increased production.[46] Each production unit produced a fixed quota amount of coal at a state-set price to be distributed by state channels to demand industries such as metallurgy, steel, and chemical production.[47] Above-quota coal could either be sold back to the state at 50 percent higher prices (and eventually 70 percent higher prices) or on the emerging free (largely illegal "black") market.[48] Coal exchanges, which were established in five cities in 1992 to reduce the extortion occurring through middlemen, had little effect and the black market continued. By June 1993 the central government allowed central state-owned mines (CSMs) to sell 80 percent of their coal production at market prices, and by 1994 decreed all coal freed from quota prices.[49] There was considerable backsliding, as many government officials had profited from arbitrage between market and state prices for coal. Also, thermal coal prices for power plants continued to be subsidized, yet Guizhou was technically the last province to abolish official state subsidized thermal coal pricing for power plants on July 1, 2006.[50]

In addition to price liberalization, reforms in the 1990s allowed progressive marketization through the organization of annual bargaining conferences (*ding huo hui* 订货会) between the major mines, power plants, and Ministry of Railways (MOR). The role of the NDRC as an active player in these sessions has gradually declined, transforming instead to a mediator role. The state-led conference was formally abolished in 2004 but the negotiation meeting continues in an evolved form named the Coal Production, Transportation and Demand Linking Session (*meitan chanyunxu xianjie hui* 煤炭产运需衔接会) as all coal contracts still must be accompanied by signed documentation from the MOR indicating that sufficient rail capacity has been reserved to transport the coal under contract.[51] Thermal coal prices on the spot market rose 25–30 percent year-on-year by mid-2004, while contract prices in China had increased by less than 10 percent. Due to this disparity, power plant managers interviewed all observed that since 2003 mines have continually renegotiated their prices and failed to deliver coal to the plant at the contract price. The domestic media has also reported openly about the extent of the problem.[52] These liberalization policies eroded coal subsidies considerably and by 2002 the spot price of Qinhuangdao coal (QHD), China's widely referenced thermal coal benchmark, had aligned closely with rising international prices. As figure 12.6 illustrates, prices of Qinhuangdao coal in China and Newcastle coal in Australia tracked well through the most recent volatility caused by rapid demand shocks in the region.

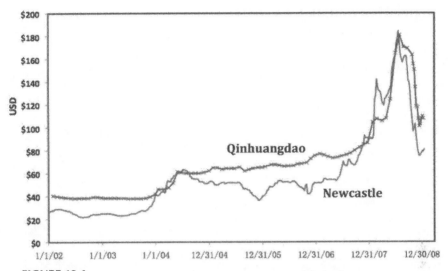

FIGURE 12.6
China's Thermal Coal Spot Prices Converge with Regional Benchmark.
Sources: Newcastle data from Reuters. Qinhuangdao data from China Coal Transport and Distribution Association (CCTD), converted with daily exchange rate data from NY Fed and calorific value (QHD: 5800 kcal/kg, NWC: 6700 kcal/kg). This graph profited greatly from discussions with He Gang and others at PESD, Stanford University.

Electric Power Industry

Processes of ownership and investment diversification have also penetrated upstream in the electricity generation industry, the result of far-ranging reforms in electric power generation.[53] As occurred in the coal industry, the financial and administrative resources of the central government proved inadequate to meet power generation demand; a shortage that by the boom years of the early 1980s became acute (see figure 12.7). Reforms pursued by the central government sought to (1) diversify sources of finance and augment state-directed capital by allowing, for the first time, noncentral government entities to invest in and build power plants; (2) raise electricity tariffs by abolishing command era pricing that only covered operating, transmission, and distribution costs and introducing "cost-plus" or "rate of return regulation" that accelerated capital repayment and guaranteed 12–15 percent returns; and (3) levy a series of national fees to create specialized funds for capital investment.

A constellation of local and regional government actors that resulted from such reforms now extends deep into the power generation sector, including provincial government investment funds, local government SOEs, grid and grid-subsidiary groups, and nuclear power firms. This complexity has been re-

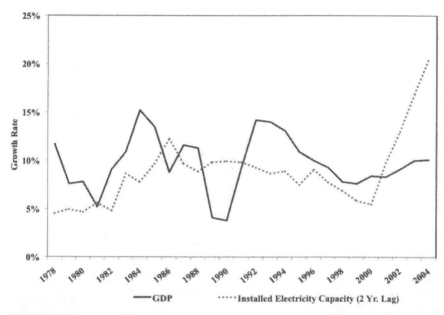

FIGURE 12.7
GDP vs. Installed Electric Power Capacity Growth. *Source:* LBNL, *China Energy Databook,* 2008. *Note:* To compensate for the average two years needed for a plant to come online, electric power growth rates were moved back two years.

cently noted by a few studies. Chi Zhang and Thomas Heller observe that "During long periods of shortage, Chinese reforms focus on getting new power on line as quickly as possible, and delegate much of the task of adding capacity to provincial and local authorities."[54] In the six years since the dissolution of the State Power Corporation of China (SPCC) that once vertically integrated regional electric grids and electric power generation, it is notable that the "Big Five" companies that were the generating assets of the SPCC command less than half of China's electricity generation market (see figure 12.8).

The energy corporation initially served as a vehicle to resolve increasingly blurred rights and claims between central and local control over energy assets during this untangling process, and also to attract foreign technology and financing to develop domestic resources under tight credit market conditions and poor fiscal capacity. Initial reforms were rather successful. For example, in 1975 China suffered from a shortage of approximately 5 GW, or 12 percent of national generating capacity; this grew to 15 GW or 16 percent by 1986.[55] As figure 12.9 illustrates, rapid increases in electricity capacity began in the late 1980s to respond both to these historical shortages as well as the fast-growing demand resulting from the expansionary economic reforms of the early

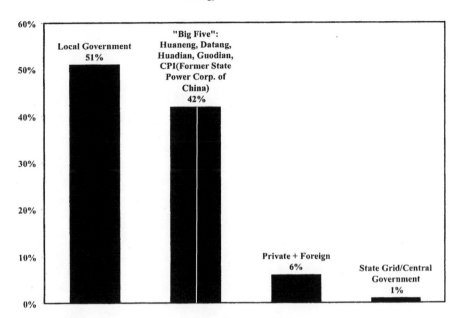

FIGURE 12.8
Ownership of Power Generation Capacity, 2007. *Sources:* China Electricity Council, 2008; Arthur Kroeber, "Enigma Variations: Unwrapping the Riddle of China's Electricity Industry," *GaveKal Dragonomics China Insight*, August 26, 2008; Author's estimates. *Note:* Figures are compiled according to "controllable capacity" by each firm.

1980s. By the late 1980s annual capacity increases averaged a respectable 15GW, through the boom of the 1990s.

More specifically, formal financial reform of the electric power industry began in 1984 with the passing of legislation that transformed direct state funding of power plant construction into loans from state banks.[56] At that time, there was no foreign or non-central-state investment in China's power industry. Price reform deepened in 1986, and was highlighted by the promulgation of the Provisional Regulations on Encouraging Fund Raising for Power Construction and Introducing Multi-Rate Power Tariff.[57] This battery of reforms increased wholesale prices and diversified sources of finance by permitting subnational government, private, and eventually foreign-invested entities to invest, in an effort to encourage investment through three main mechanisms.

To attract new investors, the reforms raised the wholesale tariffs paid to the power producers and introduced a pool purchase price (PPP) to a "cost-plus" formula that guaranteed a 12–15 percent rate of return for newly invested plants. In addition, an RMB0.02 fee was added to the end-user retail prices nationwide to raise capital for the newly established electricity construction

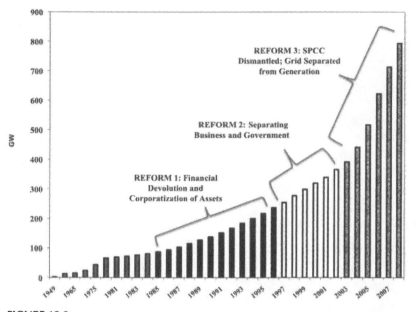

FIGURE 12.9
China's Installed Electric Power Capacity. *Sources:* Xu, *Powering China,* 37; www.drcnet.
com.cn; *NBS Electricity Power Yearbook,* various years; China Electricity Council, 2009.

fund. Lastly, a wide range of special fees and charges, such as the "fuel and transportation surcharge," were also allowed by 1986. These fees were collected by the central and local governments to finance various projects such as the Three Gorges Dam project and the "coal for oil substitution" project and a portion was also disbursed to local projects.[58] Such reforms diversified ownership, diluting the central government's share of generation assets, and also introduced sufficient subnational funding to increase generation capacity and largely solve the major power shortages of the 1980s and early 1990s.[59]

Firms such as Huaneng Group proved effective at building partnerships with foreign financial institutions and creating the foundation for rapid expansion. The prominence of electricity firms in this crucial stage of policy and economic reform is reflected in the fact that six of the original twenty-two SOEs approved by the State Council to issue shares in overseas stock markets hailed from the electric power industry.[60] Huaneng Power International, Incorporated (HPI), was established in June 1994 and in October of the same year listed on the New York Stock Exchange, issuing $1.25 billion in American Depositary Receipts.[61] By 1995 over forty power investment companies had begun operation, forming what has been characterized by some scholars as "a group of independent power producers (IPPs)."[62] In January 1998, HPI was listed on the Hong Kong Stock Exchange and in November 2001 the firm successfully issued A-shares in the domestic market. By 2002, 13 percent of the total investment in the Chinese power industry was foreign.[63]

By March 1997, another power firm—Beijing Datang Power Generation Corporation—became the first Chinese firm to list on the London Stock Exchange. In December 1996 the State Power Corporation of China (SPCC) had been established and within a few months the MOEP had been transformed into the Department of Electric Power within the SETC, with a staff reduced to fewer than twenty people. This reorganization served to separate production, including both generation and distribution, from regulatory functions. In 1999 the China National Nuclear Corporation (CNNC), which managed the country's nuclear power sector, was also split into two separate firms. One firm focused on resource extraction, nuclear processing for civilian and military use, waste treatment and safety, while the other remained responsible for the construction and execution of nuclear power plants.

The year 1996 resulted in a raft of new laws that brought legal, if not regulatory, clarity to the power industry. The Electricity Law was passed and allowed non-state entities to participate in the generating sector, while also furthering the separation of regulatory and ownership functions of power producers. Between 1998 and 2002 subsequent legislation revised and clarified regulatory changes designed to separate generation and transmission assets formally, split generation and transmission pricing, launch small-scale market power pooling trials, and elaborate future reform objectives.[64] These objectives included (1) the formal separation of generation from transmission in terms of ownership and regulation; (2) the establishment of new pricing mechanisms to internalize environmental costs more effectively; (3) the creation of competitive regional markets for the dispatching of generators; and (4) the development of market-oriented pricing mechanisms throughout the power value chain, from generation to transmission, distribution, and retail pricing.[65] Cross-subsidization through price discrimination still plagued the sector however. For example, in 2002 the average rural price for electricity was RMB0.66/kWh, compared to an urban average of RMB0.44/kWh. The largest differential between regions reached RMB0.264/kWh.[66]

The great expansion of power that began in the mid-1980s through the reforms discussed above also heralded the relative decline of central funding for such expansion. For example, between 1980 and 1994, "the annual growth rates of both power generation and installed capacity averaged more than 8 percent, while between 1980 and 1992, the share of central government investment in total power sector investment decreased from 91 percent to 30 percent."[67] The central government provided nearly half of power industry investment during 1985–1990. In the following five years, however, between 1991 and 1995, only one-third of investment funds flowed from the central government. Financial levers of influence have clearly narrowed. In the same period, local sources accounted for 42.9 percent of the total. The third-largest category of investment was foreign, equalling 9.9 percent. Moreover, the variation across regions was considerable, from provinces such as Tibet that were dominated by central state funds, at 98.7 percent, to powerhouse Guangdong market, in which only 3.5 percent of funding was from the central state.[68] Statistics for the Southern Grid reveal both the progressive efforts of local government to meet rising power demands and the necessary freedom from central guidance that the region enjoyed in order to succeed. Foreign investment shares were highest in Guangdong and Hainan (23.2 percent and 21.7 percent respectively), as were local government investments (54.1 percent and 41.7 percent).[69]

In 1998, after two years of operation, the SPCC had earned a mere RMB7.01 billion in profits, based on sales revenue of RMB260.64 billion.[70] Partly as a result of such poor performance supporting the argument of reform-minded leaders, in 2003 the firm, which controlled 49.5 percent of installed capacity, was broken up into five major generation firms (the "Big Five"). Additionally, 6.47GW of installed capacity was allowed to remain under the authority of the State Power Grid Company for eventual sale in an effort to finance power grid development, and 9.2GW was assigned to a separate firm to cover noncore business expenses.[71] (See figures 12.10 a, b, and c.)

Moving Forward: Three Challenges

China's devolution of financial investment and ownership to noncentral levels of government and firms in the core of its energy sector—the coal and electric power generation industries—has allowed the country to meet the vast majority of its energy needs, despite an initial lack of finance and technology available to the central government. Rapid economic growth has generated enormous energy demand and the vast majority of that demand has been met through domestic resources. The Chinese state's ability to manage successfully the considerable coordination of such a complex sector under such demanding conditions has been impressive. However, as China continues to grow, there are three main challenges to stable economic development that are most often cited in the literature relating to China and its energy development. The first, rising oil import dependence, is often highlighted by security and international relations scholars and has thus far been managed fairly well. The second and third challenges, namely rising energy intensity levels and environmental degradation, present far more serious long-term consequences and the potential solutions are far more complex.

Ownership	Generation Assets	Transmission and Distribution Assets
Central Government	46%	54%
Provincial and Local Government, Corporate	87%	13%

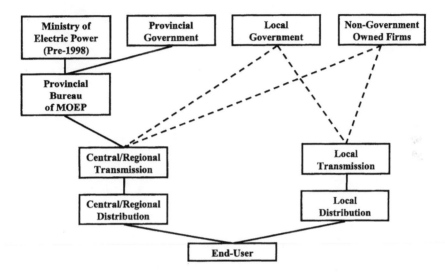

FIGURE 12.10a
Recent Evolution of Electric Power Sector Assets: A. Mid- to Late-1990s.
Source: Adapted from Chi Zhang and Thomas Heller, "Reform of Chinese Electric Power Market," 94. *Note*: As they have done, solid lines note generating capacity trusted to the provincial bureau of the ministry for operation (then placed under SPCC subsidiaries after 1997), while dashed lines note generating capacity that sells into the grid by other entities. The terms "Generation" and "Trans. + Distr." above the charts represent shares of generating capacity and electricity distributed, respectively. Figures are estimates for 1997, 2002, and 2007. See also www.buyusa.gov/china/en/power.html.

Supply Side: Oil Dependence

Despite China's high level of energy self-sufficiency, its rapidly growing oil industry is the sub-sector of the national energy market that is most dependent on imports. Arguments are often marshaled that China's dependence on politically unstable regions of the world, such as the Middle East, for one-half of its oil imports is exposing the nation—and national economic development—to unhealthy levels of supply risk. Such arguments are commonplace in the security and political debates of other nations, such as the United States. However as figure 12.11 demonstrates, even in the case of oil, China's ratio of imports to total

Ownership	Generation Assets	Transmission and Distribution Assets
Central Government	46%	54%
Provincial and Local Government, Corporate	87%	13%

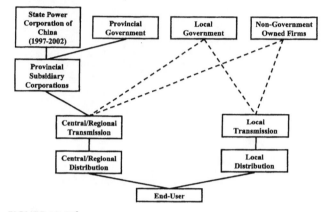

FIGURE 12.10b
B. 1997–2002

Ownership	Generation Assets	Transmission and Distribution Assets
Central Government	1%	42% ("Big Five") + 57% (Other)
Provincial and Local Government, Corporate	89%	11%

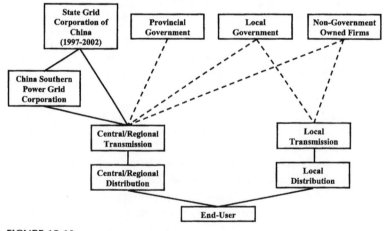

FIGURE 12.10c
C. Post–2002

consumption is considerably lower than that of regional neighbors such as India and Japan, though it is nearly double that of the United States and growing rapidly. Oil crude imports have annually exceeded oil product imports, as seen in figure 12.12, and crude imports have more than tripled in volume between 1999 and 2006. As the experiences of India and Japan make clear, oil import dependence does not, in itself, present a challenge to economic development. In economic and security terms, such supply risk can be mitigated through policies such as supplier diversification, investment in efficiency through technology, and hedging against price risk through financial instruments.

In fact the investment actions of Chinese oil firms have yielded results that fulfill the first of these policy objectives fairly well. In 1993 China imported approximately 40 percent of its crude oil from the Asian region, with the bulk (26 percent) supplied by Indonesia. As a result of the rapid decline of Indonesian production, by 2006 the share of Asian supplies was reduced to a negligible amount, and replaced largely by West and East Africa, as well as Russia (see figure 12.13). Perhaps most significantly, despite such rapid growth in imports, the overall share of supply from the Middle East remained stable, at about 50 percent. Significantly, supply lines for oil *product* imports are much more concentrated geographically and are much closer to home. The majority

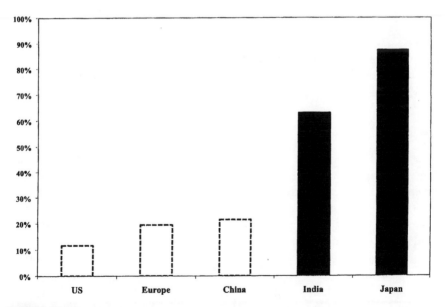

FIGURE 12.11
Oil Imports as Percentage of Total Oil Consumption, 2007. *Sources: BP Statistical Review of World Energy,* **2008; WTO Trade Statistical Database, 2008.**

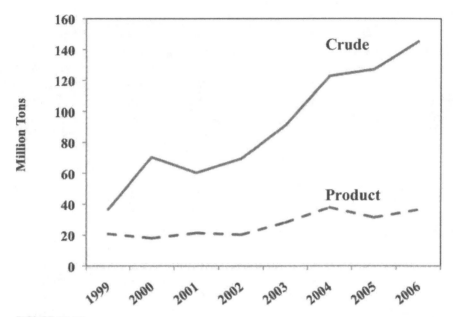

FIGURE 12.12
China's Crude and Oil Product Imports. *Source*: LBNL, *China Energy Databook*, 2008.

of product is imported from developed economies in the Asia region. Of the nearly 70 percent of oil products that are imported from Asia, 30 percent come from South Korea and 13 percent from Singapore. The Middle East provides a mere 12 percent.[72]

Demand Side: Energy Efficiency

While China's ability to deliver the energy necessary for economic growth has been considerable, and supply side management has proven laudable, its future energy (and increasingly environmental) needs are clearly more complex than simply meeting soaring consumption with *supply* side solutions.[73] The combination of a rapid corporatization of energy assets, national energy demand on pace to surpass that of the United States, and strong continued investments in heavy industry have created pressing regulatory challenges on the *demand* side of the energy equation. Past gains in energy efficiency have been impressive, and seemingly provide grounds for hope. China's energy intensity (ratio of energy consumption to GDP) dropped rapidly despite major economic growth during the 1980s and 1990s. Between 1980 and 2000 China quadrupled its GDP and only doubled its energy consumption. Indeed,

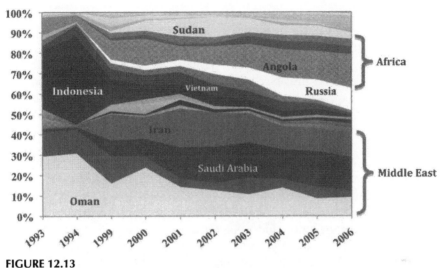

FIGURE 12.13
Chinese Imports of Crude Oil by Source. *Sources:* China Customs Bureau, various years;
LBNL, *China Energy Databook*, 2008.

Xiannuan Lin argued with much empirical support that energy conservation policies, rather than solely structural changes in the economy, drove much of the efficiency gain after 1980.[74]

However, between 2002 and 2005 this trend reversed itself, and energy consumption grew at a rate faster than economic output. In recognition of such a trend, energy intensity reduction targets were one of the few quantitative goals enumerated in the Eleventh Five-Year Plan. The plan calls for China's energy intensity in 2010 to be 20 percent below 2005 levels. This would require an annual reduction of about 4.5 percent between 2006 and 2010. These targets have not been met thus far. On March 9, 2009, the chairman of the National People's Congress (NPC) Standing Committee, Wu Bangguo, delivered the committee work report during the Second Plenary Session of the Eleventh NPC. The report specifically highlighted this failure to meet efficiency goals (italics added):

> Two major binding targets—*energy consumption per unit of GDP* and total emissions of major pollutants—fell far short of the set goals. To a great extent this showed that the pattern of China's economic development had not been transformed fundamentally: industry still holds the dominant position in the industrial structure, exports and investment still play the leading role in the demand structure, and serious problems such as mounting pressure on resources and the environment, increasing difficulty in expanding employment, and insufficient consumption still exist.[75]

As the 2007 IEA World Energy Outlook made clear, China's decentralized approach to energy growth, which has privileged supply side solutions over demand side solutions, will not meet the nation's future needs. The rise of local actors in mining and electric power generation coincided with the major reductions in energy intensity discussed above. Had such reductions not taken place and the energy intensity levels of 1980 remained static, China would have burned twice as much coal in 1995 than needed to produce that year's GDP.[76] Slowing reductions in energy intensity, combined with heightened urbanization and continued industrialization trends may be outstripping the ability of local actors to invest in domestic infrastructure, despite the current stimulus package by the central government. Ninety percent of China's coal reserves are located in the hinterland while the vast majority of its demand and industrial centers are located in the coastal areas. Failures to mitigate energy intensity will exacerbate this infrastructure strain and will increase demand growth over the next decade to much higher absolute levels. Significantly, China became a net coal importer in the first half of 2007, signaling pressures on this infrastructure.

Demand Meets Supply: Environmental Degradation

Finally, the environmental impact of continued supply side solutions delivered by a diverse range of corporate and local state actors has already registered domestically and globally.[77] The fate of the global commons, historically placed solely in the hands of the developed world, now will also be determined by major actors of the developing world. China's CO_2 and total greenhouse gas (GHG) emissions have recently surpassed those of the United States. While it is clear that the developed world, led by the United States and Europe, has contributed the vast majority of the current stock of CO_2, moving forward, the US Energy Information Agency (EIA) has estimated that China will produce well over one-quarter of world CO_2 emissions through 2030, while the United States will contribute less than 20 percent.

In terms of local environmental degradation, economic damages from China's air pollution alone were estimated to equal 3.8 percent of GDP as early as 2003 by a recent World Bank report. The cost of health damage from air pollution is projected to be 13 percent of GDP by 2020 under the "business-as-usual" (BAU) scenario, as estimated by an OECD study.[78] Reliance on domestic forms of energy will continue to generate major environmental costs.

As much of China's energy supply has successfully been met through the devolution of energy production to the local level, environmental progress may also need to depend on this decentralized approach to governance. China's vast geography and regional variation in economic development will in all likelihood require local customization of approaches to environmental protection.

Many observers credit what progress the United States has made in this regard to forward-looking state governments that legislate environmental standards more stringent than federal standards. David Vogel has written about the "California Effect" and improvements in US federal automobile emissions standards that were nudged along through such action in California, given its auto market size.[79] Decentralized approaches to regulatory reform in the case of the environment can function well, and it is often the more wealthy regions with large consumer markets that can provide momentum. As recent provincial-level energy intensity data mapped by Lawrence Berkeley National Laboratory (LBNL) graphically illustrate, China's more wealthy coastal provinces are indeed leading the way in areas such as energy intensity reduction.

Conclusion: A Fifth Centralization Attempt? (2008–)

In recognition of the conflicting interests and broad range of regulatory authorities relating to China's energy policy, energy markets, and energy security, the National Energy Leading Group (NELG) was established in the spring of 2005 to bring together the heads of thirteen ministries under Premier Wen Jiabao and provide direct leadership guidance to the sector. This leading group fulfilled the function that other leading groups have historically, serving as a temporary vehicle to discuss the challenges the nation was facing in a given sector and to design the form and content of a more formal institution that would eventually provide oversight. By March 2008 the NPC voted to establish two overarching energy-related regulatory bodies to strengthen oversight of proliferating energy firms.

The National Energy Commission (NEC) replaces the National Energy Leading Group in setting and guiding national energy strategy and policy as a supraministerial institution. The National Energy Administration (NEA) combines with the existing Energy Bureau to implement these policies, and will have its own Party Group, but will only enjoy vice ministerial status and remain under the authority of the NDRC.[80] Despite these clear advances, it is important to note that the cast of characters is still evolving and a true division of responsibilities remains unclear. The draft Energy Law, which is expected to be passed by the National People's Congress in 2010, does not yet detail authority delegation and continued uncertainty is highlighted by the fact that a vice premier has not been named to head the National Energy Commission.

The National Energy Administration will oversee national implementation of energy policy with nine departments and a staff size of 112 people—double the 50–60 staff of the original Energy Bureau, but still quite limited.[81] In all, China's national government may contain approximately 800 individuals whose work in some way is related to energy policy. In contrast, the EIA alone—an organization dedicated mainly to data gathering, analysis, and education—employed 620 people in fiscal year 2004. The US Department of Energy (DOE) employed 14,713 individuals in the same period.[82] The disparity in personnel is striking, particularly in the context of the processes of decentralization, ownership diversification, corporatization, and rapid capacity expansion that characterize China's current energy market.

In historical terms, China's central state has proven to be a capable risk manager in a critical sector undergoing considerable change. Beijing has been quite successful in allowing periodic reductions in state ownership, pricing authority, and monopoly producer rights for what is arguably the most politically critical sector of the economy. As Zhang and Heller write of the electric power industry: "Where the central government ran up against inefficient state bank lending and macroeconomic limits on state credit expansion, it allowed local governments and some foreign investors to develop a more diverse array of plants to supplement the state core."[83] Local firms and governments, pursuing economic interest, served well the goal of increasing national energy supply. Without such reforms in the energy sector China's remarkable growth story could not have occurred.

The economic interests of local actors do not align in the same manner when national policies shift toward other objectives, such as the reduction of greenhouse gas emissions and the related implementation of a national strategy to combat climate change. In the context of the global economic downturn, these reforms of the past, born during periods of high economic growth and energy shortage, are being revisited. In particular, the portfolio of ownership and financial investment in sectors such as energy, aerospace, telecommunications, and transportation is being reassessed and levels of central state ownership are being consolidated. However, this strengthening of incumbent SOE firms through consolidation, given the pronounced lack of meaningful reform in corporate governance, regulatory independence, as well as media and legal independence, may prove to be highly problematic in meeting the main challenges discussed above.

Select Bibliography

Andrews-Speed, Philip. 2000. "Reform of China's Energy Sector: Slow Progress to an Uncertain Goal." In Sarah Cook, J. Zhuang, and S. Yao, eds., *The Chinese Economy Under Transition*. Basingstoke, Hampshire: Macmillan.

———. 2004. *Energy Policy and Regulation in the People's Republic of China*, International Energy and Resources Law and Policy series, 19. The Hague: Kluwer Law International.

————. 2005. "China's Energy Woes: Running on Empty," *Far Eastern Economic Review*, June.

————. 2009. "China's Ongoing Energy Efficiency Drive: Origins, Progress and Prospects." *Energy Policy*.

Brown, Lester. 2005. "China Replacing the US as World's Leading Consumer," *Eco-Economy Updates*, Earth Policy Institute, February 16.

China Economy Supervision Center, ed. 2006. *China's Industrial Map: Energy*. Beijing: Social Sciences Academic Press.

China Electricity Council. 2009. "2008 National Electricity Industry Statistics—Brief Reports."

Chow, Daniel C. K. 1997. "An Analysis of the Political Economy of China's Enterprise Conglomerates: A Study of the Reform of the Electric Power Industry in China." *Law and Policy in International Business* 28, no. 2: 383–433.

Cunningham, Edward A. 2007. "China's Energy Governance: Perception and Reality," MIT Center for International Studies Audit of the Conventional Wisdom, March.

Downs, Erica. 2008. "China's Energy Policymaking Structure and Reforms," Testimony before the U.S.-China Economic & Security Review Commission, China's Energy Policies and Their Environmental Impacts Panel, August 13.

Ebel, Robert. 2005. *China's Energy Future: The Middle Kingdom Seeks Its Place in the Sun*. Washington, DC: Center for Strategic & International Studies.

Fesharaki, Fereidun, and Kang Wu. 1998. "Revitalizing China's Petroleum Industry Through Reorganization: Will It Work?" *Oil & Gas Journal* 96, no. 32.

Fewsmith, Joseph. 1999. "China and the WTO: The Politics Behind the Agreement," *National Bureau of Research (NBR) Analysis* 10, no. 5, essay 2 (November).

Fingar, Thomas. 1987. "Implementing Energy Policy: The Rise and Demise of the State Energy Commission." In D. Lampton, ed., *Policy Implementation in Post-Mao China*. Berkeley: Univ. of California Press.

Frye, Timothy, and Andrei Shleifer. 1996. *The Invisible Hand and the Grabbing Hand*. Cambridge, MA: National Bureau of Economic Research.

IEA. 2007. *World Energy Outlook*. Paris: IEA.

Kroeber, Arthur. 2008. "Enigma Variations: Unwrapping the Riddle of China's Electricity Industry." *GaveKal Dragonomics China Insight* (August 26).

Lawrence Berkeley National Laboratory. 2008. *China Energy Databook*.

Lewis, Joanna. 2007. "China's Strategic Priorities in International Climate Change Negotiations." *Washington Quarterly* 31, no. 1 (December 1): 155–74.

Li, Binsheng, and James Dorian. 1995. "Change in China's Power Sector." *Energy Policy* 23, no. 7: 619–26.

Li, Cheng. 2000. "China in 1999: Seeking Common Ground at a Time of Tension and Conflict." *Asian Survey* 40, no. 1.

Lieberthal, Kenneth, and Mikkal Herberg. 2006. "China's Search for Energy Security: Implications for US Policy." National Bureau of Asian Research, *NBR Analysis*.

Lin, Xiannuan. 1996. *China's Energy Strategy: Economic Structure, Technological Choices, and Energy Consumption*. Westport, CT: Praeger.

Luo Gan. 1998. "Explanation of Plan for Institutional Restructuring of the State Council." *Ta Kung Pao* (March 7). In FBIS, DR/CHI, March 10, 1998, 98-068.

National Bureau of Statistics (NBS). *China Electricity Yearbook*, various years.
———. *China Energy Yearbook*, various years.
———. Customs Bureau, various years.
Naughton, Barry. 1995. *Growing Out of the Plan: Chinese Economic Reform*, 1978–1993. Cambridge: Cambridge University Press.
———. 2006. "Claiming Profit for the State: SASAC and the Capital Management Budget." *China Leadership Monitor* 18 (Spring).
Nolan, Peter. 2002. "China and the Global Business Revolution." *Cambridge Journal of Economics* 26, no. 1 (January 1).
Nolan, Peter, and Huaichuan Rui. 2004. "Industrial Policy and Global Big Business Revolution: The Case of the Chinese Coal Industry." *Journal of Chinese Economic & Business Studies* 2, no. 2 (May): 97–113.
Nolan, Peter, and J. Zhang. 2003. "Globalization Challenge for Large Firms from Developing Countries: China's Oil and Aerospace Industries." *European Management Journal* 21, no. 3: 285–99.
Oi, Jean. 1999. *Rural China Takes Off: Institutional Foundations of Economic Reform.* Berkeley: University of California Press, 1999.
Pearson, Margaret. 2005. "The Business of Governing Business in China: Institutions and Norms of the Emerging Regulatory State." *World Politics* 57 (January).
———. 2007. "Governing the Chinese Economy: Regulatory Reform in the Service of the State." *Public Administration Review* 67, no. 4: 718–30.
Saich, Tony. 2002. "The Blind Man and the Elephant: Analyzing the Local State in China." In L. Tomba, ed., *On the Roots of Growth and Crisis: Capitalism, State and Society in East Asia*, 75–99. Annale Feltinelli.
Shih, Victor. *Factions and Finance in China: Elite Conflict and Inflation.* Cambridge: Cambridge University Press, 2007.
Shirley, Mary. 1999. "Bureaucrats in Business: The Roles of Privatization versus Corporatization in State-Owned Enterprise Reform." *World Development* 27, no. 1: 115–36.
Smil, Vaclav. 1998. "China's Energy and Resource Uses: Continuity and Change." *China Quarterly*, no. 156.
State Council Office of Economic Restructuring. 2004. "Zhongguo dianli jianguan jigou jianshe yanjiu baogao." (November).
Steinfeld, Edward. 2004. "Energy Policy: Charting a Path for China's Future." World Bank China Note, June.
Thomson, Elspeth. 1996. "Reforming China's Coal Industry." *China Quarterly*, no. 147: 726–50.
———. 2003. *The Chinese Coal Industry: An Economic History.* London: Routledge.
Vogel, David. 1995. *Trading Up: Consumer and Environmental Regulation in a Global Economy.* Cambridge, MA: Harvard University Press.
Walder, Andrew. 1995. "Local Governments as Industrial Firms: An Organizational Analysis of China's Transitional Economy." *American Journal of Sociology* 101, no. 2.
———. 1998. "Zouping in Perspective." In Andrew G. Walder, ed., *Zouping in Transition: The Process of Reform in Rural North China*, 16–23. Cambridge, MA: Harvard University Press.

Woo, Pei-Yee. 2005. "China's Electric Power Market: The Rise and Fall of IPPs." PESD Working Paper No. 45, August 16.

World Bank. 2007. *Cost of Pollution in China: Economic Estimates of Physical Damages.* Washington, DC: World Bank.

Xu, Colin, Tian Zhu, and Yi-min Lin. 2005. "Politician Control, Agency Problems and Ownership Reform: Evidence from China." *Economics of Transition* 13, no. 1: 1–24.

Zha, Daojiong. 2006. "China's Energy Security: Domestic and International Issues." *Survival* 48, no. 1: 179–90.

Zhang, Chi. 2003. "Reform of Chinese Electric Power Market: Economics and Institutions." PESD draft paper, Stanford University, January 31.

Zhang, Chi, and Thomas Heller. 2007. "Reform of Chinese Electric Power Market: Economics and Institutions." In David Victor and Thomas Heller, eds., *The Political Economy of Power Sector Reform: The Experiences of Five Major Developing Countries.* Cambridge: Cambridge University Press.

Zhou, Xiaoqian, ed. 2007. *China's Electric Power Program.* Beijing: Water Power Publishing.

Zweig, David, and Jianhai Bi. 2005. "China's Global Hunt for Energy." *Foreign Affairs* 84, no. 5.

13

Environmental Challenges

From the Local to the Global

Joanna Lewis

C HINA HAS MADE UNPRECEDENTED achievements in the past three decades. Its economic growth rates of 8 to 10 percent per year have exceeded those of any other country in the world, enabling a tenfold increase in per capita income and lifting an estimated 400 million people out of poverty. It achieved this economic growth with a decrease in energy used per unit of output, as China has become three times more energy efficient. While energy consumption and output have increased, overall air pollution concentrations in cities have decreased. Yet, these figures only begin to tell the story of China's rise, and its impact on the environment. While economic output has increased rapidly, the share contributed by energy-intensive products has also increased, causing the economy to become less energy efficient for the first time in decades. China's use of coal, which is the source of as much as 70 percent of soot, 90 percent of sulfur dioxide (SO_2), 67 percent of nitrogen oxides (NO_x), and 70 percent of carbon dioxide (CO_2) emissions in China, has increased dramatically in recent years. Despite efforts to diversify China's energy mix, the share of coal has actually risen in recent years, outpacing strong capacity increases in renewable energy.

As China enters the twenty-first century, it must decide whether it can continue to rely on its economic growth strategy of the past, which has come at the expense of its own environment. As China has grown, its environmental challenges are no longer localized—they have global reach. This is particularly true in the case of global climate change. Now the largest annual emitter of greenhouse gases, China is at the center of the quintessential environmental challenge of the twenty-first century. While most greenhouse gas emissions do not have local environmental or health impacts, the sources of these emissions—such as power plants, vehicles, and industrial facilities—also emit the air pollutants that cause more localized impacts. As a result, reducing the emissions of greenhouse gases can have both global and local benefits. As the impacts of rising global greenhouse gas emissions are more comprehensively understood, it is becoming increasingly evident that climate change will exacerbate many of China's existing environmental problems, and bring some new ones as well.

This chapter explores the current environmental challenges facing China, and examines how the linkages between the local environmental impacts being felt within China and the global environmental impacts being felt around the world may shift the attention of China's leaders to these challenges. The first section provides an overview of the current pollution situation in China and the major sources of emissions. The second section examines recent responses of China's leadership to local and global environmental challenges. The final section examines how global climate change could shape China's environmental policy response in the years to come.

China's Environmental Challenges

Rapid economic growth in China has come at a toll to both the local and global environment. The country's environmental problems include deteriorating water quality and water scarcity, air pollution in both urban and rural areas, land degradation, and increasing desertification. These environmental challenges impact the health and welfare of the current population, threaten the prospects for future generations, and challenge China's ability to sustain economic growth rates in coming decades. Most sources of pollution in China can be traced back to energy use, and particularly to its reliance on coal at the core of its energy system.

Conventional Air Pollutants

According to the World Bank, twenty of the thirty most polluted cities in the world are in China.[1] While the most populated areas in China tend to suffer from the most air pollution, the problem is most severe in the northern provinces of Qinghai, Ningxia, Shaanxi, and Shanxi, as well as Beijing and Tianjin municipalities. Each year, air pollution in China causes 500,000 to 750,000 premature deaths, and 75 million asthma attacks.[2] While the majority of pollution stems from power plants and industrial facilities, indoor air pollution from burning stoves, particularly common in rural areas, is the fourth-largest cause of mortality in China. Acid rain falls on one-third of China's territory and costs China 30 billion yuan in crop damage and 7 billion in material damage annually. Studies have estimated that poor air quality imposes a welfare cost to China of between 3 to 8 percent of GDP.[3]

As China's industrial and electricity sectors grow at rapid rates, and continue to rely on coal, pollution levels are also increasing. China's power sector is the single largest source of air pollutants, emitting about 44 percent of China's SO_2 emissions and 80 percent of NO_X emissions. Coal also has a higher carbon content than any other fuel—over 700 kilograms carbon per ton of coal equivalent (Kg-C/TCE), compared with about 400 Kg-C/TCE for natural gas—resulting in higher CO_2 emissions per kilowatt generated than any other power source. China is the largest consumer and producer of coal in the world. It relies on coal for over two-thirds of its energy needs, including approximately 80 percent of its electricity needs. Although China is also expanding its utilization of nuclear power and nonhydroelectric renewables, these sources comprise 2 percent and 0.7 percent of China's electricity generation, respectively, whereas hydroelectricity contributes about 16 percent.[4] This dominance of coal in China's energy is not expected to fall significantly as China's energy demand grows, and by several estimates may increase (figure 13.1).

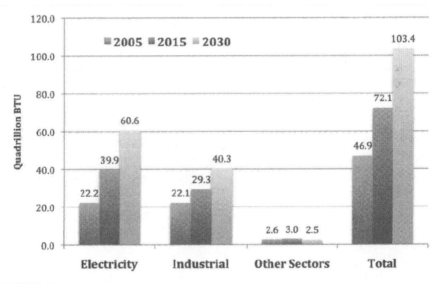

FIGURE 13.1
Current and Projected Coal Use in China by Sector. Source: Energy Information Administration (EIA), *International Energy Annual 2008*, figure 50: "Coal Consumption in China by Sector," September.

Regulation of emissions from power plants can be a major factor in reducing overall emissions, and China has relatively stringent environmental regulations in place. However, these regulations that target power plant emissions are not always effectively enforced, particularly because running pollution control equipment on a power plant can decrease the net power output, resulting in lost revenue from power sales to the plant owner. As of 2005, only 45 GW of the then 389 GW of installed thermal capacity had flue gas desulfurization units in place.[5] Table 13.1 illustrates the targets laid out in the Tenth Five-Year Plan for air pollution for 2005, as well as the actual emissions for that year. Targets for SO_2, soot, and industrial dust were all exceeded.

Water Quality, Water Scarcity, and Desertification

Water availability and water quality are critical environmental challenges in China (northern China in particular), and the situation is expected to continue to deteriorate in coming years. Water shortages throughout China have been blamed on centuries of overcultivation, as well as a lack of clear water rights and free or very inexpensive pricing of water resources. Currently two-thirds of China's cities have difficulty accessing water, and 70 percent of the water in cities is not suitable for drinking or fishing. At least 20 percent of China's water supply is estimated to be lost through inefficiencies in water use. Northern China bears the brunt of China's water challenge; water availability per capita in China is one-quarter the world average, and in northern China it is one-tenth the world average. Northern China is also home to China's most severely polluted water basins of the Liao, Hai, Huai, and Songhua rivers. Water shortages in the northern plains threaten China's agricultural produc-

TABLE 13.1
Tenth Five Year Plan Targets for Air Pollution,
Planned and Actual Emissions (million tons)

	PLANNED 2005	ACTUAL 2005	(+/− %)
Air Pollution			
SO_2	17.9	25.5	**42**
– Industry	14.5	21.7	**50**
– Domestic	3.5	3.8	**9**
Soot	10.6	11.8	**11**
– Industry	8.5	9.5	**12**
– Domestic	2.1	2.3	**10**
Industrial Dust	8.98	9.1	**1**

Source: World Bank and SEPA, *Cost of Pollution in China*, 2007.

tion, for the region produces more than 50 percent of the nation's wheat and 33 percent of its maize.

China has huge tracts of rapidly degrading grasslands, water erosion problems, and the highest ratio of actual to potential desertified land in the world. Excessive water withdrawals and land degradation in northern and western China have caused desertification to advance at a rate of 1,300 square miles per year. Four hundred million people are threatened by the encroachment of the three largest deserts, the Taklimakan (Xinjiang), Kumtag (Gansu), and Gobi (Inner Mongolia). According to a United Nations study, by 2010 there could be as many as 50 million environmental refugees in China, many fleeing the ocean of sand. Gansu Province alone reported four thousand villages at risk of being buried in drifting sand. Desertification is also linked to the spring sandstorms that inflict northern China.

A 2007 toxic algae bloom in China's third-largest freshwater lake, Lake Tai in Jiangsu Province, turned the lake fluorescent green and raised awareness of China's water challenges around the world.[6] With strong local government support, the northern arc of Lake Tai became home to 2,800 chemical plants, most of them small cinder-block factories. The Lake Tai incident, along with several other high-profile water pollution scares in recent years, has led to politically sensitive local protests. While data is hard to come by, in 2006, an environmental official noted that mass protests on pollution-related issues had risen 29 percent per year in recent years, and that there had been more than 51,000 environmental disputes related to pollution raised that year alone.[7]

China's reliance on hydroelectricity for electricity generation also has implications for the water resources for other uses. The Three Gorges Dam will provide 22.4 GW of power when completed in 2012, or roughly the equivalent capacity of twenty large coal plants. Damming the Yangtze River, however, is expected to cause increased siltation rates possibly reducing power output, as well as impacting local ecosystems.

Carbon Dioxide Emissions and Climate Change

China's role in the climate change problem has increasingly become a topic of international attention. Now the largest emitter of greenhouse gas (GHG) emissions measured on an annual basis, China can no longer ignore its contribution to this challenge, even with its relatively low per capita emissions rates (figure 13.2).

China's power sector is the largest source of CO_2 emissions in China, responsible for about one-half of energy-related CO_2 emissions. Within the power sector, about 98 percent of China's power sector CO_2 emissions come from coal use.[8] China's increase in energy-related emissions in the past few

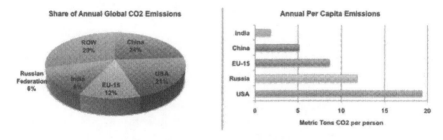

FIGURE 13.2
China's GHG Footprint. *Source*: Netherlands Environmental Assessment Agency and
BP, "China Contributing Two-Thirds to Increase in CO2 Emissions," June 13, 2008,
www.mnp.nl/en/service/pressreleases/2008/20080613Chinacontributingtwothirdstoin
creasein CO2emissions.html. *Notes*: Data are for 2007. Includes CO2 emissions from
fossil fuels only.

years has been driven primarily by demand from China's booming industrial
sector. Industry consumes about 70 percent of China's energy, and China's
industrial base supplies much of the world. For example, China today produces about 35 percent of the world's steel and 28 percent of aluminum, up
from 12 percent and 8 percent, respectively, a decade ago.[9] The IEA estimates
that the energy embedded in China's domestic production of goods for export
was 452 million tons of oil equivalent (Mtoe) in 2004, or about 28 percent of
the country's total energy consumption.[10]

Looking ahead, and recognizing that while exact projections of China's
emissions have been frequently inaccurate, the trends in China's emissions
growth are clear. As illustrated in figure 13.3, the EIA has steadily increased its
projections for China's CO_2 emissions in 2030 in its *International Energy Outlook* each year for the last five years, with the exception of a slight reduction in
the projection in 2009 based on the global economic downturn. Its projections are that China's emissions in 2030 will be in the range of 500 percent
above 1990 levels. Globally, this translates to about 40 percent of all new energy-related CO_2 emissions between now and 2030. If China's emissions
growth kept pace with this rate of 10 percent per year, it could be emitting as
much CO_2 as the entire world is today by the year 2040.

The Political Response

Today, members of China's leadership find themselves in an increasingly difficult situation. China's local environmental situation is in many contexts
degrading rather than improving, causing sporadic but increasingly worri-

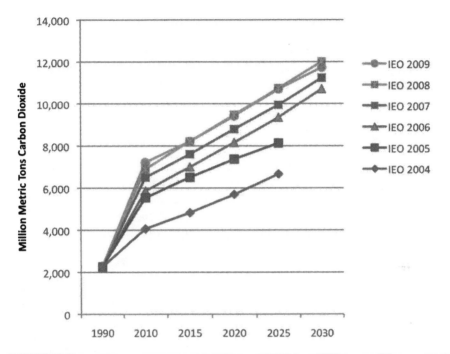

FIGURE 13.3
CO_2 Emissions Forecasts for China. *Source*: US DOE, Energy Information
Administration, International Energy Outlook (IEO) for the years 2004–2009,
reference scenario.

some signs of citizen dissatisfaction. In addition, China's contribution to global greenhouse gas emissions is recognized to have significant global consequences, causing for calls from global political leaders for increased responsibility in the form of mitigation actions.

In several areas, China's leadership is already responding to these calls for increased action to address local and global environmental challenges. Since the roots of many of China's key local and global environmental impacts are in its energy system, this is where the majority of actions will need to focus. China's reliance on coal is at the core of this challenge. Changing China's emissions trajectory will require either a substantial shift away from coal or massive investments in capturing the CO_2 emissions from coal-based energy sources. Simultaneously, China must increase the efficiency with which it uses energy resources to minimize the environmental impacts of meeting the further economic development needs of its population. Since energy-intensive heavy industry is driving the majority of energy demand, growth in these sectors must be constrained with investments shifted to light industry and service sectors.

Coal diversification, energy efficiency, and structural adjustment of the economy are, in fact, areas targeted in several of the most promising policy responses that China has implemented in recent years. This section reviews these policy responses and their effectiveness to date.

Expanding the Utilization of Low-Emission Energy Sources

Recently, the Chinese government has begun to stress fuel diversification for electricity generation to mitigate some of the environmental and health impacts of coal burning. Plans emphasize the development of natural gas and additional hydropower and include several recent transnational gas pipelines, as well as several large dams including the Three Gorges Dam.[11] Because only about 10 percent of China's total hydropower potential had been tapped as of 1995, the Open Up the West (*Xibu dakaifa* 西部大开发) program launched in 1999 to promote western development specifically calls for the development of hydropower in the western provinces. [12]

Aggressive policies also aim to promote non-hydro-renewables such as wind and biomass energy. Under the National Renewable Energy Law adopted in 2005, China has set a target of producing 15 percent of its primary energy from renewable and nonfossil energy sources by 2020, up from about 7 percent at present. For the electricity sector, the target is 20 percent of the capacity from renewables by 2020, which will require substantial increases in the use of wind power, biomass power, and hydropower. This law offers financial incentives, such as a national fund to foster renewable energy development and discounted lending and tax preferences for renewable energy projects. Although the increase in wind power in particular has been impressive in recent years, this energy source is still dwarfed by large-scale hydropower. Hydropower capacity is projected to more than double by 2020, requiring the equivalent of a new dam the size of the Three Gorges Dam project every two years.

Policies to promote renewable energy also include mandates and incentives to support the development of domestic technologies and industries, for instance, by requiring the use of domestically manufactured components. Spurred by a former requirement that new installed wind turbines contain 70 percent local content, Chinese manufacturers are now producing commercial large wind turbines selling for approximately 30 percent less than similar European and US technology. Chinese manufacturers are now producing about 70 percent of the wind turbines being sold in China and 24 percent of the wind turbines being sold globally.[13] Tax and other incentives have targeted the solar photovoltaic (PV) industry, stimulating a sixfold growth in PV production from 2004 to 2005. China is now the largest manufacturer of solar PVs in the world, accounting for 35 percent of the global market.[14]

Promoting Energy Efficiency and Targeting Heavy Industry

Between 1980 and 2000, China quadrupled its gross domestic product while only doubling its energy demand. This relationship between energy use and GDP, or energy intensity, over this time period was unprecedented in developing countries. It allowed China to use significantly less energy and emit much less pollution than it would have without this decrease in the energy intensity of its economy. For example, if China's energy intensity had remained frozen at where it was in 1977, China's energy consumption would be three times what it is today, with similar implications for GHG emissions (figure 13.4).

China's Eleventh Five Year Plan includes a major program to further improve the energy intensity of the economy, including a goal of reducing energy intensity (energy consumption per unit of GDP) by 20 percent below 2005 levels by 2010. Meeting this goal will require significant improvements in energy efficiency throughout the economy, as well as economic restructuring

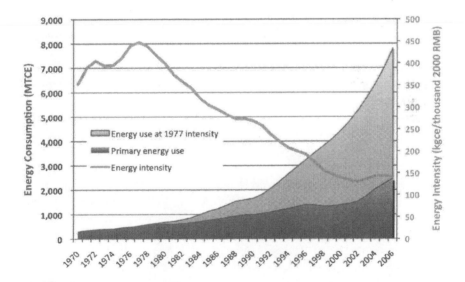

FIGURE 13.4
China's Energy Consumption: Actual and at Frozen 1997 Intensity. *Source:* Lawrence Berkeley National Laboratory, China Energy Group, *China Energy Databook,* 2008, version 7. "Table 4B.2. Actual Primary Energy Consumption and Projected Energy Consumption at Frozen 1977 Intensity."

away from energy-intensive industries. The government projects that meeting this target would reduce China's greenhouse gas emissions 10 percent below business as usual; researchers estimate that about over 1.5 billion tons of CO_2 reductions would be achieved.[15]

In order to promote aggressive implementation of this challenging target and improve local accountability, the NDRC is allocating the target among provinces and industrial sectors, and energy efficiency improvement is now among the criteria used to evaluate the job performance of local officials. There have also been increases in staffing and funding in key government agencies that monitor energy statistics and implement energy efficiency programs. In 2008 alone, China reportedly has put 14.8 billion yuan ($2.2 billion) of treasury bonds as well as $27 billion yuan ($3.9 billion) of governmental fiscal support in projects on energy saving and emission cuts.[16] While elevated implementation efforts appear to be having some impact, implementation of such centrally administered government targets has proven challenging, particularly at the local level.

To better facilitate local-level implementation, additional programs have been established to encourage specific actors to help meet this national intensity goal, including a program established in 2006 to improve energy efficiency in China's largest enterprises.[17] Together, the enterprises included in the "Top 1,000 Enterprises Program" consume one-third of China's primary energy. The group includes the largest energy users in the energy supply sectors (coal, electricity, oil) and in the largest energy-using industrial subsectors (including iron and steel). Under the program, each enterprise agreed to an energy efficiency improvement plan and to have its energy use monitored. Objectives were set for energy intensities of products produced based on advanced domestic and international standards, and incentives are offered to encourage enterprises to meet and exceed their targets.[18]

Another government effort targets the elimination of a number of small, inefficient power plants, totaling around 8 percent of China's total generating capacity, by 2010. NDRC announced in January 2007 that generators proposing new coal-fired plants will need to shut down smaller, older plants at the same time. In addition, all coal-powered plants with capacity under 50 megawatts (MW), and 100 MW generators operating for twenty years or more, will be ordered to close by 2010. Generators with coal consumption more than 10 percent above the provincial average or 15 percent above the national average are also targeted for closure.[19] Similar plant closings are planned across the industrial sector, including inefficient cement, aluminum, ferro-alloy, coking, calcium carbide, and steel plants. All cement plants with annual capacity of less than 200,000 tons were to be closed by the end of 2008, with 250 million tons of outdated cement capacity to be eliminated by 2010.[20] In the steel sector, outdated pig iron capacity is to be reduced by 100 million tons, and steel capacity by 55 million tons, by 2010.[21] NDRC has set reduction quotas at the provincial and regional levels, and provincial officials are required to sign agreements with the central government holding them accountable for their targets. Provincial officials failing to comply would be referred to the State Council, or cabinet, for potential disciplinary action.

As a result of the implementation of the measures described above to help the country mobilize toward achieving the 20 percent energy-intensity reduction goal, the worrisome trend of increasing energy intensity each year from 2003 to 2005 was successfully reversed starting in 2006. In order to meet the goal by 2010, China needs to achieve an average decline of 4 percent per year. In 2006, energy intensity was down 1.79 percent from the previous year; in 2007 it was down 4.04 percent, and in 2008 by 5.2 percent.[22] At the close of 2009, the government reported that energy intensity was down 14.38 percent from 2005 levels.[23] As a result, at the end of 2009 it appears that these elevated implementation efforts, along with the shutdown of inefficient plants, and the economic slowdown from the global financial crisis, have made China well positioned to meet its energy intensity target by 2010, although the final push to the finish line will be challenging.[24]

Counting Carbon

While estimates have been made of the potential carbon emissions savings that could accompany the 20 percent energy-intensity reduction target,[25] China had never put forth any targets that explicitly quantified its carbon emissions until late 2009. In November of that year the Chinese leadership announced its intention to implement a domestic carbon intensity target of a

TABLE 13.2
Recent Trends in Energy Intensity in China

Indicator	Unit	2005	2006	2007	2008	2009
Energy	Mtce	2,247	2,463	2,656	2,850	TBA
GDP	Billion 2005 RMB	18,322	20,449	22,982	25,848	TBA
Energy Intensity	Kgce/RMB	0.1226	0.1204	0.1156	0.1103	0.1127
Energy Intensity Reduction	% per year	-	-1.79	-4.04	-4.59	-2.2

Source: Levine and Price, "Assessment of China's Energy-Saving and Emission-Reduction Accomplishments," 2009; Chen, "Shanxi Leads China in Saving Energy," 2010.
Note: Due to revisions made to 2008 GDP figures, energy intensity is now being reported as declining by 5.2% in 2008 from the previous year. Official 2009 energy and GDP data had not been released at time of publication.

40 to 45 percent reduction below 2005 levels by 2020.[26] This target came within hours of President Obama's announcement that the United States would reduce its carbon emissions "in the range of 17%" from 2005 levels by 2020, and that the president himself would attend the UN international climate change negotiations in Copenhagen.[27]

There is no question that China's announcement of its first carbon target represents a monumental change in China's approach to global climate change. It is also important to recognize, however, that even with this target in place, growth in absolute emissions could continue to increase rapidly. Due to the nature of a carbon intensity target being a ratio of carbon emissions and GDP, whether or not such a target would reduce emissions below "business as usual" greatly depends on future economic growth rates and the evolving structure of the Chinese economy, as well as on the types of energy resources utilized and the deployment rates of various technologies, among other factors. Carbon intensity, like energy intensity, has declined substantially over the past two decades. Between 1990 and 2005, China reduced its carbon intensity by 44 percent. China is also projected to reduce its carbon intensity 46 percent from 2005 levels by 2020, while still growing its emissions by 73 percent during this same period.[28] This has led to much debate whether this domestic policy target is sufficient based on China's role in the global climate challenge.

China and the Global Climate Challenge

The key policy actions that China has taken in the areas of energy efficiency, renewable energy, and industrial policy described in the previous section, are not "climate change policies," in that they were enacted to help the country meet its broader economic development strategies and its local environmental challenges. However, many of these policies, if implemented effectively, will also serve to mitigate China's greenhouse gas emissions—some quite substantially. This is not lost on China's leadership, who released their *National Climate Change Program* report on June 4, 2007,[29] and their Climate Change White Paper in October 2008, both which describe the policies that China currently has in place that are serving to moderate its greenhouse gas emissions growth.

This recognition of the co-benefits to greenhouse gas reduction of many of China's energy sector policies, however, represented a notable change in the political discourse of the Chinese leadership on climate change, which had previously engaged in minimal discussion of China's responsibility or actions toward greenhouse gas mitigation. It wasn't until the Twelfth Conference of the Parties to the United Nations Framework Convention on Climate Change

(COP 12) in November 2006, during an informational presentation to the "Dialogue on Long Term Cooperative Action" that China climate change negotiator Gao Guangsheng gave a presentation on the "Policies and Measures of China on Climate Change Mitigation under the Framework of Sustainable Development" that outlined the contribution of China's domestic policy actions to greenhouse gas reductions.[30]

Today, while China's leadership has held firm against international pressures to cap its own emissions, it is increasingly evident that it is most likely to increase mitigation actions as a result of domestic, rather than international pressures. These domestic pressures are those described above: diversification away from coal, and restructuring the economy to be less energy- and even less carbon-intensive. It is becoming increasingly clear, however, that there is an emerging pressure that could dramatically alter China's climate change policy stance in the coming years. An increasing realization of the potential impacts that climate change may have within China has raised new concern, and may in fact become the driving force behind any future climate change mitigation strategy adopted in China.

China in the International Climate Change Negotiations

China has ratified the primary international accords on climate change—the United Nations Framework Convention on Climate Change (UNFCCC) and the Kyoto Protocol—but as a developing country, China has no binding emissions limits under either accord. It is, however, the leading participant in the Clean Development Mechanism (CDM) established under the protocol, which grants emissions credits for verified reductions in developing countries, and which can be used by developed countries toward meeting their Kyoto targets. China's position in the international climate negotiations has rarely deviated from the rest of the developing world, as collectively articulated by the Group of 77 (G-77), a group of 130 (formerly 77) developing countries.[31] The consistent position of the G-77 has been to emphasize the historical responsibility that the industrialized world brings to the climate change problem and the disparity between per capita emissions that persists between the developed and developing world. [32]

In recent years, China's alliance with the G-77 has not waned, particularly as the risk of being singled out grows due to its increasing emissions growth that put it far ahead of the other developing countries by most metrics. Despite the EU's willingness to commit to post-2012 emissions reduction targets, the absence of international commitments by the United States, the world's largest industrialized-country emitter, provides the best excuse for China to not have to adopt commitments. While China's emissions have now surpassed those of the United States on an annual basis, it will be decades before Chinese emissions surpass US emissions on a cumulative basis, measured as historic contribution of emissions to the atmosphere. As previously mentioned, China's current per capita greenhouse gas emissions would have to quadruple to equal those of the United States (figure 13.2). Consequently, if the United States were to take on credible international climate change commitments, which remains uncertain, China would face renewed pressure to revisit its delay tactics. Another key dynamic that could shift in the near term is the G-77 negotiating block. Countries within the G-77 are beginning to diverge somewhat in their positions, which could leave China in a more isolated negotiating position. Some tropical forest countries have stated a willingness to take on voluntary avoided-deforestation targets in return for compensation;[33] historically, voluntary international targets of any form have not been part of the G-77 position.

The Fifteenth Conference of the Parties to the United Nations Framework Convention on Climate Change and the Fifth Meeting of the Parties to the Kyoto Protocol (COP 15, COP/MOP 5) in Copenhagen in December 2009 in many ways marked the beginning of a new era in the global climate negotiations. Entering Copenhagen, both the United States and China—in many ways the two key players in the global climate debate due to their leading roles as contributors to global emissions—had announced domestic carbon targets, as well as a long list of bilateral energy and climate change agreements stemming from the presidential summit between Presidents Hu and Obama in November.[34] The resulting Copenhagen Accord, agreed to by both China and the United States, along with numerous other countries, marks the first international climate change agreement with documented emissions reduction actions by developing countries. It also allows for the development of a crucial international assessment of emissions statistics reported by both developed and developing countries.[35]

The measurement, reporting, and verification (MRV) of national mitigation actions was a topic that China in particular approached with much reluctance in Copenhagen. Some of China's hesitancy to take on any form of international emissions commitment stems from its concerns about energy data quality and transparency. In developing countries, where resource constraints result in limited data quality, inventories of national greenhouse gas emissions are notoriously inexact, and China has long struggled with developing an accurate inventory system for energy statistics.[36] The uncertainty associated with national inventories makes it very difficult to implement greenhouse gas reduction commitments that rely on baseline inventories and estimated annual improvements at the national level, particularly in developing countries.

Having in place a national emissions inventory system will likely be a crucial step in enabling the adoption and enforcement of any binding emissions reduction policies, whether enacted nationally or internationally. As a result, the topic of measuring, reporting, and verifying emissions reductions in China, whether from its carbon intensity target or from other domestic actions, is likely to remain a focus of both international climate negotiations and US-China bilateral discussions for years to come.

Climate Science and Projected Impacts on China

There is now a scientific consensus that human activity is altering the climate. Driven primarily by a century and a half of rising fossil fuel combustion, carbon dioxide concentrations in the atmosphere had reached 379 parts per million by 2005, 35 percent higher than preindustrial levels.[37] Average global temperatures have risen by 0.76 degrees Celsius since the late 1800s, and the effects are evident in extreme weather events, changed weather patterns, floods, droughts, glacial and Arctic ice melt, rising sea levels, and reduced biodiversity.[38] Average temperatures are projected to increase by another three degrees Celsius upon a doubling of carbon dioxide concentrations.[39] In China, the observed data show that the nationwide mean surface temperature has increased between 0.5 and 0.8 degrees Celsius over the past one hundred years,[40] and will likely increase by 3 to 4 degrees Celsius by the end of this century.[41] Even if all emissions were to stop today, the greenhouse gases already accumulated in the atmosphere will remain there for decades to come, resulting in more warming and stronger climate impacts.

A synthesis report compiled by China's leading climate change scientists stated, "It is very likely that future climate change would cause significant adverse impacts on the ecosystems, agriculture, water resources, and coastal zones in China."[42] Climate change is expected to increase the frequency and severity of storm surges, droughts, and other extreme climate events, particularly in coastal areas. Climate change could also increase the frequency and intensity of heat waves, resulting in higher mortality and morbidity from heat-related weather events. Increased temperatures over time could increase the occurrence and the transmission of infectious diseases, including malaria and dengue fever.

Impacts that are already being observed in China include extended drought in the north, extreme weather events and flooding in the south, glacial melting in the Himalayas endangering vital river flows, declining crop yields, and rising seas along heavily populated coastlines.[43] Projected impacts include a decline in precipitation by as much as 30 percent in the Huai, Liao and Hai river regions in the second half of the century.[44] Estimates of future sea level rise along China's coastline range from 0.01 to 0.16 meters by 2030, and 0.4 to 1 meter by 2050.[45] Higher sea levels increase the possibility of flooding and intensified storm surges, and exacerbate coastal erosion and saltwater intrusion. A one-meter rise in sea level would submerge an area the size of Portugal along China's eastern seaboard;[46] the majority of Shanghai—China's largest city—is less than 2 meters above sea level.[47] China's twelve coastal provinces contribute 42 percent of China's population and 73 percent of its GDP.[48] As a result, China's agricultural system, trade system, economic development engines, and human livelihood all will face new risks under a warming world.

China's leaders are increasingly recognizing the impact of climate change on China. For example, China's special ambassador for climate change, Yu Qingtai, recently stated that "climate change . . . is in fact a comprehensive question with scientific, environmental and development implications and involves the security of agriculture and food, water resource, energy, ecology and public health and economic competitiveness," and "if the climate changes dramatically, the survival of mankind and the future of earth might be impacted."[49] While scientists are still understanding the full implications of climate change for China, it is highly likely that the Chinese leadership, and in particular the leaders within the Chinese Communist Party, will act to address the impacts of climate change if they are deemed to represent a serious threat to national stability.

Many of the climate impacts that are beginning to affect China, and will become more severe in the coming decades, could initiate disruptive change, internally and externally, and therefore may elicit a response from the leadership that we have not yet seen in the face of other environmental challenges. A response that targets the causes of climate change in China, namely its coal dependence and its industrial structure, would simultaneously provide new hope for addressing local environmental concerns that also stem directly from these factors.

Conclusion

The current environmental challenges facing China are inherently linked to the challenges China's leadership faces in the energy sector, including its heavy reliance on coal, and on energy-intensive industry to fuel economic growth. These environmental challenges impact the health and welfare of the current population, threaten the prospects for future generations, and challenge China's ability to sustain economic growth rates in coming decades. The causes of many of China's local environmental challenges are also contributing to the global environmental challenge of climate change.

Most sources of pollution in China can be traced back to energy use, and particularly to its reliance on coal at the core of its energy system. Only through the aggressive promotion of low-emission energy sources including renewable energy, as well as increasing shares of natural gas power and nuclear power, can China diversify its energy system. China must aim to increase the efficiency with which it uses energy resources to minimize the environmental impacts of meeting the further economic development needs of its population. Since energy-intensive heavy industry is driving the majority of energy demand, growth in these sectors must be constrained with investments shifted to light industry and service sectors.

While coal diversification, energy efficiency, and structural adjustment of the economy are, in fact, areas targeted in several of the most promising policy responses that China has implemented in recent years, and significant efforts have been taken to promote better enforcement of regulations adopted in these areas, much more needs to result in current goals being met. To achieve more sweeping changes, additional actions will need to be taken as well. Changing China's emissions trajectory will require either a substantial shift away from coal or massive investments in capturing the CO_2 emissions from coal-based energy sources. A response that targets the causes of climate change in China, namely coal dependence and industrial structure, would simultaneously provide new hope for addressing local environmental concerns that also stem directly from these factors.

Conclusion

China's Next Three Decades

Joseph Fewsmith

A NYONE WHO HAS LOOKED CLOSELY AT THE last three decades of China's development wisely hesitates to predict China's developmental path over the
next three decades. China's reform is almost universally described as "incremental," yet as Sebastian Heilmann reminds us, there have been periods of rapid,
nonincremental change. Just looking at the economic area, the implementation
of the Household Responsibility System in the years 1979–1983 was one period
of rapid, nonincremental change. This reform was a sweeping change of sociopolitical and economic relations in the countryside that continues to reverber-
ate down to the present. One cannot imagine the growth of township and village enterprises (TVEs) or rural to urban migration without it. Both the social
order problems that find expression in mass incidents and the implementation
of village-level elections are responses to changing cadre-peasant relations that
derive from this period. One might also point to the adoption of the Decision
on the Reform of the Economic Structure in 1984 as another inflection point. It
was this decision, which aimed to introduce market-oriented reforms into the
urban and industrial areas of China, that exacerbated tensions between reformers and "conservatives," generating so much tension in the late 1980s. Another,
often overlooked, turning point came with the introduction of tax reform in
1994. Prior to this change, the reform process, in both economic and political
terms, was decentralizing. Put simply, the localities were getting wealthy and the
center was getting poorer, at least in relative terms. The tax reform dramatically
reversed these trends, and now the localities, particularly those without significant local enterprise, are starved for funds, while Beijing has become quite

wealthy. Indeed, central revenues have been growing faster than GDP for many years. Finally, the reorganization of SOEs and massive layoffs of some 50 million workers in the 1996–2000 period marked another enormous change in the economy and in state-society relations.

In other words, there is nothing in the history of the last thirty years that suggests that a straight-line projection of current trends would lead to accurate predictions of China's future. Indeed, the one area in which trend lines have been relatively consistent—economic growth—seems likely to change with important consequences to the overall political-social system. Central revenues cannot continue to outpace GDP, investment cannot continue to outpace consumption, dependence on export markets—especially after the financial crisis—cannot continue at the same pace, and industrial expansion cannot continue to displace environmental and other concerns for long. As Naughton points out, China signaled its desire to change the pattern of its growth when it adopted the Eleventh Five Year Program in 2006. But nothing happened. The momentum of the export-driven system China had built up over preceding years continued in place. Now China faces making enormous changes to its economic system under the pressures of the global financial crisis, with all the pressures on employment and exports that implies.

A major reason why the economy did not change directions quickly and easily is because the political system rewards economic growth, particularly as measured by GDP. Local cadres are evaluated in many categories, including social stability and implementation of the one-child policy, but the one category that has trumped all others has been economic growth. There has been much discussion and some experimentation in recent years of changing the cadre evaluation system and the ways in which it weighs economic growth versus other goals such as environmental protection, but, so far, there has been little change. This is something that will have to change. Somehow the cadre evaluation system will have to take into account divergent goals, which is extremely difficult because different areas have different attributes. At least measuring GDP growth appears to be fair to all areas; incorporating other goals appears to risk introducing even greater arbitrariness into the system, with unknown consequences for corruption and social order.

Sebastian Heilmann suggests that, contrary to much Western thinking, China might be rather well positioned to make these transitions. He argues that in a world increasingly skeptical of neoliberal models of economic governance, China has, rather successfully, been learning to combine practices derived from the CCP's revolutionary history, particularly policy experimentation, with planning in ways that allow a still robust, and perhaps increasingly robust, planning system to work with markets in ways that will continue to generate economic growth and social justice. Whether such a model can incorporate the diversity of welfare goals that the change to qualitative growth implies within an authoritarian, hierarchical system remains to be seen. The changes that will need to be incorporated will certainly challenge that model much more than in the past.

Change will also take place at the highest levels of the political system. Remarkably China passed with very little disruption from a political system dominated by a single strongman (Deng Xiaoping in the reform era, Mao Zedong before that) to one in which no one person can "strike the table" (*pai banzi* 拍板子) and decide matters. Political decisions must be negotiated among the leaders, particularly the Politburo Standing Committee, and the very concern with making mistakes and being forced to take responsibility appears to pressure the political system into greater consultation with policy experts, hence the proliferation of leadership small groups. As suggested in chapter 8, the political system has evolved in ways that are strikingly different than in Western democracies. In democratic polities, periodic elections bring new leadership to the fore, sometimes generating rather new approaches to policy and governing. In the Chinese political system, no one makes it to the top without extensive grooming in a number of positions, both provincial and central. The political system internalizes continuity by rolling over the leadership rather than changing it at one stroke. Thus, a new general secretary finds himself surrounded by colleagues chosen by his predecessor—and then does the same thing to his successor.

This system has brought a large degree of consistency to important issue areas over an extended period of time. As Barry Naughton has pointed out elsewhere, China has been blessed with considerable continuity and expertise in its top economic decision makers over perhaps the past two decades.[1] Expertise in such positions and the relationship between economic technocrats and political leaders cannot be assumed; it is possible that Chinese leaders will simply promote the wrong technocrats or that their relationship with the political leaders will change in ways deleterious for the economy. It is possible that China, like Japan, will "unmake" its economic miracle.[2]

There may also be increasing pressures within the political system to increase competitive pressures. Heightening competition within the political system need not take the form of democratization; the CCP talks a great deal these days about "inner-party democracy," hoping that increased choice within the party will decrease the need for real electoral competition. In 1987, the CCP adopted *cha'e* (差额) elections for the Central Committee, under which there would be 5 percent more candidates than seats. It was under this system that conservative ideologue Deng Liqun failed to be elected to the Central Committee, setting off recriminations among his supporters. In 2007, twenty years later, the numbers of candidates in excess of seats was expanded to 8 percent. The expansion of political competition among the elite thus expanded very slowly. But it expanded. And it certainly will again. Perhaps this expansion will take place very slowly, as it has in the past. But even if the ratio of candidates to seats expands slowly, say to 12 or 15 percent over the next twenty years or so, it seems inevitable that there will be greater intra-elite competition in the future. And such competition can have unpredictable results.

The likelihood of expanding and perhaps accelerating competition seems high as we move into the post–Hu Jintao era (Hu must step down as general secretary in 2012). Deng Xiaoping not only designated Jiang Zemin as his successor but was able to name Hu Jintao as Jiang's successor. But, as the political system moves into the future, there will be no ghost of the past deciding the political leadership; it will have to be decided among a group of elites of relatively equal standing. This likelihood suggests either that an extremely ingrown elite could generate dull and unexciting leaders, much as the Soviet oligarchy did in the years before Gorbachev, or that there will be an informal expansion of competition, which could produce real surprises. A hint of such competition seems to be emerging as Bo Xilai, party secretary of Chongqing, carries out a high-profile campaign against organized crime in that city.[3] Although Bo's political calculations are not clear, it appears that he is competing with other second-tier leaders, such as Guangdong's Wang Yang (who was Bo's predecessor as party secretary of Chongqing), to be promoted to the Politburo Standing Committee in 2012. If such speculation is anywhere close to being accurate, it suggests that we may see a rather different political dynamic in the years ahead.

Ren Jiantao reminds us of the importance of ideology in the Chinese political system. Western observers usually dismiss ideology, opining that no one in China believes in Marxism-Leninism any more. Whether or not that is true, ideology is one of the tools the Chinese state uses to bind the system together and delineate acceptable and unacceptable practices at lower levels. As Ren argues, China's ideological system is fundamentally against markets and liberal political change; reform has had to proceed by swimming upstream against this ideological current, pushing against the Stalinist legacy to make room for markets and now private property. Efforts by reformists to open up China's ideological system in the 1980s were met by the campaigns against spiritual pollution and bourgeois liberalization in 1983 and 1987, respectively, and finally by the military crackdown in June 1989. One of the legacies of that crackdown has been to reinforce the statism inherent in the Leninist political structure, and, while economic development has moved ahead by leaps and bounds, there has been little progress in political reform. Ren suggests that the progress of reform in the future is likely to be constrained by the ideological formulations of the past. But, if a change to qualitative growth occurs in the economy, there will certainly be pressures to rethink ideological strictures, and loosening such strictures will generate greater competition in the political system.

Up to the present, as Perry argues, social protesters have "played by the rules." Reviewing both the prereform and pre-Communist past, Perry finds that the Chinese people are doing what they have always done: using the rules the state has laid down both to protest against local officials who have violated these rules and to secure a better deal for themselves. China certainly has a contentious society, but all this conflict ultimately revolves around the distribution of benefits within an authoritarian state. Contention is not, at least in and of itself, the leading edge of democratization. Civil conflict is plentiful but civil society difficult to find.

Weller and Sun are perhaps somewhat more optimistic about evolving state-societal trends. The rapid growth in religion pushes against the strictures of the state, especially in the case of Protestantism, which has taken advantage of the "gray area" to proselytize actively. In areas such as Wenzhou, Protestantism has expanded without threatening the state, which could be a model for the future. Religion would shape society, but the state would remain authoritarian. But Protestantism is more a language of protest in Henan and other places. This form of protest appears to be different than the mass incidents Elizabeth Perry has focused on because house churches and other groups in that area do not "play by the rules." Here, there seems to be real conflict between state and society over the rules of the game. If the state remains strong and perhaps gains in strength, the odds of such confrontations changing state-society relations in a liberal direction appear very limited. Growing urbanization and marketization are likely to erode the foundations of these movements and the state will certainly use its power to confine, channel, and eliminate such challenges.

But other outcomes are possible. Jamie Horsley correctly notes the progress that rule of law has made over the past three decades, even if there remain very significant gaps. The question is how far efforts to extend the rule of law will go. The state certainly agrees to a utilitarian "rule by law" system in which it uses an increasingly elaborated legal code to regulate and control the behavior of its citizens. Can rule by law evolve into "rule of law" by which the party and state will be bound to legal codes the same way citizens are? Horsley is optimistic that the state's commitment to rule of law and open government laws, as well as its own statements calling for the party to obey the laws, will translate into a rule of law regime. Economic reform, globalization, and calls for social justice might reinforce such trends, regardless of the state's intentions. But, it might be noted, significant political reform would be required for that to occur. The role of the party would have to be reduced significantly; the dominance of local party secretaries would have to give ground to more procedurally grounded governments and more independent courts. Such changes would mark not just an incremental growth of the legal system but a profound break with the political economy as it has evolved over the past three decades. As noted above, the implementation of reform has not always been incremental, so perhaps such a breakthrough is possible.

Nevertheless, the constraints China faces are considerable, with the relationship between the center and the localities one of the most entrenched. In recent years, the center has been trying in various ways to recentralize authority, and has been quite successful in some areas, most notably the tax reform of 1994. The removal of the branches of the People's Bank of China from provincial control and their reorganization into regional banks also gave Beijing more control over monetary policy. Recently the central government has tried to exert hierarchical control over provincial-level discipline inspection commissions, but this reform does not appear to be as successful.

To control its local agents, Beijing needs to either tighten hierarchical control, which seems impractical given the size of China, or allow greater input from local citizens—or both (one could imagine a more effective bureaucratic system, responsive to Beijing's demands, combined with an electoral system, ensuring citizen input). So far, Beijing has not been able to professionalize local-level bureaucracies nor been willing to extend local democracy. As Yawei Liu points out, village-level elections have not been allowed to extend up the administrative hierarchy to the township, much less the county level. And the party's favored remedy, inner-party democracy, has proven ineffective to date. Without some combination of bureaucratic rationalization or electoral control, it is difficult to see how Beijing can better monitor its local agents and curtail behavior that both distorts Beijing's policy demands and arouses local discontent.

The political economy that propelled China's economic development over the past thirty years will be increasingly challenged over the next thirty years. China has met its energy needs largely by decentralizing the production of coal, with more than half of coal being produced in non-state mines. Such local entrepreneurship has served China well in recent years, fueling China's growth, but the highly fragmented energy sector will exact growing costs on Chinese society as pollutants will cause increasing damage to both air and water. The fragmented, largely decentralized nature of the energy sector fits well with the localized nature of China's political economy, but it will fit less well with demands to curtail dangerous and highly polluting mines. But attention both to public safety issues that have received much publicity in recent years, and to the costs to the domestic economy and global climate, which Joanna Lewis lays out in chapter 13, suggest the need to change the model that has undergirded China's political economy in the last thirty years. Yongnian Zheng's chapter 11 on central-local relations suggests why changing this model will be so difficult.

No prediction about the future is "safe," but the increasing costs of China's political economy seem clear. China's political leaders seem determined to modify the old model by adding new criteria to the evaluation of cadres, but the multiplication of criteria is likely to increase political contention within and across regions as well as arguments at the central level about the goals China should strive for (growth at all costs versus environmental protection, increasing popular participation versus technocratic decision making, etc.). Over the last three decades the Chinese system has responded to political and economic challenges in surprisingly robust fashion, which leads to the easy prediction that China will continue to modify its system in response to new challenges. The question is whether China's model of political economy can be modified incrementally or if the challenges of the future will bend that model to the breaking point. If the latter, one can expect much more rapid, if unpredictable, change than any simple projection of trends would lead one to believe.

Notes

Introduction: Three Decades of Reform and Opening

1. Frederick Teiwes and Warren Sun, *The End of the Maoist Era: Chinese Politics during the Twilight of the Cultural Revolution, 1972–1976* (Armonk, NY: M.E. Sharpe, 2008), 492–96.

2. Deng Liqun, *Shi'erge chunqiu* (unpublished manuscript), 127.

3. Deng Xiaoping, "'Liangge fanshi' bu fuhe Makesi zhuyi" [The "two whatevers" are not in accordance with Marxism], in *Deng Xiaoping wenxuan (yijiu qiwu-yijiu ba'er nian)* [The selected works of Deng Xiaoping, 1975–1982] (Beijing: Renmin chubanshe, 1983), 35–36.

4. Teyue pinglunyuan [Special commentator], "Shijian shi jianyan zhenli de weiyi biaozhu" [Practice is the sole criterion of truth], *Renmin ribao*, May 12, 1978. On the background of this article, see Michael Schoenhals, "The 1978 Truth Controversy," *China Quarterly*, no. 126 (June 1991): 243–68.

5. Yu Guangyuan, *Deng Xiaoping Shakes the World* (Norwalk, CT: Eastbridge, 2004).

6. "Communiqué of the Third Plenary Session of the Eleventh Central Committee," *Beijing Review*, 30 Years of Reform and Opening Up, www.bjreview.com/special/30yearsofreform/2008-11/29/content_167170.htm.

7. C. Fred Bergsten, Charles Freeman, Nicholas Lardy, and Derek J. Mitchell, *China's Rise: Challenges and Opportunities* (Washington, DC: Peterson Institute for International Economics and Center for Strategic and International Studies, 2008), 106.

8. Bergsten et al., *China's Rise, 106.*

9. Indeed, there is the argument that religious adherents tend to be more moral, law-abiding citizens. See Zhang Tianyong, *Gongjian: Zhongguo zhengzhi tizhi gaige yanjiu baogao* (Assault: Research report on China's political reform) (Urumqi: Xinjiang shengchan jianshe bingtuan chubanshe, 2007).

Chapter 1: Popular Protest: Playing by the Rules

1. My thanks to participants in the conference sponsored by the Pardee Center of Boston University on "Three Decades of Reform and Opening: Where is China Headed?" for their questions and comments. I am especially appreciative of the thoughtful suggestions raised by Chen Xi and Peter Lorentzen on an earlier draft of this paper. For discussions of these early reform period protests in the countryside, see Elizabeth J. Perry, "Rural Violence in Socialist China," *China Quarterly* (September 1985).

2. People's Daily online, March 1, 2006, english.peopledaily.com.cn/200603/01/eng20060301_247056.html.

3. Kevin O'Brien and Lianjiang Li, *Rightful Resistance in Rural China* (Cambridge: Cambridge University Press, 2006), 119, 127.

4. David Zweig, "To the Courts or to the Barricades: Can New Political Institutions Manage Rural Conflict?" in Elizabeth J. Perry and Mark Selden, eds., *Chinese Society: Change, Conflict and Resistance* (New York: Routledge, 2000), 132.

5. Mary Elizabeth Gallagher, *Contagious Capitalism: Globalization and the Politics of Labor in China* (Princeton: Princeton University Press, 2005), 121, 158.

6. Pei Minxin, "Rights and Resistance: The Changing Contexts of the Dissident Movement," in Perry and Selden, *Chinese Society*, 40–43; see also Pei Minxin, "Citizens v. Mandarins: Administrative Litigation in China," *China Quarterly* 152 (December 1997): 832–62.

7. Merle Goldman, *From Comrade to Citizen: The Struggle for Political Rights in China* (Cambridge, MA: Harvard University Press, 2005), 222–23.

8. Merle Goldman, *Political Rights in Post-Mao China* (Ann Arbor: Association for Asian Studies, 2007), 74.

9. Goldman (2007, 14) writes, "The beginnings of civil society facilitated the organization of groups and networks that took political initiatives without state approval."

10. Yongshun Cai, "Disruptive Collective Action in the Reform Era," in Kevin J. O'Brien, ed., *Popular Protest in China* (Cambridge, MA: Harvard University Press, 2008), chap. 8.

11. Guobin Yang, "Contention in Cyberspace," in O'Brien, ed., *Popular Protest*, chap. 6.

12. For a discussion of the contribution of "as if" politics to regime stability in another authoritarian setting, see Lisa Wedeen, *Ambiguities of Domination: Politics, Rhetoric and Symbols in Contemporary Syria* (Chicago: University of Chicago Press, 1999).

13. James L. Watson, "Structure of Chinese Funerary Rites: Elementary Forms, Ritual Sequence and the Primacy of Performance," in James L. Watson and Evelyn S. Rawski, eds., *Death Ritual in Late Imperial and Modern China* (Berkeley: University of California Press, 1988), 3–19.

14. Neil J. Diamant, *Revolutionizing the Family: Politics, Love and Divorce in Urban and Rural China, 1949–1968* (Berkeley: University of California Press, 2000).

15. The discussion of the 1956–1957 strikes is taken from Elizabeth J. Perry, "Shanghai's Strike Wave of 1957," *China Quarterly* (March 1994).

16. In the same period, numerous rural protests also erupted. Taking advantage of the relative freedom of expression encouraged by the Hundred Flowers Campaign, many of these protests espoused religious beliefs. But they were often also a reaction

against the collectivization of agriculture that was taking place at this time. See Elizabeth J. Perry, "Rural Violence in Socialist China," *China Quarterly* (September 1985).

17. Sidney Tarrow, *Power in Movement: Social Movements, Collective Action and Politics* (Cambridge: Cambridge University Press, 1994), 7.

18. Information on the wind of economism is drawn from chapter 4 of Elizabeth J. Perry and Li Xun, *Proletarian Power: Shanghai in the Cultural Revolution* (Boulder, CO: Westview Press, 1997).

19. On early protests, see Elizabeth J. Perry, "Masters of the Country? Shanghai Workers in the Early People's Republic," in Jeremy Brown and Paul G. Pickowicz, eds., *Dilemmas of Victory: The Early Years of the People's Republic of China* (Cambridge, MA: Harvard University Press, 2007), 59–79; on those of 1976 see Sebastian Heilmann, "The Social Context of Mobilization in China: Factions, Work Units and Activists During the 1976 April Fifth Movement," *China Information* 8, no. 3 (Winter 1993–1994): 1–19.

20. In "rightful resistance," according to O'Brien and Li (*Rightful Resistance*, 5) "villagers frame their claims around Communist Party policies, state laws and official values; solicit assistance from influential allies; and combine legal tactics with collective action to define their 'lawful rights and interests.'" Rules consciousness encompasses these features, but is not limited either to contemporary villagers or to a discourse of "citizens' rights." At various points in Chinese history, including the pre-Communist era, rules conscious protesters have included urbanites as well as villagers who have framed their claims in terms of community, nationalism, revolution, class struggle, and other state-authorized values.

21. Perry, "Rural Violence."

22. Thomas Bernstein and Xiaobo Lu, *Taxation without Representation in Contemporary Rural China*, (Cambridge: Cambridge University Press, 2003), 13.

23. Bernstein and Lu, *Taxation without Representation*, 13.

24. Bernstein and Lu, *Taxation without Representation*, 120–37.

25. Kevin J. O'Brien and Lianjiang Li, "The Politics of Lodging Complaints in Rural China," *China Quarterly*, no. 143 (September 1995): 759–60.

26. Bernstein and Lu, *Taxation without Representation*,141.

27. Peter Ho, "Contesting Rural Spaces: Land Disputes, Customary Tenure and the State," in Perry and Selden, *Chinese Society*, 109.

28. Heilmann, "Social Context of Mobilization."

29. Andrew J. Nathan, *Chinese Democracy* (Berkeley: University of California Press, 1986).

30. For a much more extended development of this argument, see Elizabeth J. Perry, "Casting a Chinese 'Democracy' Movement: The Roles of Students, Workers, Peasants and Entrepreneurs," in Jeffrey N. Wasserstrom and Elizabeth J. Perry, eds., *Popular Protest and Political Culture in Modern China* (Boulder, CO: Westview Press, 1994).

31. Ching Kwan Lee, "Pathways of Labour Insurgency," in Perry and Selden, *Chinese Society*, 77.

32. Lee, "Pathways," 77.

33. Lee, "Pathways," 80.

34. Lee, "Pathways," 80.

35. Chen Xi, "Collective Petitioning and Institutional Conversion," in Kevin J. O'Brien, ed., *Popular Protest in China* (Cambridge, MA: Harvard University Press, 2008), 67.

36. Ching Kwan Lee, *Against the Law: Labor Protest's in China's Rustbelt and Sunbelt* (Berkeley: University of California Press, 2007), 96.

37. Lee, *Against the Law*, 116.

38. Elizabeth J. Perry, *Rebels and Revolutionaries in North China, 1845–1945* (Stanford: Stanford University Press, 1980).

39. Chester Holcombe, *The Real Chinaman* (New York: Dodd, Mead and Company, 1895), 33.

40. Zhang Yiguan, ed., *Fengtai xianzhi* [Gazeteer of Fengtai County] (1882), chap. 4, part 5.

41. Perry, *Rebels and Revolutionaries*, 78–79.

42. William Alexander Parsons Martin, *A Cycle of Cathay* (New York and Chicago: F.H. Revell and Co., 1900), 91–92.

43. Hsiao Kung-ch'uan, *Rural China: Imperial Control in the Nineteenth Century* (Seattle: University of Washington Press, 1960), 441.

44. Rebecca Nedostup and Liang Hong-ming, "'Begging the Sages of the Party-State': Citizenship and Government in Transition in Nationalist China, 1927–1937," *International Review of Social History*, no. 46 (2001): 202.

45. Joseph Fewsmith, "An 'Anger-Venting' Mass Incident Catches the Attention of China's Leadership," *China Leadership Monitor*, no. 26 (Fall 2008), www.hoover.org/publications/clm/issues/China_Leadership_Monitor_No_26.html.

46. For elaboration of this point, see Elizabeth J. Perry, *Challenging the Mandate of Heaven: Social Protest and State Power in China* (Armonk, NY: M.E. Sharpe, 2002), introduction.

47. Peter L. Lorentzen, "Regularized Rioting: The Strategic Toleration of Public Protest in China," *Social Science Research Network Working Paper Series* (June 2008): 31. Available at SSRN: ssrn.com/abstract=995330.

48. Thomas Taylor Meadows, *The Chinese and Their Rebellions* (London: Smith, Elder, 1856), 27.

Chapter 2: Religion: The Dynamics of Religious Growth and Change

1. The first to make a similar distinction was C. K. Yang, *Religion in Chinese Society* (Berkeley: University of California Press, 1961).

2. Karl Marx, "Critique of Hegel's Philosophy of the Right," in Eugene Kamenka, ed., *The Portable Karl Marx* (New York: Penguin, 1983 [1943]).

3. Mao Zedong, "Report on an Investigation of the Peasant Movement in Hunan," in *Selected Readings from the Works of Mao Tsetung* (Beijing: Foreign Languages Press, 1971 [1927]), 23–39.

4. Ronald Inglehart, Miguel Basañez, and Alejandro Moreno, *Human Values and Beliefs: A Cross-Cultural Sourcebook* (Ann Arbor: University of Michigan Press, 1998).

5. Yang Fenggang, "The Red, Black, and Gray Markets of Religion in China," *Sociological Quarterly* 47 (2006): 93–122.

6. Adam Yuet Chau, *Miraculous Response: Doing Popular Religion in Contemporary China* (Stanford: Stanford University Press, 2005), 47.

7. Jing Jun, "Female Autonomy and Female Shamans in Northwest China" (paper presented at the annual meeting of the American Anthropological Association, Atlanta, 1994), 4.

8. Interviewed by Weller, 1985.

9. Kenneth Dean, *Taoist Ritual and Popular Cults of Southeast China* (Princeton: Princeton University Press, 1993), 65.

10. See, for example, Jing, "Female Autonomy."

11. Dean, *Taoist Ritual and Popular Cults of Southeast China,* 64, 84, 100, 211.

12. Chau, *Miraculous Response,* 48, 94.

13. Jing, "Female Autonomy," 4.

14. Gao Bingzhong, "An Ethnography of a Building Both as Museum and Temple: On the Double-Naming Method as an Art of Politics" (paper presented at the Annual Meeting of the American Anthropological Association, Washington, DC, December 2005), 5.

15. Liu Zhijun, Xiangcun doushihua yu tongjiao xingang bianquian [Rural urbanization and changes in religious belief] (Beijing: Shehui kexue wenxian chubanshe, 2007).

16. Wu Keping, "Serving Others, Saving Selves: Philanthropic Acts and Religious Revival in Eastern China" (paper presented at the Conference on Engaged Religions in Chinese Societies, Hsinchu, Taiwan, June 2008).

17. Prasenjit Duara, "Superscribing Symbols: The Myth of Guandi, Chinese God of War," *Journal of Asian Studies* 47, no. 4 (1988): 778–95; John W. Meyer and Brian Rowan, "Institutionalized Organizations: Formal Structure as Myth and Ceremony," *American Journal of Sociology* 83 (1977): 340–63.

18. This example is based on observations from Sun Yanfei's field trips to monasteries in Jiangxi in 2008.

19. *Shaolinsi fangzhang cujin lüyou yougong huozeng haohua yueyeche* (Abbot of the Shaolin Temple awarded a luxury SUV for contributions to tourism promotion), August 15, 2006, news.sina.com.cn/c/2006-08-15/095710729455.shtml (accessed November 22, 2008).

20. Raoul Birnbaum, "Buddhist China at the Century's Turn," *China Quarterly* 174 (2003): 428–50.

21. For example, *Shaolinsi wangshang kaidian Shaolinhuanxidi dabufen wangyou bu zancheng* (Many netizens disapprove of the Shaolin Temple opening an online store), June 24, 2008, www.wabei.com/news/200806/115989.html; *Shaolinsi fangzhang cujin lüyou yougong huozeng haohua yueyeche* (Abbot of the Shaolin Temple awarded a luxury SUV for contributions to tourism promotion), August 15, 2006, news.sina.com.cn/305/2006/0815/58.html; *Wangyou jibian Shaolinsi Dabeisi shushi fomen zhengzong* (Netizens debate who represents authentic Buddhism, the Shaolin Temple or the Dabei Temple], January 18, 2008, news.163.com/08/0118/02/42F5RP9T00011229.html (all accessed November 22, 2008).

22. The entire text of his speech, *Chongxin juqi yijieweishi de qizhi* (Reestablish the importance of "taking the Vinaya" as the master), can be found at the website of the State Administration for Religious Affairs of P.R.C., www.sara.gov.cn/GB/jqgy/jld/ldjh/yexiaowen/0aa507fe-918f-11db-b514-93180af1bb1a.html (accessed November 22, 2008).

23. Alan Hunter and Chan Kim-Kwong, *Protestantism in Contemporary China* (Cambridge: Cambridge University Press, 1993); Yang Fenggang, "Lost in the Market, Saved at McDonald's: Conversion to Christianity in Urban China," *Journal for the Scientific Study of Religion* 44 (2005): 423–41; Liu, *Rural Urbanization and Changes in Religious Belief.*

24. Hunter and Chan, Protestantism in Contemporary China; Leung Ka-lun, *Gaige kaifang hou de zhongguo nongcun jiaohui* (The rural churches of mainland China since 1978). (Hong Kong: Alliance Bible Seminary, 1999).

25. Carsten T. Vala and Kevin J. O'Brien, "Attraction Without Networks: Recruiting Strangers to Unregistered Protestantism in China," *Mobilization* 12 (2007): 79–94.

26. Jason Kindopp, *The Politics of Protestantism in Contemporary China: State Control, Civil Society, and Social Movement in a Single Party-State* (PhD diss., George Washington University, 2004); Ryan Dunch, "Protestant Christianity in China Today: Fragile, Fragmented, Flourishing," in Stephen Uhal-ley, Jr. and Wu Xiaoxin, eds., *China and Christianity*, 195–216 (Armonk, NY: M.E. Sharpe, 2001); Hunter and Chan, *Protestantism in Contemporary China*; Leung, *Rural Chinese Churches.*

27. Yu Jianrong, *Jidujiao de fanzhan yu zhongguo shehui wending—yu liangwei jidujiao jiatingjiaohui peixunshi de duihua* (The development of Protestantism and China's social stability—A dialogue with two Chinese preachers from 'Protestant house churches'), Leaders (April 2008); Yu Jianrong, *Zhongguo jidujiao jiatingjiaohui xiang hechu qu?—yu jiating jiaohui renshi de duihua* (Where are China's Protestant house churches headed? Dialogues with house church leaders), Leaders (November 2008).

28. Gao Shining, *Dangdai zhongguo minjian xinyang dui jidujiao de yingxiang* (The influence of contemporary Chinese popular beliefs on Protestantism), Zhejiang xue-kan (Zhejiang Academic Journal) no. 2 (2005); Xiao Zhitian, *Dangdai zhongguo zongjiao wenti de sikao* (Thoughts on religious issues in contemporary China). Shanghai: Shanghaishi shehui kexueyuan chubanshe, 1994), 73, 164; Hunter and Chan, Protestantism in Contemporary China; Leung, Rural Chinese Churches.

29. Alan Liu, "The 'Wenzhou Model' of Development and China's Modernization," *Asian Survey* 32 (1992): 696–711.

30. Cao Nanlai, "Christian Entrepreneurs and the Post-Mao State: An Ethnographic Account of Church-State Relations in China's Economic Transition," *Sociology of Religion* 68 (2007): 45–66; Cao Nanlai, "Boss Christians: The Business of Religion in the 'Wenzhou Model' of Christian Revival," *China Journal* 59 (2008): 63–87; Chen Cunfu, *Zhuanxingqi de zhongguo jidujiao—Zhejiang jidujiao gean yanjiu* (Chinese Protestantism in transformation—A case study of Protestantism in Zhejiang). Beijing: Dongfang chubanshe; Li Feng, *Xiangcun jidujiao de zuzhi tezheng jiqi shehui jiegouxing weizhi—Huanan Y xian X zhen jidujiao jiaohui zuzhi yanjiu* (The organizational features of rural Protestantism and its social structural position—Research into the

organizational dimension of Protestant churches in Y township of X county in South China). Shanghai: Fudan daxue chubanshe, 2005).

31. Cao, "Christian Entrepreneurs and the Post-Mao State"; Cao, "Boss Christians."

32. David Aikman, *Jesus in Beijing* (Washington, DC: Regency Publishing Inc., 2003).

33. Yang, "Lost in the Market, Saved at McDonald's," 439.

34. Pastor Liu Tongsu has penned a number of articles elucidating this stance. See the website of Chinese Christian Internet Mission, www.ccimweb.org/tongsu (accessed December 2, 2008).

35. From the website of the Autumn Rain Church, earlyrain.bokee.com/6803316. html (accessed December 2, 2008).

36. Vala and O'Brien, "Attraction Without Networks."

37. Vala and O'Brien, "Attraction Without Networks."

38. Cao, "Boss Christians."

Chapter 3: The Rule of Law: Pushing the Limits of Party Rule

1. The Communiqué of the Third Plenum of the Eleventh Central Committee of the Communist Party of China of December 22, 1978, *Peking Review* 21, no. 52 (December 29, 1978) at 14, www.marxists.org/subject/china/peking-review/1978/PR1978-52.pdf. The Chinese of the italicized language is "*youfa keyi, youfa biyi, zhifa biyan, weifa bijiu.*"

2. Hu Jintao, "Hold High the Great Banner of Socialism with Chinese Characteristics and Strive for New Victories in Building a Moderately Prosperous Society in All," Report to the Seventeenth Party Congress, October 15, 2007, English translation at www.china.org.cn/english/congress/229611.htm.

3. "Highlights of NPC Standing Committee Chairman Wu Bangguo's Work Report," National People's Congress, March 9, 2009, at www.npc.gov.cn/englishnpc/Special_11_2/2009-03/09/content_1487180.htm.

4. State Council Information Office, "White Paper: China's Efforts and Achievements in Promoting the Rule of Law," February 28, 2008, www.gov.cn/english/2008-02/28/content_904901.htm [hereafter "ROL White Paper"].

5. Wang Canfa, "Chinese Environmental Law Enforcement: Current Deficiencies and Suggested Reforms, *Vermont Journal of Environmental Law* 8 (2006–2007): 159, 163.

6. ROL White Paper, *supra* note 4.

7. "Post-Olympic Stress Disorder," *Economist*, September 11, 2008, www.economist.com/world/asia/displaystory.cfm?story_id=12209848.

8. Some of the themes and examples discussed in this chapter draw on the author's chapter on "Rule of Law in China: Incremental Progress," in C. Fred Bergsten, N. Lardy, B. Gill, and D. Mitchell, *The China Balance Sheet in 2007 and Beyond* (Washington, DC: Center for Strategic and International Studies and The Peterson Institute for International Economics, 2007). For a general overview of the Chinese legal system, see Jianfu Chen, *Chinese Law: Context and Transformation* (Leiden: Martinus Nijhoff Publishers, 2008). For earlier classics on the Chinese legal system, see Stanley Lubman, *Bird in a Cage: Legal Reform in China after Mao* (Stanford: Stanford Univer-

sity Press, 1999) and Randall P. Peerenboom, *China's Long March toward Rule of Law* (Cambridge: Cambridge University Press, 2002).

9. Article 5, Constitution of the People's Republic of China, as amended March 2004, English translation at www.npc.gov.cn/englishnpc/Constitution/node_2825.htm.

10. Article 3, Constitution of the Communist Party of China, as amended October 2007, English translation at news.xinhuanet.com/english/2007-10/25/content_6944738.htm.

11. ROL White Paper, *supra* note 4 (in Chinese: "*youfa buyi, zhifa buyan, weifa bujiu*").

12. See, Jamie P. Horsley, "Public Participation and the Democratization of Chinese Governance," in Yang Zhong and Shipin Hua, eds., *Political Civilization and Modernization in China: The Political Context of China's Transformation* (Hackensack, NJ: World Scientific Press, 2006).

13. Zhu Zhe, "NPC to Make All Draft Laws Public," *China Daily*, April 21, 2008, www.chinadaily.com.cn/china/2008-04/21/content_6630400.htm.

14. Jerome A. Cohen, "China's Reform Era Legal Odyssey," *Far Eastern Economic Review* 34 (December 2008).

15. Constitution, *supra* note 9, Article 126; ROL White Paper, *supra* note 4.

16. Xinhua News Agency, "Courts to Allow Easier Access to Judicial Services," February 19, 2009, www.china.org.cn/government/central_government/2009-02/19/content_17299842.htm.

17. China Law Society, "*Zhongguo fazhi jianshe niandu baogao (2008 nian)*" [2008 report on China's rule of law construction], June 3, 2009, news.xinhuanet.com/legal/2009-06/03/content_11478996.htm [hereafter "2008 ROL Report"].

18. "Association: Lawyers Play Bigger Role in China's Politics," *People's Daily Online*, October 26, 2008, english.people.com.cn/90001/90776/90785/6521573.html.

19. "*Gongyi lvshi wangluo' zai Beijing qidong, zhenghe gongyi susong ziyuan*" [Public interest lawyers network started in Beijing, pooling public interest litigation resources], March 15, 2009, www.bj.xinhuanet.com/bjpd_sdzx/2009-03/15/content_15959074.htm.

20. Joseph Kahn, "Lawyer Takes on China's 'Unwinnable' Cases," *New York Times*, December 12, 2005.

21. Xinhua News Agency, "Highlights of Work Report of China's Supreme People's Court," March 9, 2008, english.sina.com/china/1/2008/0309/149438.html.

22. Xinhua News Agency, "Highlights of Work Report on China's Supreme People's Court," March 10, 2009, english.people.com.cn/90001/90776/90785/6610940.html.

23. "Practicing Lawyers in China Reach 140,000," *People's Daily Online*, October 27, 2008, english.people.com.cn/90001/90776/6522103.html.

24. Joseph Kahn, "When the Chinese Sue the State, Cases Are Often Smothered," *New York Times*, December 28, 2005.

25. 2008 ROL Report, *supra*, note 17.

26. *Zuigaoyuan xin gongbu xingzheng anjian sifa jieshi* [SPC issues new judicial interpretation on administrative cases], *Caijing*, January 17, 2008, www.caijing.com .cn/2008-01-17/100045594.html.

27. Xinhua News Agency, "China Gives Public More Leeway to Disagree with Government Decisions," June 8, 2007, news.xinhuanet.com/english/2007-06/08/content_6217625.htm.

28. *Quanmian tuijin yifa xingzheng shishi gangyao* [Outline for promoting the comprehensive implementation of administration in accordance with the law] adopted March 22, 2004, news.xinhuanet.com/zhengfu/2004-04/21/content_1431232 .htm.

29. *Guowuyuan guanyu jiaqiang shixian zhengfu yifa xingzheng de jueding* [State Council decision on strengthening administration in accordance with the law by municipal and county governments], issued May 12, 2008, www.gov.cn/zwgk/2008-06/18/ content_1020629.htm.

30. Wen Jiabao, "VI. Strengthening Government Reform and Improvement Efforts," Report on the Work of the Government to the National People's Congress, March 5, 2007, news.xinhuanet.com/english/2007-03/16/content_5857166_5.htm.

31. Wen Jiabao, "Report on the Work of the Government to the National People's Congress," March 5, 2009, www.npc.gov.cn/englishnpc/news/Events/2009-03/14/content_1493265.htm.

32. *Hunansheng xingzheng chengxu guiding*, effective October 1, 2008, hn.rednet .cn/c/2008/04/18/1487353.htm.

33. Christopher Bodeen, "Chinese Official Talks to Striking Taxi Drivers," November 6, 2008, Associated Press, biz.yahoo.com/ap/081106/as_china_taxi_strike.html?.v=1.

34. Bodeen, "Chinese Official Talks."

35. "Public Must Be Allowed to 'Air Grievances,'" *China Daily*, November 26, 2008, www.chinadaily.com.cn/china/2008-11/26/content_7239377.htm.

36. ROL White Paper, *supra* note 4.

Chapter 4: Economic Growth: From High-Speed to High-Quality

1. An earlier version of this chapter was presented to the conference "Three Decades of Reform and Opening: Where Is China Headed?" Pardee Center for the Study of the Longer Range Future, Boston University, December 8, 2008.

The State-owned Assets Supervision and Administration Commission (SASAC) has repeatedly declared that coal is a strategic industry over which the government should exercise "*juedui kongzhili*," absolute control, meaning majority ownership (SASAC 2006; Xinhua 2006). Despite this, there has been little effective effort to actually restrict the operation of private and locally controlled mines.

2. This is in addition to the usual incentives to generate income in order to have more resources available for patronage and side payments to allies.

3. Some Southeast Asian economies, such as Malaysia and Thailand, experienced short-run investment rates above 40 percent of GDP for a short period in the mid-1990s. However, these were the result of surges of incoming foreign direct investment, and were not sustained as long as China's investment rates have been sustained.

4. Guangdong became the most populous province in 2007, according to official figures that include in-migrants who are resident long term (over six months). According to official household registration—which excludes migrants who are unable to transfer their permanent residence—Guangdong is only fourth, after Henan, Shandong, and Sichuan (NBS 2008b, 67).

5. The central government currently funds these programs in western and most central provinces, but requires the wealthier coastal provinces to fund the same programs out of local fiscal resources. This increases the impact of the policies in redistributing benefits from higher- to lower-income regions.

Chapter 5: Inequality: Overcoming the Great Divide

1. Prepared for discussion at the conference on "Three Decades of Reform and Opening: Where Is China Headed?" at Boston University, funded by the Pardee Center for the Study of the Longer Range Future, December 8, 2008.

See, inter alia, UNDP (2005, 2008), Ravallion and Chen (2004), Shue and Wong (2007), Khan and Riskin (2005), Xie and Wu (2008), Zhou et al. (2008), and several of the other items in the references to this chapter.

2. See also Khan (2004), who shows that the elasticity of poverty reduction with respect to income increased sharply in the 1995–2002 period compared to that of 1988–1995, and attributed this change primarily to a reduction in the disequalizing nature of China's growth between the two periods.

3. This comes from a policy brief distributed at the June 5, 2008, UN University launch of two works on inequality and poverty in China edited by Guanghua Wan. See Wan (2007, 2008b).

4. However, Luo and Zhu express concern about inequalities of opportunity, especially as regards education, which could "undermine long-term prospects for development" (21), and advocate continued improvement in educational services accessible to poor people.

5. In fact, however, Kuznets himself, in the original statement of the hypothesis, included among the potential causes of reduced inequality at higher levels of development the changes in policies and attitudes toward spending on social welfare that are likely to come with greater prosperity. See Kuznets (1955).

6. See Khan and Riskin (2005), who show that in 2002 the distribution of land holdings over all rural income groups was virtually equal, that is, had a concentration (pseudo-Gini) ratio of zero.

7. Urban average consumption per capita is estimated to have been 3.6 times as high as rural in 2003. See UNDP (2005, 9).

8. See Li et al. (2007) for a description of the CHIP survey.

9. The lack of a migrant survey in 1995 makes it impossible to estimate the impact of adding migrants to urban residents in that year.

10. For a start, see Aroca et al. (2008); Lin and Liu (2008); Naughton (2002); Naughton (2004); Renard (2002); Wan (2008a); Wan et al. (2008).

11. As charged by Lin and Liu (2008). See below.

12. However, the provincial sample sizes of the CHIP data used by Khan and Riskin were too small to permit a great deal of confidence in this finding.

13. Without, however, replacing it with alternative funding, a failure bound to be hurtful to poor localities.

14. See also Shue and Wong (2007).

15. See "China Plans 120 Billion Dollar Health Reform By 2011," *Medical News Today*, January 23, 2009, www.medicalnewstoday.com/articles/136552.php (accessed March 9, 2010).

Chapter 6: Economic Governance: Authoritarian Upgrading and Innovative Potential

1. Steven Heydemann, "Upgrading Authoritarianism in the Arab World," Saban Center Analysis, Brookings Institution, November 2007; for the term see also R. A. Spector and A. Krickovic, "Authoritarianism 2.0: Non-Democratic Regimes are Upgrading and Integrating Globally" (paper presented at the annual meeting of the International Studies Association's 49th annual convention, San Francisco, March 2008).

2. *OECD Reviews of Innovation Policy: China* (Paris: OECD, 2008), 45.

3. Cf. Wolfgang Streeck and Kathleen Thelen, "Introduction," in Streeck and Thelen, eds., *Beyond Continuity: Institutional Change in Advanced Political Economies* (Oxford: Oxford University Press, 2005).

4. See Murray Scot Tanner, "How a Bill Becomes a Law in China: Stages and Processes in Lawmaking," *China Quarterly*, no. 141 (March 1995): 42.

5. Cf. Sebastian Heilmann, "Experimentation Under Hierarchy: Policy Experiments in the Reorganization of China's State Sector, 1978–2008" (Working Paper No. 172, Center for International Development, Harvard University, June 2008).

6. See for example, Joseph C. H. Chai, ed., *China: Transition to a Market Economy* (Oxford: Oxford University Press, 1998); Long H. Liew, *The Chinese Economy in Transition: From Plan to Market* (London: Edward Elgar, 1997).

7. Cf. Loren Brandt and Thomas G. Rawski, eds., *China's Great Economic Transformation* (New York: Cambridge University Press, 2008).

8. Cf. Peter J. Boettke, ed., *The Collapse of Development Planning* (New York: New York University Press, 1994).

9. For comprehensive treatises on development planning written by high-ranking policymakers and advisors, see, for example, Cheng Siwei, *Fazhan jihua de zhiding yu guangli* (The setting and management of development planning) (Beijing: Jingji kexue chubanshe, 2004); Zhong Qifu and Xu Guangjian, *Zhongchangqi fazhanguihua de jichu lilun he fangfa* (The fundamental theory and method of mid- and long-term developmental programs) (Beijing: Zhongguo jihua chubanshe, 2001).

10. For striking evidence in this regard see *OECD Reviews of Innovation Policy: China.*

11. Cheng Siwei, "Lun Zhongguo sheshui zhuyi shichang jingji zhidu xia de fazhan jihua" (On development planning under China's socialist market economic system), *Gonggong guanli xuebao* 1, no.2, (May 2004): 5.

12. See Heilmann, "Experimentation Under Hierarchy," 12.

13. Li Pumin and Li Yong, "'Jiuwu' shiqi woguo jihua tizhi gaige huigu" (A look back at the reform of China's planning structure during the ninth five-year plan), *Hongguan jingji yanjiu*, no.2 (2001): 24–26.

14. *OECD Reviews of Innovation Policy: China,* 46, 80.

15. Michael Howlett, M. Ramesh, and Anthony Perl, *Studying Public Policy: Policy Cycles and Policy Subsystems,* 3rd ed. (Toronto: Oxford University Press, 2009).

16. Carl E. Walter and Fraser J. T. Howie, *Privatizing China: Inside China's Stock Markets* (Singapore: Wiley, 2006), 4.

17. See Heilmann, "Experimentation Under Hierarchy," 5–9.

18. The term "shadow of hierarchy" stems from Fritz Scharpf, *Games Real Actors Play: Actor-Centered Institutionalism in Policy Research* (Boulder, CO: Westview Press, 1997), 197–98. Scharpf points to the indirect effects of a hierarchical authority structure. Though lower-level administrators may enjoy considerable leeway in a noncoercive hierarchical environment, they still remain embedded in the overall authority structure and vulnerable to ad hoc intervention and the threat of sanctions if something goes wrong. Thus, even if hierarchical authority doesn't achieve effective control, it still affects the calculations, behavior (be it evasive or loyal), and interactions across levels of state administration.

19. *OECD Reviews of Innovation Policy: China,* 45–46.

20. Pranab Bardhan, "What Does This Authoritarian Moment Mean for Developing Countries?" The Economists' Forum, August 22, 2008, *Financial Times online (FT.com).*

21. Cf. Alan Carter, *A Radical Green Political Theory* (London: Routledge, 1999).

22. See Douglass C. North, *Institutions, Institutional Change and Economic Performance* (Cambridge: Cambridge University Press, 1990), 80–81; North, *Understanding the Process of Economic Change* (Princeton: Princeton University Press, 2005), 154.

23. Nathalie Rothschild, "Hypocrisy of Olympian Proportions: For Years Western Observers Slammed China's 'Red Authoritarianism.' Yet Today They Positively Cheer On Its Eco-Authoritarianism," August 20, 2007, *Spiked (spiked-online.com).*

Chapter 7: Foreign Direct Investment: Diaspora Networks and Economic Reform

1. This chapter was initially prepared for the "Three Decades of Reform and Opening: Where Is China Going?" conference at Boston University, December 8, 2008.

See, for example, Harding 1987; Fewsmith 1994; Shirk 1994; Lieberthal, Oksenberg, and Lampton 1992; and Khanna 2007.

2. Donnithorne 1972; Shue 1988; White 1998; and Zweig 2002.

3. Rogers 1995; Walker 1969.

4. Similar observations are made by Johnston 2008.

5. Head of the Propaganda Department Deng Liqun, a leading figure of conservative force in Beijing, became a supporter for economic reform after a trip to Japan in 1978. Japan, which was at a similar level of development with Tianjian in the 1950s, vastly surpassed the latter after two decades. See, Deng Liqun, Ma Hong, Sun Shangqing, and Wu Jiajin. 1978. *Fangri guilai de sisuo* [Thoughts upon returning from Japan]. Beijing.

6. Office of Central Compilation. 2004. *Deng Xiaoping Annuary 1975–1997* [Deng Xiaoping nianpu]. Beijing: Central Compilation Publisher.

7. *Renmin ribao* [*People's Daily*], July 21, 1989, 4.

8. See *Jingji tequ nianjian* [SEZ statistical yearbook], 1984, 148.

9. Lu Ding. 2005. "Guangdong de duiwai kaifang yu jingji tizhi gaige" [Guang-dong's openness and economic reform], in *Deng xiaoping yu gaige kaifang* [Deng Xiaoping and China's reform and openness]. Beijing: CCP History Publisher.

10. For a statistical analysis of FDI in early SEZs, see Min Ye, "Policy Learning or Diffusion," *Journal of East Asian Studies* (Fall 2009).

11. "Wang Zhen Gives Impressions on Tour of Special Economic Zones in the Company of Deng Xiaoping." *Liaowang* (staff report no. 16, 1984).

12. "A Brief Introduction to Coastal Open Cities: Dalian," in *Guide to China's Foreign Economic Relations and Trade* (Beijing: Economic Information Agency, 1984).

13. "A Brief Introduction to Coastal Open Cities: Dalian."

14. D. Jin. 1984. Congratulatory Speech at the Opening of the Symposium on Investment, in *Guide to China's Foreign Economic Relations and Trade*.

15. *Renmin ribao*, November 17, 1984, 2.

16. *Renmin ribao*, October 26, 1989, 1.

17. *Renmin ribao*, October 16, 1989, 6.

18. *Renmin ribao*, December 4, 1991, 5.

19. See, for example, Dittmer 1990.

20. Deng Xiaoping's visit was not reported by news media in Beijing but was closely followed by Hong Kong media. When those media reports circulated back to the mainland days later, some Chinese reporters were permitted to publish on the Southern Tour.

21. *Renmin ribao*, September 18, 1989, 6.

22. *PRC Statistics Yearbook*, 1995.

23. *Renmin ribao*, September 18, 1989, 6.

24. *Renmin ribao*, September 11, 1989, 4.

25. *PRC Statistics Yearbook*, 1995.

26. *Zhongguo duiwai jingji tongji daquan, 1979–1991* (Beijing: zhongguo tongji xinxi zhixun fuwu chubanshe), 401–7.

27. *Zhongguo duiwai jingji tongji daquan*, 409.

28. *Jingji yanjiu cankao* [Internal report on economic reform]. Beijing, October 12, 1993.

29. By convention, Taiwanese names usually use a hyphen between characters of given names, while mainland Chinese names do not.

30. See official website of Kunshan, www.ketd.gov.cn.

31. Lin Zi, "Dalu moujing la taishan" [The mainland tried to attract Taiwan investment], *Gangao cankao*, December 15, 2000.

32. Lin Zi, "Shanghai kaidian qule" [Open a store in Shanghai], *Gangao cankao* [Internal report on Hong Kong and Macao], December 15, 2000, 57.

33. Hong Kong and Taiwan combined. See, Lin Wandong, "Shanghai liyong waizi de tongji fengxi," *Shanghai Statistics*, November 9, 2000, 11.

34. Hong Kong *Lian He Bao*, July 16, 1993.

35. "42% of Taiwan Desktop PCs Made in—and Sold from—China," *Taiwan Weekly Business Bulletin*, August 16, 2000, 6.

36. See, Huang 2003.

37. *Lianhe Zaobao*, March 22, 1997; and *Da gong bao*, February 7, 1998.

38. Taiwan *Jingji ribao*, July 7, 1998.

39. Pan Huanyou, "Yinzi jiajie huo deshi" [Using FDI in SOE reform], *Touzi lilun yu shijian* [Investment Theory and Practice], no. 11, 1995.

40. "Dui kuoguo gongsi shixing konggu jingyin de fengxi" [Analysis of MNCs-controlled global operation], *Lilun xuexi yu yanjiu* [Theoretical Learning and Research), no. 3, 1997.

41. Wang Yaping, "Guoyou qiye gaige yu liyong waizi" [SOE reform and the use of FDI], *Hongguan jingji yanjiu* [Macroeconomics Research], no. 4, 1999.

Chapter 8: Elite Politics: The Struggle for Normality

1. William Overholt's 1993 book, *The Rise of China: How Economic Reform Is Creating a New Superpower* (New York: W. W. Norton) was ahead of its time, especially given the uncertainties prevailing in the post-Tiananmen period. More recently there have been many notable books on the subject, including C. Fred Bergsten, Charles Freeman, Nicholas Lardy, and Derek J. Mitchell, *The Rise of China: Challenges and Opportunities* (Washington, DC: Peter G. Peterson Institute for International Economics and the Center for Strategic and International Studies, 2008); James Kynge, *China Shakes the World: A Titan's Rise and Troubled Future* (New York: Houghton Mifflin Co., 2006); Thomas G. Rawski and William W. Keller, eds., *China's Rise and the Balance of Power in Asia* (Pittsburgh: University of Pittsburgh Press, 2007); and Robert S. Ross and Zhu Feng, *China's Ascent: Power, Security, and the Future of International Politics* (Ithaca, NY: Cornell University Press, 2008).

2. Wu Xiang, "Yang guan dao yu du mu qiao" [The broad road and the single plank bridge], *Renmin ribao*, November 5, 1980.

3. Chen Yun. "Jianchi an bili yuanze tiaozheng guomin jingji" [Readjust the national economy in accordance with the principle of proportionality], in *Chen Yun wenxuan* (1956–1985) [The selected works of Chen Yun, 1956–1985] (Beijing: Renmin chubanshe, 1986), 226–31.

4. Barry Naughton, *The Chinese Economy: Transitions and Growth* (Cambridge, MA: Massachusetts Institute of Technology Press, 2007).

5. William H. Riker, "Comments on Vincent Ostrom's Paper," *Public Choice* 27 (1976): 13–15, quoted in Douglass North, *Institutions, Institutional Change and Economic Performance* (Cambridge: Cambridge University Press, 1990), 60.

6. Frederick Teiwes, *Leadership, Legitimacy, and Conflict in China* (Armonk, NY: M.E. Sharpe, 1984).

7. George W. Breslauer, *Khrushchev and Brezhnev as Leaders: Building Authority in Soviet Politics* (London and Boston: Allen & Unwin, 1982).

8. "Guanyu dangnei zhengzhi shenghuo de ruogan zhunze" [Some guiding principles for political life within the party], in Zhonggong zhongyang wenxian yanjiushi, ed., *Shiyijie sanzhong quanhui yilai zhongyao wenxian xuandu* [Selected readings in important documents since the Third Plenary Session of the Eleventh Central Committee], 2 vols. (Beijing: Renmin chubanshe, 1987), 1:163–84; Melanie Manion, *Retirement of Revolutionaries in China: Public Policies, Social Norms, Private Interests* (Princeton: Princeton University Press, 1993).

9. Shaoguang Wang, "The Politics of Private Time: Changing Leisure Patterns in Urban China," in Deborah S. Davis et al., eds., *Urban Spaces in Contemporary China* (New York: Cambridge University Press, 1995), 149–72.

10. Joseph Fewsmith, *Dilemmas of Reform in China: Political Conflict and Economic Debate* (Armonk, NY: M.E. Sharpe, 1994).

11. The notion of elite politics as a game to win all or lose all was central to the thinking of Tang Tsou. See, for instance, his *The Cultural Revolution and Post-Mao Reforms: A Historical Perspective* (Chicago: University of Chicago Press, 1986).

12. Li Peng, "Full Text" of Top-Secret Fourth Plenary Session Document: "Li Peng's Life-Taking Report Lays Blame on Zhao Ziyang," in Mei Qiren, ed., "Three Interviews with Zhao Ziyang," *Chinese Law and Government* 38, no. 3 (May-June 2005): 69–84.

13. Kenneth Jowitt, *The New World Disorder: The Leninist Extinction* (Berkeley and Los Angeles: University of California Press, 1992).

14. See, for instance, Bruce Dickson, *Red Capitalists in China: The Party, Entrepreneurs and Prospects for Political Change* (New York: Cambridge University Press, 2003).

15. Gao Xin and He Pin, *Zhu Rongji zhuan* [Biography of Zhu Rongji] (Taipei: Xinxinwen, 1993) , 231–32.

16. On Deng's "southern journey," as this trip is often called, see Richard Baum, *Burying Mao: Chinese Politics in the Age of Deng Xiaoping* (Princeton: Princeton University Press, 1996), 341–68.

17. On these political developments, see Joseph Fewsmith, *China since Tiananmen*, 2nd ed. (Cambridge: Cambridge University Press, 2008), 62–77.

18. Erik Eckholm, "Beijing Sends Potential Dissidents a Message: Don't," *New York Times*, December 25, 1998.

19. Deng Liqun, *Deng Liqun zixu: Shi'erge chunqiu (1975–1987)* [Deng Liqun's narrative: Twelve years (1975–1987)] (n.d., n.p.), 11.

20. On the left, see Luo yi ning ge'er [pseudo. Wang Shan], *Disanzhi yanjing kan Zhongguo* [Looking at China through a third eye] (Taiyuan: Shanxi renmin chubanshe, 1997); on the right, see Wang Xiaoming, ed., *Renwen jingshen xunsilu* [Pondering the humanistic spirit] (Shanghai: Wenhui chubanshe, 1996).

21. John Burns, "Strengthening the Central CCP Control of Leadership Selection: The 1990 Nomenklatura," *China Quarterly*, no. 138 (June 1994): 458–91.

22. "Rule of Law" was a major theme of the Fifteenth Party Congress in 1997, and the call for standardization.

23. Gao Xin, *Jiang Zemin de quanli zhi lu* [Jiang Zemin's road to power] (Hong Kong: Jing Ming chubanshe, 1997), 58–80.

24. Tang Tsou, "Prolegomenon to the Study of Informal Groups in CCP politics," in Tsou, *The Cultural Revolution and Post-Mao Reforms*, 95–111.

25. Joseph Fewsmith, "The Sixteenth National Party Congress: The Succession That Didn't Happen," *China Quarterly*, no. 173 (March 2003): 1–16.

26. Cheng Li, "The New Bipartisanship within the Chinese Communist Party," *Orbis* 49, no. 3 (Summer 2005): 387–400.

27. "Hu Jintao zai xianfa shixing ershi zhounian dahui sang de jianghua," 2002.

28. Fewsmith, *China since Tiananmen*, chap. 8.

29. On these debates, see Fewsmith, *China since Tiananmen*, 262–69.

30. Joseph Fewsmith, "China in 2007," *Asian Survey* 48, no. 1 (February 2008): 82–96.

31. Wang Xing, Liu Yingting, and Lin Qi, "Shichanghua gaige zai chufa" [Relaunching market-oriented reform], *21 shiji jingji daobao*, April 3, 2005.

32. At the Seventeenth Party Congress in 2007, 51 percent of full members of the Central Committee retired. In 2002, at the Sixteenth Party Congress, 56 percent of full members retired, and at the Fifteenth Party Congress in 1997, 57 percent retired.

Chapter 9: Local Elections: The Elusive Quest for Choice

1. I thank Professor Joseph Fewsmith for inviting me to write this article. I also thank Heather Saul for her efforts to revise the article and her many constructive suggestions in improving the clarity of the article.

"Shiyi cunmin zizhi: qiuyi nongmin zuizhenshi de minzhu caolian" [A decade of villager self-government: The most real exercise of democracy by 900 million farmers], *People's Daily*, November 4, 2008.

2. "Shiyi cunmin zizhi." A Ministry of Civil Affairs (MCA) official told me that the amendment of the Organic Law would be deliberated and hopefully adopted toward the end of 2009. The interview with the MCA official was conducted on April 2, 2009.

3. For Peng Zhen's remarks on why direct villager committee elections were important and useful, see Yawei Liu, "Better Local Governance or More Consolidation of the State Power: Consequences of Villager Committee Elections in China," *China Perspectives* 31 (September-October 2000). See also Peng Zhen, *Lun xinshiqi de shehuizhuyi minzhu yu fazhi jianshe* [On socialist democracy and rule of law during the new period] (Beijing: Minzhu yu fazhi chubanshe, 1989), 367–68.

4. For details of the electoral experiments at various provinces, see Li Fan, *Shouhuisheng and Xiao Lihui, Chuangxin yu fazhan—Xiangzhenzhang xuanjuzhidu gaige* [Innovation and development: Systemic reform of township/town magistrate election] (Beijing: Dongfang Chubanshe, 2000). For the Buyun election, see Yawei Liu, "The Buyun Experiment," January 31, 2003, www.chinaelections.net; Liu Yawei, ed., *Gei nongmin rangquan—zhixuan de huisheng* [Returning the power to the peasants: The echo of direct elections] (Xian: Xibei Daxue Chubanshe, 2002); Li Fan, *Chengfeng erlai—wo suo jingli de1 buyun xiangzhang zhixuan* [Coming with the wind—I witnessed the direct election of the magistrate in Buyun Township] (Xian: Xibei Daxue Chubanshe, 2003); and Shi Weimin, *Gongtui gongxuan: xiangzhen renda xuanju zhidu1yanjiu* [Public nomination, public election] (Beijing: Zhongguo shehui kexue1chubanshe, 2000).

5. The residents of Xiaogang Village decided to divide the production brigade's land among individuals, thus triggering the subsequent Household Responsibility System.

6. For the second Buyun election, see Yawei Liu, "What Does Buyun Township Mean in the Context of China's Political Reform?" in Tun-jen Cheng, Jacques Delisle, and Deborah Brown, eds., *China under Hu Jintao: Opportunities, Dangers, and Dilemmas* (Hackensack, NJ: World Scientific, 2005).

7. For details of the Yangji experiment, see Jens Hildebrant, "Yangji Experiment, a Chronology," July 26, 2003, en.chinaelections.org/newsinfo.asp?newsid=9691.

8. Josephine Ma, "Yangji and Ya'an Experiments, a New Round of Political Reform?" *South China Morning Post*, January 12, 2003.

9. For details of the survey, which initially was published at the Yangji Town website, see Jens Hildebrant, "Yangji's Public Opinion Survey on Elections," February 13, 2003, en.chinaelections.org/newsinfo.asp?newsid=9719.

10. Interview with Chinese scholars, Beijing and Wuhan, December 2002 and January 2003.

11. See Xu Yong and He Xuefeng, eds., *Yangji shiyan: liangtui yixuan shuji zhenzhang* [The Yangji experiment] (Xian: Xibei daxue chubanshe, 2003). The Carter Center and the Ford Foundation sponsored the publication of this book. For more articles on the meaning of the Yangji experiment, check www.chinaelections.org/List .asp?SortID=57.

12. Ma Ya, "Wei Shengduo Juedi tuwei" [Wen Shengduo tried to overcome his dire conditions], *Fenghuang zhoukan* [Phoenix weekly], no. 1 (2005). Li Fan, a political activist in China, told the author that he was at Pingba at Wei's invitation. He was offering advice and prepared to observe the election. After Wei was taken into soft custody, Li Fan was on the run. Had it not been for some acquaintances who came to his help through sending a car, he could have been arrested by the local police. Interview with Li Fan, late August 2003, Beijing.

13. See Ying Hongwei, "Changshi zhenji zhixuan bei mianzhi de Wei Shengduo taoshuofa" [Wei Shengduo seeks clarification of the disciplinary action against him for his plotting of a township direct election], *Nanfengchuan*, February 20, 2008.

14. To find more information on the Honghe experiment, see "Yunna Honghezhou 'zhitui zhixuan' xiangzhenzhang" [Honghe Prefecture in Yunnan conducts direct nomination and election of township/town magistrates], *Banyuetan*, November 11, 2004. Also see Tang Jianguang, "Yunnan Honghezhou daguimo tuixing zhixuan tuijin xiangzhen tizhi gaige" [Honghe Prefecture promotes township/town structural reform through large-scale direct elections], *Zhongguo xinwen zhoukan* [Chinese Newsweek] 43, December 27, 2004. When The Carter Center staff sent a request to the NPC to visit Honghe and find out more about this bold experiment, its contact at the NPC was summoned in by a high-ranking official who accused the former of political insensitivity. "How could you allow Westerners to look into an electoral experiment that was unconstitutional?" he was asked. This contact also said an investigation team was dispatched to Honghe to examine where relevant laws were violated. No details of the findings were presented to the public. Luo Chongmin reportedly told the investigators that he had one head to lose and they could take it if they chose. Interview with an NPC official, January 2005, Beijing.

15. "Chongqing shouci qunzhong zhitou jueding zhenzhang renxuan" [Chongqing voters cast votes to select magistrate for the first time], *Chongqing Shibao* [Chongqing Time], April 4, 2005.

16. To see presentations by scholars at the Shenzhen Conference, please visit www.chinaelections.org/List.asp?SortID=183. There are a total of 724 articles on the Beijing district people's congress deputy elections. To access these articles, go to www.chinaelections.org/List.asp?SortID=184.

17. Yuan Dayi, "Wo shi ruhe bei 'xiehang' xialai de" [How I lost my candidacy through 'consultation'], *Zhongguo xinwen zhoukan* [Chinese Newsweek], December 8, 2003. For details of the Beijing election, see Zou Shubin, ed. *2003 nian Beijing shi quxian renda daibiao jingxuan shilu* [Report on the district/county people's congress deputy election in Beijing, 2003] (Xian: Xibei Daxue Chubanshe, 2004). For the details of the so-called Shenzhen electoral storm, see Tang Juan and Zou Shubin, *2003 nian Shenzhen jingxuan shilu* [Report on the 2003 Shenzhen elections] (Xian: Xibei Daxue Chubanshe, 2003).

18. The book series includes Shi Weimin and Lei Jingxuan, *Zhijie xuanju: zhiu yu guocheng* [Direct elections: system and processes] (Beijing: Zhongguo shehui kexue chubanshe, 1999); Liu Zhi, Shi Weimin, et al., *Shuju xuanju: renda daibiaoxuanju tongji yanjiu* [Statistical elections: study of the statistics of people's congress deputy elections] (Beijing: Zhongguo shehui kexue chubanshe, 2001); and Shi Weimin and Liu Zhi, *Guifan xuanju: 2001–2002 xiangji renmin daibiao dahui daibiao xuanju yanjiu* [Standardizing elections: a study on the 2001–2002 township people's congress deputy elections] (Beijing: Zhonguo shehui kexue chubanshe, 2003). This book was sponsored by the Carter Center.

19. Cai Dingjian, *Zhongguo xuanju zhuangkuang baogao* [Report on the status of Chinese elections] (Beijing: Falv Chubanshe, 2002).

20. Sun Jinzhong and Hou Yongmei, "'Yanse geming' tuxian meiguo zhanlue bianhua'" ['Color Revolution' reveals America's change of strategy], *Liaowang Xinwen Zhouka*, April 4, 2005.

21. "Taishi cun kaichuang zhongguo zhengzhi zhidu gaige de lingyiige xianli?" [Is Taishi Village creating another precedent for China's political reform?], www.hexun .com, September 16, 2005.

22. He Linping, "Yougan yu cunmin yifa 'ba'guan" [Thoughts on villagers recalling villager committee chair], *Renmin ribao* [People's Daily], September 14, 2008.

23. Fan Yafeng, "Taishi keneng jiushi minzhuhua de ciaogang" [Taishi is probably the Xiaogang of democratization], www.yannan.net, September 4, 2005.

24. Adam Heyd, "Here Today, Gone Tomorrow, Media Responses to the Taishi Village Incident," November 15, 2005, www.chinaelections.net/newsinfo.asp?newsid=3326.

25. *Panyu ribao*, September 19, 2005. Eventually, the Guangdong provincial government charged that both the Ford Foundation (through a professor at Zhongshan University) and the Carter Foundation (which does not exist) of paying villagers to go on hunger strike and participate in the sit-ins. A media blackout on the incident was ordered and the Carter Center has since been associated with the vast evil Washington conspiracy to undermine the Chinese Communist Party and overthrow the Chinese government through underground agitation.

26. www.cat898.com, September 20, 2005.

27. Guanzhongren, "Hu-Wen jiang minzhu baixing ting yuyin," September 5, 2005, www.chinaelections.org/NewsInfo.asp?NewsID=1989. For translation, see "Hu and Wen discuss democracy; the common people listen to the residual sounds," chinadigitaltimes.net/2005/09/hu-and-wen-discuss-democracy-the-common-people-listen-for-the-residual-sounds-guanzhongren/.

28. Sheng Huaren, "Yao renzhen zuohao xuanju gexiang gongzuo yange yifa xuanju channsheng xiangzhenzhang" [Do well in all aspects of the election work and elect

township/town magistrate legally], *Qiushi* [Seeking Truth], August 30, 2006. According to Chinese officials, a shorter version of this article was distributed as a circular issued by the Central Party Committee and the State Council.

29. See John Thornton, "Assessing the Next Phase of a Rising China," circulated online. Ironically, Wen repeated the same vision to Fareed Zakaria on September 23, 2008, during his visit to New York when he attended the UN General Assembly. In the past two years, China has done absolutely nothing in the first two areas identified by Wen. Progress in the third area is minimal, mostly as a result of the media initiatives. See the transcripts of the interview at edition.cnn.com/2008/WORLD/asiapcf/09/29/chinese.premier.transcript/index.html.

30. Jiang Zemin, "Political Report to the 16th National Congress of the Chinese Communist Party," Xinhua News Agency, November 11, 2002.

31. Hu Jintao, "Political Report to the 17th National Congress of the Chinese Communist Party," Xinhua New Agency; English version at en.chinaelections.org/newsinfo.asp?newsid=11818.

32. For more details on Hu Jintao's emphasis on grassroots democracy, see Zhan Chengfu, "Grassroots Democracy According to Hu Jintao," December 29, 2007, en.chinaelections.org/newsinfo.asp?newsid=14313.

33. See note 29.

34. See Cai Yang, "Jiedu Qingxian moshi" [Interpreting the Qingxian model], August 14, 2008, www.chinaelections.org/PrintNews.asp?NewsID=132583.

35. Back in 2002, the author went to visit officials at the MCA. During the meeting, the cell phone of one of the officials rang. It was Zhao Chaoying calling to beg for help. According to the official, Zhao cried and said he was about to break under the pressure from the provincial Organization Department. The official said he was going to do all he could to protect Zhao. I'm not sure what happened later but Zhao was able to survive and the Qingxian innovation was recognized as a good experiment to deal with village affairs.

36. See note 32.

37. "Chronology of Guaiyang 'Yibashou' Seeking Office through Competition," www.chinaelections.org/{rintNews.asp?NewsID=131947.

38. Li Jun, Speech to the 5th Plenary Session of the 8th Meeting of the Guiyang Party Committee, June 23, 2008, www.chinaelections.org/{rintNews.asp?NewsID=131948.

39. "Guiyang zhenggai bianjie" [The border of the Guiyang political reform], *Liaowang dongfang zhoukan*, www.chinaelections.org/{rintNews.asp?NewsID=132026.

40. "Guiyang zhenggai bianjie," and note 35.

41. "Chronology of Guaiyang 'Yibashou.'"

42. "Chronology of Guaiyang 'Yibashou.'"

43. Zhang Jie, "Gongtui gongxuan de1 zhengzhixue jiedu" [A political science interpretation of open nomination and open election], *Xuexi Shibao* [Study Times], November 24, 2008.

44. Jiang Zemin, *Selected Works of Jiang Zemin*, vol. 3 (Beijing: Renmin Chubanshe, 2006), see quotes at www.chinaelections.org/NewsInfo.asp?NewsID=94114.

45. Mei Ninghua, "Cong aoyunhui chenggong juban kan zhongguo zhengzhi tizhi de youshi" [The advantage of China's political system seen through the successful hosting of the Olympic Games], *Beijing Daily*, September 22, 2008.

Chapter 10: Ideology: Its Role in Reform and Opening

1. This essay uses the concept "ideology" (*yishi xingtai* 意识形态) much the way Karl Mannheim does in *Ideology and Utopia* (Shanghai: Shangwu yinshuguan, 2000), namely, that any pure and complete academic theory is a concept of utopia, and that whenever it is comprehensively combined with state power it becomes an ideology. See pp. 196–209.

2. One can most directly appreciate the connection in Mao's judgment that "the sound of the gunshots of the October Revolution carried Marxism-Leninism to China." See Mao Zedong, "On the People's Democratic Dictatorship," *Selected Works of Mao Zedong*, vol. 4 (Beijing: People's Publishing House, 1969), 411–25.

3. See Yu Guangyuan, *1978: wo suo qinli de neici lishi da zhuanzhe* [1978: That historical turning point as I experienced it] (Beijing: Zhongyang bianyiju chubanshe, 2008), 160, passim. According to the author's recollections, Deng Xiaoping in his closing speech to the Third Plenary Session of the Eleventh Central Committee raised the issues of emancipating thought, democracy, and legal rule which have influenced the development of these 30 years. The tone that Deng had set at the beginning was conspicuously different than this.

4. That the classic Leninist states of the Soviet Union and Eastern Europe began an increment process of reform in the 1950s, starting and stopping, clearly reflect this characteristic. On the entry of the Soviet Union into soft reform, see Lu Ge Pihuoya [transliteration], trans. Xu Jindong, et al., *Sulian zhengquan shi* [History of the Soviet Union] (Beijing: Renmin chubanshe, 2006), chaps. 2 and 7.

5. See *Renmin ribao* [People's Daily], Jiefangjun bao and Hongqi joint editorial, "*Xuehao wenjian zhuazhu gang*" [Study the documents well, grasp the key link], February 2, 1977.

6. See Zhu Xueqin, "A Turbulent 30 Years: The Reality of Reform and Opening," www.xschina.org/show.php?id=12711.

7. Precisely because it was like this, some people have pointed out that there was no such role as the "general architect." The exploratory nature and pauses inherent in this large of a social change reflect that there was no general architect acting as the guarantor of order. See the introduction to *1978: wo suo qinli de neici lishi da zhuanzhe*. Yu Guangyuan pointed out that there was no central report in the Third Plenary Session of the Eleventh Central Committee, and this hinted at the reality that the reform and opening guided by the CCP was a by-product of a complicated political game.

8. The use of "leftist" in this essay is intended as a neutral analytic term and does not convey any praise or condemnation. Because of this, one cannot carry out any political surmise or political categorization.

9. See Deng Liqun, *Shi'erge chunqiu* [Annals of twelve years] (Hong Kong: Bozhi chubanshe, 2006). The publication page of this book does not state the date of publication, so this author is using the date listed on Hong Kong's Book City website. See hkbookcity.com/showbook2.php?serial_no=80175.

10. "Fandui jingshen wuran de qianqian houhou" [Before and after opposing spiritual pollution], in Deng, *Shi'erge chunqiu*, 261–423.

11. For instance, after this, the reform of the CCP itself became almost a forbidden zone. If the CCP recognized the need to reform itself, it was only in such superficial ways as "inner-party reform." In contrast, in 1988 Guangdong had designed measures to abolish party groups at the provincial level; such measures would be unimaginable today.

12. See Gao Weixue, preface to *Bu yu ju" lunji* [Essays on "not going beyond the bounds] (Beijing: Dazhong wenyi chubanshe, 2003). This book contains political criticism of reform and opening and can be said to represent the thinking of the Old Left.

13. See Gong Yang, ed., *Sichao—Zhongguo "Xinzuopai" jiqi yingxiang* [Thought tide—the "new left" and its influence] (Beijing: Zhongguo shehui kexue chubanshe, 2003). One can clearly sense this proposal in the essays collected in the first volume.

14. See Deng Liqun's description of the Old Left's advocacy of using power relations behind the scenes in the chapter "Yijiubasi nian de richang gongzuo he maodun" [Daily work and contradictions in 1984] in *Shi'erge chunqiu.*

15. See Ren Jiantao, *Zhongguo xiandai sixiang maimo zhong de ziyou zhuiyi* [Liberalism in the mainstream of contemporary Chinese thought] (Beijing: Beijing daxue chubanshe, 2004), chap. 6, section 5: "Wenren siwei" [Intellectuals' modes of thought], which has an analysis of the characteristic ways of thinking of the New Left.

16. See Gong Yang, ed., *Sichao.* One can comprehensively perceive the negative influences of these proposals in the essays in the second volume.

17. This can be seen in the way the Old Left uses "spiritual pollution" and "bourgeois liberalization" as weapons to attack others. One can see something of the New Left's characteristic way of thinking from their casual way of using "liberalism" as a pretext to attack others.

18. See He Bingmeng, ed., *Xin ziyou zhuyi pingxi* [Analysis and criticism of neoliberalism] (Beijing: shehui kexue wenxian chubanshe, 2004), esp. the preface.

19. Since the 1990s, China's publishing circles have released a series of works that are representative of Western liberalism. For instance, Beijing's Sanlian Publishing House published the Series of Translations on Constitutional Government (*Xianzheng iicong*), the Chinese Academy of Social Sciences published the Series on Western Contemporary Thought (*Xifang xiandai xisiang Congshu*), and the Commercial Press released Series of Translations on Democracy (*Minzhu yicong*). All these created a fever about liberalism in Chinese-language scholarly circles.

20. See Zhu Xueqin, "1998, ziyou zhuyi xueli de yanshuo" [1998: Scholarly discussions of liberalism], *Shuzhaili de geming* [A revolution in the study] (Changchun: Changchun chubanshe, 1999).

21. This major change drew forth speculation from everywhere. To try to answer people's doubts, the CCP drew together high-level people to write *Shiqida baogao xuexi fudao baiwen* [Study guidance on a hundred questions about the 17th Party Congress] (Beijing: Xuexi chubanshe and dangjian duwu chubanshe, 2007).

22. See *Renmin ribao*, February 27, 2007.

23. Chen Kuiyuan, ""Zhongguo shehui kexueyuan gaige gongzuo zuotanhui shangde jianghua" [Talk at a CASS seminar on reform work], *Zhongguo shehui kexueyuan yuanbao*, July 26, 2008.

Chapter 11: Central-Local Relations: The Power to Dominate

1. Zheng Yongnian, *De Facto Federalism in China: Reforms and Dynamics of Central-Local Relations* (London and Singapore: World Scientific Publishing, 2007); "China's De Facto Federalism," in Baogang He, Brian Galligan, and Takashi Inoguchi, eds., *Federalism in Asia* (Cheltenham: Edward Elgar, 2007), 213–41; "Explaining the Sources of de facto Federalism in Reform China: Intergovernmental Decentralization, Globalization, and Central-Local Relations," *Japanese Journal of Political Science* 7, no. 2 (2006): 101–26; and "Institutionalizing de facto Federalism in Post-Deng China," in Hung-mao Tien and Yun-han, eds., Chu *China under Jiang Zemin* (Boulder, CO: Lynne Rienner Publishers, 2000), 215–32.

2. For a review of this literature, see Zheng Yongnian, "Institutional Economics and Central-Local Relations in China: Evolving Research," *China: An International Journal* 3, no. 2 (2005): 240–69.

3. Gabriella Montinola, Yingyi Qian, and Barry R. Weingast, "Federalism, Chinese Style: The Political Basis for Economic Success in China," *World Politics* 48 (October 1995): 50–81; Hehui Jin, Yingyi Qian, and Barry R. Weingast, "Regional Decentralisation and Fiscal Incentives: Federalism, Chinese Style" (unpublished manuscript, 1999); Yuanzheng Cao, Yingyi Qian, and Barry Weingast, "From Federalism, Chinese Style, to Privatization, Chinese Style" (unpublished manuscript, 1997); and Yingyi Qian, "The Institutional Foundations of China's Market Transition" (paper prepared for the World Bank's Annual Conference on Development Economics, Washington, DC, April, 28–30 1999.

4. Montinola, Qian, and Weingast, "Federalism, Chinese Style," 79.

5. Montinola, Qian, and Weingast, "Federalism, Chinese Style," 80.

6. Susan Shirk, *The Political Logic of Economic Reform in China* (Berkeley, CA: University of California Press, 1993).

7. Shirk, *Political Logic*, 83.

8. Yasheng Huang, *Inflation and Investment Controls in China: The Political Economy of Central-Local Relations During the Reform Era* (Cambridge: Cambridge University Press, 1996).

9. Olivier Blanchard and Andrei Shleifer, "Federalism with and without Political Centralization: China versus Russia," International Monetary Fund staff paper, no. 48, 2001.

10. The World Bank, *China: Internal Market Development and Regulations* (Washington, DC: World Bank, 1994). For a summary, see Anjali Kumar, "China's Reform, Internal Trade and Marketing," *Pacific Review* 7, no. 3 (1994): 323–40.

11. Wang Shaoguang and Hu Angang, "Zhongguo zhengfu jiqu nengli de xiajiang jiqi houguo" [The decrease in the extractive capacity of the Chinese government and its consequences], *Ershiyi shiji* [Twenty-First Century], no. 21 (February 1994): 5–10.

12. Wang Shaoguang and Hu Angang, *Zhongguo guojia nengli baogao* [A report of state capacity in China] (Hong Kong: Oxford University Press, 1994).

13. For a more detailed discussion of China's fiscal reforms, see Christine P. W. Wong and Richard M. Bird, "China's Fiscal System: A Work in Progress," in Loren Brandt and Thomas G. Rawski, eds., *China's Great Economic Transformation* (New York: Cambridge University Press, 2008), 429–66.

14. For assessments of the 1994 taxation reform, see Shaoguang Wang, "China's 1994 Fiscal Reform: An Initial Assessment," *Asian Survey* 37, no. 9 (September 1997): 801–17.

15. For a discussion of China's financial system, see Franklin Allen, Jun Qian, and Meijun Qian, "China's Financial System: Past, Present, and Future," in Brandt and Rawski, eds., *China's Great Economic Transformation*, 507–68.

16. John Burns, ed., *The Chinese Communist Party's Nomenklatura System* (Armonk, NY: M.E. Sharpe, 1989).

17. Burns, *Chinese Communist Party's Nomenklatura System*.

18. *Renmin ribao*, May 17, 1995, 1.

19. *Zaobao*, Singapore, November 21, 2006.

20. Yongnian Zheng, *Globalization and State Transformation in China* (Cambridge: Cambridge University Press, 2004); and Dali Yang, *Remaking the Chinese Leviathan: Market Transition and the Politics of Governance in China* (Stanford, CA: Stanford University Press, 2004).

21. See Zheng Yongnian and Zhang Yang, "Cong CEPA dao '9+2': zhengzhi dongle yu goujia" [From the CEPA to '9+2': Political motivations and frame], in John Wong and Li Jiangtao, eds., *Hezuo yu gongying: fanzhusanjiao jingji hezuo ji dui dongnanya de yingxiang* [Cooperation and win-win: Economic cooperation in the Greater Pearl River Delta and its impact on Southeast Asia] (Guangzhuo: Guangdong renmin chubanshe, 2006), 73–92.

22. Zheng, *De Facto Federalism in China*, chap. 6.

23. Shuanglin Lin, "China's Government Debt: How Serious?" *China: An International Journal* 1, no. 1 (March 2003): 73–98.

24. "Qi hangye you guoyoujingji juedui kongzhi, guoqi zhengti shangshi jiang tisu" [Seven industries firmly controlled by the state, SOEs listing to be accelerated], *People's Daily*, December 19, 2006, finance.people.com.cn/GB/5185910.html.

25. For a detailed discussion of this strategy, see Yongnian Zheng, *Zhu Rongji Xinzheng: Zhongguo gaige de xinmoshi* [Zhu Rongji's new deal: A new model for China's reform] (River Edge, NJ: Global, 1994), chap. 4.

26. "Li Rongrong: Guoziwei de chengli shuoming chuziren kaishi daowei" [Li Rongrong: The establishment of SASAC means investors are in place], *China News*, May 22, 2003, www.nyconsulate.prchina.chn/xw/t30193.htm.

27. SASAC data.

28. "Guoziwei fu zhuren: woguo jiang jiji tuijin guoqi renshizhidu gaige" [Deputy director of SASAC: China will actively promote the reform of personnel system in SOEs], *Xinhua*, October 25, 2006, www.gov.cn/jrzg/2006-10/25/content_423735.htm.

29. "2006 nian guoziwei gongzuo huigu" [SASAC work review 2006], www.sasac .gov.cn/2006rdzt/2006rdzt_0021/gzw/default.htm.

30. "2006 nian guoziwei gongzuo huigu."

31. "Renmin luntan diaocha: 96.5% de ren dui dangqian gongzi buman" [People's forum survey: 96.5% of responses indicate dissatisfaction about current salaries], *Xinhua*, June 5, 2007, news.xinhuanet.com/fortune/2007-06/05/content_6202484.htm.

32. "Tiaozheng longduan hangye gongzi buru wanshan guoqi zhili jizhi" [It is better to improve management mechanism, rather than adjust the wage system of SOEs in monopoly sectors], *Yanzhou Metropolis Daily*, March 19, 2007, news.xinhuanet .com/comments/2007-03/19/content_5865109.htm.

33. "Guoziwei yancha yangqi 'xiao jinku,' wei yangqi shangjiao gongli pulu" [SASAC rigorously investigates central SOES' "little treasures" to prepare for the resumption of dividends payments from central SOEs to the state], *Beijing Times*, February 16, 2007, news.xinhuanet.com/fortune/2007-02/16/content_5745865.htm.

34. "Guoqi laozong zha jiu chengle fubai 'zhongzaiqu'?" (How did SOE bosses become the "disaster area" of corruption?) *Guangming Daily*, February 1, 2007, gov.people.com.cn/GB/48380/535462.html.

35. "Longduan hangye fubai gao shouru gao, zhongyang jiang xiang longduan guoqi kaidao" [Monopoly sector has much corruption and a high income, and the central government is targeting monopoly SOEs], *Oriental Outlook*, October 26, 2006, news.xinhuanet.com/fortune/2006-10/26/content_5251320.htm.

36. Speech of Deputy Prime Minister Zeng Peiyan on the National SME Forum, September 14, 2006, available at Department of SME, National Development and Reform Commission of China, zxqys.ndrc.gov.cn/ldxw/t20061103_91615.htm.

37. See for example, Clement Kong-Wing Chow and Michael Ka Yiu Fung, "Small Business and Liquidity Constraints in Financing Business Investment: Evidence from Shanghai's Manufacturing Sector," *Journal of Business Venturing* 15, no. 4 (2000): 363–83; Alessandra Guariglia and Sandra Poncet, "Could Financial Distortions Be No Impediment to Economic Growth After All? Evidence from China," *Journal of Comparative Economics* 36, no. 4 (2008): 633–57.

38. Cited in Jiang Wandi, "Grassroots Democracy Taking Root," *Beijing Review* 39, no. 11, March 11–17, 1996, 11.

39. Lianjiang Li and Kevin O'Brien, "Accommodating 'Democracy' in a One-Party State: Introducing Village Elections in China," *China Quarterly*, no. 162 (June 2000): 465–89; and Li and O'Brien, "The Struggle for Village Elections," in Merle Goldman and Roderick MacFarquhar, eds., *The Paradox of China's Post-Mao Reforms* (Cambridge, MA: Harvard University Press, 1999), 129–44.

40. Lianjiang Li, "The Two-Ballot System in Shanxi Province: Subjecting Village Party Secretaries to a Popular Vote," *China Journal*, no. 42 (July 1999): 103–18.

41. For example, Hairong Lai, *The Causes and Effects of the Development of Semi-Competitive Elections at the Township Level in China since the 1990s* (PhD diss., Department of Political Science, Central European University, Budapest, January 2008).

42. See Lisheng Dong, "Grassroots Governance and Democracy in China's Countryside," in Zhengxu Wang and Colin Durkop, eds., *East Asian Democracy and Political Changes in China: A New Goose Flying?* (Singapore: The Konrad Adennauer Stiftung, 2008), 155–68.

43. Lianjiang Li, "The Politics of Introducing Direct Township Elections in China," *China Quarterly*, no. 171 (September 2002): 704–23.

44. "Rights-democracy" refers to citizens from the marginalized or disadvantaged social groups asserting or defending their rights by a variety of means, including competing in local elections and asserting the right to recall a delegate who was deemed incompetent, corrupt, or unwilling to represent voters' interests to a local people's congress. For a discussion of all these forms of democracy, see Li Fan, "Is Democratic Development in China Sustainable," in Wang and Durkop, eds., *East Asian Democracy and Political Changes in China*, 135–51.

45. Qiusha Ma, *Non-Governmental Organizations in Contemporary China: Paving the Way to Civil Society?* (London and New York: Routledge, 2006).

46. Cited in Zengke He, "Institutional Barriers to the Development of Civil Society in China," in Zheng Yongnian and Joseph Fewsmith, eds., *China's Opening Society: The Non-State Sector and Governance* (London and New York: Routledge, 2008), 162.

47. Zengke He, "Institutional Barriers," 163.

48. State Council, *Shehui Tuanti Dengji Guanli Tiaoli* [Regulations on the registration and management of social organizations] (Beijing: State Council, 1998).

49. Jude Howell, "NGO-State Relations in Post-Mao China," in David Hulme and Michael Edwards, eds., *NGOs, States and Donors: Too Close for Comfort?* (London: Macmillan Press Ltd, 1997), 202–15; and Linda Wong, *Marginalization and Social Welfare in China* (London and New York: Routledge, 1998).

Chapter 12: Energy Governance: Fueling the Miracle

1. According to statistics published by China's National Bureau of Statistics (NBS), China became the world's largest primary energy producer in 2009. Measured in million tons of oil equivalent (Mtoe), China's primary energy production surpassed that of the United States in 2005. The Economist, *Pocket in World Figures 2009* (London: Profile Books, 2009), 56.

2. Also based on Mtoe figures. British Petroleum, *Statistical Review of World Energy,* 2008.

3. British Petroleum, *Statistical Review of World Energy,* 2008; WTO Trade Statistics Database, 2008.

4. British Petroleum, *Statistical Review of World Energy,* 2008.

5. IEA, *World Energy Outlook* (Paris: IEA, 2007).

6. US Oak Ridge National Laboratory (cdiac.esd.ornl.gov). News release: www.ornl.gov/info/press_releases/get_press_release.cfm?ReleaseNumber=mr20080924-00.

7. For an example of this shift see Lester Brown, "China Replacing the US as World's Leading Consumer," *Eco-Economy Updates,* Earth Policy Institute, February 16, 2005.

8. Philip Andrews-Speed, *Energy Policy and Regulation in the People's Republic of China,* International Energy and Resources Law and Policy series, 19 (The Hague: Kluwer Law International, 2004), 24. Andrews-Speed is one of the careful longtime observers, arguing that while participation of the private sector is limited in the sector, local township and village enterprises have been significant players in the coal industry.

9. Such success in achieving stable energy supply has of course come at enormous environmental cost. This is particularly true in relation to coal utilization. This critical issue is addressed in chapter 13 on the environment, authored by Joanna Lewis.

10. For more on devolution and delegation as the foundation of decentralization reforms, see G. Shabbir Cheema and Dennis A. Rondinelli, *From Government Decentralization to Decentralized Governance* (Washington, DC: Brooking Institution, 2007);

Dennis A. Rondinelli, John R. Nellis, and G. Shabbir Cheema, "Decentralization in Developing Countries: A Review of Recent Experience," World Bank Staff Working Papers, No. 581, Management and Development Series (Washington, DC: World Bank, 1983); and James Manor, "The Political Economy of Decentralization," World Bank Draft Paper, August 1, 1997.

11. Andrews-Speed (2004), p. 17.

12. Philip Andrews-Speed et al., "A Framework for Policy Formulation for Small-Scale Mines: The Case of Coal in China," *Natural Resources Forum* 26 (Blackwell Synergy, 2002), 45–54.

13. Chi Zhang and Thomas Heller, "Reform of Chinese Electric Power Market: Economics and Institutions," in David Victor and Thomas Heller, eds., *The Political Economy of Power Sector Reform: The Experiences of Five Major Developing Countries* (Cambridge: Cambridge University, 2007), 77.

14. This section is a more detailed treatment of a summarized argument in Edward Cunningham, "China's Energy Governance: Perception and Reality," MIT Center for International Studies Audit of the Conventional Wisdom (March 2007).

15. Thomas Fingar, "Implementing Energy Policy: The Rise and Demise of the State Energy Commission," in D. Lampton, ed., *Policy Implementation in Post-Mao China* (Berkeley: University of California Press, 1987), 207.

16. Victor Shih, *Factions and Finance in China: Elite Conflict and Inflation* (Cambridge: Cambridge University Press, 2007), 110.

17. Shih, *Factions and Finance*, 114–15.

18. Xiaoqian Zhou, ed., *China's Electric Power Program* (Beijing: Water Power Publishing, 2007), 117.

19. Daniel Chow, "An Analysis of the Political Economy of China's Enterprise Conglomerates: A Study of the Reform of the Electric Power Industry in China," *Law and Policy in International Business* 28, no. 2 (1997): 406.

20. MOEP, "Expanding the Scale and Use of Foreign Investment to Accelerate Electric Power Development" (document no. 341, September 10, 1993), in Xiaoqian Zhou, ed., *China's Electric Power Program* (Beijing: Water Power Publishing, 2007), 826.

21. Pei-Yee Woo, "China's Electric Power Market: The Rise and Fall of IPPs" (Program on Energy and Sustainable Development [PESD] Working Paper No.45), August 16, 2005, 11.

22. Yi-Chong Xu, *Powering China: Reforming the Electric Power Industry in China* (Aldershot: Ashgate, 2002), 126.

23. Corporatization is defined as the diversification of ownership structure, and in this chapter particular attention is afforded the introduction of sub-central-state and non-state parties as shareholders "to make SOEs operate as if they were private firms facing a competitive market or, if monopolies, efficient regulation." Mary Shirley, "Bureaucrats in Business: The Roles of Privatization versus Corporatization in State-Owned Enterprise Reform," *World Development* 27, no. 1 (1999): 115. See also Colin Xu, Tian Zhu, and Yi-min Lin, "Politician Control, Agency Problems and Ownership Reform: Evidence from China," *Economics of Transition* 13, no. 1 (2005): 1–24.

24. Xu, *Powering China*, 100.

25. See the Chinese Civil Law Network, www.cclaw.net/download/companylaw.asp.

26. Philip Andrews-Speed, "China's Energy Woes: Running on Empty," *Far Eastern Economic Review* (June 2005): 17.

27. Barry Naughton, "Claiming Profit for the State: SASAC and the Capital Management Budget," *China Leadership Monitor* 18 (Spring 2006): 4.

28. Luo Gan, "Explanation of Plan for Institutional Restructuring of the State Council," *Ta Kung Pao* (March 7, 1998), in FBIS, DR/CHI, March 10, 1998, 98-068; Cheng Li, "China in 1999: Seeking Common Ground at a Time of Tension and Conflict," *Asian Survey* 40, no. 1 (2000): 122. For related WTO accession issues please see Joseph Fewsmith, "China and the WTO: The Politics Behind the Agreement," National Bureau of Research, *NBR Analysis* 10, no. 5, essay 2 (November 1999).

29. For representative works supporting this perspective, see Dali Yang, *Remaking the Chinese Leviathan: Market Transition and the Politics of Governance in China* (Stanford: Stanford University Press, 2005).

30. Margaret Pearson, "The Business of Governing Business in China: Institutions and Norms of the Emerging Regulatory State," *World Politics* 57 (January 2005): 304–5. See also Margaret Pearson, "Governing the Chinese Economy: Regulatory Reform in the Service of the State," *Public Administration Review* 67, no. 4 (2007): 718–30.

31. David Zweig and Jianhai Bi, "China's Global Hunt for Energy," *Foreign Affairs* 84, no. 5 (2005); Kenneth Lieberthal and Mikkal Herberg, "China's Search for Energy Security: Implications for US Policy," National Bureau of Asian Research, *NBR Analysis* (2006); Daojiong Zha, "China's Energy Security: Domestic and International Issues," *Survival* 48, no. 1 (2006): 179–90. Notable recent exceptions include Peter Nolan and Huaichuan Rui, "Industrial Policy and Global Big Business Revolution: The Case of the Chinese Coal Industry," *Journal of Chinese Economic & Business Studies* 2, no. 2 (May 2004): 97–113; the many writings of Philip Andrews-Speed; and Elspeth Thomson, *The Chinese Coal Industry: An Economic History* (London: Routledge, 2003).

32. Peter Nolan and J. Zhang, "Globalization Challenge for Large Firms from Developing Countries: China's Oil and Aerospace Industries," *European Management Journal* 21, no. 3 (2003): 285–99.

33. Timothy Frye and Andrei Shleifer, *The Invisible Hand and the Grabbing Hand* (Cambridge, MA: National Bureau of Economic Research, 1996); Andrew Walder, "Zouping in Perspective," in Andrew G. Walder, ed., *Zouping in Transition: The Process of Reform in Rural North China* (Cambridge, MA: Harvard University Press, 1998), 16–23; Andrew Walder, "Local Governments as Industrial Firms: An Organizational Analysis of China's Transitional Economy," *American Journal of Sociology* 101, no. 2 (1995); Jean Oi, *Rural China Takes Off: Institutional Foundations of Economic Reform* (Berkeley: University of California Press, 1999). For an overview of varying approaches to the role of the local state in economic development see Tony Saich, "The Blind Man and the Elephant: Analyzing the Local State in China," in Luigi Tomba, ed., *On the Roots of Growth and Crisis: Capitalism, State and Society in East Asia*, (Annale Feltinelli, 2002), 75–99.

34. For example, Amy Jaffe et al., "Beijing's Oil Diplomacy," *Survival* 44, no. 1 (2002): 115–34; Robert Ebel, *China's Energy Future: The Middle Kingdom Seeks Its Place in the Sun* (Washington, DC: Center for Strategic & International Studies, 2005); Linda Jakobson and Daojiong Zha, "China and the Worldwide Search for Oil Security," *Asia-Pacific Review* 13, no. 2 (2006): 60–73.

35. Philip Andrews-Speed, "Reform of China's Energy Sector: Slow Progress to an Uncertain Goal," in Sarah Cook, J. Zhuang, and S. Yao, eds., *The Chinese Economy Under Transition* (Macmillan, 2000), 113.

36. Andrews-Speed, "Reform of China's Energy Sector," 114, 117.

37. Peter Nolan, "China and the Global Business Revolution," *Cambridge Journal of Economics* 26, no. 1 (January 1, 2002): 125. See also F. Fesharaki and K. Wu, "Revitalizing China's Petroleum Industry Through Reorganization: Will It Work?" *Oil & Gas Journal* 96, no. 32 (1998).

38. Nolan, "China and the Global Business Revolution," 126.

39. Philip Andrews-Speed, S. Dow, and Z. Gao, "The Ongoing Reforms to China's Government and State Sector: The Case of the Energy Industry," *Journal of Contemporary China* (2000): 15.

40. Kenneth Lieberthal and Michel Oksenberg, "Bureaucratic Politics and Chinese Energy Development" (US Department of Commerce, International Trade Administration, 1986); Kenneth Lieberthal and Michel Oksenberg, *Policymaking in China: Leaders, Structures, and Processes* (Princeton: Princeton University Press, 1988).

41. China Economic Reporting and Monitoring Center, ed., *Zhongguo chanye ditu—nengyuan 2004-5* (Beiijing: Shehui kexue wenxian chubanshe, 2006), 102.

42. China Electricity Council, "*2008 nian quanguo dianli gongye tongji kuaibao yilanbiao,*" 2009.

43. While the growth rate did decline, the severity of the drop in LNSM growth rates during the period 1998–2002 is considered by most to be suspect due to significant underreporting.

44. Elspeth also points out the additional attractions of local mines: "Besides mitigating the shortage problem, relieving the critical lack of railway capacity on the north-south lines, and costing half as much to build and operate, LNS mines also contribute to other Chinese government objectives. They become operational much sooner, add to the wealth of peasants, help reduce rural unemployment, stem rural-urban migration, stimulate the development of rural industry and help halt the ecological damage resulting from the scavenging for firewood." Elspeth Thomson, "Reforming China's Coal Industry," *China Quarterly* (1996): 729.

45. See State Council Notice "Provisional Regulation on the Encouragement of Fundraising for Power Construction Investment and Implementation of the Multi-Rate Power Tariff," document no. 86, April 17, 1986.

46. Barry Naughton, *Growing Out of the Plan: Chinese Economic Reform, 1978–1993* (Cambridge: Cambridge University Press, 1995).

47. Bin Wang, "An Imbalanced Development of Coal and Electricity Industries in China," *Energy Policy* 35, no. 10 (2007): 4959–68.

48. Thomson, "Reforming China's Coal Industry," 745.

49. Thomson, "Reforming China's Coal Industry," 745.

50. For detailed analysis of this process, please see Elspeth Thomson, *The Chinese Coal Industry: An Economic History* (London: Routledge, 2003).

51. In late 2005 the NDRC promulgated "*Guanyu zuohao 2006 nian quanguo zhongdian meitan chanyunxu xianjie gongzuo de tongzhi*" [Notice regarding the 2006 linking of national key coal mine production, transportation, and demand], which

made clear that the NDRC had abolished the "temporary interference" of the central government in coal pricing for electricity generation and encouraged the signing of long-term contracts between coal and electricity firms.

52. "Favorable Coal Prices to Be Abolished," *China Daily*, July 23, 2004.

53. For an excellent updated review of reforms in China's electricity sector see Chi Zhang and Thomas Heller, "Reform of Chinese Electric Power Market: Economics and Institutions," in David Victor and Thomas Heller, eds., *The Political Economy of Power Sector Reform: The Experiences of Five Major Developing Countries* (Cambridge: Cambridge University, 2007).

54. Zhang and Heller, "Reform of Chinese Electric Power Market," 77.

55. See State Council Notice "Speeding Up the Development of the Electricity Industry," document no. 114, July 25, 1975; Zhang and Heller, "Reform of Chinese Electric Power Market," 93.

56. See Ministry of Electric Power Notice "Provisional Measure Transforming All Budgetary Infrastructure Fund Allocations into Loans," document no. 84, December 27, 1984. This was followed months later by the MOEP Notice "Central Government and State Council Leaders' Memo on Questions Relating to the Utilization of Foreign Financing to Speed the Building of Electric Power," document no. 54, February 26, 1985.

57. See State Council Notice document no. 86, April 17, 1986.

58. Zhang Chi, "Reform of Chinese Electric Power Market: Economics and Institutions," PESD draft paper, Stanford University, January 2003, 9.

59. Intermittent short-term shortages always existed, as is the case in most developing (and, occasionally, developed) nations.

60. The six firms are Huaneng International Joint Stock Company, Shandong Huaneng Electricity Joint Stock Company, Shandong International Power Development Company, China Harbin Power Plant Equipment Group, Northeast Electric Transmission and Transformation Equipment Corp., and Datang Power Company. The listings occurred in 1994.

61. Investor Communication company document, "In Pursuit of World Class Corporate Governance and IR"; see www.fa100index.com/images/PDF/huanengpower .pdf (accessed February 4, 2010).

62. Xu, *Powering China*, 127.

63. Woo, "China's Electric Power Market," 11.

64. Prominent examples of such legislation were State Council documents 146, 5 and 2704 of 2002; and later 2 of 2003 and 432 of 2005.

65. Edward Steinfeld, "Energy Policy: Charting a Path for China's Future," World Bank China Note, June 2004.

66. State Council Office of Economic Restructuring, "Zhongguo dianli jianguan jigou jianshe yanjiu baogao," November 2004, 150.

67. Binsheng Li and James Dorian, "Change in China's Power Sector," *Energy Policy* 23, no. 7 (1995): 625.

68. Xu, *Powering China*, 172.

69. Xu, *Powering China*, 173.

70. Matthew Miller, "Beijing's Power Sector Feels Wind of Change," *South China Morning Post*, January, 13, 2000, 10.

71. Woo, "China's Electric Power Market," 9.

72. LBNL, *China Energy Databook*, 2008.

73. For a more detailed discussion of efficiency issues, please see chapter 13 on the environment by Joanna Lewis.

74. Xiannuan Lin, *China's Energy Strategy: Economic Structure, Technological Choices, and Energy Consumption* (Westport, CT: Praeger, 1996).

75. "Full Text: Work Report of NPC Standing Committee," March 16, 2009, news .xinhuanet.com/english/2009-03/16/content_11018210_1.htm.

76. Vaclav Smil, "China's Energy and Resource Uses: Continuity and Change," *China Quarterly*, no. 156 (1998): 947.

77. For an informative view regarding China's approach to climate change, please see Joanna Lewis, "China's Strategic Priorities in International Climate Change Negotiations," *Washington Quarterly* 31, no. 1 (December 1, 2007): 155–74, as well as chapter 13 in this volume.

78. World Bank, *Cost of Pollution in China: Economic Estimates of Physical Damages* (Washington, DC: World Bank, 2007).

79. David Vogel, *Trading Up: Consumer and Environmental Regulation in a Global Economy* (Cambridge, MA: Harvard University Press, 1995).

80. The NEA will also absorb nuclear power generation authorities from the Commission of Science, Technology and Industry for National Defense (COSTIND). For an excellent discussion see Erica Downs, "China's Energy Policymaking Structure and Reforms," Testimony before the U.S.-China Economic & Security Review Commission, China's Energy Policies and Their Environmental Impacts Panel, August 13, 2008.

81. These departments include General Integration, Strategic Planning, Policy, International Cooperation, Science and Technology Energy Savings, New Energy, Coal, Electric Power, Petroleum and Natural Gas.

82. E-mail communication with US EIA staff, December 20, 2005; US DOE website.

83. Zhang and Heller, "Reform of Chinese Electric Power Market," 107.

Chapter 13: Environmental Challenges: From the Local to the Global

1. World Bank, "China Quick Facts," 2009, go.worldbank.org/4Q7SC8DU50 (accessed January 6, 2010).

2. World Bank and China State Environmental Protection Administration (SEPA), *Cost of Pollution in China,* 2007, siteresources.worldbank.org/INTEAPREGTOPENV RONMENT/Resources/China_Cost_of_Pollution.pdf.

3. World Bank and SEPA, *Cost of Pollution in China.*

4. *China Energy Statistical Yearbook 2006* (Beijing: China Statistics Press, 2007); REN21, "Renewables Global Status Report 2006 Update," 2006, ren21.org/pdf/RE_GSR_2006_Update.pdf.

5. Regulatory Assistance Project (RAP), "China's Power Sector: A Backgrounder for International Regulators and Policy Advisors," February 2008 (prepared for the Energy Foundation China Sustainable Energy Program).

6. Joseph Kahn, "In China, a Lake's Champion Imperils Himself," *New York Times*, October 14, 2007, www.nytimes.com/2007/10/14/world/asia/14china.html?_r=1&pagewanted=all.

7. Congressional-Executive Commission on China, *Annual Report, 2008*, 110th Congress, Second Session, October 31, 2008, www.cecc.gov/pages/annualRpt/annualRpt08/CECCannRpt2008.pdf.

8. International Energy Agency (IEA), *World Energy Outlook 2007* (Paris: OECD/IEA).

9. Trevor Houser, "China's Energy Consumption and Opportunities for U.S.-China Cooperation to Address the Effects of China's Energy Use," testimony before the U.S.-China Economic and Security Review Commission, June 14, 2007, www.uscc.gov/hearings/2007hearings/written_testimonies/07_06_14_15wrts/07_06_14_houser_statement.php.

10. IEA, *World Energy Outlook 2007*, chap. 9.

11. The Three Gorges Dam project currently includes twenty-six 700 MW turbines, and an additional six turbines are currently under construction, with a total planned capacity of 22.4 GW. "Sanxia jizu guochanhua yiqu chenggong" (Three Gorges Generating Units Has Been a Success Domestically), *Xinhua*, December 12, 2008, www.hb.xinhuanet.com/zhibo/2008-12/04/content_15097047.htm.

12. Philip Andrews-Speed, Stephen Dow, Aijuan Wang, Jim Mao, and Bin Wei, "Do the Power Sector Reforms in China Reflect the Interests of Consumers?" *China Quarterly* 159 (1999): 430–46.

13. Make Consulting, "WTG OEM Market Shares 2009," Wind Power Sector Research Note, March 2010.

14. "Solarbuzz Reports World Solar Photovoltaic Market Growth of 62 Percent in 2007," *Solar Daily*, March 18, 2008, www.solardaily.com/reports/Solarbuzz_Reports_World_Solar_Photovoltaic_Market_Growth_of_62_Percent_In_2007_999.html.

15. Catherine Brahic, "China to Promise Cuts in Greenhouse Gases," NewScientist.com news service, February 14, 2007, environment.newscientist.com/article.ns?id=dn11184; Jiang Lin, Nan Zhou, Mark Levine, and David Fridley, "Achieving China's Target for Energy Intensity Reduction in 2010: An Exploration of Recent Trends and Possible Future Scenarios," Report #61800, Lawrence Berkeley National Laboratory, December 2006.

16. Chinaview.com, "China's Energy Consumption per Unit of GDP Down 3.46 Percent in First 3 Quarters," December 13, 2008, news.xinhuanet.com/english/2008-12/13/content_10497268.htm.

17. Lynn Price and Xuejun Wang, "Constraining Energy Consumption of China's Largest Industrial Enterprises Through Top-1000 Energy-Consuming Enterprise Program," Lawrence Berkeley National Laboratory, June 2007, ies.lbl.gov/iespubs/LBNL-62874.pdf.

18. China National Development and Reform Commission, 2006, hzs.ndrc.gov.cn/newzwxx/t20060414_66220.htm; Jonathan E. Sinton, "China's Quest for Energy Efficiency: Its Top 1,000 Enterprises Program," OECD/IEA, June 2006, www.iea.org/Textbase/work/2006/gb/papers/ChinaQuest.pdf.

19. PlanetArk.com, "China to Require Swap of Old Coal Plants for New," February 1, 2007, www.planetark.com/dailynewsstory.cfm/newsid/40107/newsDate/1-Feb-2007/story.htm.

20. Reuters/PlanetArk.com, "China Orders Small Cement Plants to Be Closed," March 2, 2007, www.planetark.com/dailynewsstory.cfm/newsid/40623/story.htm.

21. PlanetArk.com, "China to Shut Old Steel, Power Plants in 2007—Wen," March 5, 2007, www.planetark.com/dailynewsstory.cfm/newsid/40654/newsDate/5-Mar-2007/story.htm.

22. Based on revised GDP figures for 2008 released by the National Bureau of Statistics at the end of 2009. The prior decline in energy intensity reported for 2008 had been 4.59 percent.

23. Chen Chao, "Shanxi Leads China in Saving Energy," March 10, 2010, www.china.org.cn/china/NPC_CPPCC_2010/2010-03/10/content_19576768.htm.

24. Mark D. Levine and Lynn Price, "Assessment of China's Energy-Saving and Emission-Reduction Accomplishments and Opportunities During the 11th Five Year Plan: Findings and Recommendations" (presentation to the China FAQs Network for Climate and Energy Information Meeting, World Resources Institute, Washington, DC, December 2, 2009); Alibaba.com, "Halfway Through: China's Energy-Saving Policy Analysis," March 31, 2009, news.alibaba.com/article/detail/business-in-china/100078469-1-halfway-through%253A-china%2527s-energy-saving-policy.html; Wu Chong and Si Tingting, "Bar for Climate Change Goals Set High for China," *China Daily*, November 26, 2009, www.chinadaily.com.cn/china/2009-11/26/content_9052416.htm; CCTV, "China Revises 2008 Growth Figures of 9.6%," December 26, 2009, english.cctv.com/program/chinatoday/20091226/101128.shtml.

25. See, for example, Jiang Lin, Nan Zhou, Mark Levine, and David Fridley, "Taking Out One Billion Tons of CO_2: The Magic of China's 11th Five Year Plan?" June 2007, Lawrence Berkeley National Laboratory Report (LBNL-757E), china.lbl.gov/publications/taking-out-one-billion-tons-co2-magic-china's-11th-five-year-plan.

26. Office of the State Council General, "Guowuyuan changwu hui yanjiu jueding woguo kongzhi wenshiqiti paifang mubiao" (China's State Council executive will study the decision to control greenhouse gas emissions targets), November 26, 2009, www.gov.cn/ldhd/2009-11/26/content_1474016.htm.

27. White House Press Office, "President to Attend Copenhagen Climate Talks: Administration Announces U.S. Emission Target for Copenhagen," November 25, 2009, www.whitehouse.gov/the-press-office/president-attend-copenhagen-climate-talks.

28. US DOE EIA, *International Energy Outlook 2009*.

29. Chinese National Development and Reform Commission, "China's National Climate Change Programme," June 2007, en.ndrc.gov.cn/newsrelease/P020070604561191006823.pdf.

30. Gao Guangsheng, "Policies and Measures of China on Climate Change Mitigation under the Framework of Sustainable Development" (presentation to the 2nd Workshop of the Dialogue on Long-Term Cooperative Action to Address Climate Change by Enhancing Implementation of the Convention, November 15–16, 2006, Nairobi, Kenya), unfccc.int/files/meetings/dialogue/application/vnd.ms-powerpoint/061115_cop12_dial_3.pps.

31. Joanna I. Lewis, "China's Strategic Priorities in International Climate Negotiations," Center for Strategic and International Studies and Massachusetts Institute of Technology, *Washington Quarterly* 31, no. 1 (2007): 155–74.

32. Reuters, "China to Watch Others on Climate Change Action," June 15, 2005, www.enn.com/today.html?Id=7959; P. Parameswaran, "Rich Nations Must Honor Climate Change Pledge: Developing Countries," Agence France-Presse, September 25, 2007, sg.news.yahoo.com/afp/20070925/tts-un-climate-warming-developing-c1b2fc3.html.

33. "Reducing Emissions From Deforestation in Developing Countries: Approaches to Stimulate Action," January 30, 2007, unfccc.int/files/methods_and_science/lulucf/application/pdf/bolivia.pdf (submission of views of seventeen parties to the Eleventh Conference of the Parties to the UNFCCC).

34. US DOE, "U.S.-China Clean Energy Announcements," November 17, 2009 (press release) www.energy.gov/news2009/8292.htm.

35. "Copenhagen Accord" (draft decision, COP 15), December 18, 2009, unfccc.int/resource/docs/2009/cop15/eng/l07.pdf.

36. See US General Accounting Office, "Selected Nations' Reports on Greenhouse Gas Emissions Varied in Their Adherence to Standards," GAO-04-98, December 2003, www.gao.gov/new.items/d0498.pdf; David G. Streets et al., "Recent Reductions in China's Greenhouse Gas Emissions," *Science*, November 30, 2001, 1835–37; Subodh Sharma, Sumana Bhattacharya, and Amit Garg, "Greenhouse Gas Emissions From India: A Perspective," *Current Science*, February 10, 2006, www.ias.ac.in/currsci/feb102006/326.pdf.

37. Intergovernmental Panel on Climate Change (IPCC), "Fourth Assessment Report, Working Group I, Summary for Policy Makers," 2007.

38. IPCC, "Fourth Assessment Report."

39. IPCC, "Fourth Assessment Report."

40. Lin Erda, Xu Yinlong, Wu Shaohong, Ju Hui, and Ma Shiming, "Synopsis of China National Climate Change Assessment Report (II): Climate Change Impacts and Adaptation," *Advances in Climate Change Research* 3 suppl. (2007): 6J11 (paper as synopsis of section II of the *China's National Assessment Report on Climate Change*, which was published in February 2007), www.climatechange.cn/qikan/manage/wenzhang/02.pdf.

41. Lin Erda, Xiong Wei, Ju Hui, Xu Yinlong, Li Yue, Bai Liping, and Xie Liyong, "Climate Change Impacts on Crop Yield and Quality with CO_2 Fertilization in China," special issue, "Food Crops in a Changing Climate," *Philosophical Transactions: Biological Sciences* 360, no. 1463 (2005): 2149–54.

42. Lin et al., "Synposis."

43. IPCC, "Fourth Assessment Report."

44. Elizabeth Economy, "China vs. Earth," May 7, 2007, www.thenation.com/doc/20070507/economy.

45. Lin et al., "Synopsis"; Fan Daidu and Li Congxian, "Complexities of China's Coast in Response to Climate Change," *Advances in Climate Change Research* 2, suppl. 1 (2006): 54–58; C. X. Li, D. D. Fan, B. Deng, and D. J. Wang, "Some Problems of Vulnerability Assessment in the Coastal Zone of China," in N. Mimura and H. Yokoki, eds., *Global Change and Asian Pacific Coasts*, 2001 (proceedings of APN/SURVAS/LOICZ Joint Conference on Coastal Impacts of Climate Change and Adaptation in the Asia-Pacific Region Held in Kobe, Japan, November 14–16, 2000), 49–56.

46. Economy, "China vs. Earth."

47. US EPA, "Greenhouse Effect, Sea Level Rise, and Land Use," www.epa.gov/climatechange/effects/coastal/SLRLandUse.html (accessed February 20, 2009).

48. Li et al., "Some Problems of Vulnerability Assessment."

49. Yu Qingtai, media interview, September, 22, 2007, www.chinaembassy.org.in/eng/zgbd/t366696.htm.

Conclusion: China's Next Three Decades

1. Barry Naughton, "China's Economic Leadership after the Sevententh Party Congress," *China Leadership Monitor*, no. 23 (Winter 2008), media.hoover.org/documents/CLM23BN.pdf.

2. William Grimes, *Unmaking the Japanese Miracle: Macroeconomic Policies, 1985–2000* (Ithaca, NY: Cornell University Press, 2002).

3. Wang Xiangwei, "China's Young Guns Readying for Showdown," *South China Morning Press*, January 4, 2010, 4.

Index

ACFTU. *See* All China Federation of Trade Unions (ACFTU)

About the Contributors

Edward A. Cunningham is an Ash Institute Postdoctoral Fellow at the John F. Kennedy School of Government, Harvard University, and an affiliate of the Massachusetts Institute of Technology (M.I.T.) Industrial Performance Center. In the fall of 2011 he will join Boston University's Department of Geography and Environment as an assistant professor of energy. Dr. Cunningham graduated from Georgetown University, received an A.M. from Harvard's Graduate School of Arts and Sciences, and recently received his Ph.D. from the Department of Political Science at M.I.T. He was selected as a Fulbright Fellow to the PRC, during which time he conducted his doctoral fieldwork as a visiting fellow at Tsinghua University. His primary research interests relate to energy markets, comparative political economy, industrial organization and competitiveness, and public policy. Dr. Cunningham is the author or a contributing author of several publications, including: *Global Taiwan* (M.E. Sharpe, 2005); "China's Energy Governance: Perception and Reality," *Audits of Conventional Wisdom Series* (M.I.T. Center for International Studies, 2007); "China and East Asian Energy: Prospects and Issues," Australia-Japan Research Centre (ANU, 2008); "Why Pollute? Explaining the Environmental Performance of Chinese Power Plants," *China Economic Quarterly* (September 2008); and "Greener Plants, Grayer Skies? A Report from the Front Lines of China's Energy Sector," *Energy Policy* 37:5 (May 2009).

Joseph Fewsmith is professor of international relations and political science as well as director of the Boston University Center for the Study of Asia. He is the author of four books: *China since Tiananmen: The Politics of Transition* (Cambridge University Press, 2001 and 2008), *Elite Politics in Contemporary China* (M.E. Sharpe, 2001), *The Dilemmas of Reform in China: Political Conflict and Economic Debate* (M.E. Sharpe, 1994), and *Party, State, and Local Elites in Republican China: Merchant Organizations and Politics in Shanghai, 1980–1930* (University of Hawaii Press, 1985). His articles have appeared in such journals as *Asian Survey, Comparative Studies in Society and History, The China Journal, The China Quarterly, Current History, The Journal of Contemporary China,* and *Modern China,* as well as in numerous books. His quarterly analyses of Chinese reform appear in *China Leadership Monitor,* a web publication analyzing current developments in China. He is also a Faculty Fellow at the Frederick S. Pardee Center for the Study of the Longer Range Future and a research associate of the John King Fairbank Center for East Asian Studies at Harvard University.

Sebastian Heilmann is professor for comparative government and political economy of China, the director of the Center for East Asian and Pacific Studies at Trier University, and vice chairman of the German Association of Asian Studies. Dr. Heilmann earned his M.A. in political science in 1990 from Tuebingen University and a Ph.D. in political science in 1993 at the Saar University in Germany. Dr. Heilmann has published extensively on China's political economy, with a special focus on economic policymaking and regulation. His latest publications include *Policy Experimentation in China's Rise, The Political System of the PRC,* and *The Chinese Equity Market.*

Jamie Horsley is deputy director of the China Law Center and senior research scholar and lecturer in law at the Yale Law School. Before moving to Yale, Ms. Horsley was a partner in the law firm of Paul, Weiss, Rifkind, Wharton & Garrison, establishing their first office in Beijing in 1981–1983 and managing the China practice from Hong Kong, 1986–1990; commercial attaché in the US embassies in Beijing and Manila, 1991–1995; vice president of Motorola International, Inc. and director of Government Relations for China for Motorola, Inc., while resident in Beijing (1995–1998); and a consultant to the Carter Center on village elections in China (1999–2002). Ms. Horsley lived and worked in China for thirteen years, travels there frequently, and has written and spoken on doing business with China, legal participation, and administrative dispute resolution in China. She is a director of the National Committee on US-China Relations. She received her J.D. from the Harvard Law School, an M.A. in Chinese Studies from the University of Michigan, her B.A. from Stanford University, and a diploma in Chinese law from the University of East Asia, Macao. She speaks and reads Mandarin Chinese.

Joanna Lewis is an assistant professor of science, technology, and international affairs at Georgetown University's Walsh School of Foreign Service. Her current work focuses on renewable energy industrial development, mechanisms for low-carbon technology transfer in the developing world, and expanding options for multilateral engagement in a post-2012 international climate change agreement. Most of Professor Lewis's research is based in China, and has included studies of China's energy system and policy options to promote renewable energy use and local renewable energy technology development. She is the primary technical advisor for the Asia Society's Initiative for US-China Cooperation on Energy and Climate, and an international advisor to the Energy Foundation China Sustainable Energy Program in Beijing. Previously, Dr. Lewis was a senior International Fellow at the Pew Center on Global Climate Change and a researcher in the China Energy Group at the US Department of Energy's Lawrence Berkeley National Laboratory, and has worked at the White House Council on Environmental Quality, the National Wildlife Federation, and the Environmental Defense Fund. From 2003–2004 she was a visiting scholar at the Institute of Energy, Environment and Economy at Tsinghua University in Beijing. Professor Lewis holds an M.A. degree and Ph.D. in energy and resources from the University of California, Berkeley, and a bachelor's degree in environmental science and policy from Duke University.

Yawei Liu is director of the Carter Center's China Program. Yawei Liu has been a member of numerous Carter Center missions to monitor Chinese village, township, and county people's congress deputy elections from 1997 to 2006. He has also observed elections in Nicaragua, Peru, and Taiwan. He has written extensively on China's political developments and grassroots democracy. He edited two Chinese book series: *Rural Election and Governance in Contemporary China* (Northwestern University Press, Xian, 2002 and 2004) and *Political Readers* (China Central Translation Bureau Press, 2006). He is the coauthor of *Obama: The Man Who Will Change America* (Chinese language, 2008). He is the founder and editor of China Elections and Governance (www.chinaelections. org and www.chinaelections.net), a website sponsored by the Carter Center on political and election issues (2002 to present). He is also associate director of the China Research Center based in Metro Atlanta. Yawei Liu earned his B.A. in English literature from Xian Foreign Languages Institute (1982), M.A. in recent Chinese history from the University of Hawaii (1989), and Ph.D. in American history from Emory University (1996).

Barry Naughton is Sokwanlok Chair of Chinese International Affairs Professor at the Graduate School of International Relations and Pacific Studies at University of California since 1988. Barry Naughton's most recent book is *The*

Chinese Economy: Transitions and Growth, a comprehensive survey of the Chinese economy that was published by MIT Press in 2007. Naughton has published extensively on the Chinese economy, with a focus on four interrelated areas: economic transition, industry and technology, foreign trade, and Chinese political economy. His pioneering study of Chinese economic growth, *Growing Out of the Plan: Chinese Economic Reform, 1978–1993* (Cambridge University Press, 1995) won the Masayoshi Ohira Prize. Naughton is a contributor and editor or coeditor of four books: *Reforming Asian Socialism: The Growth of Market Institutions*; *Urban Spaces in Contemporary China*; *The China Circle: Economics and Technology in the PRC, Taiwan and Hong Kong*; and *Holding China Together: Diversity and National Integration in the Post-Deng Era*. Naughton publishes quarterly analyses of China's economic policy-making at *China Leadership Monitor*.

Elizabeth J. Perry is Henry Rosovsky Professor of Government at Harvard University and director of the Harvard-Yenching Institute. Born in Shanghai and raised in Tokyo, she holds a Ph.D. in political science from the University of Michigan and taught at the universities of Arizona, Washington (Seattle), and California (Berkeley) before moving to Harvard in 1997. She served recently as president of the Association for Asian Studies and was the recipient of a Guggenheim fellowship. She is the author or editor of more than fifteen books. Two of her books, *Rebels and Revolutionaries in North China, 1845–1945* (Stanford University Press, 1980); and *Shanghai on Strike: The Politics of Chinese Labor* (Stanford University Press, 1993) have been published in Chinese translation. The latter book won the John King Fairbank prize for the best book on East Asian history from the American Historical Association. Professor Perry is currently engaged in a study of the history and politics of the labor movement at the Anyuan Coal mine.

Ren Jiantao is a well-known expert on political philosophy, history of Chinese political thought, government reform, and administrative ethics in China. He was dean of the School of Government at Sun Yat-sen University (2004–2009), vice president of the Guangzhou Academy of Political Science and Public Administration, and editor for the *Journal of Public Administration*, a bimonthly journal in Guangzhou. He has been a cooperative researcher at Harvard University (Nov. 1998–Nov. 1999), and a research fellow for the Guangdong Provincial People's Government Development Research Center. Professor Ren has directed many research projects funded by the Ford Foundation.

Carl Riskin is a Distinguished Professor of Economics at the Queens College since 1974. Riskin has been one of the pioneers of contemporary Chinese economic studies. His *China's Political Economy: The Quest for Development since 1949* (Oxford, 1987) is a comprehensive history of China, from a political economy perspective, since the founding of the People's Republic. Since 1987, Riskin has been analyzing China's changing income distribution, based upon a series of large-scale surveys carried out in China as reflected in *Inequality and Poverty in China in an Age of Globalization* (Oxford, 2000) and *China's Retreat from Equality* (M.E. Sharpe, 2001). Riskin has also done a number of commissioned studies for the United Nations Development Program. He produced the first two national Human Development Reports on China, in 1997 and 1999. He has also helped UNDP in other parts of the world, including Uzbekistan, Latvia, and Laos. For the Asia and Pacific Bureau of UNDP he produced a study of the UN response to the "Asian Crisis" of 1997–1998. Most recently, he prepared and coauthored *The Macroeconomics of Poverty Reduction: The Case of China* (UNDP China, 2004), and led UNDP's evaluation of its global program of producing national Human Development Reports (2005–2006).

Sun Yanfei is a Ph.D. candidate at the Department of Sociology, University of Chicago. She has done research on China's environmental movement and has published several articles on this topic. Currently, she is writing her dissertation on religious revival and changes in contemporary China.

Robert Weller is professor and chair of anthropology, and research associate at the Institute on Culture, Religion and World Affairs at Boston University. His current research focuses on the role of religion in creating public social benefits in Chinese communities in China, Malaysia, and Taiwan. His recent publications have included the development of the environmental movement and nature tourism in China and Taiwan in the context of economic growth. He has examined the role of local voluntary organizations as mediators between state and society in Hong Kong, Taiwan, and China, and he has consulted on poverty and unemployment relief in western China. He has written numerous books and articles on Chinese political, social, and cultural change, often with a focus on relations between religion and civic life. His latest book is called *Ritual and Its Consequences: An Essay on the Limits of Sincerity* (Oxford, 2008). Professor Weller has a B.A. from Yale University and a Ph.D. from Johns Hopkins University.

Min Ye is an assistant professor of international relations and director of the East Asian Interdisciplinary Studies Program at Boston University. Her recent publications include *The Making of Northeast Asia*, coauthored with Kent Calder (2010), and "Policy Learning and Diffusion: China's FDI Liberalization in the Shadow of Japanese Model," *Journal of East Asian Studies* (2009). She is currently a postdoctoral fellow at the Fairbank Center at Harvard University and is completing her manuscript *Embedded States and Economic Transitions in China and India: Innovative Liberalization of Foreign Direct Investment.* Ye received her Ph.D. from Princeton University and conducted research in China, India, Japan, and South Korea.

Yongnian Zheng is professor and director of East Asian Institute, National University of Singapore. He is editor of the Series on Contemporary China (World Scientific) and editor of China Policy Series (Routledge). He is also coeditor of *China: An International Journal.* He has studied both China's transformation and its external relations. His papers have appeared in journals such as *Comparative Political Studies, Political Science Quarterly, Third World Quarterly,* and *The China Quarterly.* He is the author of thirteen books, including *Technological Empowerment, De Facto Federalism in China, Discovering Chinese Nationalism in China,* and *Globalization and State Transformation in China,* and coeditor of eleven books on Chinese politics and society including, most recently, *China and the New International Order* (2008). Besides research work, Professor Zheng has also been an academic activist. He served as a consultant to the United Nations Development Program on China's rural development and democracy. In addition, he has been a columnist for *Xinbao* (Hong Kong) and *Zaobao* (Singapore) for many years, writing numerous commentaries on China's domestic and international affairs. Professor Zheng received his B.A. and M.A. degrees from Beijing University, and his Ph.D. from Princeton University. He was a recipient of the Social Science Research Council-MacArthur Foundation Fellowship (1995–1997) and John D. and Catherine T. MacArthur Foundation Fellowship (2003–2004). He was professor and founding research director of the China Policy Institute, University of Nottingham, United Kingdom (2005–2008).